The Liberating Gospel in China

The Liberating Gospel in China

The Christian Faith among China's Minority Peoples

Ralph R. Covell

Published by Baker Books,
a division of Baker Book House Company
P.O. Box 6827
Grand Rapids, MI 49506-6287

Printed in the United States of America

Library of Congress Cataloging-in-Publication Data

Covell, Ralph R.
The liberating gospel in China : the Christian faith among China's minority peoples / Ralph R. Covell.
p. cm.
Includes bibliographical references and index.
ISBN 0-8010-2595-8
1. Minorities—China—Missions. 2. Protestant churches—Missions—China. 3. Catholic church—Missions—China. 4. Missions—China. 5. Taiwan aborigines—Missions. 6. Missions—Taiwan. I. Title.
BV3415.2.C684 1994
275.1p082p08693—dc20 94-42375

With gratitude to my Sediq friends in Taiwan
who taught me so much about
what it means to follow Christ

Contents

Pronunciation Guide

a Vowel as in *far*
b Consonant as in *be*
c Consonant as in *its*
ch Consonant as in *chip;* strongly aspirated
d Consonant as in *do*
e Vowel as in *her*
f Consonant as in *foot*
g Consonant as in *go*
h Consonant as in *her;* strongly aspirated
i Vowel as in *eat* or as in *sir* (when in syllables beginning with *c, ch, r, s, sh, z,* and *zh*)
j Consonant as in *jeep*
k Consonant as in *kind;* strongly aspirated
l Consonant as in *lard*
m Consonant as in *me*
o Vowel as in *law*
p Consonant as in *par;* strongly aspirated
q Consonant as in *cheek*
r Consonant as in *right* (not rolled) or pronounced *z* as in *azure*
s Consonant as in *sister*
sh Consonant as in *shore*
t Consonant as in *top;* strongly aspirated
u Vowel as in *too;* also as in French *tu* or the German *Munchen*
v Consonant used only to produce foreign words, national minority words, and local dialects
w Semi-vowel in syllables beginning with *u* when not preceded by consonants, as in *want*
x Consonant as in *she*
y Semi-vowel in syllables beginning with *i* or *u* when not preceded by consonants, as in *yet*
z Consonant as in *zero*
zh Consonant as in *jump*

Preface

Bishop K. H. Ting of the China Christian Council has reminded us that the efforts made by the socialist regime in China to achieve social, economic, and political liberation must not be confused with what no government can do—liberate people spiritually and create a "new person in the Pauline sense."[1] An unfulfilled transcendent need in the hearts of people has led to a revival of all religions. This is particularly true of Christianity, with unprecedented numbers among the Han Chinese finding freedom in Jesus Christ.

Even more has this been true among many of China's national minorities, large groups of people on her northern, western, and southern borders. The stories of their unusual experiences are not well known:

An official of the Religious Affairs Bureau, noting that more than one half of the 480,000 Lisu in his area of control are Christians, suggests that the Christian faith be considered their official religion.

A large gathering of Sediq Christians in Taiwan celebrates in August 1989 the translation of the entire Bible in their language.

A Boulder, Colorado, opthamologist goes with his family to China to discover that the churches started one hundred years earlier by his wife's grandfather continue to prosper.

A pastor living in Kunming travels weekly to the northwest corner of Guizhou Province to minister to the large Miao community, where great revivals occurred at the beginning of this century.

Revival fires continue to burn among the Lisu, Lahu, Wa, and Yi minority peoples in Yunnan Province. Some of these groups, in cooperation with the United Bible Societies, are currently revising the Bible in their languages.

Ten thousand copies of the Lisu New Testament are reprinted at the Amity Press in Nanjing for the Lisu churches in Yunnan.

1. K. H. Ting, "Evangelism as a Chinese Christian Sees It," *Missiology* 11, 3 (June 1983): 312.

News about the minorities is not limited to church events. The Chinese government has reported recently the closing of portions of the northwest province of Xinjiang. It rightfully fears that ethnic disturbances in Kirghizia and Uzbekistan in Central Asia will spill over into China and ignite ancient hopes for independence among the same minority nationalities. Tibetans from outside China tell the world that the war it has ignored continues in Tibet, the "roof of the world," as the gallant Khans persist in resisting those whom they perceive as Chinese invaders.

Americans are learning much about China today. They have visited there by the hundreds of thousands since 1980 and gazed with wonder at many spectacular sites—the Great Wall, the Forbidden City, the Ming tombs, the unearthed terra cotta soldiers in Xian, and the strangely-shaped *karst* mountains about Guilin. Some have engaged in education, commerce, industry, and science. China has become better known to Americans of this generation than at any previous time in her long and fabled history.

Although the tragedy of Tiananmen has dimmed much of this luster, Christian people remain fascinated with exotic China. They want to learn more about the fate of their brothers and sisters in this great land. Firsthand accounts of the spread of the faith, of persecutions endured for the gospel, of signs and wonders performed in the name of Christ, and of the experiences of those smuggling Bibles and other Christian literature into China get top priority in many of our Christian publications.

But there is an untold story about the unseen minorities of China—the fifty-five nationalities who ethnically are not Chinese, but who are loyal citizens of that country and as much Chinese as the Native American is a U.S. citizen. Apart from the Hui and the Manchu, who speak Chinese, these groups all have separate languages. Their cultures, histories, and traditions differ from that of the Han Chinese. The populations of several minority nationalities exceed that of many African nations. The symbols of their life and history—Genghis Khan, the Huns, the Gobi Desert, the Dunhuang Buddhist caves in Xinjiang, the Potala Palace in Lhasa, the entrancing Tang drama and music—are prominent in China's long history.

As is true of other minority groups around the world, China's non-Chinese nationalities are poor, despised, oppressed, and bound by crippling, age-long traditions. Many of them became enthusiastic Christian believers well before liberation. Their response to Christ far exceeded proportionally that of the Han Chinese. Jesus the Liberator freed both the sinner and the sinned against. Shackles of economic exploitation, gross immorality, demonic oppression, and feudalistic bondage fell from them personally and collectively. Individuals and groups were revitalized by finding new identity in Christ. Why did some of these peoples accept Christ's freedom more easily than the Chinese did? Was it the quality of the missionaries, the methods used in the work, the focus of the message preached, or some combination of these? Or must we go beyond purely theological reasons and God-talk to examine broader historical, economic, sociological, and cultural reasons? And if we do find answers, can they help us to minister more effectively to these groups in China and to those like them in other nations?

Some minority nationality groups resisted Christ even more vigorously than did the Han Chinese: those immersed in Buddhism and Islam, as well as some with traditional folk religions. Again, why did people resist Jesus, who sought to liberate them from systemic religious oppression and slavery? Were there any critical, historic turning points that turned people away from freedom in Christ? We will probe deeply missiological issues of communication: what was the message preached? To whom was it given? Was it clear? Was it heard?

Whether of response or of resistance, the tale is a thrilling one. Single-minded commitment, heroic efforts, tragic sacrifice, and satanic opposition combine with the flow of Chinese history in a story that is largely unfamiliar to Christian people everywhere.

One emphasis today in mission is on *ta ethne* (Matt. 28:19), the peoples to be discipled in all the countries of the world. Some Christians want to "adopt a people" for whom to pray and, if possible, on whom they might concentrate efforts of evangelism and nurture. Some mission agencies have developed a "nonresident missionary" program that will enable them to focus multiple efforts on unreached peoples and areas within countries where there is limited access. All of this depends on knowing more about such peoples—their background, the history of God's working through God's people to liberate them, the results of these efforts, and the reasons for response or resistance.

This account of missions in China ends with 1949. Where the Christian message was well received, I try to bring you up to date on progress to the present. Where the message was and continues to be opposed, I will make no attempt, for obvious reasons, to give details on current efforts. Nor will I burden you with excessive documentation. For the scholars who want to know where I have gotten this material, there is a source for nearly every sentence. I will be glad to furnish this documentation if it is requested. In keeping with most recent writing on China, I am using *pinyin,* the current system of romanization, to indicate all but well-known Chinese names and expressions. A pronunciation guide is included.

Five maps will help you to locate the places named in each chapter. Map 1 (p. 14) is for general orientation. Map 2 (p. 32) helps to follow

Roman Catholic and Protestant efforts (chaps. 2 and 3) to get into Tibet from the south. Map 3 (p. 82) covers the material found in chapters 2–4 and 6–10. Map 4 (p. 106) gives the important sites in Mongolia and Manchuria. Map 5 (p. 242) shows the area where the Sediq churches are located in Taiwan. Some of the spelling on the maps may differ from that currently used on maps of China.

1

Melting Pot or Tossed Salad

Who Are the Chinese?

Time magazine for 8 July 1991 was entitled *Who Are We?* The arrival of many new immigrants, as well as the presence of older ethnic groups, causes America to question its identity. Is it one unified culture or a pluralistic society? What weight should be given to long-time, traditional values? Does each subculture constitute an enclave with its own history and values? What common factors bind the country together? J. Hector St. John de Crevecoeur, a French traveler who later became an American citizen, first raised the question of American identity two hundred years ago when he asked: "What then is the American, this new man? He is either an European, or the descendant of an European, hence that strange mixture of blood which you will find in no other country."[1] This issue has taken on new significance with the pressure of a new wave of immigration and its important political, educational, economic, social, and cultural consequences.

For China this question has been with it from its beginning five thousand years ago. When average Americans think about China, they think of the "Chinese" people—those who speak Chinese, who quote Confucius, who have an ancient, exotic script, whose land is crisscrossed by the Great Wall, and who eat rice or noodles with chopsticks. Americans assume that the people are the same everywhere, even though they speak

1. J. Hector St. John de Crevecoeur, *Letters of an American Farmer* (New York: Dutton, 1957), 39.

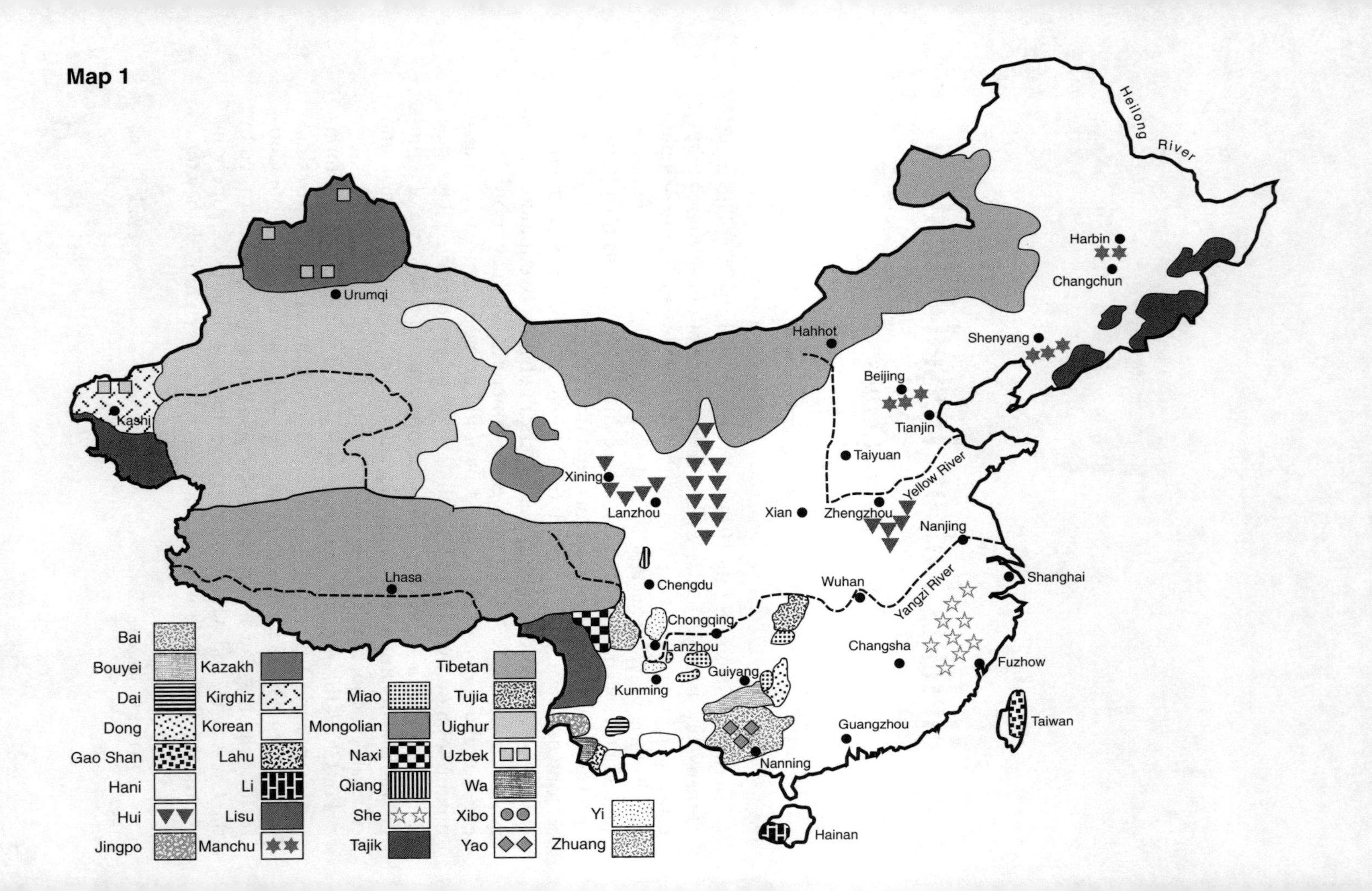
Map 1
Heilong River
Harbin
Changchun
Urumqi
Hahhot
Shenyang
Beijing
Tianjin
Kashi
Taiyuan
Yellow River
Xining
Lanzhou
Xian
Zhengzhou
Nanjing
Lhasa
Chengdu
Wuhan
Shanghai
Yangzi River
Chongqing
Lanzhou
Changsha
Fuzhow
Guiyang
Kunming
Guangzhou
Taiwan
Nanning
Hainan
Bai
Bouyei
Dai
Dong
Gao Shan
Hani
Hui
Jingpo
Kazakh
Kirghiz
Korean
Lahu
Li
Lisu
Manchu
Miao
Mongolian
Naxi
Qiang
She
Tajik
Tibetan
Tujia
Uighur
Uzbek
Wa
Xibo
Yao
Yi
Zhuang

different dialects of the one written Chinese language. Few would dream that the country has any groups to compare with Native Americans.

When the People's Republic of China drew up its first constitution in 1954, it defined the country as a "unitary multinational state in which all the *nationalities* are equal." After many years, during which ethnographers, sociologists, and historians sorted out the evidence presented by more than four hundred groups who wished to be considered a nationality, fifty-six were identified. The principal nationality was the Han people, those traditionally considered Chinese, those descended from the time of the Han dynasty at the time of Christ. This dominant group numbers more than one billion people. The other fifty-five nationalities, ranging in number from fifteen million to several hundred, live within the geographical boundaries of China, are loyal to its government, and are considered citizens of the country. If you pointedly ask them if they are Chinese, they may reply no or yes. Both answers are accurate. Or they may give you both replies, adding the explanation that they live in China and are patriotic Chinese citizens, but that they have their own unique language, culture, history, and land. To that degree they are not of the "family of Han," even though they are inhabitants of *zhong guo* (Middle Kingdom), the traditional name for China as a political state. Politically they are Chinese, but culturally they have another identity.

Even though the fifty-five nationalities number nearly one hundred million, this represents only 8 percent of China's total population. But the minorities weigh far more than they count. For example, they live in 60 percent of China's huge territory, an area larger than that of the United States, supply most of China's livestock, and have in their territories most of China's mineral resources. Their music, poetry, and customs have greatly influenced national life. Uighur music produced much of Tang dance and drama;[2] the Yi calendar led to the development of the ancient lunar calendar that is used in China today. The yin-yang duality, considered to be the thinking of the Han people, may have also come from the Yi minority. Many of these peoples live along China's "shivering spine," in areas bordering her neighbors, Commonwealth of Independent Nations, India, Myanmar (Burma), and Vietnam. Policies that the Chinese government adopts toward the nationalities quickly become decisions of foreign affairs. Where there is a concentration of members of one people group with religious views that may easily foster aspirations for independence, the Chinese government is wary. Tibet is a prime example of this, as are dissident Muslim groups in China's New Province

2. Walter J. Meserve and Ruth L. Meserve, "Theatre for Assimilation: China's National Minorities," *Journal of Asian History* 13, 2 (1979): 95–120. The authors give a fascinating account of how China's non-Han peoples have contributed to the dominant Han culture.

(Xinjiang). When there were riots in Kirgizia, Uzbekistan, and Tajikistan in Russian Central Asia in 1990, China closed off large areas of Xinjiang. It feared that these disturbances would infect the Kirghiz, Uzbek, and Tajik groups in China.

Origin of China's Minority Nationalities

When the first white settlers came to America, they found that native peoples were already there. By many means, usually violent, they displaced these Native Americans and eventually settled many of them in reservations where they live in isolation from the dominant culture. Is this the pattern that developed in China? To understand the Chinese situation we must go back even before the record of the first dynasty.

People whom we now call *Hanren* apparently lived for thousands of years in areas around the Yellow River in what is now north-central China. Early writings, ancient legends, and archaeological remains tell how a succession of cultural heroes led the people to develop basic arts and sciences. They began to relate to other small enclaves (states?) of "outside" people surrounding them. One leader in particular, the Yellow Emperor, *Huang Di,* helped to defeat these "barbarians." Over a period of time this led to the formation of the Xia dynasty (c. 2205–c. 1766 B.C.), the first political state of the Chinese people. The name *Xia* may also have had an ethnic meaning to distinguish its inhabitants clearly from the non-Xia people around them. One example of these neolithic Xia may be the community that lived in Banpo, close to the city of Xian, where a museum preserves many features of their life. To this day, the Han people view this early ancestor, Huang Di, as their Abraham, the founder of their race.

This early dynasty was succeeded by the Shang (c. 1766–c. 1122 B.C.), which was a loose federation of several states of sinitic peoples. The people of this federation viewed themselves as the center of a series of concentric circles. Eventually they called themselves *zhong guo,* the central kingdom. One of the circles surrounding the core was made up of the *sifang,* the peoples of the four directions. To the south were the *man,* to the east the *yi,* to the west the *jung,* and to the north the *di*. When the people of the central kingdom wrote the names of these four groups on the "margin," they did so with the use of the symbol of a dog, to express their contempt. Why did they look down upon the people who were not at the center? They were nomads and pastoral, unlike the agricultural Chinese, and as a result of this, they lacked the refinements of "civilization." The mission of the kingdom at the center was to civilize these barbarians and to bring them toward the center culturally. Only there could they enjoy the blessings bestowed by heaven upon its chosen people, ruled over by the emperor, who was viewed as the Son of Heaven. The people of the four directions who accepted the rule of the central kingdom, either by conquest or by assimilation, became a part of the Great Tradition and were treated as Chinese. The litmus test was not racial, but cultural. Those at the center and those at the margin, with a few exceptions, were and are probably Mongols. Some scholars have suggested minor ethnic distinctions. The finer distinction made here between Han and non-Han corresponds roughly to the contrast sometimes made between two subgroups, namely, the southern Sinids and the more northern Tungids or Mongols. The latter tend to have flatter faces, narrower eyes, shorter and squatter stature, and a more pronounced eye fold. The only important exceptions to these generalizations are the Tibetans and the original populations of the southern coastal regions (now largely vanished in pure form), neither of whom are Mongols.[3]

After a long, complex period in which many states contended for power, the Qin (221–207 B.C.) and then the Han dynasties (207 B.C.–A.D. 220) took control. By this time some of the barbarians had been assimilated by the dominant group and considered themselves to be Chinese. From the Qin (*ch'in* in the old Wade-Giles romanization) dynasty comes the country's English name, China. During the Han dynasties, the dominant people began to be referred to as Hanren, or people of Han. Over the centuries they have absorbed many features of the minority cultures. They now number more than one billion and are not homogeneous linguistically or socially, even though they possess only one written script and adhere to one basic cultural tradition.

Linguistically and subculturally, the Han may be divided into several groups—Cantonese, Sichuanese, Hakka, Fukienese, Taiwanese, to name just a few. These are large language groups, and within them are many subdivisions. A Chinese proverb notes that "every three *li* [about one mile], the dialect is different." Today in China there is much more cultural and linguistic unity than there was in the past, but the old differences cannot be erased.

In the course of history, as dynasties came and went, the Han people were influenced by and influenced non-Han peoples. The Great Wall symbolizes that China has always been nervous about her northern borders. From the northeast and northwest came hordes of invaders. They swept into China from the high plateaus of Tibet, Qinghai, and Xinjiang, from the steppes of Mongolia, and from the frigid plains of Manchuria. Among these invaders were the Xiong Nu (known as Huns to Europeans), the fierce Turks, and the wild Mongols of Genghis Khan. At times

3. Caroline Blunden and Mark Blunden, *Cultural Atlas of China* (New York: Facts on File, 1983), 16.

they came to plunder; often they set up foreign dynasties to rule over China: the Liao (907–1125) and Jin (1125–1234) in north China and the Yuan or Mongols (1222–1368) and Qing or Manchu (1644–1911) over all of China. Usually these people were absorbed into Han culture in the way "stomach juices will treat a steak," to use Dennis Bloodworth's noted phrase. But they left their cultural legacy to all of Chinese culture.

Because of the disrupting influence of the barbarian invaders from the north, many Han people moved elsewhere: to the fertile land north and south of the Yangzi (Yangtze) River, down the coast, and into Sichuan and Yunnan. One Chinese historian has noted one of these migrations early in the fourth century: "According to one record, six or seven out of every ten gentry families joined the southward march. In many cases, entire clans including neighbors and servants left their homes and travelled hundreds of miles to establish new homes south of the Yangtze River. Millions of people moved southward, probably the largest migration ever recorded in history."[4]

As the Han people moved south of the Yangzi in their massive migrations, they came into contact with Tai peoples and those belonging to the Miao-Yao groups. In Sichuan, Yunnan, and other areas farther south they met those belonging to the Tibeto-Burmese peoples. Some of these peoples, such as the Tai groups, may have already been pushed back from areas in north China. There they had contributed some features of their advanced culture, developed many centuries earlier from their original dwellings in Burma and Thailand.

As this contact occurred, the non-Han peoples were pushed back by the Han into the mountains, usually much more barren than the fertile river valleys where they had been living. Others, like the many different branches of the Miao, stayed and lived alongside the Chinese, but separate from them in their own communities. Some groups both fled and stayed. The majority of one group went into Thailand and became the Thai nation, while those who remained are the Zhuang, the largest of the minority nationalities, and the colorful Bouyei people of the province of Guizhou. Some were totally assimilated, and it became difficult to distinguish the Han from the non-Han peoples.

The non-Han minorities did not give up without a fight. Ancient Chinese dynastic annals record hundreds of uprisings. These began as early as A.D. 600 and extended into the early twentieth century. During the period of the Ming dynasty alone (1368–1644), 382 rebellions against Chinese rule are recorded. During the Qing dynasty (1644–1911), the government, although occasionally on the defensive for short periods,

4. Dun J. Li, *The Ageless Chinese: A History,* 3d ed. (New York: Charles Scribner's Sons, 1978), 140.

used harsh measures in dealing with these uprisings. The government limited the freedom of movement of the non-Han, built walled towns, established military colonies, confiscated minority lands, giving them to Chinese, and deliberately attempted to smash tribal cultures.[5] Occasionally, both in southwest and northwest China, political states made up of minority peoples challenged the central Chinese government for periods of thirty or forty years to four centuries.

Government Policy toward Minority Nationalities

Fighting, intermingling, and crosscultural pollination between Han and non-Han people went on from the beginning of Chinese civilization. This continuous struggle was given a final political settlement when the imperial armies of the Qing dynasty, between 1755 and 1792, extended China's geographical boundaries to include Chinese Turkestan, Mongolia, Tibet, and all of south China from Yunnan to Taiwan. At this time all of these people were not merely barbarians on China's borders, alternating in controlling China or being controlled by her; they were now Chinese citizens. The government needed to develop a coherent policy to deal with them within a unified state, while still recognizing ways in which they were different.

When the core of China and its outer boundaries were unified under the Qing, itself a non-Han dynasty with Manchu rulers, the minority nationalities were put under the control of the Office for the Management of the Frontiers. The very complicated bureaucratic apparatus used at the center was not applied to the margins. These groups were ruled by very nominal supervision, as in Tibet, or by military presence, or through feudal systems inherited from the past by particular peoples, as the Yi and Miao in the southwest.

When the Qing dynasty was replaced by the new Republic under Sun Yat-sen in 1912, the first flag used by the new state had five colors, representing the five "races" of China: Han, Man (Manchu), Meng (Mongol), Hui (Muslims in Xinjiang), and Zang (Tibetans). Despite acknowledging a pluralistic state, the Kuomintang government over the years put its emphasis upon *Zhongzu,* the Chinese race or nation, and not upon *minzu,* people groups. Its policy was one of assimilation. Han Chinese culture, language, and history were prominent. It was expected that all minority groups, since they were Chinese politically, should become Chinese culturally. This policy was more true in areas where the minorities had no political aspirations. Tibet considered itself independent in this period. Outer Mongolia declared its independence in 1921, and

5. Blunden and Blunden, *Cultural Atlas of China,* 38.

Xinjiang, with its large number of restless Muslims, was also virtually independent. The Nationalist government was never able to gain full political and military control over some of these volatile outlying areas.

What can be said about the attitude of the People's Republic of China (PRC), which came to power in 1949? The new government's attitudes began to crystallize even before it began to rule the country. During their Long March in 1935 from south China to their northern refuge in Yan'an, the Communists passed through many minority areas where they learned more about these peoples. In Yan'an they observed the ethnic-like tensions between the Han Chinese and non-Han Muslims. They also were aware of the nonassimilative model used by the USSR as its minorities were given political status in various republics, particularly in Central Asia. By 1938 Mao Zedong had formulated the broad outlines of the policies to be followed by his government. Minorities would be encouraged to live in autonomous areas, having equal rights with the Chinese and freedom to use their own languages and cultures, but there would be no separate states. The non-Han people would live in the same unified country with the Han Chinese.

This policy was different from that in the USSR, in that the Chinese autonomous areas would not be republics with the theoretical ability to secede from the state. Neither would the people in these areas have the same degree of internal autonomy as was available to the people in the Soviet republics. This is understandable, because the Soviet Union had a much higher percentage of minority peoples than did China, and these minorities were more equal politically and culturally to the dominant group than was the case in China.

Moreover, as June Teufel Dreyer points out, Communist theory indicates that class differences, that is, differences between the Han and non-Han and among the non-Han, can be tolerated only during transition periods leading to the time of pure socialism. When this final utopian dream has been realized, then "nationality characteristics" can be expected to disappear.[6] When they do pass away, only the dominant Han culture will remain. Will these characteristics pass away any sooner than other features of current society, such as religion? The new government was speaking of several generations, but the ultimate goal presumably is the same as the Kuomintang policy of assimilation. However, the Communists prefer to say that their goal is "integration." For this reason, they refuse to use "assimilation," the term preferred by the Nationalists, desiring instead something that, in translation, is comparable to the English "melting [pot]."

6. June Teufel Dreyer, *China's Forty Millions* (Cambridge: Harvard University Press, 1976), 261–62.

In formulating their policy toward the minority nationalities, the Communists have had to define clearly what they mean by "nationality." Ethnicity has not been played up as a major factor. One general definition is, "A nationality is a stable community which people have formed historically, having a common language, a common region, a common economic life and a common psychological quality which expresses itself in common cultural characteristics."[7] Not all of these factors need to operate in determining what group is or is not a nationality. The Hui people, for example, speak the same language as the Han Chinese, and their economic life is little different from that of the dominant culture. But they all embrace Islam as their religion, and their culture and social life express this fact clearly. Possibly 10 to 20 percent of some nationalities are dispersed in many different places and do not have a common region, but they are related to a group that is concentrated in one or several localities. People of all nationalities, totaling 414,000 and representing 3.8 percent of the city's population, live in Beijing, the capital of China, but they trace their roots to the home region of their nationality.

Before the advent of the PRC, people who were on the borderline between being recognized as Han Chinese or as a particular minority preferred being identified as Chinese. They feared the way in which society tended to discriminate against the minorities. Today, the same people often claim minority status because they wish to claim the benefits that the present regime gives to its minority nationalities.

Now that minorities are given a higher status, their leaders as well as the Chinese are combing past history to highlight the ways in which they have contributed to the national government and culture, as well as in resisting past oppression. Some writers emphasize that the early Xia dynasty included not only sinitic groups but also the Qiang, Rong, Miao, and Man, all minority peoples. To put down the An Lushan rebellion in 757, leaders of the Tang dynasty (618–906) called upon the Uighur peoples from the northwest to give help. Scholars point out that the later Tang dynasty was created by a minority people, the Shatuos of the Turkic people. A noted Yi anthropologist, Liu Yaohan, has explained in some detail how ancient Yi culture has furnished many important cultural features that make up Chinese life today.[8]

7. Colin Mackerras, "The Minority Nationalities: Modernisation and Integration" in *China: Dilemmas of Modernisation,* ed. Graham Young (London: Croom Helm, 1985), 237.

8. This material, as well as that in the following paragraph, has come from *China's Minority Nationalities,* ed. Ma Yin (Beijing: Foreign Language Press, 1989), 9–14, 18–20; Liu Yaohan, *Zhongguo Wenming Yuantou Xintan: Dao Jia Yu Yizu Hu Yuzhouguan* (A New Investigation into the Origin of Chinese Civilization: Daoism and the Tiger World View of the Yi Minority) (Kunming: Yunnan People's Publishing House, 1985).

Peasant rebellions of the past, early harbingers of the Communist liberation, are retold with a new emphasis on the role played by the minorities. The Yellow Turban uprising (205–220) at the end of the later Han dynasty included many Xiong Nu soldiers. The Dali kingdom (formerly Nan Zhao) that rebelled in the tenth century against the Song dynasty was made up almost entirely of Tai, Bai, and Yi minorities. The great Taiping Rebellion of the nineteenth century, reinterpreted as a revolt against imperialism and feudalism, included not only Han but Zhuang, Yao, Hui, Miao, Dong, and Yi nationalities. The early revolutionary movements in 1911 and 1919 had many Zhuang, Hui, Mongolian, and other peoples participating along with the Han.

Characteristics of Minority Nationalities

How can the minority nationalities be distinguished from the dominant Han Chinese? What types of relationships do they have with one another? From the table on page 27 it is evident that these people are distributed widely about the outer edges of China: northeast, northwest, southwest, central south, and southeast China. In general, only those in Guizhou and Hunan are in provinces that are not considered to be frontier or border areas. Only the Hui, indistinguishable from the Han except in religion, are scattered in any large numbers throughout China.

Minority peoples tend to be poorer than the Han Chinese, to be more nomadic and pastoral, and to live in areas where the soil is mountainous or marginal and where dry farming must be practiced. They are not nearly as advanced technologically as the Chinese and would seem to be less prepared for the present emphasis of the government upon modernization. Most of them live in rural areas or small villages and do not enjoy the amenities of the dominant society. Their social life was often feudal. Because China is a multinational society, oppressive relationships were common. Either the Han Chinese, other more dominant nationalities, or a religious or social aristocracy within their own societies kept many of the non-Han peoples in a state of virtual serfdom or slavery. Compared to the Han Chinese, their percentage of population growth has been very high, increasing from a total of 65 million in 1982 to 91 million in 1990. The percentage of increase over this decade ranges from a low of 8.73 for the Koreans to 714 for the Gelao.[9] Some of the increase may be due to new groups being added to the list of national minorities.

9. These statistics and the table on page 27 are from *Beijing Review,* 24–30 December 1990.

The minorities have regional self-government or regional autonomy at three levels: 5 autonomous regions, comparable in size to and on the same level as provinces; 30 autonomous prefectures; 122 autonomous counties. These distinctions are largely of size, but at each level there are three possibilities: one is established in areas where there is only one nationality; a second exists where there is one minority with a large local population coexisting with several other minority nationalities who have their own self-government at a still lower administrative level; a third is an autonomous area that is formed jointly by several minority nationalities and where administrative functions are shared. In some areas, relationships among the minorities and between them and the Han Chinese are complex. For example, in the Guangxi Zhuang Autonomous Region in south China, the Han inhabit the cities and towns, the Zhuang, Dai, and Bai minorities reside on the plains, and other minority peoples live in the mountains. In this ladder-like scale, each level of self-rule is practiced.

Certain conditions characterize each level of autonomy. First, the administrative head of a region, prefecture, or county is to be a citizen of one of the nationalities. This regulation does not require that the chairmen of the Party in the area be a minority person. The self-government exercised at each level is to be in accord with the language, religion, customs, and traditions of the particular minorities. Important positions in the self-governing process at each level are to be filled whenever possible by qualified minority peoples. To this end, the government has established cadre training institutes for each minority to assure that the proper quality is attained. The government attempts to give an equal status to minorities and the right to care for their own affairs. It decries any evidence of "Han chauvinism," although the tradition of thousands of years cannot be wished away this easily.

Autonomy is not to be equated with independence. No autonomous regions, such as the Tibetan Autonomous Region, are allowed to secede. In fact, when uprisings have occurred in Tibet, these have been met repeatedly with firm resistance. China does not retreat from its insistence that Tibet, historically and at the present, is a part of China. The same attitude applies to the Xinjiang Uighur Autonomous Region, where Uighurs and other Islamic peoples have shown an interest in independence. The issue of potential secession does not arise in other regions, prefectures, or counties, since these areas historically have never had political entities comparable to states. Thus the Yi people of Sichuan, hemmed in on all sides by Han Chinese or Tibetans and often dissatisfied with Chinese rule and prone to frequent uprisings, have never claimed to be a political state independent from China.

The extent of self-rule is severely limited by the fact that actions taken by local autonomous groups must be ratified by the National People's

Congress before those actions are implemented. However, even the smallest of the minority nationalities are represented in the National Congress, the highest political body within the country, as well as in local congresses. Ultimately, power in China resides within the Communist Party, and minority representation here is not enough to wield any influence.

Advantages of Belonging to a Minority Nationality

Why do people who in pre-liberation days wished to be Chinese now register as belonging to a minority group? One major reason is that the government has sought to remove not only legal discrimination, which would deny equality to minorities, but also to remove practical discrimination in everyday living. For example, the national language is no longer called the "National Language" *(Guoyu)* as it was in the Kuomintang period, but rather the "common language" *(Putonghua)*. Condescending terms to refer to certain groups, such as "Lolo" for the Yi in Sichuan, are no longer used.

The very term *minority nationality* is much more acceptable than the old term *tribe (buluo)*. The radical—that part of the Chinese character that gives the meaning—for tribal groups is no longer the "dog" radical. Efforts are being made to remove tensions that have existed for centuries between the Han Chinese and minority nationalities living in the same or nearby areas.

As China has modernized, the country's infrastructures in transportation and communication have been developed to embrace the minority areas. Peoples who once were isolated now feel an identity as part of one unified state. From the time of liberation to the present, government propaganda teams have gone out of their way to help the minorities develop a patriotic spirit and to see how they might relate this to their ethnicity. This does not mean government approval for all traditional minority culture. The government, for example, has prohibited headhunting Wa from fertilizing their crops with freshly decapitated Chinese heads.

Whereas the former government sought to unify the country around a national language, the PRC has helped to develop the minority languages, giving special attention to the scripts employed. In some cases, this has meant developing new scripts for groups that have never had a written language; in other cases it has been to change an old script that has not been useful; sometimes it has been to modify an ancient script while introducing a new romanized system. For example, when the Communists on their Long March in 1935 went through the Jianchang Valley in what is now Sichuan, they took with them to their northern headquarters at Yan'an a few of the local Yi minority. Communist linguists analyzed the Yi language and ancient script. They reduced drastically the number of symbols in this script and developed a romanized system to be used along with it. When their armies again marched into this area in March 1950, they had these new language materials ready and, within weeks, had introduced them to the Yi people.

In each of the autonomous regions, prefectures, and counties, linguists have developed grammars, dictionaries, and lexicons of specific languages. Educational leaders have promoted magazines, films, and radio broadcasts within many autonomous areas. They have encouraged local writers to record their ancient traditions, as well as to create contemporary literature. Minority anthropologists have investigated many important features of the religious, social, and cultural life of their own peoples.

An important privilege for the minority nationalities is that they are exempted from the government dictum of "one family, one child." Within these areas it is common for families to have three or four children. This helps to explain the percentage of numerical growth among the minorities.

Local officials also allow for special privileges related to various customs of the people: vacation for ethnic festival days; subsidies for Muslims to buy beef, generally more expensive than pork; help in starting Islamic restaurants in areas where there is a heavy concentration of Muslim peoples. Also, in contrast with the religious situation among the Han Chinese, a Communist cadre working among a specific minority is allowed to become a member of that group's religion, be it Buddhism, Islam, or Christianity.

Despite the efforts that the PRC has made to treat the minorities in an equal and nondiscriminatory fashion, problems remain. The suspicion still exists that the long-range Chinese policy is to have a culturally monolithic state. The minorities are restless when they see the large number of Han immigrants who are being brought into their areas, almost as if the goal is to balance the number of minorities with an equal number of Han Chinese. With any weakening of the national government will some of the more ardently ethnic and religious groups seek independence? Will foreign governments having common borders with China seek to encourage such secession? How can the Chinese government separate between religion and politics in an area such as Tibet? Can there be harsh suppression of religious freedom, alongside the claim that the Tibetans have true self-government and are autonomous in any sense? Will the economically more backward minority areas be able to participate fully in the long march toward modernization? An important question for Christians is whether Han Chinese national and local leaders will allow the continued expansion of the Christian faith where it has been unusually successful in the last one hundred years. And, even more important, where Chinese or nationality churches desire to evangelize among nationalities that have never been introduced to the Christian faith, will this be possible? Or will evangelization be hindered by the government's religious policy or by regulations developed by the China Christian Council, either on the national or local levels?

Classification of China's Minority Nationalities

How can anyone get a quick grasp of China's fifty-five national minorities? Table 1 (p. 27) gives an alphabetical listing, 1990 population figures, the language family, and the general location of China's minority nationalities. The map on page 14 also gives some idea of where these many groups may be found.

Perhaps an easier method of classification is to divide the nationalities by their language groups. Nearly all of the languages of northwest, north-central, and northeast China are Altaic. The only exception is Tajik, which is Persian, or more broadly, Indo-European. The Altaic languages have three subdivisions in China: Turkic, which includes groups like Uighur, Kazakh, Kirghiz, and Uzbek; Mongolian, which includes Mongolian proper and four other small groups; Tungus, which includes Manchu, Evenki, and three small groups. Korean may also be included under the Altaic family. The many groups of south and southwest China are divided into four subgroups: Tai, which has eight groups, including Zhuang, Dong, Bouyei, and Li; Tibeto-Burman, which has sixteen languages, including Tibetan, Yi, Lisu, Lahu, Naxi, Hani, Qiang, and Bai; Miao-Yao, which includes these two groups; Mon-Khmer, which has three groups, the most important being Wa. In Taiwan may be found the Gao Shan peoples, which have at least ten major and minor subdivisions.

We may also classify the minorities of China according to their religion: some are Muslims, some are Buddhists, some are largely Christian, and some adhere to traditional religions, often called animistic in the past. This may be too simple, for there are different combinations of religious belief in many groups. In general, however, we may say that all groups in northern China are Muslims, with the exception of the Mongols. The Mongols and Tibetans believe in Lamaism, a form of Buddhism. Nearly every group in southwest China and Taiwan has been dominated by a belief in spirits, a traditional religion. One exception is the Dai, who historically have adhered to Hinayana Buddhism. Even for groups that are Islamic or Buddhist, the principal reality is the spirit world. With the Korean people and many groups in southwest China and Taiwan, the Christian faith has gained a strong hold. Some of these people, such as the Lisu and many groups of the Gao Shan in Taiwan, consider Christianity to be their major faith.

TABLE 1

The Minority Nationalities of China (1990)

Name	*Population*	*Language Family*	*Location*
Achang	27,708	Tibeto-Burman	Yunnan
Bai	1,594,827	Yunnan	
Benglong	12,295 (1982)	Mon-Khmer	Yunnan
Bulang	82,280	Mon-Khmer	Yunnan
Bonan	12,212	Mongolian	Gansu
Bouyei	2,545,092	Tai	Guizhou
Dai	1,025,128	Tai	Yunnan
Daur	121,357	Mongolian	Manchuria
Deang	15,462	Yunnan	
Dong	2,514,014	Tai	Guizhou
Dongxiang	373,872	Mongolian	Gansu
Drung	5,816	Tibeto-Burman	Yunnan
Evenki	26,315	Tungus	Manchuria
Gao Shan	2,909 (China)	Austronesian	Taiwan
Gelao	437,997	Guizhou	
Han (Chinese)	1,042,482,187	Sinitic	Everywhere
Hani	1,253,952	Tibeto-Burman	Yunnan
Hezhen	4,245	Tungus	Manchuria
Hui	8,806,978	Sinitic	Everywhere
Jing	18,915	Guangxi	
Jingpo	119,209	Tibeto-Burman	Yunnan
Jinuo	18,021	Tibeto-Burman	Yunnan
Kazakh	1,111,718	Turkic	Xinjiang
Kirghiz	141,549	Turkic	Xinjiang
Korean	1,920,597	Manchurian	
Lahu	411,476	Tibeto-Burman	Yunnan
Lhoba	2,312	Tibeto-Burman	Tibet
Li	1,110,900	Tai	Hainan Island
Lisu	574,856	Tibeto-Burman	Yunnan
Manchu	9,821,180	Tungus	North
Maonan	71,968	Tai	Guangxi
Miao	7,398,035	Miao-Yao	South
Moinba	7,475	Tibeto-Burman	Tibet
Mongolian	4,806,849	Mongolian	North
Monguor (Tu)	191,624	Mongolian	Qinghai

Mulam	159,328	Tai	Guangxi
Naxi	278,009	Tibeto-Burman	Yunnan
Nu	27,123	Tibeto-Burman	Yunnan
Oroqen	6,965	Tungus	Manchuria
Pumi	29,657	Tibeto-Burman	Yunnan
Qiang	198,252	Tibeto-Burman	Sichuan
Russian	13,504	Indo-European	Xinjiang
Salar	87,697	Turkic	Qinghai
She	630,378	Miao-Yao	Fujian
Shui	345,993	Tai	Guizhou
Tajik	33,538	Indo-European	Xinjiang
Tatar	4,873	Turkic	Xinjiang
Tibetan	4,593,330	Tibeto-Burman	Tibet
Tujia	5,704,223	Hunan	
Uighur	7,214,431	Turkic	Xinjiang
Uzbek	14,502	Turkic	Xinjiang
Wa	351,974	Mon-Khmer	Yunnan
Xibo	172,847	Tungus	North
Yao	2,134,013	Miao-Yao	South
Yugur	12,297	Turkic	Gansu
Yi	6,572,173	Tibeto-Burman	South
Zhuang	15,489,630	Tai	Guangxi
Unidentified	749,341		

Receptivity and Rejection of Christianity among China's Minorities

Christian missionaries have sought for more than twelve hundred years to bring the gospel of Jesus Christ to the minority peoples of China. Beginning with the Nestorians during the Tang dynasty (618–907) and continuing at least until the advent of the PRC, emissaries of the cross have tried to penetrate Mongolia, Tibet, and areas in what is now Xinjiang in northwest China. Only within the modern era of Christian missions to China, in the late nineteenth century, was missionary work commenced among the many minority groups in southwest China. Dutch missionaries established churches among some minorities in Taiwan early in the seventeenth century, but no concentrated efforts were made to reach these people until about 1870.

Previous to 1949, conditions among the minority nationalities of China did not favor the Christian missionary effort. The social situation then among the minorities was diametrically opposite to what is now seen in China: minority peoples were despised; religious hierarchies oppressed them; feudalism was rampant; at best, they were second-class citizens within China; local conditions were chaotic because the central government lacked effective control; many of the groups were ravaged by infighting as well as by struggles with other groups; travel conditions into minority areas were difficult and dangerous; education for these peoples and communication with them was almost nonexistent; languages had not been analyzed or reduced to writing and there was no written literature; the planting and use of opium was the foundation of local economies; banditry and murder were everyday occurrences; and deadly diseases killed off missionaries, as well as the local people. Apart from times of special crisis, there was usually freedom for missionaries and local Christians to preach the gospel. This meant little, however, in the face of the religious, social, political, and economic bondages faced by the people.

What was the response by minority peoples to the gospel as it was preached and demonstrated to them up until the coming of the PRC? Among some groups, largely those in Taiwan and southwest China, there was an enthusiastic reception of the liberating message of Christ. People were freed from the many shackles that bound them and lived productive lives in their communities. Other groups, specifically those with the more classical religious commitments to Buddhism and Islam, resisted vigorously.

In the following chapters we will discuss both resistant and responsive groups. It will be possible to talk about only a few of the minority nationalities. We will concentrate on selected representatives within the three major religions: Islam, Buddhism, and traditional religion. This approach will give a profile of why certain minorities have either rejected or received the Christian message. The lessons in mission that can be learned from such an analysis will be helpful to those seeking to promote God's kingdom among China's minorities and among those similar to them in other countries.

The Gospel of the Kingdom of God

When Paul the apostle proclaimed the Christian message, a central theme was the kingdom of God (Acts 19:8; 20:25; 28:23, 31). Luke records also that Philip preached the "gospel of the kingdom of God" (Acts 8:12). They both knew well that the gospel of the kingdom was the liberating truth with which Jesus began his ministry (Mark 1:14).

Mark's record of Jesus' earthly ministry shows how he constantly confronted the systemic powers of evil that enslaved both individuals and entire societies. Immediately after calling Peter, Andrew, James, and John, Jesus began his public ministry by casting out a demon from a man in the synagogue at Capernaum (Mark 1:21–28). That same evening, he "drove out many demons, but he would not let the demons speak because they knew who he was" (1:34). To religious leaders, the doubters in every period, he explained that this work of exorcism was because he, the King, had invaded the strong man's kingdom and had conquered him (3:22–30). He demonstrated his kingly authority even more vividly by casting numerous demons from the body of an oppressed man (5:1–20) and by healing a young boy with a "deaf and mute" spirit (9:14–32). Little wonder then that following the crucifixion, where, in the words of Paul he "disarmed the powers and authorities, [and] made a public spectacle of them, triumphing over them by the cross" (Col. 2:15), he commanded his followers to cast out demons in his name.

The message of liberation is what both Protestant and Catholic missionaries proclaimed as they worked among the minorities of China. As the message was received, people obtained a glorious freedom far beyond anything they had previously experienced. As the message was rejected, for whatever reasons, it brought a continued subjection to what Paul called "the rulers, . . . the authorities, . . . the powers of this dark world, and . . . the spiritual forces of evil in the heavenly realms" (Eph. 6:12). These were indeed personal evil beings. Equally, they represented systemic evil that embraced the social, religious, economic, political, and cultural dynamics of human societies.

Jesus, the king of the kingdom of God, also demonstrated his authority over sickness, fear, death, sin and its power of alienation. He condemned the empty rhetoric of religious leaders, prejudice, and the useless rituals of traditional Judaism. He met every type of grassroot need experienced by the people of his day. He freed them to be servants of the kingdom to follow him and do his will.

Committed followers of Christ in the missionary enterprise have used Jesus as their model. Their message first of all has urged people to be born into the kingdom of God (John 3:5). They then have encouraged new converts to form a worshiping community that would witness to Jesus the King and be a sign of his liberating kingdom in every dimension of human society.

As Protestant and Catholic missionaries entered into China's minority areas with this message, they were overwhelmed by the needs that they saw. These needs were not necessarily different in kind, but certainly in extent, from what they viewed in their own countries. They responded with the compassion of Jesus to meeting these needs and setting people free.

This book explores the yes and no to Jesus among eleven of China's minority nationalities.[10] I do not use the words *liberating gospel* with the same political and economic emphasis that is found in liberation theology. On the other hand, I want to restore to the term the broad biblical content that it has always had in the Christian mission. The approach is inductive. In each chapter I shall give a preliminary missiological analysis of reasons for "success" or "failure." In the final chapter I shall probe more deeply into the most fundamental question raised by the missionary enterprise: the mystery of faith and unbelief—why do people divide when confronted by the liberating claims of Jesus Christ?

10. I would have included more minorities and more material on those within the eleven nationalities had it been possible to find reliable records of other groups. Any easily accessible record of Roman Catholic work among the minorities, apart from Tibet and Mongolia, is skimpy. Extensive primary research in the archives of the Paris Foreign Mission Society would undoubtedly turn up more material. The *Bulletin of La Societe Missions-Etrangeres,* found at the Catholic University of America, includes some material on the Yi of Sichuan. This is probably because Monseigneur de Guebriant, one of the later directors of the mission, was an early participant in its work among the Yi. Paul Vial's extensive work, *Les Lolos: Histoire, Religion, Moeure, Langue, Ecriture* (Changhai: La Mission Catholique, 1898), says nothing about Roman Catholic work among the Lolos. Adrien Launay in his several works mentions minority groups only in passing. Jean-Paul Wiest (*Maryknoll in China: A History* [Armonk, N.Y.: Sharpe, 1988]) says almost nothing about Maryknoll work among the Koreans in China. Nor is anything on the Koreans found in the files at Maryknoll. The same may be said about Catholic periodicals, such as *Les Missions Catholiques.* Catholic authors do not mention Catholic work among Muslims. In general, Roman Catholic scholars, apart from what they say about Tibet and Mongolia, do not highlight Catholic work among the minorities of China. They treat these groups as citizens of China and as being on the same level as the Han Chinese. Thus, it has been very difficult to give as much prominence to Roman Catholic work as I would have desired. The material is not lacking for Tibet, Mongolia, and the Yi of Sichuan. I have included in chapter 4 such material as Theophane Maguire has given in *Hunan Harvest* (Milwaukee: Bruce, 1946) on the Miao in Hunan. I have supplemented this with primary source material from the Passionist archives in Union City, N.J.

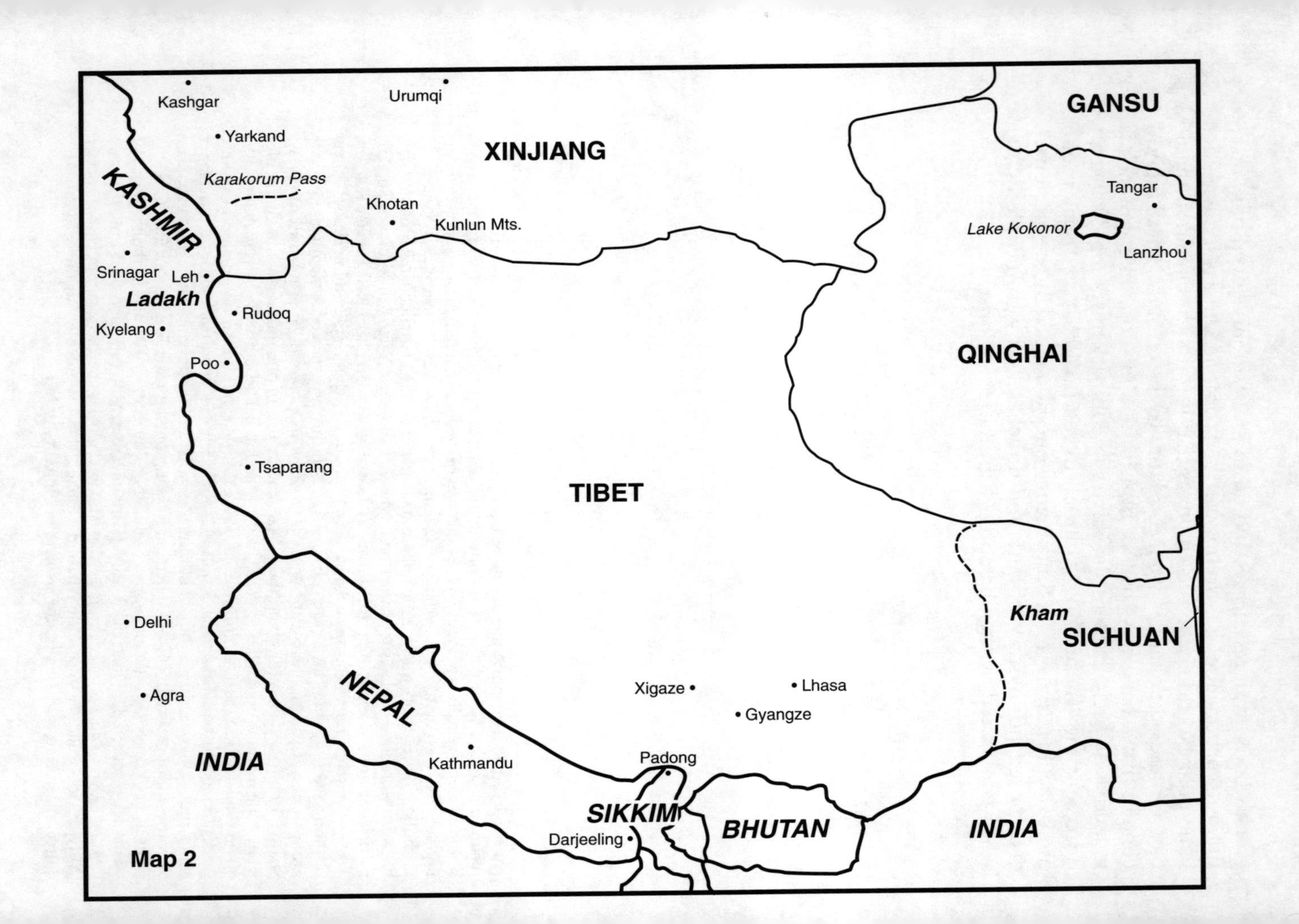
GANSU
XINJIANG
QINGHAI
TIBET
Kashgar
Urumqi
Yarkand
KASHMIR
Karakorum Pass
Khotan
Kunlun Mts.
Tangar
Lake Kokonor
Lanzhou
Srinagar
Leh
Ladakh
Rudoq
Kyelang
Poo
Tsaparang
Delhi
Agra
NEPAL
Kathmandu
INDIA
Xigaze
Lhasa
Gyangze
Padong
SIKKIM
Darjeeling
BHUTAN
INDIA
Kham
SICHUAN
Map 2

2

An Ancient Goal

The Kingdom on the Roof of the World

When asked to describe Tibet, Monsieur l'Abbe Desgodins, a Roman Catholic missionary to Tibet, replied with a simple illustration. "Take a piece of paper in your hand," he said. "Crumple it up and then open your hand and let it fall out! Nothing is flat—all you have are high points and low depressions—the steep, inaccessible, rugged mountains and the deep valleys, though which flow some of the largest and fastest rivers in the world."

This description is a bit overdone, for Tibet has high plateaus at twelve thousand to thirteen thousand feet, with surrounding majestic mountains penetrating even higher into the thin atmosphere, where, tourists confess, you fight for every breath. These plateaus are surrounded by an extensive mountainous frontier. On the south, Tibet touches the northern borders of Kashmir, Nepal, Sikkim, and Bhutan. Its eastern frontiers touch Yunnan and Sichuan. On the north it is bounded by Qinghai and Xinjiang. From time immemorial, Tibet has also been known as the "roof of the world." It has the reputation of being a cold, desolate, exotic, and mysterious land typified by a strange religion that makes extensive use of huge monasteries, tens of thousands of lamas or priests, and ever-present prayer flags and wheels. But it is just this kind of country that has had a magnetic attraction for outsiders—diplomats, traders, explorers, mountain climbers, and missionaries. Particularly for the latter, Tibet has always been a challenge. Until its ramparts have been scaled and the flag of Jesus' kingdom planted within its borders, the church will not be satisfied. So it was with both Catholics and Protestants.

Tibet and Early Roman Catholic Efforts (1600-1750)

Background

Tourists traveling to Tibet are surprised when they enter the Jokhang temple, the holy of holies of Tibetan Buddhism, to see hanging in the entrance hall a bell on which are inscribed the words *Te Deum Laudamus, Te Dominum confitemur* (We praise thee, O God; we acknowledge thee to be the Lord). How could this symbol of the Christian faith be found in this isolated citadel of heathendom? Who were the missionaries who brought this bell to Tibet?

Abbe Huc, an early Catholic historian who in the mid-nineteenth century would himself go to Lhasa, notes that during the Middle Ages Catholic missionaries traveled everywhere with the gospel: "These preachers of the Gospel became nomads with the Tartars of the Desert, and worked their way through the lofty snow-covered mountains of Thibet into the seemingly impregnable fortress of Buddhism."[1] Of whatever Christian communities developed as a result of these first sacrificial efforts, no permanent results remained.

An Italian Franciscan, Friar Odoric of Pordenone, traveled in China from 1322 to 1328. In his extensive goings and comings through Central Asia, he may have gone into Tibet during the period of Mongol rule in China. It is not inconceivable that he could have given a Christian witness in that land. Again, however, no records or results remain to give any credence to this possibility.

The most credible evidence of the first missionary efforts in Tibet comes from the early seventeenth century. This is to be expected, for several reasons. The religious awakening that produced the Protestant Reformation in Europe in the sixteenth century also brought renewal to the Catholic church. A new burst of missionary enthusiasm came with the founding of new missionary orders, particularly the Society of Jesus, but also the Capuchins, who were to be assigned a special role in reaching Tibet. In 1622 the Congregation for the Propagation of the Faith was founded and gave coherence and unity, under the direct administration of the papacy, to Catholic missionary activity. Extremely important for the ultimate development of local Catholic churches around the world was the founding in 1663 of the Paris Foreign Mission Society. This

1. M. l'Abbe Huc, *Christianity in China, Tartary, and Thibet 1844–46*, vol. 2 (London: Longman, Brown, Green, Longmans, and Roberts, 1857), 249.

agency's primary purpose was to send out secular priests, not religious clergy, for evangelizing and church planting around the world. These activities within the church, as well as the climate of exploration and discovery in the sixteenth and seventeenth centuries, set the stage for vigorous worldwide Catholic outreach.

What was the political status of Tibet at this time? Then as now, when people thought of Tibet, they saw it related in some vague way to China. Yet it had an aura of independence. Missionaries saw themselves as going to Tibet, not to China. From 1582 to 1610 Father Matteo Ricci, an Italian Jesuit, was working his way through south China toward Beijing, its capital in the north. He never thought of his goal as including Tibet, nor did the administrative jurisdictions of the church group China and Tibet as one entity.

From before the advent of Christ until the fifth or sixth century, separate, wild tribes of nomads, referred to by the Chinese as Qiang, occupied the area that today is called Tibet. However, they did not have any identity as a separate, distinct group of people until the time of Songtsen Gampo. This remarkable leader has been compared to Alexander, Genghis Khan, and Napoleon. Born in 617, Songtsen Gampo unified these disparate tribes. From them he developed an empire that extended west to Samarkand, north to Mongolia, and south into India, presuming to call the Bay of Bengal the "Tibetan Ocean." As he went east into China, he plundered the capital at Xian and took a Chinese princess for a wife. Continuing until the tenth century, this kingdom left a permanent imprint of traditions, culture, language, and religion over the entire area.

Politically, Songtsen Gampo's vast empire split up very quickly after his death and reverted to hundreds of fiefdoms and small feudal states. For a time, even the commitment of the people to Buddhism, introduced through Gampo's two wives, one Chinese and the other Nepalese, waned.

When the Mongols ascended to power in China in the thirteenth century, they received tribute from the larger Tibetan states in return for not interfering in their affairs. This arrangement lasted until 1240 when Godan, a grandson of the famed Mongol leader Genghis Khan, plundered several villages in Tibet. Surprisingly, he then enlisted a famous abbot, Sakya Pandita, to instruct him in Buddhism. Thus began a relationship between the Mongol rulers and certain lamas in Tibet, by which the latter accepted the rulers' protection in exchange for giving them religious instruction. Ultimately, this produced the Tibetan theocracy, with its concept of the Dalai Lama as the spiritual and temporal ruler of Tibet. The cozy relationship between a Mongol leader and a lama also introduced Tibetan Buddhism, often called Lamaism, to the Mongols, who became its strong patrons. Kublai Khan, during his reign as emperor of

China (1260–1294), built Buddhist monasteries in Mongolia and at his court in Kambaluc (Beijing). He also appointed Tibetan monks to important positions in China and Mongolia.

When the Mongol dynasty lost its control over China in 1368, Tibet was left virtually independent. Shortly before the demise of the Mongols, Tibetan Buddhism, largely a product of Indian and Chinese Buddhism, went through a period of reform that gave it its unique identity. The Martin Luther of the Tibetan highlands was Tsong-kaba, who, according to tradition, was born miraculously to a mother who had been unable to conceive. His mother shaved his head when he was three years old and threw his white flowing hair outside the tent. A great tree, revered by the faithful in following centuries, instantly sprang up. He retired to meditate and pray in order to purify his heart. At this critical juncture he met a lama from the west, probably a European missionary according to later Catholic speculation. This man instructed him in doctrine for several years and then died suddenly. Following his teacher's death, Tsong-kaba retired to a new place called Lhasa, "land of the spirits," where he received disciples and instructed them in the reformed faith. Those who followed him became known as the Yellow Cap lamas, to distinguish them from the older, traditional Buddhists who were called the Red Caps.[2]

When Altan Khan, a descendent of the great Mongol khans, was ruling over Mongolia's reduced empire in 1578, he invited Sonam Gyatso, the Tibetan lama who was in charge of the Yellow Caps, to meet him at what today is Qinghai Lake. They formed a cordial relationship that led to Altan's conversion to the new Tibetan form of Buddhism and to its spread through evangelistic efforts by Gyatso and others throughout Mongolia. Out of gratitude, Altan Khan gave to Sonam Gyatso the title *Tale* (Dalai), a Mongolian term meaning "ocean." He considered the lama's knowledge to be as deep as the ocean. The title was more than an empty name; it gave the Yellow Caps, and Gyatso, further claim to be supreme over all Buddhist rivals in Tibet and Mongolia.

Sonam Gyatso was already considered to be the reincarnation of a former lama, himself a reincarnation of Gedun Truppa. Truppa had founded in 1447 a great monastery in Xigaze that had three thousand monks. So with the title recently given to him, Sonam Gyatso was considered to be the third in this line of succession. For a while the term *Dalai Lama* was only honorific. But when Lozang Gyatso assumed this title in 1622 as the fifth successor, another Mongol khan conferred on him both the spiritual and temporal power to rule over Tibet. Shortly

2. *Huc and Gabet Travels in Tartary, Thibet and China 1844–46,* vol. 1 (London: George Routledge and Sons, 1928), 79.

after this, he designated Lhasa as his capital and began construction of the Potala, the great palace that was to belong to him and his successors to the present day.

The role of the Dalai Lama is not hereditary; the term is an oxymoron in a celibate priesthood. The selection process is both mysterious and complicated as monks seek to find the baby boy in whom the spirit of the former Dalai Lama has become reincarnated. Political elements as well as religious ones make the selection to be even more difficult than the so-called apostolic succession. For example, the Tibetans believe that reincarnation is a common phenomenon that occurs with hundreds of lamas. Therefore the Dalai Lama is often selected according to power dynamics within and without Tibet. The current Dalai Lama, born in 1935 and now in exile in India, is the thirteenth in this role and comes from a peasant family of the Amdo region, now belonging to the Chinese province of Qinghai.

Although the figure of the Dalai Lama has given a theoretical unity to Tibet, much as the pope has to the Roman Catholic church, the country has remained divided. Often, the lamas, the nobles, and the Dalai Lama were pitted in an ongoing battle to gain control. The Dalai Lama has controlled the central kingdoms of U and Tsang and the three kingdoms of Ngari, the territory that is usually considered to be Tibet. But outside of this more limited sphere were the "independent Tibetan kingdoms of Laddak, Spitu, Kulu, Kangra, Mustang, Sikkim, Bhutan and Dergue. Added to these were the large principalities of Amdo and the warring kingdoms of Kham." Since 1850, some of these independent kingdoms were taken over by British India—Ladakh, Spitu, Kulu, and Kangra. Sikkim, Bhutan, Mustang, and Dergue continued independent. Others, principally Amdo and Kham, were ruled over off and on by Chinese warlords whose power was reigned in only partially by Beijing until 1949.[3] The uncertainty of the boundary lines between Tibet proper and the eastern kingdoms, and between the latter and China proper, as well as the uncertainty of who ruled what, added greatly to the problems of both Catholic and Protestant missionaries in taking the gospel to "Tibet." They never were sure where they were and who was opposing them for which reasons! China may have believed that she controlled Tibet, but Tibet certainly believed that she was independent. Theory aside, each was busy with its own affairs, and, in practical politics, sovereignty and suzerainty were moot questions.

3. For the quotation and the other material in this paragraph I am indebted to Michael Peissel, *Cavaliers of Kham: The Secret War in Tibet* (London: Heinemann, 1972), 7. Amdo was included in the new province of Qinghai, and Kham's territory until 1949 was divided into Tibet proper and the new Chinese province of Xikang.

The Work Begins

Roman Catholic missionaries had worked in China proper and among the Mongols in the thirteenth and fourteenth centuries. The story of the Jesuits entering China in the late sixteenth century is also well known. However, Catholics did not concentrate on Tibet until the 1620s, near the end of the Ming dynasty. The missionaries were all Jesuits, and, courageous and intrepid, they appeared not a bit awed by the formidable obstacles before them. The Jesuit trailblazer for this pioneer effort was Antonio de Andrada, a Portuguese, who used Agra, the capital of Mogol, south of the present New Delhi, as his base. His initial interest was aroused by reports of the existence of Christian communities, survivals from some earlier witness for Christ. He and a companion, Manuel Marques, disguised themselves as Buddhist pilgrims and in 1624 joined the caravan of the Great Mogol that was going to Kashmir. Faced with dangerous circumstances when their disguise was about to be uncovered, they stopped at the city of Tsaparang. Here the king, queen, and princes gave them a warm welcome, fed them, allowed them to preach, and permitted them to build a chapel. Supplied with a document from the king guaranteeing him liberty in his work and freedom from harassment, Andrada returned to Agra for reinforcements.

The king responded well to Andrada's ministry, becoming an enthusiastic inquirer who learned doctrine, memorized Catholic prayers, and volunteered to lay the cornerstone for the new church. Alarmed at this turn of events, the lamas who counseled the king persuaded him to go to a famous monastery where his brother was the Grand Lama. Upon his return after two months of study, the king held several public conferences at which missionaries and Buddhist lamas discussed such weighty topics as the nature of God and reincarnation. The work continued to go forward and many believed, including the royal family.

When word of these happenings reached Lhasa, the Dalai Lama sent a Mongol prince to Tsaparang with his army. He put down this religious uprising, taking the life of the Christian king. Andrada, who had been transferred from Tsaparang, sought the help of the king of Ladakh, then called Great Thibet, but this king did not wish to interfere in a civil war that pitted the Yellow Caps against all the religious groups opposing them. What had been a promising beginning fell victim to internal strife in Tibet.

Other Jesuit missionaries reached Ladakh, Lhe, and Rudoq, to the southeast, and Christians numbered nearly four hundred. The king of Lhe attacked the Christian community, imprisoning both believers and some Jesuit fathers. He made slaves of several of the Christians and brought them to Lhe.

Even during this early period, the missionaries wished to reach Lhasa. In attempting to reach this goal, they stopped in what is now Bhutan. With the permission of the king and queen, they built a church and baptized twelve people, including the queen's niece, who was a daughter of the king at Lhasa. Father Estevao Cacella had a profitable, short ministry in Xigaze, but he died before the work could be established firmly. Times were chaotic and over the next twenty years the work prospered or was abandoned as local conditions improved or worsened. Believers numbered in the hundreds, but no records remain to show if there was any continuity with new thrusts into Tibet in the following century.[4]

In the next Catholic effort, missionaries reached Lhasa itself. In 1704 several Capuchin friars went to Tibet, but within five years the mission was abandoned, largely because there were not enough missionaries to replace those who died or became sick. The vision of reaching this distant land, however, had not disappeared. Students studying in Rome knew about this pioneer effort. One of them, Ippolito Desideri, waded his way through a maze of Catholic bureaucratic procedures to become a missionary. He finally reached Lhasa, called then the capital of Third Tibet, 18 March 1716.

Desideri committed himself to learning the language and the culture. After only a few months of diligent study, combined with intensive discussions with Tibetan lamas on their faith, he prepared an apologetic work. This book summarized "the great important Truth that there is but one Faith leading to Heaven and eternal salvation."[5] He presented this book to the king and discussed with him all aspects of the Christian faith. Although the king and his advisers concluded that this teaching was completely opposite from what they believed, they did not interfere with Desideri, even providing him with a small chapel in which he held daily Mass.

In 1717 Desideri moved two miles away from Lhasa itself to continue his studies at a famous monastery, plunging ever more deeply into the complex mysteries of Tibetan Buddhism. It soon became apparent, even as others learned later, that the most learned of the lamas were not able to answer his questions. So he prayed to God for light on Buddhism, and was thankful to understand finally all of the subtleties and abstruse matter. With this new, God-given light he affirmed: "Having by my aforesaid diligence discovered the site of the enemy's camp, the quality of their

4. The material concerning Andrada and other early Jesuits comes from two sources: C. Wessels, S.J., *Early Jesuit Travellers in Central Asia 1603–1721* (The Hague: Martinus Nijhoff, 1924) and Huc, *Christianity in China, Tartary, and Thibet,* 2:249–71.

5. Fillipo de Fillipi, *An Account of Tibet: The Travels of Ippolito Desideri of Pistola, S.J. 1712–1727* (London: George Routledge and Sons, 1932), 99. Subsequent material about Desideri is also from this source.

arms and their artifices, and provided myself with arms and ammunition, towards the end of November I resolved to challenge them and begin war. In the name and by the aid of God, I commenced to confute the errors of that Sect and to declare the truth of our Holy Faith."[6]

At this point disaster struck. The Mongols invaded the country, Lhasa was taken, and the king and his ministers were deposed and murdered. A few years later in October 1720, China and its emperor took over Tibet and ruled the country through a body of ministers, some of whom were Chinese, Mongols, and Tibetans.

Equally disastrous were the bungling administrative decisions of the Catholic church. Its leaders decided that the province of Tibet was to be worked not by the learned Jesuits, of whom Desideri was a worthy example, but by the Capuchins. Unfortunately, Capuchin interest in Tibet had been lukewarm, and their commitment to the language and culture was minimal. After Desideri obeyed the Society's General and left Tibet, the Capuchins carried on as best they could, opening a small dispensary, translating catechisms, distributing literature, and commencing chapel services. By 1742 they counted twenty-seven baptized adult converts and double that number of interested inquirers. More than twenty-five hundred children, most near death, were baptized to gain eternal salvation. Lack of cultural sensitivity resulted in some unwise action by a number of converts, such as refusing to revere the Dalai Lama by bowing and not performing some expected activities. A vicious persecution followed, and the mission to Tibet was closed, with the fathers hastily retreating to Nepal. The last salvo in the battle that Desideri wanted was ended. The Tibetan lamas were the victors. Other Catholics reached Lhasa, and the Protestants always had it as their elusive, if not vain, goal. No subsequent efforts in Tibet proper would ever attain this high a degree of success.

Fathers Huc and Gabet Travel to Lhasa

After the Capuchins abandoned their missionary effort in Tibet in the 1720s, Catholic missionary work languished for one hundred years. Much of this was caused when the pope, dismayed by the tragic rites controversy in China, dissolved the Society of Jesus in 1774. But in 1846, Abbe Huc and Father Gabet, both of the Vincentian Order and living in Beijing, undertook a long exploratory trip that took them through Manchuria, Mongolia, and Tibet. The first of the unequal treaties between China and the western powers was being signed, and the Protestant missionaries were only now entering into the five open treaty ports. However, quite a few Roman Catholic fathers, whose orders had been in

6. Ibid., 106.

China off and on since 1600, were scattered throughout the country. They were able to travel at this time without regard to the new treaty arrangements that restricted religious workers to the coastal areas. Huc and Gabet faced no opposition as they went to Tibet. They stayed for long periods at major monasteries and had extended discussion with the lamas.

The fathers were surprised at the shape of Tibetan Buddhism. Huc commented:

> Upon the most superficial examination of the reforms and innovations introduced by Tsong-kaba into Lamaism, one must be struck with their affinity to Catholicism. The cross, the miter, the dalmatic, the cape, which the Great Lamas wear on their journeys or when they are performing some ceremony out of the temple; the service with double choirs, the psalmody, the exorcisms; the censer, suspended from five chains, which can be opened or closed at will; the benedictions given by the lamas extending the right hand over the heads of the faithful; ecclesiastical celibacy, spiritual retirement, the veneration of saints, the fasts, the processions, the chaplet, the litanies, the holy water—all these are analogies between the Buddhists and ourselves.[7]

How did they explain this? They concluded that Tsong-kaba's teacher, the one whom he had described as having a "great nose and eyes that gleamed as with a supernatural fire," was a European Catholic missionary, who, tragically, died before completing his instruction in the faith. Here again is one of those historic enigmas that raises the question, What if—?

As they traveled toward Lhasa, Huc and Gabet had specific missionary goals that they did not seek to conceal. One was to translate a short account from the time when the world was created to the period of the apostles. They put this in the form of a dialogue between a lama of the Lord of Heaven and a Buddha. The people who saw the first draft of this were intrigued by specific names of people and places and certain dates. How different from the lamas' quasi-mythical records or formal, logical reasoning!

When they reached Lhasa, Huc and Gabet found the Tibetan regent friendly. He allowed them to set up a little chapel in their home for worship and to explain to those who came the meaning of the large picture of the crucifixion hanging on the wall. The regent was up to date in his understanding of dialogue: "Your religion is not the same as ours. It is important we should ascertain which is the true one. Let us, then, examine both carefully and sincerely. If yours is right, we will adopt it. How

7. *Huc and Gabet Travels in Tartary, Thibet and China 1844–46,* 2:79.

could we refuse to do so? If, on the contrary, ours is the true religion, I believe you will have the good sense to follow it."[8]

Unfortunately, the Chinese ambassador was extremely antagonistic. The presence of these missionaries, not yet tolerated even in China, would harm Chinese-Tibetan relationships, he claimed, and he ordered them to leave. To the regent and some receptive lamas he justified his action by affirming that the teaching of the missionaries would ultimately destroy the lamas and their religion.

Posttreaty Efforts by Catholic Missionaries to Evangelize Tibet

The Catholic church usually operates by clear administrative procedures. Early in the seventeenth century, the Society of Jesus was responsible for the initial missionary thrusts into Tibet from India. This responsibility was transferred in the 1720s to the Capuchins, and Desideri, well-prepared for effective work among the Tibetans, was forced to leave Lhasa. In 1808 the Sacred Congregation established the Tibet-Hindustan apostolic vicariate and committed it to the Capuchins, who used Agra in India as their base of operations. In March 1846 Tibet was separated from India and made an apostolic vicariate and committed to the Foreign Mission Society of Paris (La Societe des Missions-Etrangeres de Paris). To this mission agency, not an order but a society of "seculars," was given the responsibility for evangelizing many of the minorities in China. Its specific purpose was to send out missionaries from the Diocese of Paris who would make all due haste in raising up indigenous priests to take over the work. This sets the stage for the Catholic missionary outreach to the frontier areas of China in the nineteenth and twentieth centuries.

Just what is an apostolic vicariate? This was an entirely new development in Catholic missionary strategy. From one standpoint, it avoided the stranglehold that the *Padroado* had given to Spain and Portugal on Catholic missionary work. A vicar apostolic bore the title of an extinct see and therefore he could be appointed directly by the pope and under the direction of the Propaganda to a Protestant or pagan land. This was done where the lack of patronage by a Roman Catholic state made the usual approach of using diocesan bishops impossible. The see that a vicar apostolic occupied was called an apostolic vicariate.

When the Foreign Mission Society (hereafter known as MEP) received jurisdiction over Tibet, there may have been as many as five thousand Christians in that land. These were mostly among the Chinese, but with a few Tibetans and "half-breeds" (offspring of Tibetans and other peoples such as Lissous or Loutze). Charles Renou was the society's first

8. Ibid., 196.

missioner to try to reach Tibet from China. He went through Litang and Batang in far west China. When he pressed on toward Lhasa in 1848, disguised as a merchant, he was apprehended by Chinese authorities and sent back to Canton. Not to be deterred, he traveled to Yunnan and, using the same ineffective disguise, headed northwest to the lamasery of Tserou, where he was welcomed warmly. The resident living Buddha, believing Renou to be a Chinese merchant, gladly put him up and gave him some Tibetan lessons!

Renou had some missiological questions that he directed to Rome. What should he do about polyandry, an arrangement in which a woman had several husbands? Did Paul's principle apply—that is, if she became a Christian, must she stay with the first husband, even if he refused to believe, or could she choose among those who converted? Or if none believed and wished to leave her, could she marry a Christian? Given the lack of fish, vegetables, and eggs, could a convert be excused from fasting or abstinence from meat? The pope, by special decrees, responded positively to both these requests.[9]

In the 1850s news traveled slowly. The seminary of the Foreign Mission Society in Paris was dismayed by Renou's first attempt to reach Lhasa. Not knowing of his successful passage through Yunnan, its leaders determined that the mission would be accomplished better from the Indian side, via Assam or Bhutan. This proved to be even more tragic: Nicolas Krick and Augustin Bourry were massacred by the wild Michemis in 1854, and efforts to travel through Nepal and Sikkim also failed.

So, it was back again to square one—the China side. Renou headed northwest from the province of Yunnan and in 1854 established a station in Bonga, where he built a vicarage and a private chapel. His main work was to compose a book of doctrine in the Tibetan language, which would be of help in evangelism and would enable him to instruct Chinese and Tibetan children. Very shortly the promising beginning was brought to an abrupt end. Renou was attacked, beaten, and then chased from the city by crowds whom the lamas had stirred up. He retreated to Kiangka, southwest of Batang.

9. Adrien Launay, *Histoire de la Mission du Tibet* (Paris: Desclee, de Brouwer et cie, 1930), 215, 216. Other material in the history of Catholic missions in Tibet during this period has come from several sources: "La Mission du Thibet," *Annales de La Societe Missions-Etrangeres de Paris* (July-August 1934): 147–53; numerous articles from 1860 to 1900 in *Les Missions Catholiques,* published by Propagation de la Foi et de Saint-Pierre Apotre; Adrien Launay, *Memorial de la Societe des Missions-Etrangeres,* 2 vols. (Paris: Seminaire des Missions-Etrangers, 1912–16); various issues of *Bulletin of La Societe Missions-Etrangeres;* various issues of *Catholic Missions,* published by the Society for the Propagation of the Faith in New York, beginning in 1907; *Annales de la Propagation de la Foi;* Gaston Gratuze, *Un Pionnier de la Mission Tibetaine le Pere Auguste Desgodins (1826–1913)* (Paris: Apostolat des Editions, 1968). Apart from very important quotations, I will not give full annotation.

Monseigneur Thomine Desmazures was appointed vicar apostolic of Tibet in 1857, and by 1861, with several colleagues, he determined to push on toward Lhasa. He wanted to establish his base in the Tibetan capital, the equivalent of Rome to Catholics and Mecca to Muslims. Equally important, he wanted to test France's recently completed unequal treaty with China. Would Tibet, supposedly controlled by China, be considered under the provisions of this treaty? Would there be freedom to preach there, even as supposedly there was freedom to preach everywhere in China?

Desmazures soon found out. When the party reached Tchamutong, north of Ouisi and west of the Salween River, it was stopped by a very hostile group of lamas who did not allow it to proceed. The party stayed stubbornly for several months, pleading vainly the treaty provisions that the missionaries thought afforded them a kind of protectorate. Leaving a few of the fathers on the scene, Desmazures went to Beijing to press his case for the Tibetan mission. The Chinese government complacently refused to intervene. It denied, without much logic, that Tibet was included in the recently negotiated treaties. The French legation was of no more help. It accepted with little complaint the Chinese interpretation of the treaties, even though some months earlier it had assured the French missionaries that the Treaty of Tientsin included Tibet. This was the hardest blow to take—even the mother country had betrayed them. To the missionaries at the time this was the death blow to an effective work in Tibet. Gratuze, the biographer of Auguste Desgodins, one of Desmazures's companions, commented bitterly, "The hope that the missionaries had of seeing Christ reign in the capital even of Llamaism was, if not lost forever, very strongly compromised."[10]

The same reasoning applied to the ravaged Bonga station of work. Neither the Chinese government nor the French government was going to intervene if the problem was in Tibet proper. Father Chauveau, successor as vicar apostolic to the disappointed Desmazures, who retired to France, was left with only one course of action. He needed to find a safe city along the frontier, that area between China and Tibet where neither Tibetans or Chinese had permanent control, and make that the center of the mission work. Here, at least, despite the often chaotic conditions, there could be appeal to the Chinese and French governments. The city chosen was Dajianlu, later to be renamed Kangting by the Kuomintang. It was officially the capital of what the missionaries came to call Chinese Tibet or the Sichuan frontier of Tibet. This could be a base for reaching out to other territories to the south, referred to often as the Yunnan frontier of Tibet that were under Chinese control: Bomme, Yerkalo, At-

10. Gratuze, *Un Pionnier de la Mission Tibetaine,* 134.

entze, Ouisi, and other smaller villages. To the west was the city of Batang, much closer to "independent" Tibet, but still largely under Chinese control. From these several cities along the edges of Tibet, the missionaries prayed that divine Providence would ultimately open its tightly closed doors, "Open Sesame," the apostolic prayer using the oft-closed flower as an analogy of an inaccessible land.

In the years leading up to the chaos of the Boxer Rebellion, the Tibetan lamas in Chinese territory, oft-inept Chinese officials, and zealous priests struggled with each other for some temporary advantage. At least eight stages can be identified: an attack on a mission station; retreat by missionaries with dispersion of local Christians; protests by the missionaries to Beijing, local officials, and the French government; consultations at some level with all involved; assurances that the situation would be rectified; a waiting period to see if promises would be met; final assurances that this type of thing would never happen again; return of the missionaries and Christians and continuation of the ministry. If the damage inflicted resulted in considerable loss of life or extensive damage to property, the Chinese government might make an indemnity payment. For example, after an attack upon Batang and Bomme in 1875, a payment of eleven thousand francs was made to MEP for repair, for articles that could not be replaced, and for general losses.

The religious lamas and the Chinese officials who opposed the missionaries always listed the incursion of a foreign faith, preached by foreign missionaries, to be their main objection. Specifically, the Frenchness of the missionaries portended that France had political interest in Tibet. Officials often searched missionaries' homes and persons for maps, descriptions of where they had traveled, and any other evidence to substantiate such charges.

Colonial powers had never grabbed any of Tibet's territory, but Russia, Great Britain, and China had for many years played the "Great Game," the power struggle among them for influence in Tibet and in Central Asia.[11] Even a small country like Nepal, unified by Gurkha kings in the late eighteenth century, invaded Tibet in 1788 and in 1855. A British expedition led by George Bogle advanced into Xigaze in 1774, seeking trade agreements. Another British expedition, headed by Younghusband and assisted by the Chinese representatives in Tibet, reached Lhasa in 1904. The result was a treaty with the Tibetans which gave the expedition trade rights through Gyangze, the third largest city in Tibet. Little wonder then that the Tibetans were nervous about a French presence whose motives puzzled them. Add to this China's usual fear of foreigners, abnormally heightened in the posttreaty period after

11. Jeremy Bernstein, "A Journey to Lhasa," *The New Yorker,* 14 December 1987, 68–69.

1860 when it sought to reform and to resist increased western pressure. This set the stage for the Chinese to resist to the death the incursion of religious outsiders, even in distant Tibet.

Of course, religious opposition was also a major factor. After one bad incident in the late 1860s, two imperial legates, acting on behalf of the Dalai Lama, ignored in a written reply to the missionaries the matter of the people they had killed and the houses they had destroyed. They mentioned only that they had had their religion for a long time and had no need for a foreign one. In their view, the new religion was not only foreign, but also false. With this as their premise, the lamas blamed the missionaries for every untoward local event, be it the great Batang earthquake, an infestation of field mice, changes in the seasonal weather, drought, floods, and every other calamity!

Jittery missionaries were even more alarmed when they heard about the Tientsin massacre of 1870, in which several Catholic priests and nuns were killed as a result of the people misunderstanding their conduct of an orphanage. Father Chauveau felt that it was only a matter of time before the repercussions from this tragic event would reach Tibet and further inflame the anti-French sentiment.

Support for the missionary cause often came from strange places. Monseigneur Chauveau reported that Sir Jung Bahadoor, the royal regent of Nepal, had written a letter to Tibetan authorities that called for them to respect the treaties granting French missionaries the liberty to preach their religion in Tibet and to reimburse them for their losses. This letter caused consternation among officials in Lhasa, since they highly respected their Nepalese friend and his advice.

Not all of the conflicts the missionaries experienced were among themselves, the Chinese, and the Tibetan religious leaders. Chinese officials and the lamas were always in tension with one another; the "Mahometans," spread widely through Chinese Tibet, hated both the Tibetans and the Chinese, and in the mid-1870s destroyed the Kumbum monastery, widely known outside Tibet because of Abbe Huc's account of his experiences there; the "Lyssous" (Lisu?) to the south revolted every five or ten years against the Chinese, who sought every excuse to annihilate them; the "Lou-tze" (Lolos?), also to the south and close to the Salween River, were known to be savage and rebellious. This part of the world was not friendly to the gospel of Christ, with its message of reconciliation!

Missiological Issues in Catholic Work (1846-1900)

What was the specific work of Catholic missions in Tibet in the late nineteenth century and how and why was it done? The daily schedule in most of the stations and compounds where missionaries, staff, and converts lived was predictable: rising at 5 A.M.; one-half hour of prayer, followed by study until breakfast; study or work until noon; after lunch, work until 6 P.M.; evening prayers in both Tibetan and Chinese; supper; an explanation of the catechism in Chinese and in Tibetan. Everyone went to bed at 9 P.M. On Sunday there was detailed doctrinal instruction in Tibetan.

The compounds were often elaborate. In Bomme, for example, the missionaries had a large, two-story home, and nearby was the home of the farmers, presumably converts, who cultivated large areas of land near to the two homes. Only the plot of land being farmed had a low wall about it. No city seems to have existed at the place where the missionaries lived, but from their residence they went easily to scattered villages close by. For purposes of protection, missionaries sometimes erected modest forts. This further enraged the lamas, as they interpreted this to mean that the missionaries were building military establishments to further the French presence. The village of Bonga was often referred to in French as Bongadzong, the fortress of Bonga.

In the small town of Batang, the missionaries had a walled compound in which, apart from living quarters, there was a stable, a barn, a place to keep pigeons, a garden for vegetables, and some irrigation ditches. Agriculture was an essential part of the work in each area, and the missionaries tried to find a more sedentary livelihood for converts who, up to this point, may have been nomads.[12]

As they preached in villages where they lived or in nearby areas, how were the missionaries received? In Bonga, the common people were more impressed by the progress that they saw than by the attacks made on the missionaries. Whenever a missionary went off to Beijing for business, rumor had it that he had been granted the rank of Mandarin. So local people concluded that the missionaries had some clout, and that there were practical advantages for seeking their protection. Ministries of compassion to orphans and to others in need also attracted local people to the Christian faith. Missionaries started schools for young people and helped them to get a rudimentary education. Adult converts, who needed to go through a catechetical process before being baptized, were not numerous. Many children were baptized: those in families with adult believers, but more often pagan children at the point of death.

Adrien Launay, a noted Catholic church historian, gives a detailed account of outreach from Bonga into several surrounding villages, some Tibetan and others of small minority groups. In the early 1860s, Desgodins and several colleagues went to the village of Songta, the home of the

12. Drawings of these homes and compounds are printed in *Les Missions Catholiques,* 23 July 1875, 353, 359.

Melam people, a subgroup of the Loutze. The whole village welcomed them, fed them bountifully, and then listened as Desgodins explained the Christian faith, emphasizing the advantages that would come to them if they believed as a village. He stressed the protection they would receive under the provisions of the new treaties.

All of the people, led by their chief, considered this proposal, and then unanimously prostrated themselves on the ground. This indicated to the missioners that the Melam were willing to embrace Catholicism and to place themselves under its protection. The missionaries then exhorted them to love God and not to serve the devil. They were not clear how not to serve the devil. Six sorcerers, charged with using drums to chase demons, came to the missionaries and said, "We want to be good Christians. Can you deliver us from the control of the demons?" Desgodins had a ready-made formula: "Be loosed by Jesus and Mary! Embrace the crucifix. Make the sign of the cross. Dismiss them [the demons] in peace." The sorcerers, upon request, then brought their drums used in exorcism, since they were no longer of use to them. Fetishes used in heathen worship were thrown into the river by one of the orphan boys from Bonga. The same procedure was used in the neighboring village of Longpou. The missionaries were ecstatic and overwhelmed with such an ingathering of converts. In these two villages a total of 323 persons were prepared to believe. "How like the experience of Peter with the miraculous catch of fish in the Lake of Galilee," they exclaimed.

Readiness to believe did not eliminate ongoing superstitious beliefs or practices. In the city of Aben, one of the priests observed that, after the village's profession of the faith, some sorcerers were still offering sacrifices. When questioned, they explained: "In Tibet it is the custom never to send someone away without a present. Because of this we are making a sacrifice of incense to the demons as we send them away." The ceremony was simple: "We have served you well in these last years, but from now on we no longer will serve you. We ask you not to be angered at our new choice!" While laughing at this, the fathers noted that this ceremony of honor for these "devilish imps" was pardonable in view of the ignorance of the neophytes.

The fathers questioned the motives of some of these people movements to Christ, pointing to another conversion that they claimed was from "more pure motives." The chief of the lamasery of Tsadam, located in the village of Tchrana, believed and, over a period of time, led his fellow lamas to the faith. The village, released from bondage to the lamas, also committed itself to Catholicism. But there was the problem of all the idols in the lamasery. Gathering the lamas together, one of the fathers took an axe to these "diabolical figures" and disemboweled several of them. This incident was blown out of proportion through rumor by those not present, who reported that the father had dragged the idols to the river and cast them in. Deciding that this behavior could be twisted to their disadvantage by lamas in neighboring villages, the missionaries resolved to do it no longer.[13]

Many missionaries felt the need to use visual objects to reinforce the faith in the hearts of new converts. Father Carreau in his preaching each month told his listeners that in visiting pagan homes he found many indications of unbelief: ancestral tablets, some type of statue of an idol, a holder in which to put incense sticks. "But," he complained, "when I visit your homes, I see no signs either of paganism or Christianity!" He exhorted them to have some functional substitutes—images of the Holy Virgin, statues of Saint Joseph and angels, and a crucifix. Not objects of faith, but aids to faith, these would focus the thinking of the converts.

Catholic Missions from 1900 to 1950

What could the Catholic church report as a result of this half-century of its modern presence in Tibet? Many missionaries martyred, several dead of natural causes, various stations built, destroyed, rebuilt, and then destroyed again, numerous complaints made to the government, and a total of 1,433 baptized converts.[14] Was it worth the cost? The answer was given in ongoing commitment to the calling of Christ. Various missioners had proposed that Tibet be consecrated to the Sacred Heart of Mary. They were not about to abandon this goal.

Some adjustments were called for. One was to reestablish a witness to Tibet from India. To this end, Father Desgodins, a veteran from the China task force, was sent to Padong, a city not far from Darjeeling and to the south of Sikkim. In British India and thus not subject to the constantly changing conditions found in China, this area was then included in the vicariate of Tibet. Desgodins did the expected things, but spent most of his time writing a Tibetan-Latin-French dictionary that was useful for future missionaries. Another emphasis in the Padong work was a ministry to orphans and children. As a result of this compassionate outreach, the government made a grant of eight hundred acres of forested land for a Christian village, which became the station of Maria Basti.

On the China side, the killings continued. Four missionaries died in 1905 alone and their names were added to the Gold Book of Necrology at the MEP Seminary in Paris where they had studied. The workers in Dajianlu hoped against hope that if France had no influence in the area,

13. Launay, *Histoire de la Mission du Tibet,* 384–91.

14. M. Louis-Eugene Louvet, *Les Missions Catholiques au XIX Siecle,* "L'Eglise de Chine, 1800–1890" (Paris: de Brouwer et Cie, 1898), 173.

possibly the British could step in the gap, a hope that was sparked as a result of the recent Younghusband expedition and resultant treaty that opened trade opportunities through Sikkim. This was a vain hope, except for a few more openings through Sikkim for missionaries on the India border. In 1924, in a realistic and symbolic move of reduced expectations, the vicariate of Dajianlu was renamed from Mission of Tibet to Mission of Dajianlu. At that time, this mission had two bishops, fifteen French missionaries, three indigenous priests, and forty-eight hundred baptized converts. More than one-half of these were Chinese, about two-fifths were Tibetans and Loutze, and a few were Nepalese.

In December 1930, Father LaFonde of the Canadian Franciscans went to Dajianlu to establish a leprosarium. Located at Mosimien, two days' journey south of the city over very treacherous roads, the leprosarium was operated by the Franciscan Sisters of Mary. Was this a response to some rather lavishly funded American Protestant works of mercy in Tibet? The American journal *Catholic Missions,* in its February 1926 issue, had plastered a slogan across one page: "A missionary without funds is as helpless as soldiers without weapons." A frequent complaint of all Catholic missionaries was that whatever success Protestants had, it was because of their vast expenditures—they bought converts!

Whatever the motivation, those suffering from leprosy came as pagans, but gradually were led by this compassionate ministry to follow the true God. They attended Mass regularly, made the sign of the cross, and regularly repeated six Pater and six Ave. Outward formality only? Possibly, but for people in these circumstances it represented progress toward a fuller understanding of the Christian faith.

Over the years from 1900, many educational projects were inaugurated by the Catholic missionaries in Dajianlu. These included a seminary, a school to train catechists, who in the Catholic scheme did most of the direct evangelization, an orphanage, a home for the aged, schools for Tibetan and Chinese virgins, and parish schools. The church also ran a hospital and a dispensary. Converts may have been relatively few, but they were well cared for by a broad range of services.

Missionaries were not sure how to interpret events of May 1919, when the Chinese government recognized the independence of Tibet. Was this not merely a belated acceptance of what had seemed to be a fact since the advent of the Chinese republic in 1912? Would this edict affect the work being done along the borders of Tibet? Would Great Britain possibly use its influence with Tibet to press for religious liberty? Plainly, the church saw that it was caught up in the dynamics of power politics, and spiritual solutions would not win the day.

Catholic missionaries were not as quick as Protestant missionaries to leave the area entirely in times of national crisis. They stayed on in 1912 when the new Chinese republic was formed and in 1927 during the conflict between Nationalist and Communist forces. In 1911 Father J. B. Charrier, for example, went west from Dajianlu a twelve-days' horse journey and lived in a small hut for three years with an aged Roman Catholic Tibetan priest, along with ten or twelve other tenants. Eventually, he bought a tent and lived in it for another four months. Knowing that it would be dangerous for him to go farther into the interior, he sent a catechist to go several days' journey west in an evangelistic effort.

How did Catholic and Protestant missionaries in Tibet get along with each other? Protestants had the usual complaints against Catholic doctrine and some of the methods. They were glad to use Roman Catholic medical facilities in Dajianlu and their hospitality along the trails from Lijiang to Yerkalo. In some cities where more missionaries were concentrated, as Dajianlu, times of tension arose. One Catholic father recalls that some of the Protestant groups displayed their zeal against "their [Catholic] neighbors," but, seeing that this got them nowhere, developed a more cordial and friendly attitude. He had praise for certain Protestant missionaries, such as Dr. Shelton of the Foreign Christian Mission.[15]

The monks of Saint Bernard from Switzerland made a unique and creative effort to demonstrate Christ's compassion along the Yunnan borders of Tibet. A branch of the noted Hospice of Saint Bernard, located at Mont Joux pass in the Alps and founded in the eleventh century to protect travelers from the Saracens and winter storms, it founded a hospice in 1933 on the pass of Mount Latsa. This was just to the west of the small village of Weixi, itself 175 miles northwest from Dali, an important city in west Yunnan. Like all Catholic work, this was no lone effort. Several years earlier Monseigneur de Guebriant, Superior of the Paris Foreign Mission Society, had discussed with Pope Pius XI the need for missioners who would be able to endure the hardships of working in the high mountains of west Yunnan. They decided to invite the monks of Saint Bernard to take up this work. After preliminary survey work, the Swiss priests selected this 12,464-foot-high peak, located on the natural trade route between China, the Salween Valley, Burma, and Tibet.

The purpose of the monks of Saint Bernard was to minister to all in need who traveled over those high mountain trails in trade and commerce. Much of their work in winter was done on skis or snowshoes. Their most valuable helpers were huge Saint Bernard dogs—half Swiss and half Tibetan. In the city of Weixi, the monks, helped by the Cluny Sisters of Saint Joseph and two Tibetan nuns, ran a mission school attended by children from Sikkim, Nepal, Bhutan, and Tibet.

15. "Les Missions Protestantes et le Thibet," *Bulletin de la Societe Missions-Etrangeres,* September 1928, 544–51.

The most effective Catholic work in the 1930s and 1940s was done along the Yunnan borders of Tibet. An important city for this was Yerkalo, which, depending on local circumstances at a particular time, was in either Chinese Tibet or independent Tibet. When a mission station was first formed here in 1887 by Christians driven from Bonga, it was in Tibetan territory. Shortly after that it reverted to China until 1932, when it was retaken by a Living Buddha from the nearby village of Sogun. Through the years the Christians at Yerkalo had suffered much for their faith, and the little local cemetery was filled with the burial plots both of French priests and of Tibetan Christians.

The most recently martyred of the Catholic priests was Father Maurice Tournay, a Saint Bernard missionary to Tibet, who came to north Yunnan in 1935. He commenced his work in education at Weixi and then at Hualopa, a few hours away. His approach to education was innovative. He wrote plays for his students that resembled the medieval mystery plays, with their drama of the confrontation between angels and devils. These dramas had practical themes: how to overcome avarice, how to defeat an opium-smoking habit. Not strictly religious in nature, but touching critical issues of local society, they attracted both Christian and pagan audiences.

Tournay took every possible opportunity to preach. Once he accompanied a colleague, Father Andre, to Patong, two hours to the south of his school. He had studied Tibetan only for one month, and Father Andre jokingly told him, "You sing the Mass, and I'll preach." Tournay refused to accept this easy way out and replied, "Trust me. I'll preach."[16] Since he had made such good progress in spoken Tibetan, Tournay traveled extensively through the entire area.

Much of his time Tourney spent encouraging the Tibetan pastor and his flock at Yerkalo, now totally in control of lamas who hated the Christian testimony in this city. They continued their pressure, threatening Tournay with death and trying to force the Christians to apostatize. He sought to no avail to rectify these situations and finally retreated to Shanghai. From here he made appeals to international agencies to put pressure on Tibet to recognize the rights of Christians in Yerkalo. Following these failures, and with the tacit approval of Monseigneur Riberi, the Catholic Apostolic Nuncio in China, he determined to travel directly to Lhasa and lodge his protest there.

Any such attempt must be secret and avoid the lamas who seemed more numerous than the mountains. Tournay disguised himself and

16. Robert Loup, *Martyr in Tibet: The Heroic Life and Death of Father Maurice Tournay, St. Bernard Missionary to Tibet* (New York: David McKay Co., 1956), 110. The material in subsequent paragraphs about Tournay is taken from this book.

joined a small caravan that first went south and then directly toward Lhasa. Unfortunately, someone apparently informed on him, the caravan was ambushed, and Tournay was cruelly assassinated. Humanly speaking, his last mission failed. But only eternity will tell whether the memory of his martyrdom and that of so many more over an eighty-year period will yet be the seed of an ongoing witness for Christ in Tibet. A recent observer of Christianity among China's minority nationalities has reported: "There are several hundred Tibetan Roman Catholics in Northern Yunnan, and one church has been reopened in Tibet itself."[17] No Protestant witness among Tibetans from the China side seems to have had such enduring results. But then there have been few Protestant missionaries who have died directly for their faith on Tibet's frontiers.

Missiological Summary

Looking back on 350 years of Catholic efforts in Tibet, whether from India or from the Sichuan or Yunnan borders in China, what missiological observations can be made? Statistically, compared with Protestants (see chap. 3), the number of Roman Catholic converts was not paltry. Dajianlu was recorded as having 5,301 converts in 1948, but it is not certain how many of these were Tibetans.[18] Likewise, it is impossible to analyze general statistics for Yunnan and determine how many of the 1,000 converts reported for the cities of Deqin, Gongshan, and Weixi in northern Yunnan were Tibetans. Nor are there any statistics for Yanjing (Yerkalo) and Mangkang in Tibet.[19]

Catholic work in Tibet, no matter how widely dispersed in both India and China, was unified through the Congregation for the Propagation of the Faith. Not that missionaries always agreed on how the work was to proceed! Yet, there was a basic unity in their diversity. News of the work in Tibet was published widely through Catholic publications in many languages. Among Catholic lay people and prospective missioners, a tradition of sacrifice and commitment was established of which they could be rightly proud.

Catholic missionaries were ready for martyrdom; in fact, celibate and without family responsibilities, they welcomed it. They did not come and go from their posts of service in times of national crisis in China.

17. Anthony P. B. Lambert, "The Challenge of China's Minority Peoples," *Church Around the World,* April 1991, 9.

18. One set of Catholic statistics for 1949 gives twelve hundred Catholics in Tibet and three thousand Tibetan Catholics in China. E. R. Hambye, "Tibet," *New Catholic Encyclopedia* (New York: McGraw Hill, 1967), 14:151–52.

19. Jean Charbonnier, *Guide to the Catholic Church in China 1989* (Singapore: China Catholic Communication, 1990), 118–19, 120–21, 146–47, 152–53.

Some of this, of course, was because they were French, and their government did not order them about in the same way as Great Britain did with its citizens. When attacked in their local stations of work, they made strategic retreats, but were back in place often before wisdom dictated it. Although they engaged in works of mercy and ministered to the whole needs of people, their prime concern was evangelism. They lived by a simple creed:

> The Catholic Church alone has the mission of leading all men along the road of salvation. Neither Protestant missionaries nor those sent by other dissenting and separated churches have any authority to preach and evangelize. Christ gave no other mission than that which He entrusted to the Catholic Church. Truth is but one, and the Catholic Church is the sole depository of this truth. . . . Their eternal destiny has been entrusted to the zeal and apostolic activity of the Church. Souls will be saved in proportion to this zeal and this activity of the Church in fulfilling her mission.[20]

To carry out this task in Tibet, the MEP missionaries made extensive use of catechists. These pioneered in difficult and inaccessible places where the presence of a foreigner might obstruct the work. They felt this policy to be better than that of Protestant missionaries who themselves itinerated widely in the distribution of literature. Because of the length of their service along Tibet's borders, the missionaries were able to develop rich resources of catechists, local priests and nuns, schoolteachers, and other helpers in the work.

In their evangelization, the missionaries aimed at entire villages, although they were glad to welcome individuals as well. Their relatively larger number of converts is because they were able to take advantage of these mass conversions, or what today would be called people movements to Christ. For this to happen, they had to swallow hard at some of the crass motivation that led people to their initial interest in Christianity. This, they reasoned, could be corrected later in the catechetical process. Were they as rigorous as they might have been in carrying out their postconversion discipleship? Were they too lax in dealing with some superstitions? Was the process of declaring one's faith a bit too automatic—almost like a formula? Did they acquiesce too easily to a new convert's desire for protection under the treaties? Did their dependence on France and its protectorate over them ultimately hinder or help them in their work?

In dealing with the need to liberate those struggling with demonic oppression, these missioners had routinized formulae, with centuries of

20. Paulo Manna, *The Conversion of the Pagan World,* trans. Joseph McGlinchey (Boston: Society for the Propagation of the Faith, 1921), 10.

church tradition behind them, to renounce the devil and all of his evil works. This renunciation, along with the pledge to follow Christ, was an indispensable tool in promoting the conversion of entire villages.

Wherever the missionaries established permanent stations of work, they engaged in a full range of activities: hospitals, dispensaries, catechetical schools, major and minor seminaries, hospices, a variety of schools for children and virgins, care for orphans and children. They were holistic before the term came into vogue.

Missionaries were prepared to live a simple life among Tibetan nomads. Unencumbered by families, they lived modestly with their Tibetan coworkers and learned well the life and culture of the Tibetan people. They were not obsessed with the need to "get to Lhasa." Once this journey to the capital of Tibetan Buddhism proved impossible legally in the early 1860s, they abandoned it as a dream and concentrated on more attainable goals.

Were they wise in building some of the huge, European-like cathedrals in out-of-the-way places? The church erected at Tchronteu, a few days' journey from Weixi, in the wilds of northern Yunnan hardly seemed appropriate for that context where Tibetans and Chinese lived together with wild Lyssous. Was this any better than their critique of the Protestants, particularly Americans, who used "all the methods of the modern apostolate, without very much success"?

The Catholic effort to reach Tibet, beginning in the early seventeenth century in India, came to an end as an outside missionary effort in 1949. Now to the church has been given the baton to reach out to the roof of the world. It has inherited the legacy of a noble missionary effort that will inspire it in this future task.

3

Tibet

The Last Country to Be Evangelized Before Jesus Returns?

Introduction

The natural amphitheater at Old Orchard, Maine, a lovely site along the rugged northeastern seacoast, was filled to capacity with an expectant crowd of several thousand people. This was Monday morning in the summer of 1886, one day after "Simpson Sunday," the name given to the last day of the convention that was having its first of many meetings under the direction of A. B. Simpson. The speaker was the famous William E. Blackstone, whose book *Jesus Is Coming* had sold more than a million copies in thirty-six languages. Weaving prophecy and world evangelism together in one indissoluble cord, he gave a ringing challenge: "God seems to be holding back that little place [Tibet] to be the last field entered just before his coming." For Simpson, always interested in world missions, this was the final catalyst that led him in 1887 to form the mission board that later was called The Christian and Missionary Alliance.[1]

The field of primary focus for the new mission organization was Tibet. Young people were recruited and mobilized by catchy slogans to go to this distant land: "A chain of mission stations from Shanghai to Tibet,"

1. William Carlsen, *Tibet: In Search of a Miracle* (New York: Nyack College, 1985), 36.

and "To place a missionary on Tibetan soil and keep him there." That Tibet had not yet received the Christian faith was not because it had been neglected. Roman Catholic missionaries had tried to enter this land from the early 1600s. Noted explorers had investigated its mysteries. And, since 1853, nearly thirty-five years before Blackstone's clarion call, German, English, and Swiss missionaries of the Moravian Mission had been trying to go into Tibet from India.

The Longest Continuing Protestant Mission among Tibetans

The first Christian missionaries to reach Ladakh, often called Little Tibet or British Tibet, in the province of Kashmir in far northern India, were probably Nestorians. The record they left in the seventh century was not much—a Georgian cross inscribed on a boulder above a lotus. This is the same symbol as on the more famous stele in Xian, the capital of China when the Nestorians first came into that country about 635. The few letters in the Syrian script described the traveler as "Charansar who has come from Samarkand." At the bottom of the inscription is the name *Ysax* (Jesus). What influence did these missionaries have? How long did they stay? Who and how many responded to their message? Could it be that they had some influence on the development of Lamaism, that unique brand of Buddhism found in Tibet and Mongolia?

We know little about the Nestorians, but the Moravians have left a clear record of their ministries. In contrast with many twentieth-century evangelical groups, the Moravians did not need any special motivation to do missionary work, nor did they have a separate mission agency. The church itself was a missionary church, sending out its first missionaries to the West Indies in 1732.

That intrepid pioneer, Karl Gutzlaff, sometimes called "the grandfather of the China Inland Mission" because of the ways he motivated Hudson Taylor, challenged the Moravians to begin a mission in Mongolia. Blocked from going to Mongolia via Russia, China, Tibet, or India, their first missionaries, A. W. Heyde and E. Pagell, settled down in Kyelang, a Tibetan village in the province of Lahul, which later would be administered by Great Britain. A second station was opened at Kunawar in 1865 and a third in 1885 in the city of Leh, farther to the north in the province of Ladakh, the native state under the control of the Maharajah of Kashmir.

Over the next few years missionaries and their local colleagues entered other cities and outlying villages. One station in the small city of Poo to the southeast, called "the child of sorrow of the Tibetan mission," faced all the obstacles that might be expected from its location only eight miles from the Tibetan border.

These early workers itinerated as much as the weather, high altitude (eleven thousand feet), and severe geographic obstacles would permit. More important, they settled in areas where they lived and carried out a full range of evangelistic, educational, medical, literary, and agricultural ministries. The direct, tangible results of this activity were little. The first baptisms did not come until 1865. Even by 1908 the mission could count only 139 baptized members. However, in contrast with Protestant work among Tibetans from other points in India or from China, this work had stability, continuity, and a holistic approach that produced the most solid Tibetan converts, local evangelists, and churches.

Moravian Missiological Principles

In addition to opening a school for women and girls and a medical work, the mission in its early years in Kyelang tried to meet the economic needs of the people. It bought waste land on the hillsides, built courses to bring in water, imported cattle and sheep, and employed needy people on a model farm. While helping to allay poverty, this project spawned selfishness and dishonesty that brought it to an end. Dividing the land into separate farms, rented out among Christian families, proved to be no better. A superficial Christianity was produced by those who were motivated economically to become Christians. Furthermore, non-Christians saw these economic projects as being competitive and boycotted the Christians. With reluctance, the missionaries found it necessary to close Kyelang station, which had such a long legacy of sacrificial work, and where Heyde and his wife, the first pioneers, had lived for forty-eight years without a furlough.

Despite the failure of the Kyelang project, the missionaries did not slack in trying to meet economic needs. They started a weaving technical school in Leh in 1939. By teaching people how to weave camp blankets popular among army officers serving in the foothills of the northwestern frontier of India, it helped to meet the needs of Christians and non-Christians alike. After they sent many looms out to neighboring villages, the Queen of Ladakh learned of the project and sent her royal weaver to learn the new method in weaving that was being used. Later this work was expanded into an industrial school. Here students were taught how to make carpets and rugs, very valuable trade items when there was almost a total stoppage of Central Asian trade during World War II.

Proclaiming the Good News of the kingdom was central to all that the Moravian missionaries did. Basic to this, of course, was the Bible, and from the very beginning in 1856, the mission gave itself to Bible translation, finally completing a translation of the Tibetan Bible in 1948. This long-time, sacrificial commitment involved several missionaries, as well as a number of gifted local Christians.

The process was begun by a learned missionary-linguist, H. A. Jaeschke, a direct descendent of the first Moravians who came to the colony at Herrnhut. Coming to the field when he was forty years of age, he already knew seven European languages well and a smattering of Sanskrit, Persian, and Arabic. As soon as he arrived in India, Jaeschke went to Ladakh and lived for three months with a family in a nearby village. Following this intensive immersion in the language—the term used today is "bonding"—he returned to Kyelang and enlisted the help of some educated lamas. Two of these were exiles from Lhasa, suspected incorrectly in 1854 of having a part in the death by poisoning of the Trashi Lama, second only to the Dalai Lama. The elder of these never became a Christian, but, at his death, he implored the missionaries to care for his twelve-year-old son. Later this son, Yoseb Gergan, became the most important Tibetan Christian leader in the area and contributed greatly to the translation of the Bible into Tibetan. The younger of the two exiles believed in Christ and was baptized as the first lama to become a Christian in western Tibet.

Many obstacles blocked progress in translating and producing the Bible: whether to use a colloquial vernacular or classical Tibetan, Jaeschke's method; terms for God, Savior, and sin, just to name a few; the death of different translators at various stages in the process; World War II, which made it impossible to set the type in Great Britain; and, finally, how to get the precious manuscript through enemy lines between Leh and Lahore. One of Jaeschke's successors was August Hermann Francke, whose ancestor of the same name had led the pietists at Halle and taught Count Von Zinzendorf. He became a well-known authority on Tibetan literature and a specialist on the history and archaeology of western Tibet. Yoseb Gergan took over after Francke and worked tirelessly to produce a one-volume edition of the Tibetan Bible, which was brought to completion by other Tibetan helpers two years after Gergan's death.[2]

Having a Bible in process and wrestling with terms in the colloquial dialects, as well as in the classical language, meant that catechisms, tracts, Scripture portions, and other literature were prepared to serve both in evangelism and in Christian nurture. As they evangelized, whether in small chapels or church buildings, along dusty trails, in bazaars, at book stalls, or in the Gospel Inn, a hostel for travelers, the missionaries and Tibetan evangelists were seeking to fit the message to the context.

Missionaries learned from their Tibetan colleagues that repeated one-to-one witness to someone with an educational background was far bet-

2. This exciting account is told in Chandu Ray, "Story of the Tibetan Bible," in *The Missionary Challenge,* reprinted from the Association for the Free Distribution of the Scriptures, London.

ter than a public sermon. People were not used to listening to long discourses. Even more difficult, their experience with the lamas led them to expect that religious messages were not really understandable, only ritual to which they need not pay much attention.

Whether one was speaking in public or to one person, using words that communicated was important. The usual term for God, at least in the classical language used by Jaeschke, was *Konchog,* the "most precious one," a term referring to the Buddhist Trinity—Buddha, the disciples, and the teaching. Savior was translated as *Skyabsgon,* "the Great Merciful One Chanrezig," who delivers people from the sorrows of repeated transmigrations. Were these expressions specific enough to carry true Christian meaning? Only with much teaching to transform and modify them for Christian use.

Framing Christian truth in stories (those that might parallel some of the parables of Jesus) and interspersed with the pithy, wise sayings used by Tibetan storytellers was essential if the message was not to be viewed as foreign. The fear of being viewed as foreign caused the missionaries to give top priority to raising up a corps of local evangelists. In the first few decades, when most of the witness was done by the foreign missionaries, few results were seen, but from the 1890s on they had not only several well-trained evangelists, but also the children of these evangelists who were following in the steps of their fathers. Yoseb Gergan often had special training classes for evangelists, helping them particularly in knowing how to communicate in a colloquial manner. These local leaders were the foundation of the work, and increasingly the missionaries decreased their work in the government of the churches and in outreach.

Most of the leading evangelists had been won to Christ either by missionaries or by other evangelists. Trained in mission schools, those run either by the Moravians or by the Church Mission Society in Srinagar, they now assumed pastoral responsibilities, along with evangelism, in outlying areas around the main centers of work. Where possible, the evangelists did itineration during the summer months, but their main responsibility was to develop and nurture groups of believers. This task was much easier in western Tibet than in the east where the people were more nomadic and did not live in villages. It was important, they believed, not only to proclaim the gospel but to live it out in a long-term contact with people in their neighborhoods.

The gospel was communicated by many methods. A favorite approach was to use a "magic lantern" and show slides of the life of Jesus, an old version of the modern evangelistic film *Jesus*. Tibetans were always attracted by a Tanka, a cloth banner or scroll on which were painted in the center the head of Christ, and around it in a circular fashion eight scenes from the life of Christ, with a parable in each of the four corners. Creative evangelists, imitating Tibetan religious practices, made use of "wayside pulpits," rocks on which they had chiseled or painted Scripture portions.

A. H. Francke developed the novel idea of a monthly Tibetan newspaper for limited distribution, and this method was continued spasmodically over the years. His aim was to "disseminate Christian truth, and to educate the Tibetan as regards the advance of knowledge and to give him a wider understanding of the great world in which he lives." A 1930 edition has articles on health, scientific progress in England, news of temperance reform in the Kyelang area, an exposition of Matthew 6, and a moving testimony of salvation by Yoseb Gergan.

One of the more productive places for witness in Leh was the Gospel Inn, referred to as the "pub" by some critics. It afforded hospitality for travelers and pilgrims, as well as their ponies, yaks, and donkeys. A Bible woman and an evangelist treated simple illnesses, sold books and Gospels, ran a small grocery store for late-night arrivals, and treated animals for foot sores. Often, even ecclesiastical dignitaries who might have been expected to stay in hostels run by nearby monasteries opted for the Gospel Inn. The witness was not exclusively to Tibetans. Leh, at least in the summer, was a cosmopolitan city: Turki pilgrims going to or coming from Mecca, travelers from Lhasa, merchants from Central Asia and from India, English big-game hunters and their entourages, explorers, vacationers from the hot plains, and nomads from the high plateau coming to buy and sell.

Gospel portions were bound like Tibetan books in looseleaf covers between red or yellow cover boards wrapped in linen and tied with a string. Scripture was printed on a rough, fibrous paper so that it might be much more similar to local books. Evangelists were careful to warn the people that Gospel portions should not be put on an altar and worshiped. A very low literacy rate made it imperative for Christian workers to use care in distributing these booklets.

Always there was opposition, varying in proportion to how frequently local lamas had been back to Lhasa for a refresher course in their religion. In general, however, there was less religious opposition in this area than in China, where the Christians were more exposed to chaotic conditions and where no government was in effective control. Apathy and indifference, as well as a growing materialism, were constant enemies. Religion to most of the people was a ritual, and they saw no need to change to something new. Local evangelists often were confronted with the demonic. Ga Puntsog related two incidents in particular: one in which he showed compassion to a fellow traveler and consequently persuaded him to cut down a sacred tree where pilgrims offered sacrifices, and one in which he was able to control a cow, claimed to be demon-possessed, by cutting off the charms that had been hung about its neck.

Baptism was the real point of decision, even as it had been in the period when the New Testament was written. While individuals were gladly welcomed, the hope was always held out, but never realized, that entire villages would convert to Christ. Before baptism, inquirers were questioned openly before the entire congregation, including any unbelievers who might be present. All candidates were expected to learn the Ten Commandments and the Lord's Prayer before being baptized. Christian workers did not confuse godliness and cleanliness, never making an issue of the need to wash off the grease that most people used to keep warm at this high altitude.

Despite the relatively low number of converts, the Moravians established several churches in this area with hundreds of Tibetan Christians, much better than the record of other Protestant groups, whether in China or India. Christian influence in Leh and the entire area extended beyond the size of the churches. Missionaries reported that villagers near Kyelang reported an indigenous movement to abolish the brewing and drinking of beer as an aid to the stability of the community. They saw this as the "leaven of the working of the Kingdom of Heaven in the community."[3] Liberation, both spiritually and socially, was coming to the people.

A Hasty Plan: The Tibetan Pioneer Mission

The possibility of evangelizing Tibet from her southern borders was not lost on other mission agencies. This included India, Nepal, Bhutan, Sikkim, and Burma as bases of penetration. The Indian border itself was tightly closed. Great Britain strictly observed its 1904 treaty with Tibet, which read in part, "No foreign power shall be permitted to send either official or non-official persons to Tibet, no matter in what pursuit they may be engaged . . ."[4]

But one approach from British territory was through Darjeeling, both a city and a district, carved out from Bhutan, and the nearby bazaar town of Kalimpong. In this general area were missionaries from many boards: Methodist Episcopal, Church of Scotland, Assam Frontier Pioneer Mission, Scandinavian Alliance Mission, Indian Christian Mission, The Christian and Missionary Alliance, the Finnish Free Church, Worldwide Evangelistic Crusade, Pentecostal Missionary Union, many inde-

3. Materials to describe the Himalayan mission of the Moravians have come from several sources: *The Moravian Missionary Atlas 1908* (London: The Moravian Church and Missionary Agency, 1908); *Moravian Missions,* published monthly; *The Moravian Quarterly of the London Association in Aid of the Moravian Missions.*

4. W. Mann, "Tibetan Work on Indian Border," *Christian Alliance Foreign Missionary Weekly,* 9 September 1922.

pendent groups, and the Tibetan Pioneer Mission. Not all groups continued through the years. New groups entered the area after the Dalai Lama fled from Tibet to India in 1959, bringing with him thousands of Tibetan refugees, who were organized into a total of fifty-three Tibetan settlements.[5]

Darjeeling was the "queen of Indian hill stations," a cosmopolitan city where many groups of people were found, including Tibetans who came and went in a variety of trading ventures. Connected by the Darjeeling-Himalaya railway to major Indian cities, it was only 75 miles from the Tibetan border, much closer than most China-based mission stations. Lhasa was only 347 miles distant, and Tibet's two other large cities, Xigaze and Gyangze, were about 200 miles away.

The Tibetan Border Mission was located in Bhot, a triangle in India on the borders of both Tibet and Nepal. Like most stations of work along the borders, it was a major trade center with Tibetans coming and going when the roads were open. Although they were not permitted to go into Tibet, local evangelists made regular evangelistic treks into the Mount Kailash area, sixty miles into Tibet, where a small church, a mixture of Chinese and Tibetans, was established.[6] An unusual response to the Christian message came when a convert from the Finnish Free Church Mission got a post under the British government in Chumbi, within the Tibetan border from Kalimpong, in the early 1900s. He and his assistant, also a Christian, engaged in low-profile witness, with the result that sixty people responded to Christ and were baptized.[7]

At best, the result of all these several efforts was sparse. Tibetans were not ready for Christianity, whether behind or beyond their borders. One of the more prominent attempts—a hasty effort that failed, at least from the India side—was the Tibetan Pioneer Mission, headed by Annie Taylor, an unusually courageous and persevering British woman. Taylor started her missionary career in China in 1885 with the China Inland Mission. Forced home by tuberculosis, she lived with a married sister in Darjeeling during her recovery period. Encouraged by opportunities to contact Tibetans here, she spent one year in 1890 learning Tibetan. This led to the conversion and discipling of Puntso, a young Tibetan man who became her helper. She tried during this period to live in Sikkim, not yet an English protectorate. Despite disguising herself as a Tibetan, she was

5. Five Tibetan congregations are known today. These are the Moravian Church in Leh, Ladakh; in Rajpur, Kalimpong, and Buxa Duars, India; and in Mangan, Sikkim. All of these are small churches. G. Tharchin and Dave Woodward, "Tibet," in *The Church in Asia,* ed. D. E. Hoke (Chicago: Moody, 1975).

6. E. B. Steiner, "With Tibetans at the Crossroads," *The Missionary Review of the World,* September 1938, 395–98.

7. Ibid.

recognized by British officials and ordered to return to Darjeeling. She opted instead for a nearby lamasery. Even here people were forbidden to relate to her or give her anything to eat; in fact, at one time, they gave her poison mixed with rice and fried eggs. This did not upset her. Of this and other obstacles, she observed, "I have always found that persons who set out for the mission field in the expectation that they are going to their death usually do die. For my part I have always believed that I shall live as long as God has work for me to do."[8]

After her time in Darjeeling, Annie Taylor returned to China, where she made an attempt in 1892 to reach Lhasa, that holy land of Tibetan Buddhism. Only three Europeans had ever reached there at this time, and for mission enthusiasts, even her attempt ranked as a victory. The trip itself, which brought her within three days' travel of her goal, was peril upon peril. She was betrayed by a Chinese companion, robbed, abandoned by her carriers, and confronted by numerous dangers before she finally arrived back in Dajianlu. A contemporary evaluates this episode: "It changed the whole face of missionary interest in Tibet. It sent a thrill round the world . . . for solitary splendour and sudden quickening power no deed in the whole history of missions will rank higher than this of the lone woman who opened the closed door and deliberately walked through the country carrying her life in her hand for Christ's sake and the Gospel's."[9]

Apparently some people questioned whether a woman should do this work, because *China's Millions,* the organ of Taylor's mission agency, spoke of the need for women apostles. Returning to England, she spoke to huge crowds of mission enthusiasts, some of whom volunteered to go with her as a missionary band to evangelize Tibetans from India. This was portrayed as one of the final steps in fulfilling the Lord's command to preach the gospel of the kingdom in all the world for a witness to the nations and as hastening his return. Organized as the Tibetan Pioneer Band, actively supported by Hudson Taylor (no relation) and the CIM, and given a rousing sendoff at a farewell meeting at London's Exeter Hall, scene of ongoing missionary enthusiasm, Taylor and her recruits headed to Darjeeling.

Living first at the small village of Gnatung in Sikkim, the group faced opposition from the captain of a British fort. Following this, they lived in some nearby caves and then in a hut at this outpost. Eventually, most of the group moved to Kalimpong. Disputes over living styles, Taylor's direction in the work, and personal differences caused the band to break

8. Isabel Stuart Robson, *Two Lady Missionaries in Tibet* (London: S.W. Partridge and Co., n.d.), 49.

9. Ibid., 79.

up, with some members staying in India and others going to China to work with the CIM. Taylor herself piggybacked on the British treaty with Sikkim in 1893 to live in Yatung in the Chumbi Valley very close to the border. Her work with Tibetans produced no visible fruit, and by 1903 she became an army nurse to British troops in the area. She called her small home "Hope College," but she finally returned a disappointed woman to Great Britain, with hope deferred of entering Tibet either from China or from India.

A Three-Pronged Approach from China

Continuing Protestant mission efforts to gain access to greater Tibet, in contrast to the much earlier work around Little Tibet, the Ladakh area in India, began in the late 1880s and early 1890s. One thrust was from the northwest area of China, either from the cities of Xining or Lanzhou, in Gansu Province and later Qinghai. The Assemblies of God, Scandinavian Alliance Mission, the China Inland Mission, and The Christian and Missionary Alliance spearheaded these efforts. Another line of approach was from south-central China, through the "marches of Sichuan," via the cities of Songpan, Dajianlu, Litang, and Batang. The groups involved here were the China Inland Mission, the Foreign Christian Mission, Worldwide Evangelistic Crusade, and a number of independent missionaries. The final door was up from Yunnan, "south of the clouds," the most productive area for Roman Catholics, through Dali, Lijiang, Weixi, and Atentze, and on to Batang. Only the Pentecostal Missionary Union sent its missionaries into this area.

Where Is Tibet?

The question for all of these missionaries was simple and yet complex. Where was Tibet? At issue was where Lhasa's jurisdiction ended and where China asserted her control. The answer depended on which government was stronger and wished to flex its muscles. In general, China did not wish to clarify the problem, for, from her standpoint, everything belonged to her. She was not prepared, however, to expend the energy, manpower, or money to take it all. From the China side, everything up to Dajianlu, in the central section, belonged to China. Tibet clearly possessed the territory from Lhasa, her capital, through Chamdo in eastern Tibet, or Kham. West of Dajianlu and east of Chamdo was the disputed area. Often it was a conglomeration of native states with princes who only tipped their hats to Lhasa. Anarchy ruled; lamas and nobles did whatever they wished.

After the British expedition into Tibet (1903–1904), Zhao Erfang marched a Chinese army into Lhasa, took control of the capital, ousted native princes in the disputed area, and created a new province extending from eastern Tibet to Dajianlu. In the process he destroyed many lamaseries and drove out the oppressive lamas. This arrangement lasted until the Qing dynasty collapsed in 1911, bringing down as well the new provincial administration in eastern Tibet. Attempts were made to mark the border—the Yangzi River at Batang, an actual wall twenty miles west of Xining, crude barriers with military posts in other places. Control passed back and forth, bringing either exhilaration or disappointment for the missionaries whose work and safety depended on stability. The presence of at least three different large groups of Muslims, particularly about Xining and Lanzhou, with loyalties vacillating between the Tibetans and Chinese, only added to the confusion. With some modifications, the same situation prevailed in the northern and southern centers of work.

A large section of northeast Tibet was included in Qinghai Province when that province was established in 1928. Very quickly the well-armed Muslim soldiers gained authority by military might over the Tibetan lamas.[10]

It was a toss-up with the missionaries as to whether they wished for Chinese or Tibetan control. Each had its advantages and disadvantages. Both groups were exclusive and ethnocentric, hating the presence of foreigners and the Christian faith but willing to use them if it meant hospitals or schools for their benefit. Missionaries were pragmatists: whatever promoted the gospel and best served their personal and institutional needs was preferred. Anything could be accepted, even violent Muslim attacks on Tibetan lamaseries, as divine Providence opening up the closed gates of Tibet before Jesus returned.

The fact that everybody had to work in Chinese Tibet, the name given to this disputed area, and could not get into Tibet proper meant that no group concentrated exclusively on Tibetan work. In the south and central areas churches were constituted of tribal groups, Chinese, and a few Tibetans. About Xining, Lanzhou, and the Hezhou-Daozhou area where The Christian and Missionary Alliance worked, congregations were made up of Chinese, Tibetans, and a few Chinese and non-Chinese Muslims. This made language learning difficult and thwarted any real attempt to contextualize the gospel for Tibetan audiences.

Even had they been able to enter Greater Tibet, the missionaries would have found that such centers as Lhasa, Xigaze, Gyangze, and Chamdo were created by the Chinese and populated largely by Chinese or those of marriages between Tibetans and Chinese. Tibetans in this area were nomadic, did not live in villages as they did in Little Tibet, and were scattered widely in ever-moving communities. They could be reached

10. Leonard Street, "Chinghai Province," *China's Millions,* September-October 1948, 54.

only by nomadic missionaries or as they came to trade in Chinese cities. These trading centers about the periphery of Tibet were critical in missionary strategy. Protestants, even as the Roman Catholics before them, recognized that the hundreds of lamaseries in Tibet, housing tens of thousands of lamas, were the only sizable population concentrations and thus the key to reaching the country.

Obstacles in the Work

The obstacles faced by Christian workers were formidable. First were personal obstacles, which included the difficulty of the terrain, isolation and loneliness, the difficulty of adjusting to the food and other living conditions, the sense of oppression living this close to the demonic, and learning a difficult language. Second were the political and ecclesiastical barriers, such as the problem of getting into Tibet proper, the control of the priestly class and the power of the lamasery, the seeming indifference of the people to sincere religion in the midst of a pervasive religiosity, the constant struggle among rival groups in eastern Tibet, and hostility to foreigners. Third were the social obstacles of illiteracy, ignorance, polyandry, and the extreme economic oppression by the lamas. Their exploitation of the serfs with unjust taxation produced brigandage and banditry that killed not a few missionaries and made it impossible for them to concentrate on Tibetans in a mixed population. Missionaries sometimes were persecuted directly and driven from their stations of work. Death was a constant possibility for local Christians. Converts did not easily forget the "Christian convert who was sewn into a fresh yak skin by merciless priests and placed in the broiling sun until the contraction of the skin squeezed the life out of his frame."[11]

In these chaotic conditions, some missionaries carried arms, usually visible weapons such as rifles and shotguns. These usually scared bandits off before any trouble erupted. Many were the occasions when visibility was not enough, and the missionaries defended themselves by firing at attackers.[12]

Signs of Hope

Where sin abounded, hope abounded even more! For every setback and difficulty, mission executives and their missionaries were perennially optimistic. As early as 1879 Hudson Taylor exclaimed that the Chefoo Convention of 1876 permitted the British government to send an expedition from India to China (it never occurred) and that this development

11. Leslie Lyall, *A Passion for the Impossible* (Chicago: Moody, 1965), 158.
12. Robert Carlson collection 205, tape 2A in archives, Billy Graham Center, Wheaton College, Wheaton, Ill.

could be "pregnant with the most important results."[13] A. B. Simpson predicted in 1893 that within five years the walls of Tibet would go down like those of Jericho if God's people only claimed this victory by faith. The Sino-Japanese war of 1894 was interpreted to mean that China's defeat might humble her and be a harbinger of hope. This was felt to be one more indication that the present dispensation of God's work in the world was coming to an end.[14] Even after the Boxer Rebellion of 1900 forced all missionaries to leave Dajianlu, they returned to find a long list of Chinese inquirers who might be able to influence the Tibetans. The revolution of 1911, which temporarily gave more control over eastern Tibet to the Tibetans, was interpreted as a new open door. CMA missionaries in Gansu were confident that since General Feng Yuxiang, a Christian general, was in command of forces seeking to quell a rebellion in that area in the 1930s, this would be to their advantage. Each outbreak of fighting when Muslims ravaged Tibetan villages, supposedly making them more open to the gospel, was accepted as the beginning of a spiritual harvest.

J. H. Jeffrey, in charge of CIM work in Chengdu, Sichuan, issued an appeal for prayer in 1937, because several events indicated "that the time is opportune for a missionary advance." What were these events? They included a changed political climate because of factions in the Tibetan government, a priesthood discredited since it could not predict the coming of the Communists, and the "destruction of many important lamaseries and the slaughtering of hundreds of lamas, thereby depriving the non-Chinese people of their spiritual guides."[15]

Missiological Principles in Chinese Tibet

As they lived in hope confronted by overwhelming obstacles, how did these servants of God carry on their work? How did they put feet to their prayers? Everyone, to a lesser or greater degree, engaged in wide itineration, lasting anywhere from a few weeks to six months. A deep sense of urgency, rooted in evangelical revivalism, motivated the missionaries. Jesus was returning soon, and after that the door of salvation would be permanently closed. Results were not measured in converts, since there were very few, but miles traveled, days away from home, the number of tracts distributed, usually in the tens of thousands, lamaseries visited, and promising contacts. Some of these itinerants had not been in the country

13. Hudson Taylor editorial, *China's Millions,* 1879, 29.

14. *Annual Report of the International Missionary Alliance,* 1894, 33. This was the forerunner of *The Alliance Weekly,* the missionary publication of The Christian and Missionary Alliance.

15. J. H. Jeffrey, "The Tibetan Border: An Appeal for Prayer," *China's Millions,* August 1937, 157.

even for one year, and their language ability was minimal. Hudson Taylor reasoned that such travel was justified, for it helped produce more missionaries and more mission stations, as well as getting Scripture out widely.[16] But there was a deeper reason, a theology of itineration formed in the 1920s and based on the philosophy of Roland Allen, whose *Missionary Methods: St. Paul's or Ours?* became a "Bible" for many missionaries. Allen was an Episcopalian missionary to China who became disgusted with missionaries who settled down, built up an array of institutions, and never got beyond their compound walls. By contrast, he claimed, Paul came into an area, preached the gospel, left a few able converts as leaders, and went on his way, trusting the Holy Spirit to complete the work he had started. Paul's methods were good for the situation in the Mediterranean world, where synagogues formed a womb for the development and birth of most new converts, but the approach was hardly proper for China in general or the minority areas in particular. If people were interested in the gospel, they were given tracts, talked with possibly for an extended period of several hours or even days, and then left until the next visit. This might not come for another year.

Some missionaries used tents and worked out traveling agreements of friendship with local leaders, permitting them to go along with nomads in their tent villages as they moved from place to place. If the trips extended for two or three months, it required that the missionary take several pack animals to carry food, literature, and other necessary supplies and that he be accompanied by numerous coolies. This method provided for a period of extended contact with people, with much more possibility of their understanding the gospel. It also afforded protection in bandit country. How did the missionaries reciprocate for this ongoing hospitality? Usually they hosted these leaders when they came into villages to replenish their supplies.[17]

Nearly every Tibetan family had one of its male members serving as a lama in some noted lamasery. Therefore, missionaries in their itineration made every effort to make friends at these religious centers, to ask for hospitality, to distribute literature, and to engage in systematic teaching for several days. The population of Tibet was concentrated at these places. Only here could a missionary find a large and usually attentive audience for his preaching. Many of the lamas recognized the danger the missionaries posed to their religious system and refused to welcome them to their headquarters.

Petrus and Susie Rijnhart, independent missionaries, centered their work about key lamaseries. Settling down in Chinese Tibet near the Kum-

16. *China's Millions,* March 1881, 29.
17. George Kraft, "On Tibetan Grasslands," *China's Millions,* May-June 1949, 28–29.

bum lamasery, famed because it was founded by Tsong-kaba, the Martin Luther of Tibetan lamaism, they learned the language from a monk who lived there. When a Muslim rebellion brought danger to the area, the *kanpo* in charge of the lamasery invited them to come and live there. This provided the opportunity for personal evangelism and for extended discussions about religious truth. Mrs. Rijnhart, a medical doctor, also treated the Chinese, Tibetans, and Muslims wounded in the vicious struggle.

Living in or near a lamasery and seeing it both as an object of their work and as a base for moving out to surrounding little lamasery-related communities involved missionaries as mediators in local struggles. For example, the head lama at the Labrang monastery died, and one of his younger relatives attempted to seize the property, which really belonged to the monastery but which the lama had taken illegally. This relative unwisely went to the local Muslims to get help in settling a purely Tibetan dispute. The result was that the monastery was burned down, and the corpses of hundreds of Tibetans covered the temple grounds. At this juncture, Tibetan friends of J. P. Rommen, a CMA missionary in the area, approached him to intercede with the Muslim general that he not go on a rampage and burn the surrounding Tibetan homes. In talking to the general, the missionary not only represented the Tibetan cause. He also spoke of the freedom he hoped he would now have to travel about where Buddhism had been so devastated and do missionary work.[18]

Missionaries often developed good relationships with local clan leaders who had varying degrees of influence in this nebulous power vacuum where Chinese and Tibetan authority waxed and waned. These clan chiefs promised to give the missionaries free rein in their limited areas, if their work included not merely evangelism, but also education and dispensaries. A prime example was Victor Plymire, an Assembly of God missionary who made his headquarters in Tangar, fifty miles east of Kokonor in what is now Qinghai Province. One day Ga Lo, chief of the Kantsa tribe, visited him from his home eighty miles west of Tangar, established a friendship, and eventually requested that the two make a blood covenant. This ceremony, to be made as priests chanted out to their gods, would result in Plymire and Ga Lo cutting their wrists and mixing their blood to seal the covenant. Ga Lo promised that the entire tribe would then be open to the Christian faith. Although he refused this attractive offer, Plymire tried to keep the doors of friendship open.[19]

18. J. P. Rommen, "Another Foothold for the Gospel in Tibet," 7 June 1919, 168–69, and A. R. Fesmire, "Tibet Open—Forward March," 21 June 1919, 202–3, in *The Alliance Weekly: A Journal of Christian Life and Missions.*

19. David Plymire, *High Adventure in Tibet* (Springfield, Mo.: Gospel Publishing House, 1959), 66–68.

The itineration, the obsession of missionaries and constituencies alike, was to get to Lhasa, more important to Tibetans even than Rome was to Roman Catholics or Mecca to Muslims. Its attraction was magnified because it was forbidden, was hidden behind almost impassable mountains, had seldom been reached by Europeans, and epitomized symbolically the coming victory of the gospel. Nearly everyone dreamed of going there to preach the gospel and to establish the Christian church.

Some went beyond dreaming and laid elaborate plans to go, usually impelled by what they interpreted as the voice of God urging them on. We have already mentioned Annie Taylor's attempt, which so inspired the English-speaking Christian world. A more tragic attempt was made by the Rijnharts. After their time at the Kumbum monastery, they moved on to Tangar, which was on the route to Lhasa. They visited widely in that area, making many friends with Muslim officials who at this time were in control of that immediate location. Because she was a trained doctor, a graduate of the Women's Medical College in Toronto, Mrs. Rijnhart opened a dispensary and treated many patients. Here also the Rijnharts made friends with four *kushoks* who represented the Dalai Lama and looked after his interests here. Possibly encouraged by these friendly contacts, they decided that they would press on to Lhasa. Friends tried to dissuade them, but to no avail. Murphy's law took over immediately—anything that could go wrong did go wrong! They were faced with incredibly bad weather, bad trails, the suspicions of religious leaders who did not know them and had no reason to accord them the respect they had had in Kumbum or Tangar. Their guides deserted them and then, to add misery upon misery, their one-year-old son, carried on the father's back, died suddenly. They had the sad task of burying him under rocks along the trail.

Belatedly, seeing their hopes dashed, the Rijnharts headed back toward Dajianlu along a more southerly trail than the one they had followed from Tangar. Apparently a gang of brigands was trailing them, and when Mr. Rijnhart left to pacify a hostile-looking group they saw in the distance, he never returned. For two months, with little shelter and food, Susie Rijnhart struggled on courageously to return to China. Finally she reached Dajianlu and friends at the CIM home there, who initially mistook her for a Tibetan tramp. When she returned to Canada to recuperate, a close friend observed that she had "changed from a bright, dark-haired girl into a quiet, white-haired woman." Although beset with tragedy, her journey, like that of Annie Taylor, had a fairy-tale result. As she spoke in Canada and the United States, her testimony and vision motivated the Foreign Christian Missionary Society to open a mission on the border of Tibet. Dr. Rijnhart was in the first party to be sent out. Three years after her return to Dajianlu, she married James Moyes, one of the CIM missionaries who had met her on her return from Tibet. By this time her health was failing badly, and she returned to Canada with her husband, only to die suddenly 7 February 1908 after giving birth to a son.[20]

Twenty-five years later, during the time when most missionaries had retreated to Shanghai and Beijing because of unrest in China, Victor Plymire of the Assemblies of God set out on a similar pilgrimage. Starting again from Tangar and accompanied by forty-seven yaks, two Tibetan and three Chinese helpers, he headed west on what he called an evangelistic trip. When faced with the inevitable opposition, he requested permission to go to Lhasa but was turned away fifteen miles short of his goal. From here, however, he could see the sun reflecting from the golden Potala Palace, the huge residence of Dalai Lama. With no sense of history, he commented, "Suffice it to say that I carried the Gospel where no other had ever been able to go." Satisfied that this was "mission accomplished," a radical revision of his original hope, he left Tibet by Leh in Ladakh to the south.[21]

Not everyone had the same compulsion to reach Lhasa. As D. E. Hoste, who succeeded Hudson Taylor as general director of the CIM, and his colleagues evaluated the Tibetan situation, they concluded that this high-profile approach of foreigners trying to penetrate Tibet was questionable. In an editorial in *China's Millions* Hoste observed: "The opinion of some, well-qualified by years of experience to judge, is that probably the regions under consideration will be best evangelized by Chinese and Tibetan Christians, of whom there is now a small church at Tatsienlu."[22]

Even though this analysis was most appropriate in 1907, shortly after England and Russia had concluded a treaty that prohibited outside interference of any type in Tibet, it continued to be relevant through the years. Tibetans resented interference by outsiders, particularly the English, and it threatened them profoundly when anyone tried to penetrate their borders.

And yet, more itinerant Protestant missionaries died at the hands of bandit gangs than by the intrigue of religious leaders. Danger lurked behind every rock and at every mountain pass. Dr. Albert Shelton, a member of the Foreign Christian Mission Society, was the best-known missionary doctor along the Tibetan border in the first two decades of the twentieth century. Skilled as a surgeon, fluent in Tibetan, compassionate

20. Robson, *Two Lady Missionaries in Tibet,* 114–60. See also Archibald McLean, *The History of the Foreign Christian Missionary Society* (New York: Revell, 1919), 115–19.

21. Plymire, *High Adventure in Tibet,* 113–14.

22. *China's Millions,* April 1907, 57.

in his ministry to people, he ministered to both Chinese and Tibetans in many war situations and was respected equally by all, who recognized him as a man of God. Some of these contacts gave him hope that he might be able to establish a hospital in Lhasa. Before this became even remotely possible, he was gunned down by brigands twenty miles south of his station at Batang.

William Ekvall Simpson of the Assemblies of God, born in Tibet, familiar with several dialects of Tibetan, ideally suited by temperament and lifestyle to travel as a nomad with the Tibetans and to give a relevant Christian witness, was also killed by bandits in the Kokonor region as he was traveling alone. Such senseless deaths added to an ongoing debate among missionaries as to whether they ought to carry firearms to protect themselves in emergency situations.

What literature were the missionaries using in their itineration? Very soon after their arrival among Tibetan peoples, the missionaries began to produce simple gospel tracts. Later, they translated portions of the New Testament into a colloquial, eastern Tibetan that would serve their purposes better than the classical New Testament produced by the Moravians in Little Tibet. Early in 1918 the Tibetan Religious Tract Society established a printing press at Dajianlu. This expedited greatly the availability of necessary literature. The press sent bundles of tracts to all mission stations in both China and Tibet and also sent tracts to each Tibetan lamasery that could be reached by means of the Chinese postal service. During 1918, Theo Sorensen of the CIM prepared special tracts that contrasted and compared the Buddhist and Christian explanations of God, creation, human origin, sin, and salvation. Interesting letters were received from many lamaseries, indicating that, despite apparent outward indifference, there were lamas with sincere religious questions.[23]

Although Tibet had a written language, adapted from the Sanskrit and introduced from India along with the Buddhist religion, very few people were able to read. The effectiveness of a literature ministry then was questionable, unless that ministry was accompanied by oral proclamation and teaching. Early missionaries to China felt the oral approach was the only proper method of communicating God's truth. Certainly then it was a bit presumptuous for missionaries to claim Isaiah 55:10–11 as a justification for every tract and Gospel portion:

> As the rain and the snow
> come down from heaven,

23. "Report of Tibetan Religious Tract Society, 1919," printed in *The West China Missionary News,* February 1919, 17–19.

and do not return to it
without watering the earth
and making it bud and flourish,
so that it yields seed for the sower and bread for the eater,
so is my word that goes out from my mouth:
It will not return to me empty,
but will accomplish what I desire
and achieve the purpose for which I sent it.

Central Station Ministries

All Protestant mission groups trying to evangelize Tibetans had a main base from which they worked and from which they itinerated. In these central stations what kind of activities were they engaged in? Visiting non-Christians, preaching services for adults in homes, in rented chapels, or in a permanent building, providing services for children and young people, running schools for children or a dispensary or hospital, distributing literature, and engaging in some type of technical training were among the options.

Some groups, such as the Foreign Christian Mission Society, first in Dajianlu and then Batang, and The Christian and Missionary Alliance, south of Lanzhou, were specifically committed to mission-station work, although their missionaries also itinerated widely. The China Inland Mission established a large hospital in Lanzhou, but its main ministry there was directed more toward the Muslim minorities.

The Foreign Christian Mission (FCM), the mission arm of the Disciples of Christ in America, saw a full-service ministry as the best strategy to reach Tibetan peoples. One of its members observed, "One of the big obstacles to work in this area is money. Many independent groups try to get something going, but they do not have enough perseverance in terms of money when the converts are not too many."[24] To get money when they had decided to use it was never easy along the isolated Tibetan borders. As much as a year's supply in silver ingots was sometimes brought in by horse, despite the danger of robbery. The more usual method was to get cash from merchants in Batang, after their representatives in other parts of China had used missionary drafts to buy their merchandise.

Missionaries with the FCM usually had a liberal arts education, some type of systematic Bible and missions training, and possibly a technical education as well. They threw themselves enthusiastically into all phases of the work in Batang. They ran a kindergarten, as well as a school for older students. A hospital was erected, and from this base Dr. Shelton and

24. Marion H. Duncan, *The Mountain of Silver Snow* (Cincinnati: Powell and White, 1929), 95.

other doctors did mobile clinic work in the surrounding area. A church was quickly formed, and Sunday classes for both Chinese and Tibetan children were commenced. One missionary led the Chinese class on one side of the room, and Dr. Shelton led a Tibetan class on the other side. The wives did visitation in many country homes, seeking to win the women and children. Missionaries engaged in efforts to help the poor, the beggars, and destitute children to acquire a vocation from which they could make a living. To achieve this goal they taught people to weave rugs, to make soap, to make shoes, to farm and garden. Early results from these varied ministries was good.

Mr. Ogden's great revival (1911) began, and more than two hundred came in that raw land, in that young station, confessing their sins of robbery and murder and trying to quit opium and wine-drinking, asking that he go into their homes and tear down idols, which he gladly did, leaving in their places the Lord's Prayer.[25]

Church services were always crowded, but as with every other group and its audience and converts, Chinese usually outnumbered the Tibetans. This good beginning was slowed but not disrupted by the revolution of 1911, with missionaries needing to leave the area.

The initial response was hindered when the local people saw more clearly what the missionaries were about. The Tibetan-Chinese principal of the FCM school noted that people were hesitant to send their children to the school. Parents were alarmed that their children, within the first three days of entering the school, no longer believed in the gods of their family, had accepted the idea that all people were created equal, and believed that democracy was the best political system![26]

The Christian and Missionary Alliance (CMA) commenced its work south of Lanzhou in Hezhou and Daozhou with hopes of reaching the Tibetans. William Christie and his companions pressed boldly into Labrang and other lamasery areas. Although rebuffed by riots and personal attacks, they, with new recruits, continued to occupy a variety of cities: Minzhou, Baoan, Lhamo, Lintao, Hezhou, and others. Here they preached, visited, did simple medical work, handed out literature, and organized believers into small churches. Gradually, given the response by the Chinese and the indifference of the Tibetans, they gravitated toward Chinese work. The original vision of reaching the Tibetans before Jesus returned was lost. It helped a bit to divide the missionaries into a Chinese team and a Tibetan team.

25. Flora Beal Shelton, *Sunshine and Shadow on the Tibetan Border* (Cincinnati: Foreign Christian Missionary Society, 1912), 124.

26. Duncan, *Mountain of Silver Snow,* 87.

By the late 1920s the old fire was rekindled. This was not so much from a new spiritual vision as from the way in which the missionaries saw God using Islam to break the oppressive hold of Buddhism over the people. Specifically, the Muslim rebellion of 1928–1930 destroyed the old city of Daozhou, which the missionaries had used as a base to go into Chinese Tibetan country, and forced them as refugees into the great lamasery centers of Labrang, Hehtso, and Rongwu. Only as refugees fleeing from possible Muslim wrath were the missionaries welcome among the ordinarily suspicious priests in these religious strongholds.[27] But this backdoor vision and new activities still did not open the Tibetan door to Jesus. Results were as few as always.

The China Inland Mission established a small church, along with a Sunday school, in Dajianlu and had hopes that this small group of believers, not aided as were other groups by foreign money, would be able to evangelize the Tibetans. It was a Roland Allen-type dream that was not effective for Tibet.

Beginning in 1885, Cecil Polhill of the CIM had pioneered in Xining, now included in Qinghai Province. Many faithful CIM missionaries used this as a base to penetrate further west in Chinese Tibet, particularly to follow up Tibetans who had lodged in the Tibetan Gospel Inn that the mission established there in 1923.

Disputes over the extent of the gifts of the Holy Spirit disrupted the work of the CMA along the Gansu-Tibetan border. William W. Simpson, one of the pioneers of the CMA who worked with Christie, "received the baptism of the Holy Spirit" and spoke in tongues at a convention of missionaries at Daozhou in 1912. Unwilling to compromise his newfound convictions in dealing with fellow missionaries or mission executives in America, Simpson resigned from the CMA and joined with the Assemblies of God in 1915. He returned to Daozhou in 1918 under these new auspices. He soon reported that many ordained preachers of the CMA as well as lay people had left that mission and joined with him in revival efforts. He and his new colleagues opened work to "bring Pentecost to the people" in Minzhou, Gweite, Rongwo, Labrang, and twelve other stations and outstations in the next few years. He tells of hundreds of seekers baptized in the Holy Spirit. After a period of time, this novelty wore off and produced no more lasting results than did his previous labors.[28]

27. Robert L. Ekvall, *Gateway to Tibet* (Harrisburg, Penn.: Christian Publications, 1938), 144–46.

28. For this dispute and its ramifications see W. W. Simpson, *Evangelizing West China* (Springfield, Mo.: General Council of the Assemblies of God, 1932); *Dictionary of Pentecostal and Charismatic Movements* (Grand Rapids: Zondervan, 1988), 787; *Christian and Missionary Alliance Weekly,* April 1892, 237, and July 1892, 13–14; Gary McGee, *This Gospel Shall Be*

Church divisions produced more church divisions. Pentecostal bodies multiplied in China, even along the Tibetan border. As a result the more responsible groups, such as the Assemblies of God, found it necessary to distance themselves from those who doctrinally, ethically, and methodologically did not represent the truth as they understood it.[29]

The Faith in Context

How sensitive were the missionaries to the Tibetan context and the people's extreme outward religiosity—so pervasive, one missionary commented, that even horses stopped at rocks chiseled with prayers and religious expressions? Certainly they lived and spoke the language of common need: how to deal with sickness, death, sorrow, pain, and hopelessness. They arranged rooms to meet Tibetans on their own terms, sitting on the ground. They often immersed themselves for long periods in Tibetan life—in their homes and in the marketplaces—to learn the language and the customs of the people.

Religious sensitivity was harder to come by for those who believed they had the truth. One missionary described a Tibetan prayer meeting as "dull and stupid . . . useless and wicked." Another brother, commenting on the need to adjust the presentation of the truth to the Tibetan mind, noted that "you cannot have truth for each land separately. There is one law of gravity and it cannot be adjusted." How different the comments of Susie Carson Rijnhart: "Yet there is something pathetic in this spectacle of heathen worship, and it is not, in my opinion, the part of the Christian missionary to assume an air of ridicule and contempt for the religious ideas and practices of peoples less enlightened than his own; for in every religious service, however absurd or degraded from the Christian view-point, there is some feeble acknowledgment of and groping after the one great God to whom all men and nations are alike dear."[30]

Tibetan converts did not come easily. Most missionaries waited for several years, even ten to fifteen years, to accept their first convert. Many of the converts were the domestic help of the missionaries. Some converts went on to be stalwarts in the faith. Aki Tan Tsen, formerly a Bud-

---

Preached (Springfield, Mo.: Gospel Publishing House, 1986), 57–67; David W. Myland, *The Latter Rain Covenant and Pentecostal Power* (Chicago: Evangel, 1910). The Assemblies of God reported that it had forty-five churches and 2608 communicants in northwest China in 1951. This number does not distinguish between Chinese and Tibetan communicants. See Wardella Plymire, comp., *Assemblies of God in China,* an unpublished manuscript held at Central Bible College Library, Springfield, Mo.

29. "Groundwork for Organization of China Assembly of God," from Wardella Plymire.

30. Susie Carson Rijnhart, *With the Tibetans in Tent and Temple: A Narrative of Four Years' Residence on the Tibetan Border, and of a Journey into the Far Interior* (New York: Revell, 1904), 111.

dhist priest, left the priesthood because of disillusionment. After becoming seriously ill, he spent five years worshiping idols endlessly as he sought to be healed. When he was at the point of death, William Christie of the CMA befriended him and over a period of time led him to faith in Jesus. Liberated from his past bondage, he began to work with the mission, first in menial capacities and ultimately as an evangelist. Unfortunately, he was the only evangelist the CMA could claim in the northwest.[31] Two other Tibetans who were liberated by Jesus had significant testimonies. Chi Fah-chia was beaten by the lamas and imprisoned in one lamasery for refusing to follow old religious practices. When he finalized his decision for Christ, he asked the missionary to replace the twenty-foot prayer flag in his courtyard with another equally long flag inscribed with the words, "The kingdom of God is at hand; repent and believe the gospel" (Mark 1:15).

An elderly man from the Lake Kokonor region stayed at the Gospel Inn for several weeks, listening attentively to the message given in the large preaching hall. When he decided to follow Christ, he came to the front of the hall, bringing his *khata* (scarf of blessing). Using both hands, he presented it to God with the prayer, "Thou are the true God, and I will serve thee to the end of my days."[32]

Impact went beyond converts. When the British mission under Colonel Younghusband came to Lhasa in 1904, the Dalai Lama took refuge in Kumbum monastery near Xining for one year. Here H. French Ridley of the CIM saw him several times. They struck it off well, and the Dalai Lama later sent him a personal portrait. Ridley, reporting on his several conversations with this noted religious leader, said that the Dalai Lama had stated that "Christianity is a progressive force and Buddhism would decay before it."[33]

Demon oppression was rampant in this part of the world. Lamaism was a combination of Indian Buddhism and the old Bon (spirit) religion that put its priority on casting out demons. So when Jesus was preached, it was a confrontation between his kingdom and the kingdom of Satan. Christie, a pioneer missionary with the CMA, recounts how a husband brought to him his wife, handcuffed and restrained by four strong men. Christie prayed for her in the name of Jesus for one hour, and the demon-possessed woman was liberated and went on to walk faithfully in the Way.[34] The pages of *The Alliance Weekly* were filled with many ex-

31. *The Alliance Weekly,* 31 January 1925, 71.

32. *Challenge of Central Asia* (London: World Dominion Press, 1929), chap. 6, "On the Borderland of Tibet," 90.

33. Mrs. Howard Taylor, *The Call of China's Great Northwest, or Kansu and Beyond* (London: Religious Tract Society, n.d.), 136.

34. *The Alliance Weekly,* 9 February 1918, 297.

amples, more than recorded in any other mission publication, of people healed from a variety of ailments. The land was "well-watered" with tract and Scripture distribution, people learned many good trades and went on to productive livelihoods, and many important relationships were developed. These results are not to be despised, but the missionaries wanted something more. And when the "something more" was not achieved in the numbers they desired, goals were greatly scaled back. When the CMA work was closed down in 1949 with a few converts and no Tibetan churches, one official commented: "The goal of 60 years ago for the Kansu-Tibetan border has been realized, for eastern Tibet is now open to the message of the cross."[35]

A New Strategy?

What thought did the missionaries give to any change of strategy that might have produced more satisfactory results? J. Houston Edgar, a missionary with the CIM, rued the fact that Protestant missionaries were not getting at the information needed to evangelize Tibet. In many cases, he lamented, they know less than the Roman Catholic missionaries did seventy-five years ago. And when they do have the facts, they fail to occupy all of the possible sites in the "lama-controlled areas of West China." He appended a map, outlining in detail his suggestions, to his article and pled that these areas not be "redarkened by un-Christ-like indifference."[36]

Edward Amundsen, one of the original members of the Tibetan Pioneer Mission and later affiliated both with the CIM and with the British and Foreign Bible Society, said the need was first for the light of the gospel and then for power that would liberate Tibet. "Power, mere force, would curb Lamaism and deliver those who through fear of death are all their lifetime subject to priestly bondage. Many a Tibetan is longing for such a deliverance, but it is not for us to advocate. If God should choose this method we can only say well and good, but it will surely come as a rebuke to a section of the Christian church for having failed to do its duty."[37]

One Protestant missionary, George Patterson, working independently as a Brethren in Tibet from 1947 to 1952, wanted to hasten God's deliverance. He sided openly with one political group within Tibet's complex of mutually struggling factions, the Khambas. By this he hoped to gain a political and military victory over both the reactionary government in

35. Alfred C. Snead, ed., *Missionary Atlas: A Manual of the Foreign Work of the Christian and Missionary Alliance* (Harrisburg, Penn.: Christian Publications, 1950), 103.

36. J. Houston Edgar, "The Exploration and Occupation of the Centres on the Tibetan Marches," *Chinese Recorder* 50 (September 1919): 607–12.

37. Edward Amundsen, "The Hinterland of China," *Chinese Recorder* 41 (September 1910): 591.

Lhasa and the approaching armies of the People's Republic of China. Such a strategy, deplored by most of his missionary colleagues in Dajianlu, would produce justice for the Tibetans, he claimed. Furthermore, he thought it would enable him as a missionary to develop a new foundation for Tibetan culture, one that would have the gospel as an essential ingredient. The plan did not work. His partner, Geoffrey Bull, was imprisoned for three years, and Patterson barely escaped to India. From this base and from England, he has continued until the present to press for Tibetan rights before international bodies, with full assurance that this is God's will. Tibetan leaders outside of China, including the Dalai Lama, have indicated that Patterson has been a better friend to them than the United States, Great Britain, or India.[38]

Patterson might not have succeeded, but Amundsen's hope has been accomplished. Tibet has been liberated by China, and the common people have been freed from the priestly economic, religious, and social oppression that held them in bondage for centuries. But to Tibetans outside of China, and perhaps for many still in the country who dare not speak, the old bondage has been replaced by a new one that still does not permit the Chinese church to proclaim and live out the gospel of the kingdom in that land. The day of spiritual liberation is still to come.

Marku Tsering, a Britisher with a Tibetan pseudonym, has written *Sharing Christ in the Tibetan World,* in which he analyzes in detail the type of strategy that might be effective for Tibetan Buddhists. His main emphases are upon the need to learn the language better, to understand and be more sensitive to the culture, to analyze the social structure, and to try to convert families. If Chinese Christians yet have the opportunity to live and work in Tibet, these suggestions may well be guideposts for them to follow.

Meanwhile, the labor of one century has not been without some ongoing fruit. A small Chinese-Tibetan church continues to meet and witness in a small village to the west of Kangding (the new name for Dajianlu). In the Gansu-Tibetan area where the CMA once worked, at least five churches, a mix of Chinese largely but a few Tibetans, are still serving Christ enthusiastically. One report indicates more optimistically that as many as ten thousand Tibetan believers are in the area around Hezhou.[39] On the southern borders of Tibet the witness for Christ continues. In some places missionaries have the opportunity to arrange for

38. Patterson has written several books, some repetitive of earlier ones. The most recent one is *Requiem for Tibet* (London: Aurem, 1990). Geoffrey T. Bull has written about his imprisonment in *When Iron Gates Yield* (London: Hodder and Stoughton, 1955).

39. Dan Harrison, "Broken Vessels Called to Missions," *The Great Commission Handbook 1994* (Evanston, Ill.: Berry Publishing Services, 1994), 11.

training the children of Tibetan nobles in mission schools, an arrangement worked out between the Dalai Lama and the Indian government.[40]

The big issue is not the future of Christianity in Tibet, but the very future of Tibet itself. In all of Tibet's temples and monasteries the monks have been reeducated to intone a special mantra: "Tibet has never been independent in the past, Tibet is not now independent, and Tibet will never be independent."[41] The Dalai Lama has been quoted as saying, "Tibetans will soon be no more than a tourist attraction and relics of a noble past."[42] Whether or not it is time to play the requiem for Tibet, Christians everywhere will be concerned for this land on the roof of the world that has faced such difficulties in the past half-century.

40. David Woodward, unpublished manuscript, *Sky-High in Tibet,* 316.

41. "Tibetan Culture Lives On Despite China's Hard Line," *The Christian Science Monitor,* 21 July 1993, 1. China has publicized widely the 4 September 1993 inauguration ceremony in Xigaze for the stupa and memorial hall for the remains of the Bainqen (Panchen) Lama. (Li Haibo in *Beijing Review,* 1–7 November 1993, 17–21; see also Xin Fuyong, "The Search for the Great Living Buddha," *China Today,* North American edition, November 1993, 30–33.) Is this any more, however, than religious tokenism—restoring the shell of Buddhism while systematically destroying its essence? See "Report from Tibet—China's Undercover War on Religious Life," *The Christian Science Monitor,* 4 November 1993.

42. "Tibetan Culture Lives On," 356.

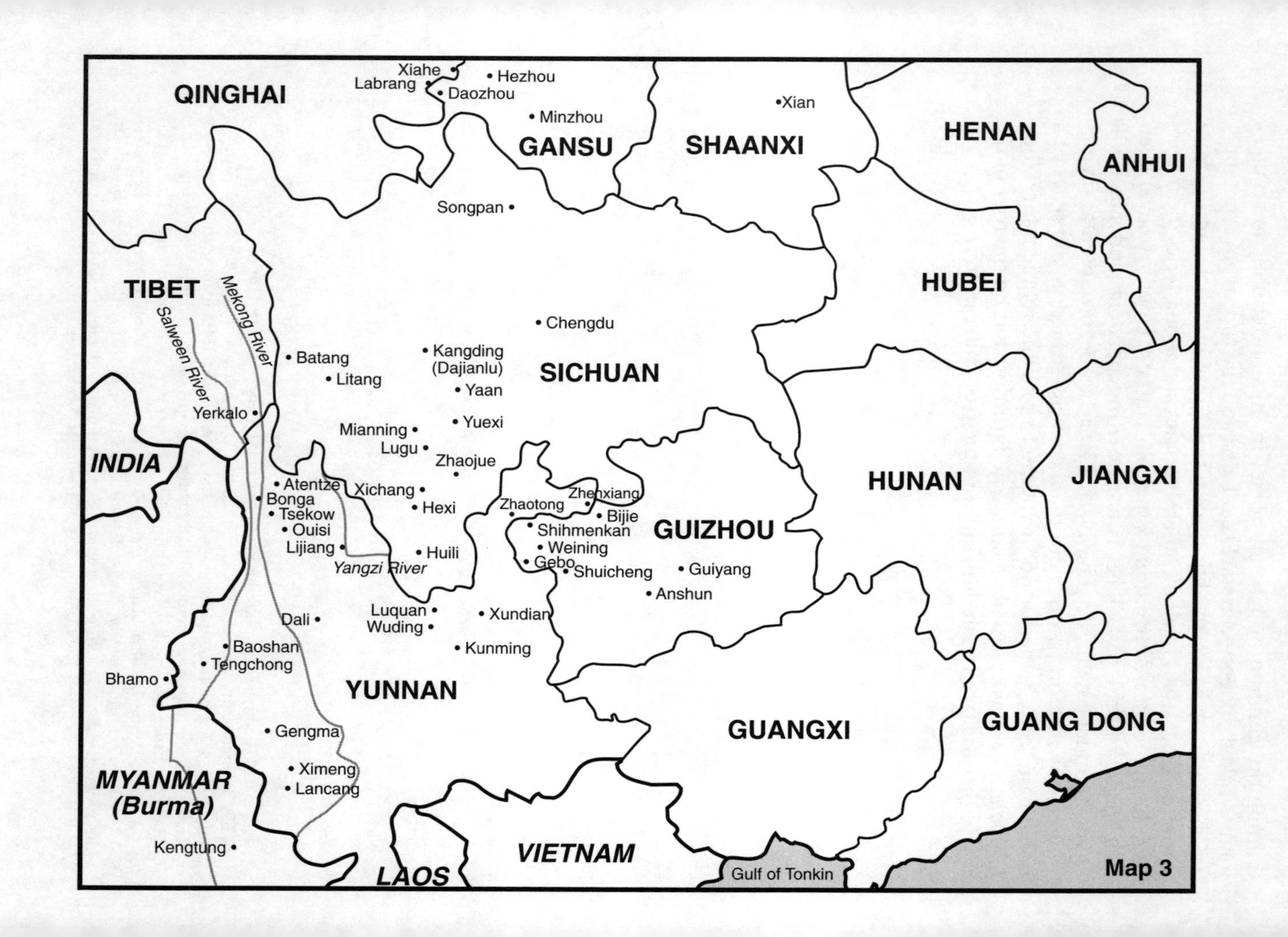
QINGHAI
Xiahe
Labrang
Hezhou
Daozhou
Minzhou
GANSU
SHAANXI
Xian
HENAN
ANHUI
Songpan
TIBET
Mekong River
Salween River
HUBEI
Chengdu
Batang
Litang
Kangding
(Dajianlu)
SICHUAN
Yaan
Yerkalo
Mianning
Yuexi
Lugu
Zhaojue
INDIA
Atentze
Bonga
Tsekow
Ouisi
Lijiang
Xichang
Hexi
Huili
Yangzi River
Zhaotong
Zhenxiang
Bijie
Shihmenkan
Weining
Gebo
Shuicheng
GUIZHOU
Guiyang
Anshun
HUNAN
JIANGXI
Luquan
Wuding
Xundian
Kunming
Dali
Baoshan
Tengchong
Bhamo
YUNNAN
GUANGXI
GUANG DONG
Gengma
Ximeng
Lancang
MYANMAR
(Burma)
Kengtung
LAOS
VIETNAM
Gulf of Tonkin
Map 3

4

The Despised Serfs of Southwest China

The Liberation in Christ of the Miao

Introduction

The four Miao near the small village outside of Anshun had never experienced anything like this. The tall, gangling foreigner with the blue eyes and the light hair had invited them to eat with him in the little roadside eating place. Could he mean it? Did he know who they were—poor, oppressed hill people, less than dirt under the feet of the Chinese who thoroughly despised them? "It must be a mistake," they thought. They refused politely, but the white man, seeing their hesitation, even confusion, insisted that they eat together. With this simple act of human courtesy, James R. Adam took a step of friendship with the Miao that would lead to the first and most remarkable of the people movements to Christ in southwest China. Tens of thousands of Flowery and Black Miao in both Guizhou and Yunnan provinces now recognize Jesus as Lord. Equally important, the turning of the Miao to the Christian faith sparked similar movements among the Yi and Lisu in Yunnan.

Who Are the Miao?

Even before the Christian era, ancestors of the Miao lived in the western part of present-day Hunan and then in the eastern portion of today's Guizhou. Their name, usually recorded as Mao, appeared periodically in Chinese documents during the Tang and Song dynasties (618–1279). Beginning in the third century of the Christian era, they were either moved or taken as captives to Yunnan and western Guizhou. Eventually their dispersion, which caused them to be more widely scattered than any other minority group in China, reached as far as Thailand and Laos, where they became known as Hmong.

Although pockets of Miao have remained "wild" and fiercely independent, most of them have come progressively under the control of the Chinese or other minority peoples, particularly the Nosu. In the Zhaotung area of northeast Yunnan, for example, Nosu or Yi landowners, referred to as *tu mu,* "earth eyes," ruled over huge estates until the advent of the Qing dynasty in the mid-seventeenth century. The new Chinese rulers brought the earth eyes under nominal control, but were wise enough not to strip them of their power and privilege. With no demand laid upon them apart from paying regular taxes, these powerful Nosu landowners created a kingdom of their own within the Chinese empire. Here they ruled arrogantly over their serfs and slaves: some Chinese whom they had taken captive and tens of thousands of Flowery Miao in five hundred villages. The situation was similar in other areas of Yunnan and Guizhou, except that in some cases the Chinese exercised relatively more authority. The Chinese in the southwest despised no other group as much as they did the Miao; the most reviling insult that a Chinese could make against one whom he hated was to call him a Miao. Many Chinese called them "men-dogs or men-wolves." They believed that the Miao had tails and claimed that when a child was born, the soles of its feet were cauterized to harden them and make them incapable of being tired.[1]

This intense Chinese hatred of the Miao, reciprocated when possible, had developed over many centuries of Chinese oppression and Miao rebellions. Chinese oppression had two sources: the desire of the Ming and Qing dynasties to extend their bureaucratic control into areas that had long been autonomous, and the pressure of Chinese settlers moving into Miao-populated districts, pushing the Miao even farther south and into the mountains and taking their land. The Ming dynasty rulers (1368–1644) tried to separate Chinese and Miao territory completely, setting up stone guardposts, establishing guard stations, and building border walls. About 1650, the Miao rebelled, tore down the guard stations, and, as was the case in eastern Germany in 1989, demolished the border wall between themselves and the Chinese.[2]

When Qianlong was ruling over China (1736–1795), Chinese, pre-

1. Joseph-Marie Callery and Melchior Yvan, *History of the Insurrection in China with Notices of the Christianity, Creed and Proclamations of the Insurgents* (New York: Harper and Brothers, 1853), 52–54.

2. Shunsheng Ling and Yihfu Ruey, *A Report on an Investigation of the Miao of Western Hunan* (Shanghai: Academia Sinica, 1947), 165–68.

tending to be traders, entered Miao territory, mistreated the people, and tried to lead them into thievery, provoking a large Miao uprising. A mass immigration of poor Chinese peasants, intent on taking more Miao land along the Hunan-Guizhou border in the early 1790s, led to another rebellion in 1795. This was put down in 1806, but only by using thousands of Qing soldiers recruited from seven provinces. Even though the wall had been demolished, the Chinese tried again. Their problem was how to sustain the ongoing contingent of four thousand soldiers occupying 830 guard posts. Their solution, hardly popular with the Miao, was to allot nearly thirty-five thousand *mu* of land to be farmed for feeding the soldiers. Called *tun fields,* they were used largely by the Chinese, but after the rebellion was suppressed, some of them were distributed to the law-abiding Miao who had not been involved in the uprising.

This was not a lasting solution. Some tun fields were rented to either Chinese or Miao, largely the former, who then exacted oppressive taxes from the renters. This led to another series of rebellions. In 1832 the Miao rebellion was directed by the Golden Dragon King, who dressed in imperial yellow robes. He declared that the government had lost the mandate of heaven and proclaimed his intention of overthrowing the Qing dynasty. Eventually this rebellion fizzled, and its pretentious leader was executed. The biggest rebellion came in the mid-nineteenth century (1851–1874), when rebel forces gained control of nearly the entire northwest area of Guizhou Province. During this same period, many dissident Miao were among the forces in the Taiping Heavenly Kingdom, which established its capital in Nanjing and nearly succeeded in overthrowing the Qing dynasty.[3]

S. Robert Ramsey sums up well the devastating effects of this centuries-long struggle between the Miao and the dominant Chinese:

> The results were brutal. In the aftermath most of the survivors were scattered, launching the Miao into an era of migration. Many of the population groups known as Black Miao went southwest into Hunan and Guangxi. The Red Miao drifted directly east to Hunan. Some of the White Miao migrated northwest into Sichuan. The Flowery Miao took a southwestern course into Yunnan, some eventually ending up in Vietnam. The Blue Miao dispersed in several directions.[4]

3. Other material on the Miao rebellions may be found in Ma Yin, ed., *China's Minority Nationalities* (Beijing: Foreign Languages Press, 1989), 344; John Fairbank, ed., *The Cambridge History of China,* vol. 10, *Late Ch'ing, 1800–1911, part 1* (Cambridge: Cambridge University Press, 1978), 132–33; and Flavia Anderson, *The Rebel Emperor* (New York: Doubleday, 1959), 25, 45, 67.

4. S. Robert Ramsey, *The Languages of China* (Princeton: Princeton University Press, 1987), 279.

Dispersion was not the only result. Even more serious was the damage done to the psyche of these sensitive, shy mountain people. They saw themselves as the lowest of the low, the despised scum of the earth, almost like wild animals being hunted and killed in the mountains. Added to the military and economic oppression was their slavery to rampant debauchery, opium, and whiskey, and the ever-present evil demonic forces. A recent Chinese researcher has stated that "hopelessness had become a way of life for them."[5]

Miao Religious, Social, and Cultural Life

The Miao belong to the Miao-Yao language family, which, along with Tai, Sinitic, and Tibeto-Burman, is one of the four major branches of the Sino-Tibetan grouping in China. However, its life as a minority people is very similar to that of the Tibetan-Burman peoples, such as the Nosu, Lisu, and Lahu. For example, the Miao, like most of the other groups in Yunnan's "ethnological garden," have stories, not too unsimilar from the biblical accounts, of creation and the flood. Unlike the Naxi around Lijiang in Yunnan, the Miao do not have an ancient script that gives a pictorial representation of the flood.[6] The Miao also have an account of "lost books," eaten from their backpacks by fish as they tried in ancient days to swim across the swollen Yangzi River.

Many of the minorities in Yunnan and Guizhou (also the Gao Shan of Taiwan) have stories to explain why there is only one sun. The Miao tradition relates that originally there were six suns, but their intense heat dried up everything. So the people conferred and decided to shoot all the suns except one. To shoot the actual suns was too difficult, so they shot the reflections in the lake of five of them. This so frightened the sixth sun that it refused to come out, leaving the land in continuous darkness. How would the people lure this sun out, so that it would be unafraid? They got a tiger to roar, but this only scared it more. The mooing of a cow made it feel better, but not good enough to come out. Finally the people tried a rooster. When it crowed, the sun peeped out, and the people were overjoyed! The sun decided to stay out, and, in gratitude, gave the rooster a red comb to reflect its own brightness. Thus, the people conclude, that is why each morning the sun comes out when the rooster crows.[7]

5. Zhang Tan, *"Zhai Men" Qian Di Shihmen Kan Jidu Jiao Wen Hua Yu Chuan, Dian, Qian Bian Miao Zu She Hui* (The Stone Threshold in Front of the "Narrow Door": Christian Culture and Miao People's Society on the Border Regions of Sichuan, Yunnan and Guizhou Provinces) (Kunming: Yunnan Educational Publishing House, 1992), 30.

6. A. Kok, "A Tradition of the Deluge," *The Chinese Recorder,* September 1914, 563–66.

7. William H. Hudspeth, *Stone Gateway and the Flowery Miao* (London: Cargate, 1937), 16–18.

Miao religious life was characterized by the people's fear of evil spirits and their attempts to placate them. They were a haunted people. The spirit world was controlled for them by the shaman-curers, whom the missionaries called wizards, and also by magicians who manipulated the demons for their own purposes. These religious figures were involved in many ceremonies in which sacrifices were made to the demons in order to rescue people from sickness, to resolve village conflicts, to deliver people from the consequences of breaking taboos, to gain the favor of ancestors, and to be cleansed after some unusual events.

One shaman in particular used the missionaries' foreign religion to enhance his reputation, invoking the name of the Trinity and engaging in a modified Christian ritual. Norma Diamond points out that "Pollard was particularly appalled by a shaman who put red dye into a pond and then proceeded to 'baptize' some 200 people in the redeeming blood of Jesus in a fairly imaginative ceremony. Some time later Pollard adds a note saying 'he died later of virulent smallpox.'"[8]

A sinister aspect of the Miao religious cult was the special role of certain women who controlled the use of *gu,* a type of black-magic poison. Its use with secret rituals, incantations, and fetish-type objects killed enemies. It also had the potential of being a love potion. All Chinese living near Miao villages were desperately afraid that the poison could be used on them, and any unusual activity among the Miao raised this specter.[9]

In the view of one missionary, no religious ritual was more important than the "worship of the door." Actually, a more important designation would be a purification ceremony. The day for this ceremony had to be determined by a wizard or a sorcerer. After a propitious day had been selected, the door was closed at dusk, but only after the house had been swept clean. A young female pig was killed and its blood was drained into a hole under the door jamb. The pig was boiled with millet and eaten by the household. Then the family had a long period of silence. Eventually all retired for the evening, except for the father and the eldest son, who waited until an hour or two before sunrise to complete the ceremony. The father, acting as a household priest for this ritual, ate some meat and then reverently recited a set phrase: "We worship thee, O door. Keep away sickness, keep away disease, keep away slander, keep away all that is injurious." This was not a community or even a neighborhood event—only the family residing in that house attended the service.[10]

8. Norma Diamond, "The Miao and Poison: Interactions on China's Southwest Frontier," *Ethnology* 27, 1 (January 1988): 9.

9. Ibid., and Ling and Ruey, *Report on an Investigation,* 306–9.

10. Hudspeth, *Stone Gateway and the Flowery Miao,* 21–22.

Nearly all of the Miao are farmers and grow their own food, but when the missionaries first came, they did not own any land. Their food is simple: steamed wheat, maize, oats, millet, and vegetables, and meat as a luxury about once a month. Their possessions are few, only what is needed for farming and preparing their food. They live in small villages or hamlets, in houses that usually resemble Chinese homes in appearance.

Every Miao village had what was called a flowery house, where young men and women got together for sexual orgies. At festival times such trysts went on for several days, and the Miao were the laughingstock of the Chinese and their neighbors. The sexual liaisons of the young people were fueled and perpetuated by the Miao fondness for anything alcoholic. Moderation was unknown to them—they drank until they were drunk. Drunkenness then led to all varieties of personal and societal evil. Depending on the policy of the national government or of local officials at any given time, the growing and use of opium was either encouraged or prohibited.

The Entrance of the Christian Faith

Protestant mission efforts in Guizhou began in 1877, but it was only in 1896 that the China Inland Mission made specific efforts to evangelize the non-Chinese peoples around them. Samuel Clarke started his ministry among the Black Miao at Panghai. The Chinese opposed this work from the beginning, but the missionaries took their stand firmly on the political privileges given them by the unequal treaties of 1842 and 1858. "We told them quietly that we were there by treaty right; we had our passports, the high provincial authorities knew we were there, as did the local magistrate at Tsingpinghsien, and we intended to stay."[11] Clarke and several who followed him in the following five years evangelized widely, established schools in many villages, and taught both the Miao and the Chinese with a romanized alphabet.

The Boxer Rebellion in 1900 disrupted missionary work all over China. Its disastrous results, however, were foreshadowed in 1899 when W. S. Fleming of the CIM and the first Black Miao convert, Pan Sheoshan, were murdered near Guiyang. Apparently Pan was suspected of importing arms to fuel another Miao uprising. The Black Miao responded well to the gospel over the years, but the real harvest of converts came in the work directed by J. R. Adam of the CIM in the area about Anshun.

Adam opened his first chapel and a small boys' school for the Flowery Miao in 1899, but his work attracted the Chinese as well as their minority neighbors. How was he to handle both groups at the same time? He put

11. Samuel R. Clarke, *Among the Tribes in Southwest China* (London: CIM, 1911), 144–45.

this question to Hudson Taylor, the general director of the CIM, who exhorted him simply, "Go on, dear brother, and do the best you can for both!"[12] He followed this advice, with growing results until 1900, as inquirers came from 250 hamlets and villages in the surrounding area. When the Boxer turmoil erupted, he and his colleagues were in great danger. The Empress Dowager had issued an edict to all provinces to kill the foreigners. The viceroy in Guizhou not only disobeyed this order; he sent an escort to accompany missionaries fleeing for refuge to Shanghai. Following this chaotic period, Adam was not certain whether anything would remain of this incipient movement. Particularly was he fearful when he learned that a military official and a noted village headman had gone throughout the entire district, threatening with death any who would opt for this foreign religion.

Some of Adam's fears were justified. Only twenty chose to be baptized at his first baptismal service in 1902. But a network of villages had been established, and the gospel was carried rapidly by the people themselves into many villages, both of the Flowery Miao and the River Miao.[13] In a very short time hundreds of them had believed in Jesus and were willing to follow him. Adam, B. Curtis Waters, and others of their colleagues baptized many of these new converts, organized them into churches, and mobilized them to reach into the many villages where the Christian message had not yet come. By 1907 the missionaries could speak of twelve hundred communicants.

One matter troubled Adam. Some of these who came to him at Anshun had obviously traveled very long distances. Not welcome or safe at Chinese inns along the way, they carried all their provisions with them in goatskin bags, and camped out in the hills, where they rolled up in sheep's-wool rugs. Samuel Pollard once compared their coming with that of the Magi who sought out the Christ child in the stable at Bethlehem:

> Not a few Magi coming from the East with gorgeous presents, but a great number of poor men setting out over hill and through valley to find out the Great Secret . . . if any one had to choose a people to teach and train, surely he would pass by these Hwa Miao, and select a people whose outlook seemed more promising. So we think. So does not God think. He often does a startling thing, a new thing. The serfs in the dirty villages, the poor in the homes of poverty, the ignorant in the grip of the wicked

12. This early account of Adam's work comes largely from his own account in "Pentecostal Blessing among the Aborigines of West China," *China's Millions*, January 1907, 10–15.

13. The term *Chuan Miao* may be translated as either the Sichuan Miao or the River Miao. The term *chuan* means "river," and it is the second syllable of the term for Sichuan, which means literally "four rivers." When not used of the Miao in Sichuan, it usually refers to the Miao who live close to the river.

> medicine men—these appealed to the love and sympathy and chivalry of the Great God. He treated them as He did the serfs in Egypt. He heard their groaning, He remembered His covenant with Jesus, He saw and He took knowledge. The people knew nothing of God and never cried to Him. But God knew them and the time for His working came.[14]

When Adam learned that these weary travelers had come to him from the Zhaotong district, three days' distance from northeastern Yunnan, he urged them, with unusual Christian charity, to visit Samuel Pollard, the Methodist missionary in charge of the Chinese work in that city. Although Adam's reputation for kindness was already widely known, the inquiring Miao were not as sure about Pollard. But they were willing to give him an opportunity, and the miracle of a mass turning to Christ was repeated.

Pollard had been in charge of the Methodist work among the Chinese in Kunming. After about ten years, he moved to Zhaotong in northeastern Yunnan to carry on the same kind of work. From this outpost, much closer to minority peoples than in Kunming, he developed an interest in the independent Nosu living north of the River of Golden Sand in what he called Babuland. He made one trip into this dangerous territory, escaping both a Chinese-planned ambush and an attempt by a noted chief to forge a family alliance with him by marrying him to his daughter. Later, a number of these wild Nosu from Huili crossed the river and arrived at his home at Zhaotong with an invitation to come and teach them. Had it not been for the pilgrimage of Miao to his door at this time, he probably would have accepted the invitation to go to Nosuland, then and now one of the most unreached areas in China.

The Miao, who streamed out of the mountains by the hundreds to visit Pollard in Zhaotong, were as impressed by him as their compatriots in Anshun to the southeast had been with Adam. They knew that Pollard and others like him were called *yang ren,* foreigners, but they thought this phrase meant "shepherds."[15] So they hardly knew what to expect! Very quickly, however, they concluded, "We are one family with you." At first Pollard was nonplussed. Where do you put two hundred visitors? And how do you feed them? Fortunately, they had brought along their own oatmeal, regular fare for them on long journeys. Pollard spread them out in his home, in the vacant space in the compound, and in the school

14. Samuel Pollard, *The Story of the Miao* (London: Henry Hooks, 1919), 47–48.

15. The term *yang* in this context can have two meanings, for which two separate Chinese characters with the same pronunciation are used. One means "ocean," and by implication those "from over the ocean," or foreigners. The other means "sheep" and the total phrase means "men who care for sheep" or "shepherd." These illiterate mountain people mistook one phrase for the other.

building next to his home. At first, they wanted him to teach them how to read Chinese, a request that he worked hard to meet. Then they began to inquire about the gospel, the message that seemed to motivate him to treat them with a courtesy and dignity that they had never received from the Chinese.

Pollard made his first trip to Miao mountain homes in 1904. Like Adam in Anshun he preached, taught, baptized converts, and organized them into churches. But he could not carry on an effective work among the people with his base in faraway Zhaotong. Some center had to be found in the mountains; so he persuaded one of the leading chiefs to give him a plot of land, twenty-three miles from Zhaotong, across the provincial border in Guizhou Province. Here he ultimately erected a chapel, a home, and educational facilities for all facets of the Miao work. This site, known as Shihmenkan (Stone Gate), became the center of the Methodist Miao work. Three other subsidiary centers were developed, and from these radiated outward a network of sites for the development of the work. Within three years more than one thousand converts had been baptized.

But this was not the end! Two Miao lepers farther west in Yunnan in Wuding county had heard about the Jesus their Zhaotong and Anshun brothers were talking about. They came to Zhaotong to learn more. They had hoped to be healed from their disease, but they learned about healing from sin and returned joyfully to tell their fellow villagers about this new message. Soon they requested that Pollard would send a missionary to their villages. Overwhelmed by his own expanding ministry, Pollard could only request that the CIM assign one of its workers to this promising new work. Its leaders sent Arthur Nicholls, then stationed in Kunming, to go to Sapushan in the eastern part of Wuding county.

Feeling the need to learn more about the Miao, Nicholls visited Shihmenkan for several months. When he returned to Sapushan, he brought with him two of Pollard's helpers on loan, a rough translation of Mark, other books of instruction, and a hymnal using the tonic sol-fa system. Little wonder that the Miao Christians scarcely realized that two missions were working in the area and always saw the church among them as one. Adam of the CIM had sent converts to the Methodists, and they in turn had helped to start the CIM work in the Sapushan area. No turf wars here!

Very shortly Nicholls established chapels in five areas, and the work gained the same momentum as it had shown in Anshun and Shihmenkan. Whole villages turned to Christ from idolatry, witchcraft, debauchery, and various levels of drug addiction. Freed from these oppressive burdens, their economic picture brightened, and their lives and societies took on a new dignity. Once converted, the Miao had a desire to share the message with other minority nationalities, particularly the Gobu and the Lisu. In 1932 the CIM estimated that the Miao church in the Wuding area numbered about two thousand with several thousand more in the wider Christian community.[16]

In the years previous to the advent of the People's Republic of China in 1949, other mission groups such as the Seventh-day Adventists, the Presbyterians, the Anglicans, the Brethren, and various Pentecostal agencies came into areas populated by the Miao minorities and sparked further growth. Since 1949, the Miao church has gone through the same vicissitudes as did the Chinese church, advancing when the government followed its policy of religious freedom or retreating in times of difficulty: early land reform, the Great Leap Forward in 1958, the Cultural Revolution from 1966 to 1976, and the more recent period following the Tiananmen incident in June 1989.

Through it all, the church has moved forward. In the Wu Mao mountain area of Guizhou Province (including Gebo, Bijie, Shuicheng, and Heshan), formerly worked more by CIM missionaries, Miao Christians in 1986 were estimated to be seventy thousand. This number includes Big Flowery Miao, Small Flowery Miao, Water Miao, and some Yi minority people.[17] Tony Lambert, in a more recent estimate, puts the number of Miao Christians in all of Guizhou at three hundred thousand, with thirty thousand more in Wuding county of Yunnan and a large number also in Luquan county.[18] Growth continues about Anshun in Guizhou and even more markedly in the Sapushan area of Yunnan. The people are still poor, but many have their own land and, because the feudal system has been abolished, they are no longer serfs. Their Christian faith is sincere and simple, without all the trappings to be found in an urban center. One observer has written:

> They witness to God, not by appearance, but by their living. Their mouths are not filled with theological terms or Biblical messages. Pastors do not wear ties, white shirts and dark blue pants; nor do they carry the Bible with them everywhere. What they wear are work clothes; what they carry are agricultural tools. They carry bamboo baskets with heavy loads on their backs . . . the Miao Christians are a blessed community. They follow Christ family by family. Around 80% of the villagers are believers. This enables them to enjoy the blessings of God's life in a community of fellowship.[19]

16. T. Mulholland, "Amongst the Tribes," *China's Millions,* July 1932, 131.

17. Zhang, *"Zhai Men,"* 237–38.

18. Tony Lambert, "The Church among the Hill Tribes" in *The Phoenix Rises,* ed. Leslie Lyall (Singapore: OMF), 1992.

19. Wong Tak Hing, "A Pilgrimage to the Mountains: A Visit to Miao Churches in Guizhou Province," *Bridge: Church Life in China Today* 24 (July-August 1987): 9–10.

This is what happened among the Miao. How did it happen and why? What philosophies guided these early Protestant missionary pioneers and their successors? What were their methods? Did they differ at all in their approaches? What were the dynamics that led the Miao to turn to Christ?

The Dynamics of the Protestant Miao People Movement

The Missionary from Scotland

Is the hero made by circumstances or do the circumstances make the hero? This tantalizing question, posed many decades ago by Thomas Carlyle, has never received a definitive answer. Among the Miao, the character and the personality of the messengers were tied inextricably with the context in which they found themselves. J. R. Adam, a CIM missionary belonging to the Free Church of Scotland, was the key figure in the early development of Protestant work among the Miao. Untiring in travel to hundreds of villages, outgoing and friendly, fluent in the Miao language, he baptized nearly seven thousand of the Miao, probably more than any other missionary among this people.

Early in the work Adam sifted out those with potential for leadership and brought them into his own home for weeks of concentrated discipleship. These initial disciples took the lead in preaching to and teaching the many hundreds who later would respond in this snowballing movement. Adam and his colleagues continued their hands-on ministry, to the extent of their time and energy, but continued outreach and the grounding of the work depended on these informally trained leaders.

Adam aggressively confronted Miao society with the claims of the gospel. After several people in a village were ready to confess the name of Jesus publicly, Adam called for a bonfire, at which time all of the spirit paraphernalia was burned. What was the spirit paraphernalia? It included drums used in sacrifice to the evil spirits, sorcerers' wands, charms such as necklaces, and soul packets of charms prepared by the sorcerers to help mothers protect their children from evil influences. Adam allowed no one to be baptized who had not made a clear break with the demon world.

Even when only a few people in a village had believed, Adam, along with these converts, took the initiative in tearing down the houses used by the young people for their sexual orgies. He helped in sweeping out all remaining signs of idolatry, in cutting down spirit trees, and in finding and destroying all traces of opium, opium pipes, and lamps. He negotiated with the Nosu *tu mu* to allow their serfs to confess Christ and interceded with officials to protect converts from unlawful treatment. Under his prodding, magistrates reluctantly agreed to issue proclamations that gave Christians their lawful rights in society. Officials, like many of the landlords, needed convincing initially that the turning of the Miao to Christ was not a plot whereby the Miao would rise in yet another rebellion and use their secret poison to kill them.

Anxious relatives once reported to Adam three cases of girl snatching, when non-Christian Miao had abducted Christian girls to marry them against their will. Adam wrote to the culprits' landlords, who were greatly disturbed that their tenants had involved them in this illegal practice. The girls were quickly returned to their homes.

While a people movement may have a large number of hangers-on who never commit themselves fully to Christ, there must be a solid core at the center to give necessary stability. Because of this, Adam and his group of catechists took great care in preparing and in examining the inquirers who presented themselves for baptism. No one was eligible who had not believed for at least eighteen months. The questioning was a rigorous, time-consuming, intensive process. In each village large numbers were waiting to be baptized, and the period for examination might extend from early morning until past midnight.

The men were examined one by one, but the women, although they were questioned individually, came in groups of three. Questions ranged over the entire spectrum of Christian doctrine and practice: God's character, the Trinity, the incarnation, redemption, mediatorial intercession, the second advent of Christ, opium, wine, immoral practices, idolatry, and superstitious rites. The missionary and his national colleague were usually assisted by as many as twenty or thirty church members who advised them on each candidate. Miao Christians made an issue also of smoking pipes. They wanted to add the following verse to the well-known hymn, "Take my pipe and let me be clean and wholly sweet for thee."[20] When the interview itself was concluded, each candidate was asked to recite or sing a hymn, to quote a passage of Scripture, and then to stand and pray. A satisfactory prayer was the seal on a person's acceptance for baptism. No unmarried people were received for baptism, since it was felt the temptations to sin in the sex-saturated Miao society were too great.

Those who passed the examination were baptized two by two in rivers near the village. After baptism, each person was given a biblical name that would distinguish him or her from other Christian brothers and sisters. Many Miao had no personal names. They were designated only by number, such as "old three," "big sister," or "little two." This new system worked well for the Miao, who saw it as a great advantage to have a personal name. The difficulty came with so many converts

20. A. G. Nicholls, "Among Miao Outstations," *China's Millions,* December 1922, 182.

and the relatively few common biblical names. It was not unusual to find converts with names such as Jehoshaphat, Sosthenes, Jeconiah, and Tryphena![21]

Christian Miao were liberal in their giving. Each family gave grain, and this was used for the support of evangelists. Some of the money given by the churches was sent to the British and Foreign Bible Society, and another portion to the West China Tract Society. From the beginning, it was common practice for the people to provide the materials and labor to erect their own buildings for worship. These were not grass-thatched shanties. The church building erected in Gebo, later to be the center of the work, was 105 feet by 36 feet and included rooms for the evangelists and missionaries, as well as the chapel for worship.

The missionaries emphasized the need for the Miao to observe the Sabbath, a policy that always puzzled non-Christian Miao, the Nosu, and other minority peoples. "We can hardly make a living in seven days! How can they get by when they work for only six days?" Probably by working even harder! Samuel Clarke reported that the Christian Miao did two days of work on Saturday, but they brought in only one-half of the harvest that night. They hid the other half, presumably from their landlords, and then brought it in on Sunday.

Several years after the Miao people movement began, Adam started a Bible school in Anshun. Students came for periods of four to eight weeks. With a better grasp of the Christian faith, they were able to help the missionaries in their wide itineration, as well as to give leadership in their local village. CIM missionaries in the areas about Anshun and Sapushan established primary schools. This gave a basic foundation for those who went on to study at the several tribal Bible schools. A hospital was erected in Anshun to meet the physical needs of minority peoples in all of the surrounding area.

Early Protestant work among the Miao had depended heavily on the use of the Chinese language, but by 1909 Adam completed a translation of Mark, as well as a hymnal and a catechism, in one of the dialects of the Flowery Miao.[22] Adam died 11 August 1915, killed by lightning as he stood by the door inside his house. The churches he had founded were unattended by other missionaries for one year, but this did not cause them to waver in their faith. A good foundation had been laid, and it stood firm over the years. But like any group movement to Christ, the

21. This material is from J. R. Adam, "Pentecostal Blessing among the Aborigines of West China," *China's Millions,* January 1907, 10–15; and B. Curtis Waters, "Further Tidings about the Revival among the Aborigines," *China's Millions,* February 1907, 26–30.

22. In the area where Adam worked there were three varieties of Flowery Miao: the Great Flowery Miao, Flowery Miao, and Small Flowery Miao. The various Miao groups receive their names from the headwear of the women.

initial impetus can be lost. As he traveled among the Miao churches in Guizhou in 1943, Eric Northgate noted the need for revival to eliminate some of the "original rubbish" from the Miao churches. He concluded that the biggest need was a new generation of leaders with a passion to evangelize the many non-Christian Miao.[23] This was difficult in the time remaining before 1950, but in the purifying process since that time, many untrained lay leaders have arisen. They, along with the few trained pastors, are leading the Miao church into the future.

The Champion of the Oppressed

More than any other missionary, whether among the Miao or others of China's minority nationalities, Samuel Pollard stands out as a man who fought against oppression. In the words of the editor of the *West China Missionary News,* "It was to him these long suffering, sinning and sinned against thousands made their first appeal in hope of a deliverer."[24]

Pollard was the right man at the right time for the right people. When the Miao people first crowded into his courtyard at Zhaotong, a wave of fear swept over their Chinese neighbors and their Nosu landlords. Why are the Miao going to see this foreigner? What could he possibly have that they would want? It must be a plot! People knew that a Miao rebellion was in the works. They guarded their wells carefully, for this is undoubtedly where the Miao would drop their poison. In a short time, all the people in Zhaotong and the surrounding area would be dead. Little wonder, given these irrational fears, that officials and landlords alike wanted to cut off this movement.[25]

And so they exerted every type of pressure on the Miao inquirers and converts. They had not counted on Pollard. He was equal to the task. Often, it was a question of authority: who had the most? Pollard? The landlord? Where people were badly in debt, Pollard bargained with the landlords to reduce their rent. He argued with them to eliminate the need for paying the annual tribute of wine, suggesting that a cash payment would be a good substitute. If a landlord took a second wife, Pollard insisted that the Christians ought not to have to pay again a marriage fee, as they had done when he married his first wife.

23. Eric Northgate, "Among the Tribes," *According to Plan: The Story of the Year 1943,* a CIM annual publication, 80–83.

24. November 1915, 1.

25. R. Elliott Kendall, one of Pollard's biographers, points out that without the presence of the missionary as a stabilizing influence, the Miao could well have engaged in another peasant revolt, like the many in their past history, at this time. They had much of which to complain, and their movement to Christ in some sense released tensions that in earlier days would have produced a full-scale rebellion. See Kendall, ed., *Eyes of the Earth: The Diary of Samuel Pollard* (London: Cargate, 1954), 80–81.

One of Pollard's first clashes was with the Chinese magistrate at Weining who did not wish him to go into a particularly dangerous area to preach. Finally, the magistrate proposed issuing an edict of toleration granting protection and freedom for western men in proclaiming the Christian faith. Pollard rejected this, insisting that the Miao Christians must have the same protection. Whenever people threatened to persecute the Christians, Pollard sent their names to the district magistrate. Whenever necessary, he went directly to the British Consul-General at Kunming. Many pre-teen and teenage girls were members of the Miao churches. Pollard went out of his way to protect those who had been violated physically and mentally by their landlords. He strongly opposed the efforts of landlords to mobilize their serfs to fight the Chinese.

Pollard waged war constantly on the sinners and sinned against in Miao society. His most vigorous battles were with the wizards, who held such tight control over the people. When he came into a village where there was even mild interest in the faith, he took the initiative in cutting from the necks of the people the strings that the wizards had forced on them. When wizards attended his evangelistic services in the villages, he prayed publicly for them to rid themselves of evil spirits. He taught the Christians how to pray for God's protection from evil spirits after they had trusted in Christ. These new Christians saw Jesus as the great Liberator from this evil demonic world, but it took constant encouragement to resist the ongoing pressures that they experienced. W. H. Hudspeth, Pollard's successor at Shihmenkan, confessed like many missionaries before and since that "as a rule I don't believe in devils but these wizards seem to have communications with a whole world of demons." He went on to explain one of the unbelievable things done by these men—putting a white-hot chain about their necks without being harmed—and challenged those who doubted him to send in their explanation. Along with his converts he learned that however one might explain the wizards and their wizardry, the only effective answer to their opposition was prayer.[26]

Pollard was not only the protector of the Miao; he was also a lawgiver, the person who helped shape their response to the gospel within their culture. Nothing made the Miao more despicable to the Chinese than the Festival of Flowers on the fifth day of the fifth lunar month. At this time the young men and women gathered for five days on the hillside to play pipes, sing love songs, and give free rein to their passions. Pollard substituted a festival filled with games, races, lantern shows, and preaching. Harvest ceremonies and Christmas gatherings were other occasions

26. W. H. Hudspeth, "A Miao Quarterly Meeting," *The West China Missionary News,* January 1917, 13.

for the people to experience community life that substituted for much that was not helpful in their past.

Pollard was an evangelist, but his interests broadened beyond this to include justice in society. "He accepted the rudimentary social institutions which were indigenous to the tribes, modified and moralised them, and created a higher conscience."[27] This led him often to insist on church discipline against wayward members who heartlessly violated tribal codes of conduct that would not have happened even in their pre-Christian days. Church leaders knew how well Pollard had learned their customs, and under his prodding they saw how Christian principles gave new meaning and application to the best within their own culture.

Concerned by the continuing poverty of the Miao, Pollard worked out a plan to help them own their own land. Merely to save money at home was unwise, for the landlord might lay his hands on it. He organized a savings club, and each participant made a weekly payment to the missionary until enough had been saved to purchase a little plot of land. Several hundred Miao church members joined this club and learned how to beat the landlord system.[28] Pollard and Hudspeth hoped to develop an industrial mission among the Miao, but their attempt to teach these farmers how to use a Chinese loom and engage in weaving failed. A medical ministry in Shihmenkan met the physical needs of the Miao, but it and the schools there, at least in the early stages of the work, never detracted from the church-centric nature of Pollard's work.[29]

Missionaries at this stage of history were still heavy-handed, and Pollard, Adam, CIM missionaries among the Yi and Lisu, and William Young among the Lahu fit this pattern. Working with local Christian leaders who were always willing to follow his advice, Pollard forbade infant betrothals, set the marrying age of men at twenty and of women at eighteen, and forbade bridegrooms to give dowries (buy wives) at weddings.

Missionaries familiar with Pollard's work about Zhaotong and that of Adam and the CIM near Anshun felt that Pollard did not insist upon new converts knowing much of the Bible as a prerequisite for baptism. He was less interested in the propositions understood by new converts than in their experience with Christ and their ability to articulate clearly their own conversion.

Pollard thought theologically about the movement in which he was involved. Since the Miao were largely illiterate and since they had been liberated from the control of evil spirits, he believed that the central motif

27. Kendall, *Eyes of the Earth,* 335.

28. Walter Pollard, *Sam Pollard of China* (London: Seeley, Service and Co., 1928), 180.

29. See Zhang, *"Zhai Men,"* 265. The author argues that in the 1930s and 1940s the Methodists seemed more concerned with "indirect preaching" or "educational preaching."

of his approach should be through holy communion. He referred to the Miao turning to Christ as a "sacramental movement." Therefore, before Christians were organized into churches, he used the communion service, rather than preaching, as the means best able to bring the heart of the gospel before the people.[30]

Pollard's message was important, but his character as a messenger was even more crucial. He itinerated almost constantly among the people, living with them and sharing his life with them. Nothing heightened his credibility more than the time when he was nearly beaten to death by the retainers of two landlords, including two Miao. This near-tragedy, which put him out of the work for one year, gave him an extraordinary identification with the people. Not only was he willing to stand with the oppressed in their agony; he was prepared to suffer the same oppression.

Eventually the man most responsible for the savage beating was apprehended and sentenced to death. Pollard intervened to save him from execution. He stated to friends: "When I'm better, I want that man to come and have a meal with me. Jesus Christ died for that man, and I want to see him saved."[31] This spirit of forgiveness and reconciliation modeled for the Miao the heart of the Christian gospel.

A colleague, Henry Smith, called Pollard "lustrously human . . . he escaped the bane of a true manhood—officialism and professionalism."[32] He was a man of captivating charm, given to hearty laughter, a self-deprecating person who never took himself too seriously. An optimist even in the midst of the most trying circumstances, he saw the bright lining in every dark cloud. In every village where he ministered, children and young men and young women were naturally attracted to him. His colleagues noticed the large number of children who were part of any Miao gathering. The Miao church was not merely an adult church, but a family church. Pollard was an unusually good communicator, and his books, sermons, and lectures conveyed the truth in simple, concise, understandable terms.

Pollard cooperated well with the missionaries of other groups, particularly the CIM, and did not wish to build his own kingdom. He confessed that he was a loner. He did not wish his own policies in the work vitiated by the example and teaching of any other who might work intimately with him. This tendency did not apply to his work with the Miao church. Nothing worried him more than that the Miao might see the church as "an institution belonging to the foreigners and not to

30. Kendall, *Eyes of the Earth,* 102.

31. William H. Hudspeth, "Reminiscences of the Late Rev. S. Pollard," *The West China Missionary News,* February 1916, 7.

32. Pollard, *Story of the Miao,* 10.

them."[33] At the beginning of the Miao ministry, Pollard started the quarterly meeting, at which time the preachers gathered together at Shihmenkan to develop methods in the work, to work out relationships between churches and their preachers, and to deal with cultural matters of concern to the people. At one meeting, for example, it was decided that the wives of preachers sent into areas where unbelievers were in a majority should make no change in the way they put up their hair, lest it be misunderstood. On one occasion, Pollard and the leaders concluded that where Miao and Nosu villages were closely intertwined, Christians from the two groups should meet together in common worship, using whatever language was common between them.

At the quarterly meetings the missionary and the preachers discussed the sensitive issues that were troubling them. The question of the second advent of Christ was raised repeatedly. The time of his coming had puzzled many believers, and when the overzealous among them fixed definite dates, many members left the church. How should one deal with wild rumors that hurt the work? A common one viewed baptism as a kind of magical ordeal: baptisms were administered in a large tank, and if the persons being baptized still had too many sins, so the gossip went, they would sink; if their sins were truly cleansed, they would rise to the surface. By this logic, older persons should be baptized first—they were old and it did not matter what happened to them; also, by this stage of life, they probably did not have as many unconfessed sins!

Like Adam in Anshun, Pollard used the Chinese language with many Miao. Ultimately, however, it was necessary that a hymnal, catechisms, and the Bible be translated into Flowery Miao. He did most of the first draft of the New Testament, but this was revised by William H. Hudspeth, who joined Pollard in 1909, and by Arthur Nicholls of the CIM. Published in 1917 and using matrices of the Miao script that had been prepared in Tokyo, this edition sold eighty-five hundred copies. When these matrices were destroyed by the earthquake of 1923, the next edition (1931), also revised by Hudspeth and Nicholls, was done by lithography. By this time the church had grown to thirty thousand members, and twelve thousand copies were printed. From the beginning of the work among the Flowery Miao, missionaries had been traveling into Black and River Miao areas, and New Testaments for these groups were published respectively in 1936 and 1939.

For his translation work among the Flowery Miao, Pollard developed a unique, nonromanized script, borrowed, he asserted, from a syllabic used by a missionary among a group of North American Indians. This

33. William Alexander Grist, *Samuel Pollard: Pioneer Missionary in China* (London: Gassell and Co., n.d.), 271.

script was accepted well by Miao Christians as their own written language. It raised their sense of self-esteem and gave them an identity they, an oppressed people, would not otherwise have had.[34] The Pollard script continues to be used today, not only for the Miao churches he founded, but by some other tribal groups as well, such as the Black Yi in Yunnan. It is clumsy, and although it has been modified for use by typewriters and computers, it will be changed in current translation projects coordinated by the United Bible Societies in Yunnan.

What was the truth that most met the need of the despised Miao? One Christian expressed it well: "I did not use to understand the meaning of the suffering endured by Jesus on the cross. But now we [Miao] have suffered all forms of cruelty that have punished us. This has caused us to know something of the Lord's teaching . . ."[35] Remarkable Protestant missionary pioneers trailblazed the work among the Miao. Within a period of sixteen months (from August 1915 to December 1916), Adam, Pollard, and Samuel Clarke died. Their work was ended, but God's kingdom among the Miao continued under their capable successors and the Miao leaders whom they had trained so well. The thriving Miao church in Yunnan and Guizhou is the best testimony to the foundations they laid. One Chinese scholar has noted that, compared with the past, the work in the Wu Mao mountain area, particularly in Gebo, is prospering much better than in Shihmenkan, once considered the center of Miao work. He traces this to CIM policy that promoted a less institutionalized, more evangelistic, and more indigenous model that fit in the Miao context.[36]

How will this church face the changes that modern Chinese society will bring to it? More Miao Christians now are learning Mandarin, wearing Chinese clothes, and using electricity, radios, television sets, refrigerators, and tape recorders in their homes. The younger generation no longer cares for the old customs, nor do they relish traditional folklore, songs, and dances. Young people are addicted to drugs, common in Yunnan with its back door leading into the opium "golden triangle" in Myanmar, Thailand, and Laos. Will these changes benefit or hurt their villages and their churches? Pastors being trained to minister in and to these churches at the Minority Bible Training Institute in Kunming will

34. Norma Diamond, "Christianity and the Hua Miao: Writing and Power," unpublished paper by the author, a professor at the University of Michigan. Diamond cogently argues that most China scholars engaged in minority studies see the minorities as in an earlier stage of human history. Hence, to have a script of their own, as a "civilized people," helped the Miao to refute this view

35. Zhang, "*Zhai Men,*" 52, quoting from "The Miao People's Saviour," a small booklet published in Hankow in 1939.

36. Zhang, "*Zhai Men,*" 225–86.

need to have a high-priority new agenda to deal with the profound economic, social, cultural, and spiritual changes that confront them.

Passionist Fathers among the Miao in Hunan Province

When Theophane Maguire of the Passionist fathers first went to China in the 1920s, he "wanted to do something for God that would be the hardest thing he could think of."[37] He got what he wanted, but it was not that romantic. In the foreword of *Hunan Harvest,* Richard Cushing observed:

> Here are no startling mass conversions, no pilgrimages of the mighty to the feet of the crucified Christ, no peals of thunder to announce the herald of the great King . . . missioners are needed in pagan lands in *every* generation. Each pagan generation has only one chance to hear the message of Christ. Tomorrow they will be old, dead. Unless *we,* the people of our generation, get to them *now,* they will remain pagan. Christ on the cross will have thirsted in vain for their souls.[38]

Three of the sixteen counties assigned to the Passionists in Hunan were inhabited largely by the Miao.[39] This was in the western part of the province of Hunan where it intersects with the borders of Sichuan, Guizhou, and Guangxi. Maguire was assigned to the county of Yungsui, "Eternal Tranquility," which had a mixed population of about sixty thousand Chinese and Miao. He began his work modestly by teaching in a Chinese city and by opening a dispensary. On his first visit to a Miao village, with only a beginner's ability in Chinese and no knowledge of the Miao language, he used one of his domestic helpers to serve the Mass. He felt fulfilled by this first effort: "It was our Eucharistic Lord's first visit to this part of the great world which He created, and it might have reminded Him of the poverty of Bethlehem . . . to pronounce the words of Consecration that bring Christ to a tiny corner of the earth until then unvisited by Him, is worth the hardships and sacrifices of a lifetime."[40]

Since there were many villages, it was more convenient for the Miao to come to Maguire in a central location. He found it difficult to instruct

37. This is a quote from a letter of Maguire of 30 March 1926. Letters from him and others of the Passionist fathers are found in their archives in Union City, N.J.

38. Theophane Maguire, C.P., *Hunan Harvest* (Milwaukee: Bruce, 1946), viii–ix.

39. The entire area of their work in Hunan was called technically the Passionist Vicariate of Yuanling, Hunan. It occupied an area equivalent to Delaware, Connecticut, Massachusetts, and Rhode Island. In 1934 there were about twenty-five hundred Roman Catholic believers, but it is impossible to tell how many of these were Chinese and how many were Miao. This material is found in a file titled "The Passionists in China."

40. Maguire, *Hunan Harvest,* 68–69.

them, since their knowledge of Chinese was poor. Even his short Sunday sermon was beyond their comprehension. So, after leading Mass, he used a catechist and a Miao interpreter to explain to them the central doctrines of the faith. The Miao here were not too influenced by Buddhism with its many idols, but their sacrifices to spirits and observance of the ancestral rites were stumbling blocks to belief.

Despite the scattered nature of the Miao villages and homes, Maguire carved out time for itinerating. The results were sparse. He baptized babies during famine times, used the "special faculty of confirming, granted to isolated missionaries," and held Masses in many homes. These were useful, he felt, since God would surely bless these people, where "even unknowingly, they had offered their humble homes to another Bethlehem."

Although Maguire was glad to be called father, a prestigious title with the Miao, this proved of little help in getting any solid Christian content to the potential converts. Most of the conversations on doctrine needed to be done by a catechist in the evening hours, long after Maguire had retired. He hoped that the Chinese language would be sufficient to instruct them, but at any rate, "the work cannot wait until I know Miao." Even as he confessed the compulsive urgency that drove him and his colleagues, he confessed that "their religion is not clear in my mind nor their superstitions."[41]

Gradually a few Miao converts were baptized. These had to meet in a crude home, since Maguire's superiors had agreed that there had to be more converts before a chapel could be built for their worship. The best way to get more converts was to make the best possible use of native catechists, who made the first contact with the local people, did the initial discipling, and, if a priest was not available, did the follow-up.

From missionary correspondence, it is clear that the biggest internal obstacle in the Passionist work was the failure of the missionaries to gain a good grasp of either the Chinese or the Miao language. Headquarters and the missionaries did not give priority to language learning, since they depended largely on local catechists. William Westhoven, writing to headquarters in 1926, complained: "We have been put out of the nest as little birds. In six months we have not studied Chinese more than six hours. We have been sent to souls too quickly—before we are able to explain doctrine. It would be far better to wait another year or two and do language study. We can't go on like this."[42]

Little wonder, then, that in Hunan there does not appear to have been any large-scale turning of the Miao peoples to Christ. But, in fairness to

41. Maguire, "In Two Miao Villages," *Sign,* August 1926, 55.
42. Letter of William Westhoven, 9 October 1926.

these dedicated missionaries, it must be observed that this area was a political volcano. Brigand bands killed three of the Passionist fathers in 1929. The area was exposed to Communist guerilla activity because of the Chinese Soviet Republic that had been operating for several years in nearby Guangxi. Conflicts between the Communists and the troops of Chiang Kai-shek created unstable conditions, making it necessary for missionaries to flee repeatedly to Hankow or Shanghai. They had confidence in Chiang's plans to gain political power, but were deeply disturbed that he had decided to become a Methodist and "go through water," thus entangling himself with "the Prods."[43]

The Miao people in Hunan had been oppressed badly by the Chinese over a long period, but remained more independent in spirit than those in Guizhou and Yunnan. This too contributed to their reluctance to adopt a new faith. Their troubled and unstable territory had been off-limits to both Protestant and Catholic missionaries in the late nineteenth and early twentieth centuries. Consequently there had not been such a long preparatory exposure period to the Christian gospel as there had been in Guizhou and Yunnan. Spiritual liberation and the freedom in Christ to "strike off the shackles of the enslaved" in economic and social bondage had not yet come.[44]

43. These materials on the political situation and on Chiang are found in various materials in the 1931 Passionist files in Union City, N.J.

44. Maguire, *Hunan Harvest,* 188. In his recent book on the Passionist work in Hunan, Casper Caulfield gives little detail on the work among the Miao (see *Only a Beginning: The Passionists in China, 1921–1931* [Union City, N.J.: Passionist Press, 1990]).

5

The Christian Mission North of the Great Wall in Mongolia and Manchuria

Introduction

Throughout her long history China has been afraid of the various peoples to her north. If they did not conquer her and set up an oppressive dynasty, they plundered her borders, toying with her as a puppet and extracting gifts and privileges to guarantee her peace and security. From the time of the Qin dynasty (221–207 B.C.) China's emperors built and repaired various segments of what today is called the Great Wall (or "long wall") to seal off her northern borders from these pesky barbarian peoples. China may have thought her Middle Kingdom culture was superior, but she feared the alleged cruelty of these steppe peoples and their use of the new military technique of men on horses, armed with bows and arrows. The only comparable threat in the recent past has been that of the Soviet bear, poised to devour a small country and impose on it the yoke of Communism.

But there was a time in history when these fearsome peoples stood passively at a crossroad, both for themselves and the entire world. United under the dynamic leadership of Genghis Khan in a kingdom that stretched from the Pacific Ocean to the Black Sea and the Baltic, they were faced with a dilemma. Which of their three borrowed religions—Buddhism, Islam, and Christianity—would they embrace as their own? More than at any subsequent period in world history, the door was open for the peoples of Mongolia and Manchuria to accept the liberating message of Jesus. Had they done so, this huge area of China would not be

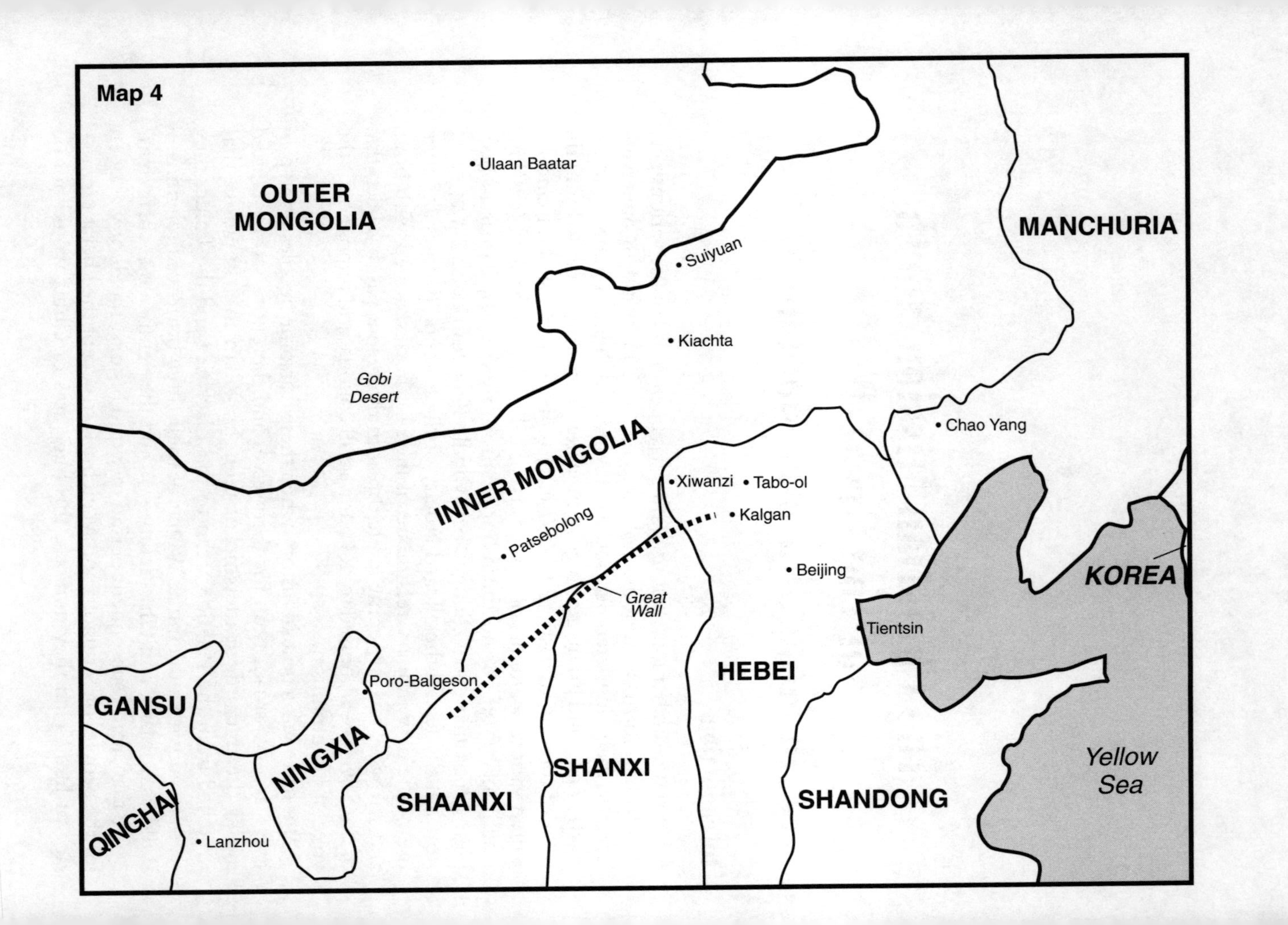
Map 4
Ulaan Baatar
OUTER MONGOLIA
MANCHURIA
Suiyuan
Kiachta
Gobi Desert
Chao Yang
INNER MONGOLIA
Xiwanzi
Tabo-ol
Kalgan
Patsebolong
Beijing
KOREA
Great Wall
Tientsin
Poro-Balgeson
HEBEI
GANSU
NINGXIA
SHANXI
Yellow Sea
SHAANXI
SHANDONG
QINGHAI
Lanzhou

dominated today by Lamaism, Buddhism, and Islam that have closed the door tightly to any effective gospel witness.

The northern boundaries of China include three different cultural areas: Mongolia, Manchuria, and Turkestan. Mongolia, the center piece of this triad, is located on a high plateau stretching south from the Siberian forests in the far north to the northern boundary of China proper. In the north peoples were hunters and herders. In both the south and north, nomads and farmer nomads were common. Where there was transition between these two economies pastoral nomads were found. The more southerly region was referred to as "steppes, those rolling plains of grass and scrubland punctuated by high mountain ranges."[1] Two-thirds of Mongolia's huge area was the Gobi Desert, referred to by the Chinese as the *han-hai* (dry sea) or as *wumao zhih di* (the land of no hair). Although it is not a desert in the classic sense of a vast area of shifting sands, it separated Mongol groups, north, south, east, and west, from one another and impeded any unification.

To the west of Mongolia this steppe country continues to the Baltic Sea and Hungary. Occupied largely by Turkic peoples and separated by the Pamir Mountains into what some have called Chinese Turkestan and Turkestan, this area is at sea level. The population of Turkestan has been concentrated in oases that surround deserts, such as the Tarim Basin and the dry steppe. Manchuria is east of Mongolia and separated from it by the Khinghan Mountains to the north and the Jehol Mountains in the south.[2] Mongolian peoples may be found in both Turkestan and Manchuria. Although these areas are not a part of political Mongolia, their Mongolian peoples are a part of the larger cultural Mongolia.

Extent of Early Christian Faith

The great nomad empires that threatened China all originated in the northwest area of what is today the People's Republic of Mongolia. This applies to the Huns (*Xiong Nu* in Chinese, 209 B.C.–A.D. 155), the two

1. Sechin Jagchid and Paul Hyer, *Mongolia's Culture and Society* (Boulder, Colo.: Westview, 1979), 16.

2. I will describe missionary efforts in Central Asia or Chinese Turkestan in chapter 7. I am not including a separate chapter on Manchuria since the Manchus, although "officially recognized as a minority, have in fact been Chinese for a long time." S. Robert Ramsey, *The Languages of China* (Princeton: Princeton University Press, 1987), 216. The Manchu or Qing dynasty controlled China from 1668 to 1911 and, after the initial period, were largely Sinicized. Although many mission groups worked in Manchuria, they never succeeded in planting distinctive Manchu churches using the Manchu language and culture. The Manchu language has its greatest usefulness as a historical tool to study the source material of the Qing period (Ramsey, 217). The only minority group in China that continues to use a dialect of the Manchu language is the Xibo, who live in Xinjiang Province (Ramsey, 215).

east Turkish kingdoms (roughly 552–734), the Uighur empire (745–840), and finally the Mongols in the twelfth to fourteenth centuries. With the exception of the Mongols, none of these peoples ruled over China; they found it more profitable to receive revenue from China and even to prop up her native dynasty with direct military aid to keep the money flowing. Manchurian peoples such as the Khitan (907–1125) and the Jurchen (1115–1234), known respectively as the Liao and Jin dynasties, waited in the wings. When native Han Chinese dynasties were reduced to weakness, they moved in to conquer.

The religion dominating the life of these several peoples, particularly the Mongols, was shamanism. It was filled with magic, divination, and the ecstatic, even mystical, relationship of witches with supernatural beings. These might be a supreme sky deity, subordinate gods, or the powers of the natural world, such as rivers, mountains, and the heavenly bodies. Shamanism is vulnerable to more structured, classical religions, and many competitors entered the fray over the years.

The first outside religion introduced into Mongolia (including both Inner Mongolia, belonging to China, and the independent People's Republic of Mongolia to the north) was Nestorian Christianity. Nestorian missionaries traveled overland from Persia into China about 635. Welcomed warmly by the reigning emperor, Tang Tai Zong, the Nestorian church prospered for two centuries, until 845, when, along with the Buddhists, it fell into disfavor and was persecuted out of existence in China proper. At this time it had hundreds of monasteries, possibly as many as two thousand religious workers, monks, and teachers, and tens of thousands of adherents. Many of these persecuted Christian believers became Muslims or joined the Jin Dan Jiao, a powerful secret society in northern China.

During the time that they were active in China, and certainly after they were dispersed by persecution in the late Tang dynasty, the Nestorians worked among Mongol-Turkic groups in Mongolia who would later be unified under Genghis Khan. To what extent did the Nestorians penetrate among the Uighur people, who were the ruling power in Mongolia from 745 to 840? Little agreement can be found among the scholars. One author claims that they were viewed as "Christian Uigur Turks" at the time when they were deposed from their capital at Karabalgasun by the Kirghiz people in the second half of the eighth century.[3] Other authors affirm that the Uighurs adopted Manicheanism from its missionaries during the time they were occupying China's capital at Loyang, right after they helped the Tang dynasty defeat the rebel An Lu-

3. See John Stewart, *Nestorian Missionary Enterprise: A Story of a Church on Fire* (Edinburgh: T. and T. Clark, 1928), 137.

shan. Manicheanism then became their state religion in the eighth and ninth centuries, and only later, when most of them were pushed out of Mongolia and moved to Urumqi and Hami in what is now Xinjiang, did they become Buddhist and Christian.[4] We do know that during the eleventh and twelfth centuries the Christian population of Xinjiang grew to such numbers that the city of Kashgar became the site of a Nestorian metropolitan with twelve bishops associated with him. The cities of Turpan and Maness were also centers of Christianity. When the Franciscan missionary William of Rubruck traveled through Uighur territory in the thirteenth century, he still found Nestorians in all their towns. Many Uighurs were also employed by the Mongols when they ruled both Mongolia and China, and some of these were committed Christians.

How normative was Nestorian Christianity among the Uighurs? Exceptions cannot be made the rule, but two Uighur Christians, Mark and Sauma, were of particular significance in the thirteenth century.[5] From devoutly religious families and tonsured as monks in Kambaluc (Beijing), they decided in the late 1270s to visit the holy sites of their Nestorian faith. As they traveled west through Mongolia and Central Asia, they were given an enthusiastic welcome by the inhabitants of these areas where there were many Nestorian communities. After their arrival in Persia, Mark, through a series of unusual circumstances, was made metropolitan of Cathay and then, only two years later in Baghdad, under the name of Mar Yaballaha III, he was elevated to the post of patriarch of the entire Nestorian church. His ability to speak the Mongol language made him a decided asset in a Mongol empire that extended from China in the east to the Ukraine in the west. A few years later Sauma traveled through the capitals of Europe and was received with both enthusiasm and surprise by Christian leaders who saw how closely akin his faith was to theirs.

When Genghis Khan came to power about 1200, he conquered the dominant tribes in Mongolia, incorporated them into his own Mongol kingdom, and then went on to take north China by defeating the ruling Manchu Jurgen people (Jin dynasty). Included in this involuntary union were the Ongkut, Kerait, and Naiman, and the Tartars further to the east. The name of the latter, also spelled Tatars, was applied to the Mongols after they came to power.

4. Christopher Dawson, *The Mongol Mission* (New York: Sheed and Ward, 1955), x, xxiv; Jagchid and Hyer, *Mongolia's Culture and Society,* 189; Igor Rachewiltz, *Papal Envoys to the Great Khans* (Palo Alto: Stanford University Press, 1971), 45–46, apparently come to the same conclusion.

5. Dawson, *Mongol Mission,* xxviii, believes that Sauma was Ongkut rather than Uighur.

In uniting these tribes, the Mongols not only gained military and political power; they also exposed themselves to the Christian faith and a more sophisticated civilization. One notable example is that the Mongols took over the script of Sogdian, an Iranian language, which was introduced to them by the Uighurs. The Keraits, or at least a number of their rulers, became Nestorian Christians by about 1000 and exercised influence in the Mongol kingdom as officials.

A well-known legend tells of the conversion of the Kerait king in 1007. Out hunting, he was trapped by a severe winter storm, lost his way, and despaired of life. From nowhere a man appeared and led him to safety, afterward imploring him to believe in Christ. He knew little of this faith, but when he returned to his camp he asked Christian merchants to give him instruction in the religion of Jesus. After his commitment, he received help from a nearby metropolitan who sent preachers and teachers to baptize his people. He affirmed that two hundred thousand believed with him at this time.[6] A later Kerait king, Unc Khan, defeated ultimately by Genghis Khan in his unifying process, was thought to be the Christian leader Prester John. European Christian leaders hoped that this legendary figure would unite with them in defeating the Muslim hordes who threatened to overrun Europe and who controlled the Holy Land.

After Genghis Khan conquered the Keraits and the Naimans, he took some of their Christian princesses as wives for his sons. One of these, Sorkhaghtani, became wife of Tolui, his fourth son, and bore him two of the most important khans, Mongke and Kublai. Yuan dynastic records indicate that these two emperors built a "temple of the cross," a little Christian chapel, for her where she could worship in Nestorian fashion. Hulagu Khan, another son of Tolui, had a wife who was described as "the believing and true Christian queen."[7]

The Ongkuts, another Turkic people, were originally in northern Mongolia but then moved to the northern bank of the Yellow River, referred to as Ordos or Tenduc (Tangkut) and now a part of the Chinese province of Gansu. Here they developed a widespread Christian culture, witnessed to by many Christian crosses subsequently found by archaeologists and missionaries. They used these crosses, with dozens of minor variations in style, to wear on their persons, to be set up on their houses, and to be painted on their churches.[8] One of the Ongkut kings, known only as King George, left the Nestorian faith for Catholicism under the urging

6. Stewart, *Nestorian Missionary Enterprise,* 143–44.

7. Ibid., 159.

8. See two articles by P. M. Scott in *The Chinese Recorder,* February 1930, 104–8, and November 1930, 704–6. Both articles are entitled "Some Mongol Nestorian Crosses."

of John of Montecorvino in 1294, bringing many of his people with him. They all returned to their original faith following the death of George.

In addition to the Keraits, the Ongkuts, and the Uighurs, who clearly had many Christian adherents, the possibility exists that other peoples were also Christian to some degree: the Kitans or Kitai, the Merkites, the Moal, and the Uriyan-gakit.[9] During the time of Mongol ascendancy, these other peoples found it to be an advantage to be thought of as Mongols. And just as the German language has been used in Germany, Switzerland, and Austria by some people who are not German, so the Mongol language was used by all of these other peoples in its various, mutually intelligible dialects.[10]

The Catholic church in Europe made every effort to send political and religious emissaries to visit the Mongol capitals. They had several reasons: the legend of Prester John, their belief that Nestorian Christianity was deficient, their desire to convert the Mongol khans and their peoples, and their hope that converted Mongols might help them recover the Holy Land from the pagan Muslims. This vision was set in motion by the Conference of Lyons in 1245, when Pope Innocent IV asked the Dominican and Franciscan orders to go to Asia and contact the Mongols. The Dominican effort was rebuffed by a Mongol general, but the Franciscan John of Plano Carpini and a companion managed to reach Karakorum, the Mongol capital, where they viewed the coronation of Guyug Khan. John was not able, however, to attain either his political or religious goals. In fact, Guyug was incensed to think that, in pressing for his conversion to Christ, these missionaries wished to bring him under obligation to them: "If thou sayest I am a Christian, I adore God and reject other religions how dost thou know whom God absolves and in favour of whom he dispenses mercy? How are thou so sure of these things as to pronounce such words?"[11]

The next major effort to gain rapport with the Mongols was made by the Franciscan William of Rubruck, who was dispatched in an unofficial capacity to the Mongolian court by Louis IX of France and the pope. His mandate was religious: to give spiritual nurture to Christians in the Mon-

9. Stewart, *Nestorian Mission Enterprise,* 153–57. Alphonse Mingana in *The Early Spread of Christianity in Central Asia and the Far East: A New Document* (Manchester: The University Press, 1925), 23, points out that "the Uriyan-gakit were Christians and had in 1298 a Christian queen."

10. Ramsey, *Languages of China,* 202, comments that "a visitor from Ulan Bator, say, would probably have fewer difficulties in Inner Mongolia than a Bavarian would in Low German-speaking areas. The common practice of dividing the Mongolian spoken in Mongolia into three different languages—Khalkha, Oirat, and Buriat—therefore seems to be more a matter of convenience than linguistic reality."

11. Stewart, *Nestorian Mission Enterprise,* 158.

gol kingdom and to preach the gospel. Traveling first through Russia brought him into contact with the Great Horde, and from there, with the blessing of Batu, the grandson of Genghis Khan, he went on in 1284 to the great Khan, Mongke, in Karakorum.

William's fascinating observations about life in the Mongol court are recorded in his *Itinerary,* an account to rival Marco Polo's description of his travels through China.[12] He was surprised at the cosmopolitan society that he found: Mongols in control, but helped voluntarily and involuntarily by many Europeans from France, Germany, and Hungary and by Asians from Georgia, Armenia, Persia, Turkish kingdoms, and China proper. Some Catholic sources claimed that Mongke was converted to the Christian faith, but William's material shows that the great khan depended heavily on soothsayers.

William wished to evangelize the Mongol court. He found this difficult, because his unofficial status allowed him to speak only when spoken to and not to initiate a religious conversation. He also felt that he was compromised by what he viewed as the corrupt lives and doctrines of the Nestorians. Even more of an obstacle was his own overbearing and aggressive attitude. Mongke reportedly complained to him: "The nurse at first lets some drops of milk into the infant's mouth, so that by tasting its sweetness he may be enticed to suck; only then does she offer him her breast. In the same way you should persuade us, who seem to be totally unacquainted with this doctrine, in a simple and rational manner. Instead you immediately threaten us with eternal punishments."[13]

Before he left Karakorum, William was asked by Mongke to participate in a debate about religious truth that pitted the Christians against the Muslims and the Buddhists. This debate, as well as several others held in the following decade, were inconclusive in convincing the great khan of ultimate truth. Over a period of time, the representatives of Tibetan Buddhism gained the favor of Mongke's successors.

One of these successors, Kublai, who ruled China from 1260 to 1294, asked the father and the uncle of Marco Polo to request the pope to send "one hundred teachers of science and religion to instruct the Chinese in the learning and faith of Europe." He was not ready to convert to *Yelikowen,* the Mongol term for Christianity, but he wished to explore all religious options. At any rate, Kublai's request was never honored. A papal interregnum, the difficulty of travel over the long, arduous route, and the uncertainty of what the khan had in mind contributed to this failure by

12. Selections from the *Itinerary* may be found in several places. One good source is Bertold Spuler, *History of the Mongols Based on Eastern and Western Accounts of the Thirteenth and Fourteenth Centuries* (Berkeley: University of California Press, 1972), 88–114.

13. Rachewiltz, *Papal Envoys,* 136–37.

western missionaries to respond.[14] Who can estimate the neglect of an opportunity to influence the destiny of an entire people?

The first missionary to China proper during the Mongol dynasty was John of Montecorvino, an Italian Jesuit, sent by Pope Nicholas IV in 1294 to Kambaluc (Beijing) shortly after the death of Kublai. As a result of his thirty-four years of work in the Chinese capital of the Mongols, he received approximately one hundred thousand converts into the Roman church. How many of these were Europeans, Armenians, or Persians, whose languages he could use? Han Chinese? He and the friars who followed him never bothered to learn Chinese! We have already mentioned the accession of King George and a large number of his Ongkut Nestorian followers. He acquired some skill in either Mongolian or Turkish and translated the gospel and the Psalms into this tongue. Possibly many of his converts were "foreign," but a sizeable number could have been Mongols, living and working within China proper. From the present perspective of the People's Republic of China, these would not be foreign, but one of its minority nationalities. Likewise, the Mongol dynasty itself is considered to be Chinese and not foreign.

What was the depth of the Christian faith among these various peoples in Mongolia in the twelfth to fourteenth centuries? Was it comparable to the Christianity forced on the Saxons by Charlemagne? Both groups of Christians were probably superficial or even heretical in their initial commitments. In Europe, although the process of forced conversions may be regretted today, it was this or nothing. The resource bases of Christianity were close enough, either in Rome or in the British Isles, for sending dedicated missionaries and establishing monasteries that could nudge the incipient faith toward a more mature stage.

This type of ongoing nurture was not possible in Mongolia or Chinese Turkestan. Nestorian Christianity does not appear to have had such resources. We do not read of scores of dedicated missionaries or of centers committed to the nurture of the Christian faith. With some exceptions, the rulers who called themselves Christians did so only to cover all the bases. They did not wish to overlook any deity who might bless their campaigns and deliver them from a variety of calamities. Very few made a specific commitment to Christianity, forsook local deities, and claimed the Christian God to be their only God and his Scriptures to be their sacred book. Their tolerance left open all the options, and where the Christian church could have entered through this door, it stumbled and fell. Today we can only talk about what might have been.

14. The origin and meaning of the term *Yelikowen* is not certain. A good case may be made that it is related to the Arabic *a lo ha* and probably means "the God religion" or "those who worship God." See Jiang Wenhan, *Zhongguo Gudai Jidujiao ji Kaifong Yotairen* (Ancient Chinese Christianity and the Jews of Kaifeng) (Shanghai: Zhi Shi Press, 1982), 96.

The Entrance of Tibetan Lamaism into Mongolia

The religious winner for the peoples within Mongolia was the Buddhism found in Tibet. A sect of Mahayana Buddhism, this variety has many bright festivals and ceremonies and a more elaborate hierarchy of gods than is usually the case with other forms of Buddhism. More important for the Mongolian context, Lamaism has many mystic or tantric elements that appeal uniquely to people with a background of shamanism.

Mahayana Buddhism first came into Mongolia through the Tujueh, a Turkic people, who ruled in Mongolia during the Tang dynasty (c. 720). This was not Lamaism, but it laid the foundation for it. The next step in the process of abandoning shamanism was when the Mongols conquered the Uighur people and absorbed some of their Buddhistic faith. More significant was when the nephew of the leader of one branch of Tibetan Buddhism came to the Mongolian court and instructed both Mongke and the young Kublai, converting a number of people at the capital. When Kublai began his reign, this tutor of Tibetan Buddhism was elevated to the rank of imperial tutor, and Kublai established a new department in his government to oversee Tibet and to direct all the religious activities of his kingdom.

When the Mongols lost their power in China in 1368, Buddhism also lost its influence among the peoples of Mongolia. After Dayan Khan brought unity among the various Mongol subgroups in the latter part of the fifteenth century, his grandson invited Tibetan lamas to reestablish the Buddhist faith. It was the reformed Yellow Sect, founded by the great Tibetan reformer Tsong-kaba, that prevailed. At this time Sonam Gyatso was given the title of Dalai Lama, and he was followed by a Mongol successor who was the only non-Tibetan in the series of Dalai Lamas. The Tibetan lamas who came at this time interpreted reincarnation in such a way that present religious personages in Mongolia were reincarnations of former great Mongol leaders. This put the reinvigorated faith solidly in the context of Mongolian lineage and hastened its acceptance by the people.

Mongolia, like China proper, was a land of suffering. One author has commented that "shamanism gave neither security for the struggle of life nor consolation in the hour of death, but Buddhism offered both with an emphasis on compassion, hope for a future life, benevolence, peace, and institutions for a more sophisticated culture. Consequently, Lamaism was accepted by both the elite of society and the masses."[15]

15. Jagchid and Hyer, *Mongolia's Culture and Society,* 182. Natsagdorji, "The Introduction of Buddhism into Mongolia," *The Mongolia Society Bulletin* 7 (1968) stresses that neither force nor the majesty of Tibetan Buddhism led to Buddhism's success in Mongolia. He notes that "the Yellow Faith, in contrast to shamanism, prohibits the shedding of blood and teaches quiet patience. This helped the people believe they could eradicate the basis of suffering, find

The Christian faith, whether in its Nestorian form or in the early Catholic effort by the Franciscans and Dominicans, had not met this need. Would it be any different as the Protestants and Catholics tried once again in the nineteenth and twentieth centuries?

Modern Protestant Missionary Penetration to the Peoples of Mongolia

The London Missionary Society Pioneer Effort among the Buryat Mongols

The first modern Protestant effort to bring the gospel to the peoples of Mongolia is filled with surprises and suffering. It begins with the tragic flight of the Kalmuk people, a Mongol group, to Russia. Buddhist in faith, they had fled from China to establish a new home along the lower Volga River north of the Caspian Sea in 1616, only to find that they faced more problems in their adopted country. Here they were the objects of oppressive missionary efforts by the Greek Orthodox Church, who sought to suppress their Buddhist faith and convert them, even forcibly, to Christianity. One of the khans responded, and after his baptism, with Peter the Great acting as his godfather, he brought his own horde into the Christian fold. The Christians, numbering as many as three thousand by 1737, were given a separate place to live near Stavropol on the Volga River, and a few Scripture portions and prayers were translated into their language.

The pressure became unbearable by 1761, and a huge group of six hundred thousand Kalmuks tried to return to China. Pursued by Russian cavalry who slaughtered them unmercifully, winter and summer, through their eight-month flight, fewer than half survived the ordeal. Once they reached China, they were given special protection by the Qianlong emperor. Marshall Broomhall commented that "it was a modern version of the Exodus, save that the Russian Pharaoh did not perish in any Red Sea."[16]

Before the Kalmuks fled Russia, the Moravians presented them with a less pressured Christianity. I. J. Schmidt contacted some of these missionaries and made a translation of the Gospel of Matthew into the Kalmuks' tongue, classified as a western Mongolian dialect. When this Gospel was circulated, it stirred up great interest among political and religious leaders of the Buryat Mongols. They collected money for the Russian

---

rebirth in the future life, and possess happiness in that life. This appealed to people who were exhausted by war and were seeking freedom from strife" (p. 11).

16. Marshall Broomhall, *The Bible in China* (London: CIM, 1934), 126–27.

Bible Society, formed in the chaotic days when Napoleon was retreating from Moscow, to translate this Gospel into the Buryat dialect. Prince Galitzin of the Buryats assigned two of his scholars to this task. By 1827 they had completed the translation of the entire New Testament, although only the four Gospels and Acts were printed at this time. In the process, these two Buryat nobles were converted to Christ and became the instruments for continued Christian outreach to their own peoples.[17]

The Kalmuk plight and the surprise of a Buryat translation, stimulated by non-Christians, encouraged the London Missionary Society, formed in 1795 as the second Protestant mission agency for world outreach, to begin work in Siberia in 1818. The center of their work was the small town of Selenginsk, about 160 miles southeast of the city of Irkutsk and under the jurisdiction of Irkutsk Province. Nearby was the famed Lake Baykal, the largest and deepest freshwater lake in the world. This placed them just south of the Chorinsky Buryats and north of the Mongols in China.

Could the missionaries have come to this base for work from the China side? Only if they had not been observed, for this was well before the unequal treaties that opened China to missionary presence and work. Entering through Russia had the great advantage that they gained the patronage of the Russian emperor Alexander, who gave them a grant of land as well as seven thousand rubles to aid in erecting the mission buildings. When the first missionaries, Mr. and Mrs. Stallybrass and Mr. and Mrs. Rahmn, left Saint Petersburg for Irkutsk, they stopped in Moscow for an interview with the emperor. The Imperial Majesty promised to pray for God's blessing on their work and granted them special permission to teach the Christian message to the Buryat people and to prepare a translation of the Bible in their language. He went out of his way to arrange for details of their travel, so that in every city they were welcomed and treated with great respect.[18]

Very soon William Swan joined Stallybrass and his wife, and the two men committed themselves to twenty-five years of linguistic work: preparing a dictionary and a lexicon and translating the Bible into literary Mongolian, understandable by Buryats and Mongols, both in Siberia and in Mongolia. In God's providence they were aided in their work by the two Buryat nobles who had already used the Kalmuk Gospel of Matthew as a basis for their translation into the vernacular Buryat tongue. They completed the entire Old Testament and were able to get a good start on

17. Ibid., 128–29.

18. "Buriat-Mongolian Mission, Siberia," *The Evangelical Magazine and Missionary Chronicle* 11, n.s. (July 1833): 328–31.

the New Testament before a change in the political and ecclesiastical wind made it necessary for them to leave Siberia.

Living and working here was not easy. The climate was very cold, forcing the Rahmn family to move to a more temperate area. Houses, log-built with the seams caulked with moss, were not convenient or comfortable. The workers were isolated from the outside world and often from their fellow missionaries. Travel was laborious. When the season and weather were right, the missionaries could ride horses. At other times, when roads and paths were snow-covered, they used a *kabitkie,* something like a sled that served as well for overnight lodging when there were no inns around.

After a few gospel tracts were translated and printed, the missionaries squeezed out the time to itinerate, to visit in homes, to converse with lamas in temples, and to distribute literature as widely as possible. The usual method was to carry a tent and to follow the people in their migrations. Often missionary husbands had to do this on their own, although Mrs. Stallybrass did as much as she could, despite bearing six children in their first twelve years on the field.

The obstacle confronting the missionaries was a pervasive suspicion. Why would they, educated foreigners, come to such an isolated place and work with the uncultured Buryats and neglect the more sophisticated Russian people? "Who but a man that loves dirt would rather frequent dirty Buriat huts than drink tea and vodka and play cards in an elegant Russian house?"[19] Both the Buryats and the Russians believed that the missionaries must have ulterior motives. Their frequent travel to follow migrating Buryats or to reach those in distant places created misunderstanding. Despite the general freedom in the work accorded them by the emperor, every advance in the work, such as printing a portion of Scripture or tracts, had to receive special government permission.

Converts did not come without a struggle. The people's loyalties were to their Buddhist faith, and they recognized the Dalai Lama in Tibet as their religious leader. Shamanism, with its many nature deities, continued to make up the stuff of their daily living. When converted, they characterized their past life as being in darkness, unbelief, ignorance, idolatry, and without peace. As a neglected, backward people, they rejoiced to know that God did not make any distinctions between rich and poor. They had a new identity as people liberated from the bondage of their past life.[20]

19. James Gilmour, *Among the Mongols* (London: The Religious Tract Society, 1882), 63.
20. Letter from Swan in *Missionary Magazine,* a replacement of the older *The Evangelical Magazine and Missionary Chronicle,* October 1937, 499–500.

The small number of converts led, as it invariably does, into institutional work. The missionaries tried to establish general schools, but they found that these did not attract students because of the "insensibility of the people to the value of education, their religious prejudices, their poverty, and their migratory habits." They felt better about seminaries that provided a liberal education to both Buryat young men and women. These, they affirmed, were a seedbed for the gospel; even if there were few converts, those trained in these schools, which instructed them in Latin, Russian, English, and other subjects, would produce a better class of Buryat people.

Government favor easily turns into government disfavor. And so it was with this pioneer mission effort among the Buryat Mongols. The spark that produced the crisis was that a powerful, intelligent, and influential Buryat, who had been an outspoken critic of the missionaries, resolved to become a Christian. The Greek Orthodox Church was alarmed that the conversion of such a prominent person would promote too much growth among this foreign mission. With this as a pretext, the Russian government in 1840 sent officers to each of the three stations of the mission at Selenginsk, Ona, and Khodon. Assembling the converts, they examined them carefully to see if the missionaries had taught them in a manner that would make them unpatriotic. They apparently found nothing incriminating, and the matter seemed to be closed.

Later that year, however, the synod of the Greek church issued a decree, confirmed by the emperor, that the mission must be terminated. The stated cause was that the mission in its work and doctrine did not conform with the views of the church and the government. The decree elaborated that when the missionaries instructed the heathen, they "remained in the state of their former heathendom." Furthermore, the authorities asserted that the missionaries "do not act to the advantage of the orthodox faith, but even secretly propagate the errors of infidelity." The decree went on to forbid them to act any longer as missionaries, or even to call themselves by that name.[21]

Had the missionaries continued only in their more secular work and agreed not to preach the gospel, they might have been able to remain. This was hardly their goal, and they refused. Many of the converts continued in the Christian faith under the umbrella of the Greek church.

21. The material about the expulsion of the missionaries from Siberia may be found in part in Charles S. Horne, *The Story of the London Missionary Society* (London: London Missionary Society, 1908), 142–45, and *The Report of the Directors to the Forty-Sixth General Meeting* (London: William Tyler, Bolt Court, Fleet Street), 73–74. Of most value is the material found in the Archives for World Mission record group no. 59, H–2118, Russia box 3, 1838/40, no. 41 and 1840/42, no. 42.

And, to its credit, this church began a specific mission to the Buryats that fit specifically its own understanding of mission.

The sacrificial example of this initial, systematic Protestant effort to reach the Mongols inspired all subsequent efforts to enter Mongolia. James Gilmour, himself memorialized as a missionary great, relates movingly how he visited Selenginsk and noted the stone-built enclosure with the four graves of Mrs. Yuille, two of her children, and Mrs. Edward Stallybrass. Going on to another site, he found two other graves, one of a second Mrs. Stallybrass.[22] All who later worked in Mongolia sought to emulate the spirit of the persevering trailblazers who had tried in vain to open this area to the gospel message.

During the years that William Swan was in Siberia, he expressed himself on important missiological issues. Published in 1831, his letters to his close friends do not mention specific dates and names. They do speak indirectly to problems with which the missionaries were struggling. The LMS was always short on personnel for Siberia, and Swan wondered whether it might be better to follow the old Moravian pattern of sending out groups and forming Christian communities, rather than depending on isolated individual missionaries or couples. Although favoring the Moravian structure, he questioned whether missionary piety alone was a sufficient qualification for dealing with the intricacies of pagan thought.

Swan also struggled with the relation between the gospel and the world. Should missions devote so much attention to barbarous or semi-barbarous groups (read: Buryats), when so much of the civilized world was not Christian? Or is it true that the gospel will help such people become civilized? If converted, they will indeed be "brought under the power of principles on which the whole structure of civilization may be reared," but this will not happen automatically; missionaries must aid in this or it will only be a partial work.

What will give credibility to the work of missions? Swan refused to think of what he called "power evangelism":

> But as no Christian missionaries, at least none deserving of the name, now pretend to the possession of miraculous gifts, and must meet opposers and objectors on other ground, it becomes a serious question how they may best accomplish the task of setting before the heathen the Gospel accompanied with such proofs or arguments in its favor as may be convincing alike to the rude and savage, and to the refined and civilized worshippers of idols.[23]

22. Gilmour, *Among the Mongols,* 56–58. See also Charles R. Bawden, *Shamans, Lamas and Evangelicals: The English Missionaries in Siberia* (London: Routledge and Kegan Paul, 1985) for a full description of this LMS work.

23. William Swan, *Letters on Missions* (Boston: Perkins and Marvin, 1831), 179.

Proofs of the truth of Christianity could not be drawn from history for such an uneducated people. The only hope, he affirmed, was the truths of the Christian faith, which were internally verifying. He said nothing about depending upon the favor of a friendly government.

Modern Protestant Mission Efforts (1870–1949)

When the first modern Protestant missionaries in China reached out in their efforts to Mongolian peoples, they had as a goal both the present Inner Mongolia in the People's Republic of China and Outer Mongolia, now the People's Republic of Mongolia.[24] Living in these areas were Han Chinese, not as many as at present, Mongolians, and other presently recognized minority nationalities, such as Daurs, Evenkis, Huis, Koreans, Manchus, and Oroqens.

The first missionary to devote himself to work among the Mongols was John Gulick of the American Board of Commissioners for Foreign Missions. He reached Kalgan, 140 miles northwest of Beijing, in 1865. This city, meaning "a great gate" in Mongolian, was literally the gate in the Great Wall through which traders, missionaries, and diplomats headed north to the Mongolian plateau. If Gulick were the first missionary, surely the most noted of the early pioneers was James Gilmour, sent to Beijing in 1870 by the London Missionary Society when he was only twenty-seven years old. His inspiration in taking up this difficult mission was a conversation he had with Mrs. Swan, the sole survivor of the initial LMS effort in Siberia. This was not a good time to come to China, but it had its advantages. The Christian community was alarmed by the Tientsin Massacre on 22 June of that year, when Chinese mobs attacked a Catholic orphanage. Before the riot was over "ten Catholic sisters, one foreign and one Chinese priest, the French Consul and his Chancellor, four other French men and women, three Russians, and a number of Chinese, including some of the orphans, were killed."[25]

The Beijing foreign community prepared to flee the rising danger, but Gilmour chose to go north first to Kalgan and then, one month and sev-

24. Although the work among Mongols was concentrated in geographic Mongolia, there were many other scattered Mongol groups: the Kalmuk Mongols on the eastern part of the Tian Shan Range; the Elsin-gol Turguts of Central Asia; the Kokonor and Tsaidam Mongols; the Ili and Tarbagatai Mongols of Zungaria; the Altai Mongols of Xinjiang; the Tannai Oleut Mongols of north Manchuria. These several groups may have made up as many as sixty separate tribes. Some missionaries located in Gansu, Xinjiang, and Manchuria worked with these Mongols, often using only the Chinese language as their point of contact. See Mildred Cable, Frank Houghton, R. Kilgour, A. McLeish, R. W. Sturt, and Olive Wyon, *The Challenge of Central Asia* (London: World Dominion Press, 1929), 67, 72. Mongols are also dispersed in small groups in Sichuan and Yunnan.

25. Kenneth Scott Latourette, *A History of Christian Missions in China* (London: SPCK, 1929), 350.

eral hundred miles more, across the desert to Kiachta. Even this far north, he was still not in Mongolia, and so he went even farther into the desert. Here he made friends with a nomadic lama living in a tent, got permission to live with him, and started his language learning. This was modern-day language bonding with a vengeance! Even here, he found the lama was teaching him classical Mongolian. He needed to balance this with a more vernacular patois that he picked up from visitors to his friend's tent.

Gilmour returned to Beijing to spend the winter in the Yellow Temple that was frequented by Mongols coming to barter or sell. In the spring of 1872 he made another extensive tour, traveling one thousand miles, riding on camels, oxen, donkeys, in carts, and walking. A *tarantass* or sled did better when he faced snow-covered roads. He usually took his own tent with him on these long itinerations, modifying it, however, much to the Mongols' amusement, to give him better protection from the wind and the sun. He did not put much stock in preaching; the Mongols were not used to anyone speaking for an extended period. Far more useful, in his opinion, were personal conversations in which he used a large picture poster to make his point clear. He learned enough about medicine to give simple treatment to those who had obvious physical needs, even overseeing a hospital near Beijing for one year.

In vain Gilmour pleaded with the mission society to send reinforcements to help him. The problem was alleviated only slightly in 1874 when he married, almost sight unseen. Mrs. Gilmour was city-bred, not accustomed to living for weeks on end in a tent with little privacy. She did far better than Gilmour or his friends expected, but eventually the burden of a small family kept her at home in Beijing or Tianjin.

When he returned to China in 1884 from a furlough to England, Gilmour changed his strategy, no longer continuing in his wide itineration to the north and northwest. Now he went to the northeast and was content until his death in 1891 to live in the city of Chao Yang. His interest in the Mongols never flagged, but most of his time was increasingly spent with the Chinese. After his wife died in 1885, leaving him with three boys, he sent the two oldest to live with an uncle in Scotland. The thirteen-month-old youngest son he entrusted to a friend in Tianjin, but the infant soon died and was buried next to his mother in Beijing.

In his latter years, Gilmour took an ascetic turn in his lifestyle. He ate poorly, usually abstaining from meat, since this was the practice of the Mongolian Buddhists. He shaved his head, dressed like the local people, lived where they lived, and to all outward appearances was not a foreigner. He commented to his mission board: "It is the foreign element in our lives that runs away with the money. The foreign houses, foreign clothes, foreign food, are ruinous. In selecting missionaries, a physique able to stand native houses, clothes, and food should be as much a *sine qua non* as health to bear the native climate."[26]

After his twenty-one years of labor in Mongolia, what could Gilmour show for his sacrifice and commitment? Possibly two Mongol converts. He saw greater results among the Chinese, and he undoubtedly laid the foundation in his catechism and tracts for the limited fruit seen by his successors in their ministries.

Protestant Missiological Principles

Gilmour's contribution goes beyond those he influenced directly. His life has been an inspiration to countless hundreds of new recruits for world mission. Furthermore, his reflection on the gospel for Mongolia and on the nature of the obstacles confronting God's work there have ongoing value. Many Protestant missionaries bewailed the "hardness of the Mongolian heart," but few took the time, at least in writing, to analyze the precise nature of the difficulty. The prime obstacle, as Gilmour saw it, was that the Mongol felt that Christianity is superfluous. With an array of colorful ceremonies, with grand temples, with many more volumes of sacred Scripture than the thin Scriptures of the Christians, the Mongolians feel they have all that is needed! To think seriously about Christianity poses the problem that Buddhism might be false, an incomprehensible idea. And the idea that Christianity might be true is even more absurd, since it surely would have gotten to Mongolia faster than it did.

To consider the Christian faith seriously raises another question: why all the variant churches preaching this doctrine if it is true? Theological issues were important for the thinking Mongol: What about three gods? What happened to those who died before the coming of Jesus? Who died without hearing of Jesus? How is the future state to be reconciled with the concept of transmigration? Why did God not prevent sin and evil from coming into the world? Do good works have no value at all? Is not the Christian doctrine of salvation too easy—no sense of karma, of reaping what you sow—just forgiveness through faith? How do you prove that the Christian Scriptures are more true than the Buddhist canon? And, is it right for a loving God to send people to a hell that is eternal and that has no way for its punishment to be alleviated? Gilmour had some problems with this last doctrine, although he did not speak about it publicly. In general, he had an open attitude on doctrinal questions that encouraged long discussions about the heart of the gospel. He knew that with the power of the lamas and the bigotry of the community, "it is very doubtful if a consistent native Christian could subsist on the plain among

26. W. P. Nairne, *Gilmour of the Mongols* (London: Hodder and Stoughton, n.d.), 152.

his Buddhist countrymen."[27] This line of thought never led Gilmour to consider the possibility of working toward village conversions—people movements to Christ. We shall note later how both Roman Catholic and Protestant missionaries started colonies in which they established Mongol inquirers and believers in new communities, but this was a method of extraction rather than of transformation.

Gilmour had many doubts about the methods that he and others were following. He questioned the usefulness of long itineration, although this was the substance of his initial approach, and he may have engaged in it more than others did. Far better, he believed, to reach Mongols from a Chinese base, and, if possible, by training the Chinese to evangelize. Mongols broke their migratory patterns to come to Chinese communities, and this, affirmed Gilmour, was the time and place to win them to Christ. He did not follow through to show how a church might be formed among new believers. Individual Mongols often joined Chinese churches, but this was not the bridge over which many would pass.

Second, Gilmour did not believe that Holy Scripture, in part or in whole, ought to be the first literature to be given to inquiring Mongols, whether on itineration or when they came to Chinese centers. The Bible had too many unfamiliar proper names and doctrines and teaching that were strange even to an educated Mongol. Given the fact that the Mongolian language had a "slight indefiniteness," he felt it far better to use gaudy, multicolored books that were very short and could give a brief introduction to the Christian faith. The Bible societies did not allow their colporteurs to sell tracts along with the Bibles, but he suggested that a Bible man and a tract man might travel together.

This is just a different form for an old argument. When Protestant missionaries first came to China, the *summum bonum* of evangelism was to preach the message orally. Literature should never be distributed, they thought, without a clear public presentation of the gospel. The difficulty of the Chinese language forced them to get into writing and distributing faster than they wished, for they felt the urgency to do something for God. Critics pointed out that one reason for the alleged heresies of the Taiping Heavenly Kingdom was the wholesale distribution of Scripture to the rebels without any accompanying explanations to make the truth clear.

Gilmour granted that "Buddhism is an elaborate and in many respects a grand system, but in one thing it fails signally, that is, in producing holiness."[28] And, in trying to lead the Mongols toward holiness before they had experienced God's grace, Gilmour showed an uncharacteristic rigidity. For example, he had very strong anti-tobacco feelings, and in his preaching

27. Gilmour, *Among the Mongols,* 226.
28. Ibid., 214.

he told the people they did not deserve good harvests from God because of their smoking. He claimed that it was useless, harmful to the body, and took money from them that could have better been spent on clothing. Possibly this was a true social analysis, but it was hardly a good initial emphasis among people whose religion was one of merit and works.[29]

Even before Gilmour's death and right until the advent of the People's Republic of China in 1949, other Protestant groups were seeking a foothold for work in Mongolia. Agencies from the Scandinavian countries had a special interest in Mongolia. Some of these became interested from the travel accounts of Sven Hedin, a noted Swedish explorer and scientist who traveled widely in Mongolia, Central Asia, and Tibet. Gilmour's *Among the Mongols* was circulated widely in Scandinavia and had a particular appeal there in raising up recruits. The Swedish Mongol Mission stationed missionaries about Halong Osso, a small Mongol center eighty miles north of Kalgan. The Swedish Alliance Mission, working in association with the China Inland Mission, had workers in Chahar and Suiyuan, early names for two of the provinces of Mongolia. The Scandinavian Alliance Mission, later known as The Evangelical Alliance Mission (TEAM), had its principal work at Patsebolong, just north of the Ordos Desert.

Other missions that made a significant effort to reach the peoples of Mongolia were Christian Mission to Many Lands, the Irish Presbyterian Mission, the Assemblies of God, and the Danish Mission Society. The ministries of these various groups followed a predictable pattern: a center, probably along the border with China, where missionaries carried on evangelism, educational work, and a medical clinic or hospital. From this base they reached out in itineration for shorter or longer periods to travel with the ever-moving nomads. Whatever the effort, whatever the sacrifice, the results varied little—very few Mongols came to Jesus Christ. And these few converts were never formed into an ongoing, purely Mongol church that could be a sign and symbol of the kingdom of God among its own people.

Anything the missionaries did seemed to create suspicion. It might be lengthening the tent sides, writing a diary, taking an early morning walk, selling books and tracts at a very low price and at an obvious loss, showing compassion where obviously there was no personal gain. Anything good was given an evil twist: Stuart Gunzel observed that wherever the missionaries went, it was obvious that Satan had arrived first.[30] We can

29. Richard Lovett, *James Gilmour of Mongolia* (London: Religious Tract Society, 1893), 193–95.

30. Stuart Gunzel in a news article in *Missionary Broadcaster of the Scandinavian Alliance Mission,* 1937, first quarter, 21.

debate whether this heavy a theological conclusion was necessary: people were responding naturally to new lifestyles and new teaching by a strange outsider. But, whatever the explanation, these suspicions hindered people in accepting the Christian message.

Nothing was more damaging to the struggling work in Mongolia than the Boxer Rebellion of 1900. Five of the SAM missionaries to Mongolia were brutally murdered, their heads carried to the Boxer leaders for rewards, and their bodies burned and buried.[31] All the work in Mongolia and along its borders was closed down, and missionaries took the quickest routes to flee the Boxer madness. Frans A. Larson led a group of six American missionaries and six Swedish missionaries, with their six children, on a frantic, two-month flight from Beijing to Kalgan to Hara Oso to Urga and then across the border into Russia, through Saint Petersburg and on to Moscow. They left Beijing on Muslim carts, hiding from prying eyes that might recognize them as foreigners, and with their luggage wrapped in yellow oilskins to disguise it. During this frightening journey, with dangers on every hand, they retained their sense of humor, composing the *Song of the Urga Pilgrim:*

> Farewell to the plains of the flowery land!
> We flee from the rage of the fierce Boxer Band.
> Both Yankees and Swedes form our strange Gypsy throng;
> Our caravan moves, we are inching along.
>   Inching along, we are inching along.
> At the pace of a snail we are inching along.
> Our horses are hardy, our camels are strong.
> We all shall reach Urga by inching along.[32]

N. J. Friedstrom of the SAM developed an industrial and agricultural colony at Patsebolong as a means of creating a stable center to which Mongols could come and where they might enter into a Christian community. Large tracts of land were obtained, and from these, one thousand acres were rented out to the Mongols for cultivation. Fifty families were a permanent part of the colony, and others came and went. A converted Mongol preacher was responsible for religious services, and an evening school was started where people were able to study the gospel. This effort, an innovative one for Protestants, had the aim of helping the Mongols break with their tribe or clan and of bringing them under the influence of Christian teaching.

31. *Missionary Broadcaster of the Scandinavian Alliance Mission,* 1925, first quarter, 13.

32. James Hudson Roberts, *A Flight for Life and an Inside View of Mongolia* (Boston: Pilgrim, 1903), 182.

The idea was fine, but the strategy was poor. The SAM was not able to recruit adequate help for this work. As a result all the tasks—financial accounts and payments, irrigation, running of home industries, marketing produce, caring for the school and the clinic—had to be handled by two people, Friedstrom and his wife. An even bigger problem was that Chinese migration into the area increased greatly. Soon there were many more Chinese than there were Mongols. And, since they were much more responsive to the gospel than were the Mongols, it was easy for the work to gravitate in their direction. No more than two or three Mongols became Christian. Friedstrom concluded that a Christian settlement was one of the best ways to reach the Mongols, but that this approach demanded an "order of industrial missionaries."[33] The colony ministry limped along with new superintendents and some increase in missionaries, but it was brought to a close in 1931 when Chinese authorities confiscated the hundreds of acres that the mission had. The Swedish Mongol Mission had a "Mongol settlement" eighty-five miles north of Kalgan, but this did not produce any better results.

Significant Protestant Missionaries

Few missionaries were able to establish the kind of rapport with the peoples of Mongolia that would lead them to consider seriously a break with the shackling traditions of their life in Buddhism. James Gilmour incarnated himself within the level of the common people in Mongolian society and became almost one with them. He never seemed at home, however, with local rulers in the various Mongol kingdoms. He was too intense and singleminded to enter into their joyous celebration of life. Despite his desire to win Mongolians to Christ, he seemed to relate better to the Chinese at Chao Yang, many of whom he influenced greatly.

Frans A. Larson, often referred to as "Larson, Duke of Mongolia," was a maverick among missionaries in Mongolia. First inspired by Gilmour's *Among the Mongols,* he came to Mongolia in 1893 when he was twenty-three years of age and served there with The Christian and Missionary Alliance until 1900. During these early years as a single missionary, he made friends with the Prince of Ordos, one of the small sovereign states in Mongolia. He lived in this nobleman's house for three months, refused the offer of a Mongol wife, and learned from the prince's wife many rules of Mongolian etiquette. After marriage and his harrowing experiences in leading missionaries to safety during the Boxer uprising, Larson left the CMA and worked several years with the Mongol Ore Company and then with a railway company doing survey work across Mongolia. All of

33. N. J. Friedstrom, "Mission Work in Mongolia," *Chinese Recorder* 43 (1912): 455–62.

the mission property and work in Mongolia had been destroyed during the chaos in 1900, and the future work of the mission was uncertain. Furthermore, he needed more money to support adequately his growing family.

When this work was finished, Larson took a position with the British and Foreign Bible Society, crossing and crisscrossing Mongolia in every direction to distribute copies of Scripture. By this time the Bible or portions of it had been translated into classical Mongolian, Buryat or northern Mongolian, Kalmuk or western Mongolian, and Khalka or eastern Mongolian. The question was how to distribute these Scriptures to the right people. This was Larson's task. He was not merely a disinterested colporteur. He himself, along with A. F. Ambland of the SAM, had worked for many months on a revision of the classical Mongolian. They had been assisted by Ponsok Searim, Commissioner of Customs of the independent state of Outer Mongolia, who had been released from his official duties in government for the task of Bible translation. A unique, unprecedented event—a Buddhist government releasing a high official to help in a Christian translation![34]

Larson left his family in Kalgan during the winter months and at a new home in Tabo-ol, ninety miles north of Kalgan, for the summer. During these months of intense itineration, he lived as the people lived, entering into their various sporting events and rollicking in their hunting parties. Young and old Mongols alike found in him a kindred spirit who enjoyed life and who sought at the same time to introduce them to the living God. He had a close rapport with the Living Buddha, a supposed incarnation of the historic Buddha, and once spent two weeks in his residence in Urga. He knew most of the nobles of the country and the most important lamas, both men and women.

Larson resigned from the Bible Society in 1913 and went to Beijing, where he served as Mongolian representative in the Chinese capital and later as adviser on Mongolian affairs to Yuan Shikai, then serving as president of China. When Outer Mongolia declared its independence from China in 1919, he left Beijing and retired to his ranch home at Tabo-ol with his family. Larson was a far different spirit from Gilmour, although no less dedicated to the people's liberation. During one period of his life he tells how, in his commitment to the superiority of western civilization, he tried to persuade the nobles to build railways and develop a postal service. They replied rather tartly that they would just as soon not have outside news. He did not remain this committed to civilizing Mongolia, but his zeal for the country's spiritual liberation did not slacken. He had a position of great influence in many circles, but the concrete,

34. Broomhall, *The Bible in China,* 130–31.

spiritual results of his work were probably no greater than those of Gilmour.[35]

Another missionary who had a significant impact in Mongolia was Stuart Gunzel of the Scandinavian Alliance Mission. Attracted first to his adopted country by the story of those martyred in the Boxer Rebellion, Gunzel dedicated himself to influencing significant Mongol leaders who, if converted, could make a difference in their own society. He bought two tents and, at the invitation of Prince De, a dominant figure in the new local government, studied at his palace in eastern Mongolia. Later he located at Zhao Ho in Suiyuan in Inner Mongolia, and from this base he itinerated widely with a traveling team, whose evangelists he himself had trained and whose camels and camping outfit had been supplied by an interested friend in Chicago. As usual, people were highly suspicious and even reticent to receive the literature offered to them.

Ongoing Results

The Japanese invasion of north China in the 1930s, the civil war between the Nationalists and Communists in the 1930s and 1940s, and the tensions produced by an Inner Mongolia autonomy movement in the mid-1930s brought most mission work to an end in Mongolia. Each mission could speak of a few converts, some of whom lasted better than others. But there was no ongoing Mongolian indigenous church. Everyone had solutions as to what might have been done differently or better: more schools, more systematic unified approaches to specific areas, more mobile medical work, more translated books. Even though the missionaries could not be in Mongolia proper, efforts at Bible translation continued. In 1951 Gunzel, for example, took the lead in a translation effort that produced a revised Mongolian New Testament in the old, up-and-down Mongolian script introduced through the Uighurs, and not in the Cyrillic script inherited from Russia.

Inner Mongolia, an autonomous region within the People's Republic of China, is still closed to the direct impact of the Christian faith. A new day has dawned, however, for the People's Republic of Mongolia (PRM), known originally as Outer Mongolia, an area that missionaries were never able to penetrate effectively. John Gibbons, who first went to this country in 1972, and his Mongolian wife, Altaa, recently translated the New Testament into modern Mongolian, and five thousand copies were published by the United Bible Societies in 1990. Upon reading this recently published New Testament, a young computer scientist working for the government department exclaimed, "In ten days

35. Most of the material on F. A. Larson comes from the book by him, *Larson Duke of Mongolia* (Boston: Little, Brown, and Company, 1930).

I made a decision. I wanted to believe in something!"[36] The goal is to finish the Old Testament by 1996. The Mongolian Bible Society has been established in Ulaan Baatar, the capital, and bookstores are selling the New Testament and Christian booklets. The *Jesus* film and a Christian cassette are available for use by a small church that is now holding services in the Mongolian Business Center in Ulaan Baatar. In the spring of 1990 the Far East Broadcasting Company began Christian radio broadcasts into Mongolia, focusing particularly on the PRM but hoping also to reach listeners in Inner Mongolia. The government is now committed to the traditional Mongolian script for literature, which is also used in Inner Mongolia.[37] The American Assembly of God reports that four churches have been established in the capital. Several branch meeting points have also been opened in the surrounding area. The mission's field director for Asia estimates that there are six hundred to seven hundred believers.[38]

But even as the door has swung open by a slight crack for the Christian faith, the collapse of the Moscow-dominated Marxist regime in the PRM has brought a renewal in Yellow Cap Buddhism and in a rehabilitation of Genghis Khan, whose memory and exploits have been eclipsed by that of Lenin over the past seventy years. Although the Communist regime has been abandoned, officials of this former regime continue to dominate the political scene. As political instability continues and as Mongolia reaches deeply for her spiritual roots in an ancient national hero and in Gautama Buddha, the Christian faith will be resisted as strongly now as it has been in the past four hundred years.

The Only Mongol Christian Community

When the Mongol dynasty was overthrown in 1368 and replaced by the Ming dynasty, there were about thirty thousand Roman Catholic Christians. These were largely either Mongols or Alans, Caucasians who were brought into Asia, most of them prisoners, by the Mongols. With the expulsion of the Mongols at the dynastic change, Christianity, at least in China proper, disappeared. After the Jesuits, spearheaded initially by Matteo Ricci, reached China in the early seventeenth century, they found Chinese Christians who had fled for refuge into Mongolia because of periodic persecution by the Qing dynasty rulers. Many of these were at Xiwanzi, a small city north of Kalgan.

36. *Word at Work,* American Bible Society, summer 1992, 18.

37. This material is found in the *Bible Society Record* of the American Bible Society, July 1991, 14–15.

38. *Mountain Movers,* January 1993, 12.

The Jesuits were replaced in Beijing and its environs by the Lazarists in 1785. In the early 1800s a Chinese priest, Matthias Xue, and a French Lazarist, Joseph Mouly, came to Xiwanzi and baptized several hundred converts, largely Chinese. The Apostolic Vicariate of Mongolia was established in 1840. In 1865 it was transferred from the Lazarists to the Congregation of the Immaculate Heart of Mary, known more popularly as the Scheut missionaries, named after a small village outside of Brussels.

Four Belgian priests, including the Scheut founder, Theophilus Verbist, arrived in 1865 and commenced the work that the missionary order would continue until 1949. Like everyone else who ever worked in Mongolia, they were overwhelmed by the immense size of the country—"it could be ten vicariates," they exclaimed. By 1883 the vicariate was divided into three parts: central, eastern, and southwestern Mongolia. Because of its central location and its historic significance, Xiwanzi became the center of all of the educational, compassionate, and ecclesiastical ministries of the Catholic church.

Despite the order's early intentions to make a significant impact on the local people, "Missions in Mongolia" quickly became "Missions amongst the Chinese in Mongolia."[39] The question, as usual, was, Where are the Mongolians? The southern section of the country, running east to west and just north of the Great Wall, the area where it was most convenient for missionaries to live and work, had increasingly been colonized by the Chinese. The central section was occupied by more Mongols, but they were selling their land to the Chinese and moving farther north. The northern section, beginning about four hundred miles north of the Great Wall and extending to the border of Siberia, was incapable of cultivation, and here is where the Mongols continued their nomadic life with no disruption by the Chinese. Comprising what is now Outer Mongolia, as well as some of Inner Mongolia, this area was untouched either by Catholic or Protestant work.

In 1875 Fathers De Vos and Verlinden made a long journey west from Xiwanzi to the country of the Ordos, where the local inhabitants were a remnant of an early Turkic empire that had ruled from Manchuria to the Caspian Sea from early in the seventh century until they were overcome by the Uighur empire in 745. The area was now divided into a number of small fiefdoms, ruled over by kings whose favor was necessary if the gospel was to be preached. Therefore, as the missionaries continued on their long itineration, they went out of their way to court the favor of these rulers. In each place they showed their passports as well as the *loung piao,* the decree of the emperor written on yellow paper and authorizing them to preach their Catholic faith. They stayed with the King of Djoun-

39. J. Leyssen, *The Cross over China's Wall* (Peking: The Lazarist Press, 1941), 39.

gar for one week, held Mass in a room he provided for them, and welcomed many high-ranking Mongols who came to inquire of their religion. These conversations led them to translate some prayers, a catechism, and the Decalogue into Mongolian.

King Wouchenta received them with great pomp and opened up the way for them to confer with his subjects. Very openly he exclaimed: "Things of the soul are not my affair—to each person is given liberty to be a lama or a black man. And if my people wish to worship the Lord of Heaven, they can do it in all security. I see from your passports that I am to give you aid and protection. You can count on me."[40]

When the two missioners visited the village of Ningzhaoliang, located on a caravan route that led north into Mongol territory, they were appalled at the devastation wreaked by the Muslims in 1869. Coming from Shaanxi, Gansu, and the Kokonor area, the followers of Muhammad had burned temples and lamaseries and killed a large number of people. The adult lamas had all fled, but many local Mongol children, taken at ten years of age from poor families to be raised in the priestly caste, were left behind. De Vos and Verlinden saw this ravaged area as a prime ground for planting the gospel seed and also for adopting these abandoned children and raising them to be schoolteachers, catechists, farmers, artisans, and apostles for the Mongolian Catholic church of the future.

Several workers were sent into this area, converts were made, and this initial fruit of missionary work was eventually formed into the Mongol Christian community at Poro-Balgeson. Located north of the Great Wall at 107.3 latitude and 37.5 longitude, this work became the only enduring work that the Catholics had among the Mongols. All other efforts at evangelization, no matter how well buttressed by money and people, were to no avail. Other Mongol converts in the western area of the field were joined to this community, and converts in the central and eastern sections were absorbed into Chinese congregations or communities.

By 1940 Catholic converts in Mongolia numbered two hundred thousand, and the church leadership included "eight Bishops, 260 foreign and 168 Chinese priests, 55 native brothers, 68 foreign and 161 Chinese sisters. These are assisted by about 600 catechists and more than 1,000 school teachers."[41] The Catholics aided people caught up in the agony of pestilence, drought, famine, and war, rescued many infants from death, ran hospitals and medical clinics, ministered with compassion to all types of physical needs, planted churches, and established seminaries

40. This statement and the other material on the trip to "les Ordos" is found in *Les Missions Catholiques* (15 October 1975 and 4 June, 11 June, 18 June, 25 June, 2 July, and 9 July issues). The statement is from the 2 July issue, 326.

41. Leyssen, *The Cross over China's Wall*, 138.

for training the clergy. Like Protestant missions, they suffered grievous losses during the Boxer uprising. Alarmed that between 1910 and 1930 eighty-four of their missionaries died from typhus, the mission helped to send a Chinese graduate of the Catholic medical school at Aurora University, Shanghai, to Poland in 1931. Here he learned the technique for typhus immunization from its founder, Rodolph Weigl. Upon his return, he worked in Fu Ren Catholic University in Beijing, from which base he prepared the vaccine for foreign missionaries in typhus-threatened areas. Despite all of these significant accomplishments, a major portion of the original goal—"to seize from Satan these poor Mongol people"—was not attained.

Catholic Missiological Principles

But even to have a Mongol Christian community, such as the one at Poro-Balgeson, was a result that the Protestant missionary force never achieved. What was the nature of this community? It was of one piece with other Catholic "reductions" established by the Scheut fathers in Ordos and, to a more limited extent, in the central and eastern sections of the country. The missionaries bought up large tracts of marginal or unusable land, often available to them as reparation for lives lost and property damaged during the Boxer Rebellion. Reclaimed by intensive irrigation, this land was then provided to converts and those who wished to embrace Christianity. The mission usually made available to them a house, kitchen utensils, oxen, carts, seed, and other things necessary for daily living. The tenants were required to pay for maintenance of the facilities. The instruments for work and the domestic animals were loaned and continued to belong to the community. The precise financial arrangements depended on how many in the family could work and the number of the people to be fed. The mission usually asked the farmers to give them the first crop and possibly one-third of the harvest each year. It used this money to buy more land, to establish schools, to build churches, and to do works of mercy.[42]

These reductions were built sturdily with thick walls and guard posts. They looked very much like forts dotting the Mongolian countryside. Frequent local skirmishes among Mongol tribes, the danger from bands of cruel brigands, and the ever-present threat of a Muslim attack made

42. *Catholic Missions Annals of the Propagation of the Faith,* April-May, 1944, 8–9, 16–17, 22–23. I have also used in this discussion of Poro-Balgeson the following materials: Joseph Van Oost, *Au Pays des Ortos (Mongolie)* (Paris: Editions Dillen et Cie, 1932); Carlo van Melckebeke, C.I.C.M., *Service Social de L'Eglise en Mongolie* (Bruxelles: Editions de Scheut, 1968); Joseph Van Hecken, C.I.C.M., *Les Reductions Catholiques de Pays des Ordos Une Methode d'Apostolat des Missionnaires de Scheut* (Schoneck/Beckenried, Suisse: Administration der Neuen Zeitschrift fur Missionswissenschaft, 1957).

this to be a necessary precaution. And, unfortunately, there was hostility from many Mongols who resented that the Boxer settlement had given to the missionaries land they viewed as their own, who opposed the Catholics' active part in settling the Chinese in their territory, and who resisted conversion to the Catholic faith.[43]

How much pressure was there to convert? Each family admitted had to attest in writing its willingness to convert to Catholicism, to promise to study the catechism and to observe the regulations of the village and of the church, and to obey the commandments of God. This document had to be signed by the head of the family, his wife, and all of the children able to do so. Catholic priests and the catechists led in the instruction of new tenants, a process that might extend from several months to two years, before baptism was administered. All in the community were expected to observe adoration, praise, the service of God, obedience to the divine commandments and to ecclesiastical discipline, to receive the sacraments, to recite prayers both publicly and privately, and to practice works of charity. The priests took special care to avoid internal disputes among the tenants and to prohibit adultery or the use of opium. This closely-monitored discipline sought to reproduce on the plains of Mongolia a "Catholic life-style that has been developed over five centuries in Europe."

Most Catholic missionaries and scholars have not found fault with the use of this methodology. J. Leyssen has commented:

> Generally speaking . . . catechumens are at first moved towards conversion by some worldly motive, but no one whose heart is sympathetic will think ill of the poor creatures for that, since they have been taught from childhood to pursue earthly ideas almost exclusively and to make pipes from every reed. Hence they cannot be expected to refrain all at once as if by magic from taking advantage of such occasions of material profit as are afforded by the approach of the missionary, and from purely supernatural motives to follow the priest whom they had been accustomed to mistrust and whose doctrine, besides, is opposed on many points to their millenial traditions.[44]

Van Hecken called it the "evangelization of the poor," and, while admitting that it produced a "class church," he noted that it elevated the economic status of the people.[45]

43. Jagchid and Hyer, *Mongolia's Culture and Society,* 192–93.

44. Leyssen, *The Cross over China's Wall,* 126–27.

45. Van Hecken, *Les Reductions Catholiques,* 100. Jolanda Jansen in a recent monograph, "A Comparative Study of the Missionary Approach by Mgr. Theodor Rutjes CICM and Mgr. Martinus Poell OFM," notes that both Rutjes, who worked in eastern Mongolia, and Poell "were preoccupied to raise as quick and as high as possible, the number of converts without bothering too much about quality" (p. 7).

A chapel erected within the walled village of Poro-Balgeson was used for daily services by the residents, but another one was built away from the village to which outside, nomadic Mongols could come for Sunday or Friday services. This was a method ideally suited to the context of a nomadic people, who found it convenient to ride by horse or camel right to the door of the church building.

The Christian faith among the Mongols at Poro-Balgeson was totally destroyed by the Boxers in 1900, but it was rebuilt following this disaster and soon attained a population of about one thousand Christians. It continued until the advent of the People's Republic of China when, along with all other reductions, most of its activities were closed down. Yet, the Mongol Christians have remained steadfast in their faith in Christ, a perseverance that shows that the beginning material motive, always suspect and in need of defense, has produced a solid commitment to the Catholic church and to faith in God.

The Protestant and Catholic effort to reach Mongols for Christ in this vast expanse north of China proper was a noble one, filled with unusual sacrifice, steadfast commitment, and tragic loss. Many Chinese came to know Jesus the Liberator, but the Mongols, so close to the Christian faith from 1100 to 1400, continue to resist the message of liberation that might free them from their spiritual bondage, from poverty and economic oppression, and from the shackles of an ancient tradition.

6

Evangelism on the Perpendicular among the Lisu People of Yunnan

Introduction

Isobel Kuhn, who along with her husband, John, was one of the China Inland Mission pioneers among the Lisu in Yunnan Province, remarked as she was dying, "When I get to heaven, I will be leaning over the parapets to see what God continues to do among my beloved Lisu." From heaven's perspective she may not be surprised. But for earthbound viewers, what has happened is almost beyond belief. By the advent of the People's Republic of China in 1949, the Protestant work of about forty years among these people, some of whom refer to themselves jokingly as the monkey people, had produced a church of 20,000 believers. Now among the 480,000 Lisu in Yunnan, officially-counted church members number 80,000, with at least one church in each Lisu village. Some observers claim that the actual number of Christians may be as high as 200,000. Local government officials in the Nujiang Lisu Autonomous Prefecture claim that one half of the Lisu population is Christian, and that it would be proper to call them a "Christian people."[1]

In the Chinese language the name *Yunnan* means "south of the clouds," an appropriate title for a province known for its salubrious climate and whose principal city, Kunming, is called the "city of eternal spring." Yunnan is also a "positive racial crazy-quilt" of at least twenty-four different minority peoples, often living not separately in areas tightly

1. Ming, "The Lisu Christians," *Bridge: Church Life in China Today* 43 (September-October 1990), 18–19.

isolated but intermixed with one another. In a short period, a traveler may pass through the villages of several different groups.

Yunnan may be divided into two separate geographic sections: western Yunnan with its towering north-south mountain ranges that are cut through by three of the world's great rivers—Salween, Mekong, and Yangzi; and the Yunnan-Guizhou plateau to the east with its mildly subtropical weather, where most of the Han Chinese are found. Isobel Kuhn described this land of minority peoples more popularly as perpendicular: in the northwest at the highest altitudes are found the Lisu; a bit lower among the subtropical forests are the Kachin (Jingpo in Chinese); still lower are the Palaung (Blang or Benglong); and on the hot plains surrounded by beautiful bamboo groves are the Shan (Tai or Dai).[2]

As Catholic and Protestant missionaries preached the gospel of God's kingdom at different altitudes in western Yunnan, they welcomed many believers and founded churches among the Dai and Jingpo peoples that continue to grow and prosper. Small communities of believers were established among the Bai and the Hani, and only a few isolated believers among other groups, such as the Naxi in the Lijiang area. The greatest response in western Yunnan was among the Lisu, Lahu, and Wa peoples. The pioneer Protestant mission among the Lisu was the China Inland Mission, whose first missionary, George Clarke, traveled to Yunnan overland from Shanghai and began to reside in Dali in 1881.

The CIM's early interest in the minority peoples was a natural result of its conviction that entrance into China's Yunnan via Bhamo in Burma was better than to reach it by the long journey from Shanghai. As early as 1866 Hudson Taylor showed J. W. Stevenson a map of the Burma-Chinese border and asked him to pray about going to China through this back door. These early plans hit a snag when Augustus Margary, an English vice consul, was killed near the Burma-China border in 1875 by a Kachin tribesperson as he was waiting the arrival of an exploratory British trade mission. Margary's family was Christian, and its members prayed that his death might open widely what had been a nearly closed door. This prayer was partially answered by the Chefoo Convention of 1876 that greatly facilitated travel from Burma into Yunnan. The back route into China was opened even more widely by 1898 when Burma was annexed by Great Britain.

The CIM stationed missionaries in Bhamo by 1881, and they began work both among local people and the tribespeople in the surrounding

2. Mrs. J. O. Fraser, "The Need of the Unreached Tribes," *China's Millions*, November 1937, 215. Her description applies to western Yunnan and not to the Yunnan-Guizhou plateau. It was she who talked about "life on the perpendicular" in work among the Lisu.

area. This was a frontier area, and the work was hindered by many strange diseases, by the often bellicose attitude of the several groups of tribespeoples, and by marauding animals, such as tigers, that wandered freely through Bhamo's streets. Gradually the CIM made plans to send more workers into Yunnan. George Nicoll made a special plea at the CIM Annual Meetings in London in 1889 for workers for Yunnan, Guizhou, Hunan, and Sichuan. "As more missionaries go out to reach these peoples in distant China," he exclaimed, "there will be less need for doctors of divinity to write large books to prove the truth of Christianity."[3]

Christian work was not easy at this time in Yunnan. The province was still unstable as a result of the Muslim rebellion from 1855 to 1873. This had poisoned relationships between the Muslims and the Chinese, particularly in the west around Dali, where the Muslims had organized their political state. But encouragement came with the conversion of a few people among the Minjia near Dali and the interest of the Jingpo or Kachin, as they are called in Burma. In 1897 a missionary reported a tale that, in a variety of forms, was common among the Jingpo, the Lisu, and other southwestern minority peoples: "The Jingpo have a tale that the Great Spirit gave writing to one of the ancestors of our race. It was written on leaves. One day it got wet and was spread in the sun to dry. When our ancestor was not watching a buffalo came and ate it up."[4]

Still, by 1900, the CIM reported only twenty-five converts among the tribes for all of Yunnan. The first missionary to the Lisu was G. E. Metcalf, who went initially to the Miao center at Sapushan, north of Kunming, and then learned of an extensive movement among the Lisu to the west. Shortly after this J. O. Fraser, later to be called the apostle to the Lisu, came to China and began systematically to start the fire of faith that later would spread like wildfire in northwestern Yunnan.

Who Are the Lisu?

The Lisu minority is related culturally and linguistically to the Yi and is classified among the "Loloish" peoples of China. Living largely in western Yunnan, these peoples are found north of Kunming near Yunnan's northern border with Sichuan and also are scattered around the Xichang and Yanbian counties in Sichuan. Like many other minorities in Sichuan, Guizhou, and Yunnan, they may be divided into the fiercely independent "wild" Lisu who are in the upper reaches of the Salween River and the "tame" Lisu who live farther to the south and who have been more sinicized by their contacts with the Chinese peoples.

3. *China's Millions,* August 1889, 125.
4. *China's Millions,* March 1898.

The ancestors of the present-day Lisu lived along the Jinsha River ("River of Golden Sand," the name of Yangzi along the Sichuan-Yunnan border). In their early history during the first millennium of the Christian era, they were controlled by the Wudeng and Lianglin tribes. At the time of the Mongol dynasty (1271–1368), they were ruled by the government's local administration at Lijiang, and then they moved into the Salween Valley where they were oppressed by Naxi and Bai feudal lords. Off and on for two hundred years, they rebelled against this oppression, with little relief. When they revolted in 1801–1803 the government repulsed them with great ferocity, using an army of ten thousand soldiers recruited from three provinces. These years of oppression, particularly during the nineteenth century, caused them to leave their homes in the far west and move east to their present home straddling the border between Burma and China.[5]

The Lisu migration eastward did not eliminate their oppression, whether by the sinicized Yi, by the Chinese, or by other more warlike minorities. As late as 1939, local officials and landlords in Eduoluo Village in Bijiang county tortured and killed 237 peasants out of a population of 1000 in the village. To physical torture and oppression over the years was added the economic burden of exorbitant taxes.[6]

The Lisu followed the traditional religious pattern of their ancestors in what used to be termed animism. They viewed themselves as descended from animals, and totemism has been prominent in their belief system. Although the people had a clan system, it was not based on hereditary succession, and over a period of time their social and political organization became decentralized and did not provide social and economic cohesiveness. Their scattering among other ethnic groups only contributed to the decentralization of their life.

The prevalent economic pattern was a feudal landlord system, with large landholders—Lisu, Chinese, or other tribes—and serfs. In time the best land was controlled by a few, and more and more of the peasants became landless and carried on their farming activities either on rented land or as hired farmhands. This led to poverty among many, and made the growth of a quick-cash crop like opium to be very attractive, even to Lisu converts.

5. The material in this paragraph comes largely from Tian Jukang, "Cementation of Segregatory Tribes—The Protestant Church among Minority Nationalities in Yunnan," unpublished paper, 1990. Charles Peterson, a CIM missionary who worked among the Lisu, told me that the name *Lisu* means the "come-down" people, whose home was in Tibet and who followed the Salween, Mekong, and Irawaddy rivers in coming down into China and Burma. Personal conversation, September 1992.

6. Ma Yin, ed., *China's Minority Nationalities* (Beijing: Foreign Languages Press, 1989), 270.

Mass Movement to Christ among the Lisu

The first Catholic missionaries came to Yunnan in the early 1800s, when the Paris Foreign Mission Society took up responsibilities in the Zhaotong area. Here its members worked among the Yi and the Miao. Eventually, as a part of their thrust into Tibet from the southern route through Lijiang, Catholic missionaries contacted Lyssous in the Atentze area. In 1898 the Roman Catholic Father Jen Anshou established a work at Bai Halo in the Nujiang area. Eventually there were several churches and more than one thousand members among the Nu, the Lisu, and the Tibetans.[7] The opposition was intense, and at one time six priests were killed in what became an international incident.[8] Yunnan has never been a strong area for Catholic work, whether among the Han Chinese or minority peoples, and little can be found at present that is continuous with its early beginnings.

To understand why the Protestant Lisu church is so strong today, it is necessary to examine carefully the work of James Fraser, whose life and ministry have inspired many young people to give themselves in missionary service in China and elsewhere.[9] Converted in his college days in Great Britain, Fraser brought an engineer's training and an analytical and disciplined mind to the tasks of mission among the Lisu. Single for twenty of his thirty years in China, Fraser gave himself with little distraction to language learning, to prayer, to wide evangelistic itineration among Lisu villages, and to discipleship. He was a gifted musician and during visits to Shanghai put on classical concerts for the public. When he was in a Chinese town for only a day or two, he often rented a piano and immersed himself in an afternoon of music. Other missionaries always encouraged him on visits to their homes to play their little Estey organs.

The Lisu people "cherished vague longings for the teacher and deliverer they expected, who would bring books in their language and good news for their people." Lisu evangelists made much of the fact that the term for Jesus in their language, "Jesu," was the same in tone and nearly identical in pronunciation as the name *Lisu*, designating their people. "Jesus of the Lisu—was He not their Coming One."[10]

7. *Lisu Zu Jiansi* (A Short History of the Lisu) (Kunming: Yunnan People's Press, 1983), 65–66.

8. *Lisuzu Shehuilisi Diaocha* (A Historical Investigation of Lisu Society) (Kunming: Yunnan People's Press, 1981).

9. The material on Fraser comes from some of his articles in *China's Millions,* from articles by others on Lisu work, and from the book by Mrs. Howard Taylor, *Behind the Ranges: Fraser of Lisuland in S.W. China* (London: Lutterworth, 1944).

10. Taylor, *Behind the Ranges,* 182.

Fraser's Missiological Principles

Very early in his ministry, Fraser discovered that he was in a spiritual battle. Ignorance was not the reason that the Lisu were not Christians. Even when Fraser had planted the good seed of the gospel on the spiritually dry ground, no fruit sprang up. A few people who had early responded to the gospel in several different villages turned back to their old practices. Often their families were afflicted with serious sickness, and they assumed that this was the attack of demons, displeased that the people were not sacrificing to them. As in the parable Jesus told about the sower sowing his seed, so here Satan was taking away the seed and binding people even more thoroughly in his firm control.

Fraser himself felt particularly vulnerable, often having long, serious bouts of depression from which he was delivered only by prayer. He recognized that this was enemy territory and that physical obstacles were but one more manifestation of this. Slippery trails, marauding bands of robbers, a variety of illnesses, and attacks by the wild Kachin tribespeople were constant dangers. In some villages, when demon-priests practiced their occult wizardry, the spiritual opposition was particularly intense. Nothing frightened the people more than the presence and control of the evil spirits in their lives. Lurking in certain places, ready to take quick advantage of any violation of age-old taboos and traditions, demanding sacrifices and the allegiance of the people, and holding them in fearful bondage, evil spirits were the obstacle to the Christian message. Once Chinese soldiers tried to take Fraser captive, but he sneaked out of the village at night as the Christians sang loudly. It was not uncommon for officials to tear down chapels in villages.

The intensity of this spiritual battle forced Fraser to devote himself to long periods of prayer and to a renewed examination of what Scripture had to say about demonology. He disagreed with those missionaries who thought that demons were a figment of people's imagination, whether in the period of the early church or among the high mountains of Yunnan. He reflected long on how the ministry, death, and resurrection of Christ had made Satan a defeated foe. The spiritual war had been won, but guerrilla battles were still being waged in the personal lives of these people who, for the first time, were being presented with the gospel of Christ.

Because of the demonic oppression that the people suffered, Fraser was inflexible in his conviction that no conversion to Christ was complete unless it included a total sweep of all the paraphernalia used in demonolatry. This, he believed, must also include the shelf in the living room of the house on which these objects were placed. The break with the old life must be thorough, for where there was a reversion from the faith, the first thing the people did was to restore these customary objects used in their demon worship. To leave any remnant of these would be to open the door for a much wider turning away from Christianity.

Fraser and his colleagues frequently were confronted with demon possession, often so violent that, like one Gospel account, a boy was at the point of throwing himself into the fire. Fraser engaged in no theatrics to exorcise the demon, only asking others to join with him in united prayer until "the power of the name of Jesus" brought deliverance. Once a professing Lisu Christian claimed to have the gift of prophecy, and what he said seemed to come true. One day Allyn Cooke found him shaking in a partial trance. When the "prophet" did not respond directly to Cooke's query, "Do you confess that Jesus Christ has come in the flesh," Cooke concluded he was possessed by a demon and cast it out.[11]

To deal with this type of opposition to the Christian faith was a great trial to Fraser's patience. He was tempted to move about rather impulsively from one center to another, probing here and there to see where the soil was the ripest. Not that he did not itinerate widely—he traveled much over this difficult terrain. But he preferred to concentrate on certain areas, even though no fruit was immediately apparent. For him to do it this way was a greater challenge to pray until the "walls of Jericho fell down." Prayer was the main weapon in the spiritual battle to liberate the Lisu from their demonic bondage, and he continued at it with great perseverance. He also encouraged his friends in Great Britain to organize small prayer cells and join with him in reaching the Lisu. One unexpected danger arose. Before the Lisu movement had shown any signs of its eventual momentum, General Director Hoste of the CIM had planned to move Fraser to Sapushan in east Yunnan to help reap the bountiful harvest among the Miao. Fortunately, this rather arbitrary administrative decision from faraway Shanghai never occurred.

During one of his prolonged periods of prayer, Fraser came to the understanding that the Lisu, like the Miao before them in Guizhou and eastern Yunnan, came best to Christ by families, or even by many families in what he and others then called mass movements to Christ. The Lisu themselves were influenced to see this by what some of them knew about the Miao turning to Christ in the Sapushan area where there were also many Lisu villages. Each day Fraser kept faithfully at his preaching—in the open air, in tea shops, in Chinese inns where he often stayed at night, and around Lisu firesides. Increasingly, however, he focused not just on individuals, but on the bridge they might give into their families. The clan system among the Lisu was strong, and unless the village elders

11. Allyn Cooke materials, CIM collection 215, box 4, files 1–10, Billy Graham Center Archives, Wheaton College, Wheaton, Ill.

approved, it was difficult for even the father in one home to do away with the family altar and sacrifices so crucial in demon worship.

To those who objected that such a mass movement could not really be spiritual and produce lasting results, Fraser replied, "although there is much that is superficial, the same could be said of revivals in the homeland; but in both cases there is a solid work of the Spirit of God that remains and bears fruit."[12] A people movement, as it is now called, did not mean that every family member would make a wholehearted decision for Christ. It did mean that all responsible family members would publicly disavow and leave all aspects of demon worship in an initial step of repentance. This kept the door open for further decisions and meant that everyone was moving along the path toward conversion, rather than turning against one another as to what step should be taken.[13] Whether initially by individuals or by families, the chief object in becoming Christians was to be freed from bondage to evil spirits. For new converts Jesus was the great Liberator from demons. This aspect of the gospel attracted them the most, and only at a later time, following extended periods of instruction, did they sense how Jesus was also the Savior from sin.

In addition to demon worship and the ancestral rites related to it, obstacles to faith were the use of opium and the use of whiskey. When Lisu were converted, they had no idea that they would be expected to give up opium in all its usages: growing, harvesting, selling, transporting, smoking. In fact, they often praised God that government inspectors had not found and destroyed their opium. Fraser was not prepared to compromise on this issue. When Christians refused to destroy their opium, he kept after them until they complied. If the Christians faced an obnoxious local official who tried to force them to plant opium, he quickly took their side. This kind of situation was often handled by the Christians paying a fine in lieu of planting opium, but one official insisted that the fine itself be paid in opium.

12. J. O. Fraser, "Mass Movements among the Aborigines," *China's Millions,* November 1937, 205.

13. Fraser explained his approach in a 7 February 1916 letter to his prayer circle in Great Britain: "When these tribespeople turn to the Lord *en famille* it does not necessarily mean that every member of the family is whole-hearted about the matter—indeed this is seldom the case—but it does mean that the responsible members of the family turn from Satan to God with a definiteness otherwise lacking. When, accordingly, I speak about so many Christian 'families' I mean families where those responsible have removed all vestige of demonolatry from the home. Much, of course, remains to be done after this, but you feel you have, in a sense, already landed your fish when this step has been taken, and thank God for the haul. In some cases a younger member of the family will turn Christian while the others hold back; he cannot then tamper with the household demonolatry. He may be quite sincere, and of course you receive him, but, as I say, such converts are apt to be unstable." Taylor, *Behind the Ranges,* 131.

Rice whiskey was imbibed most heavily at wedding feasts. Fraser knew that he could not make a biblical case for total abstinence, but he knew that if the people did not abstain totally, they would not be able to stop with moderate use. Drunkenness was a curse to the daily life of the people, leading inevitably to robbery, killing, rape, and other crimes. One of the more notable fruits of conversion was the new order and stability to be found in the Lisu villages as people found new life, and a new lifestyle, in Jesus Christ.

Despite the many obstacles that he faced, Fraser reaped the first fruits of his labors in 1916 as hundreds of families turned to Christ. A firm beginning had been made, with small fires of faith lit here and there through the mountains. Now, like a fire roaring through the underbrush and along the tops of the trees, it reached into many villages, ultimately bringing thousands into the kingdom of God. Fraser never saw this as his kingdom. He always recognized the contributions of the other groups working among the Lisu and the other minorities intermixed with them: the English Methodists, the American Baptists, the Vandsburgher Mission, the Swedish Free Mission, the Pentecostal Missionary Union, and the Assemblies of God. The CIM was working with the Hua (Flowery) Lisu, and others were working with the Black Lisu or other related peoples. The CIM had come first and had the largest missionary force in this part of China, but they and others did not wish to get involved in turf wars.

What was the gospel that Fraser preached to the Lisu? Its basic component was judgment. Fraser believed that the judgments in Revelation—the seals, trumpets, and vials—would come upon the earth very soon, bringing great suffering to everyone. So many of unrepentant humanity would be killed that it would be impossible to cope with the wild animals. The only way to escape, ultimately to heaven, was to repent and trust Jesus. The focus, clearly, was materialistic—deliverance from present suffering.[14]

As families or entire villages believed, what were the requirements for baptism? Three basics have already been noted: destroying the paraphernalia of demon worship, giving up planting opium, and refraining from use of whiskey. The premise for these prohibitions, of course, was that a person had made a positive confession of Jesus as Lord. But the spirit of legalism could well have been more important in the thinking of the people:

> These Lisu are mere grown-up children and have to be treated as such. I now see that strict rules must be made and enforced in these matters. I

14. Allyn Cooke materials.

have never had a better conscience over anything than when ruthlessly mowing down these peccant poppy heads. Our Lord not only healed the blind, lame and halt of His day, but cursed the barren fig tree and drove the buyers and sellers out of the temple. Sometimes we also have work of such nature to do.[15]

Because of widespread immorality, unmarried girls were not accepted for baptism unless their parents or older brothers were Christians. Since Lisu church rules prevented a girl from marrying until she was eighteen, very few young women were baptized. In Lisu society, the young women were prone to sexual sin, often running away with non-Christian men.

The usual period of waiting before inquirers were baptized and counted as converts ready to join Lisu churches was two years. How did Fraser justify such a long period?

> The time is ripe for baptisms and the formation of churches. We will baptize hundreds. None have been baptized until now. We are not overly conservative. We feel, however, that two years is not too long to keep these tribespeople waiting. They are emerging from deeper superstition and ignorance than our Chinese converts, and are inclined to look on baptism as a kind of magical rite which will afford better protection from evil spirits.[16]

Where churches had already been formed, its leaders helped to examine the candidates for baptism. The final choice, however, was left to the missionary, who in the early stages of the work did all of the baptizing.

This long time for preparation did not lessen the need for ongoing discipleship to build up the converts in their new faith. Even after they were baptized, the minds of the people, "having been cleared for ploughing and sowing when they first 'turned Christian'" could easily become overgrown with weeds again.

> What is the use of opening your gospel of Mark and expounding it verse by verse when the people's minds are filled with ideas about British officials coming along, seizing all converts and taking them away for soldiers? Or if they have been told by the heathen . . . that we missionaries are paid emissaries of the King of England, sent out as spies and to seduce the simple Lisu with some deep purpose, they are not likely to get a very clear idea of the gospel message, are they, if you simply preach from a book and do not meet them on their own ground?[17]

15. J. O. Fraser, "On the Road in Yunnan," *China's Millions,* January 1923, 5.
16. J. O. Fraser in news article in *China's Millions,* May 1922, 75.
17. Fraser, "On the Road in Yunnan," 6.

Discipleship was far different from what it was in Great Britain. Fraser confessed that he often got impatient with the people, since to his quick mind they seemed so slow. Not used to thinking analytically, lacking Christian background, and living in a society reckoned backward from the western perspective, they tended to see the Christian faith as another fetish to ward off evil influences. Principles for Christian living were easily turned into new sets of taboos that would keep the demons from biting them. So the questions he had to deal with in discipleship reflected the externalities of the faith, not those matters related to the worship and adoration of their new Lord:

> And you have to spend such a lot of time over mere externalities, rules and regulations, etc. as to whether a Christian, though not growing opium himself, may work for a heathen on the latter's opium fields, or whether pickled beans may be eaten (they are pickled with liquor), what to do when your son's fiancee is still in a heathen family and the latter insist on being given liquor to drink at the wedding, whether an opium-smoking convert may be allowed to come to worship, whether children of heathen Lisu should be allowed to study (the converts, until they get word from me to the contrary, usually refuse to allow heathen children to study, and even turn them away when they want to come to services!), whether you may wash clothes or hunt game on Sundays, etc.[18]

Fraser was a great advocate of each-one-teach-one in the Christian community. On one occasion when he was teaching the catechism to a group of young believers, he said, "This is all I will teach you until you have taught this in a neighboring village."[19]

Many church regulations for the maturing church dealt with family issues. Should a man pay for his bride? The churches decided no. Who then would provide a marriage feast and buy clothes for the bride? The groom's parents were given the first responsibility, and the bride's family was asked to prepare the wedding trousseau. The Lisu used to have a custom that gave the widow's children to the grandparents on the dead father's side and not to the mother if she married again. The Lisu churches decided that, unless the grandparents on the father's side had no sons to support them, the children should go to the mother.[20]

The questions the people raised and their decisions were probably a reflection of the struggles through which Fraser himself went as he tried to determine how he and fellow missionaries should live and minister in Lisu society. An early effective relationship with one village developed

18. Ibid.
19. Letter from Charles Peterson, September 1992.
20. Cooke materials.

because he felt God led him to give a gift of money to help defray wedding expenses for a young Lisu man, an act of compassion directly in conflict with usual mission policy. On the other hand, he was overzealous in forbidding some things, such as "pelting everybody with carrots, potatoes and other root-vegetables" as a part of a wedding ceremony, something like the throwing of rice at weddings in America or Great Britain. He traced this custom's origin to demon worship, and then he was afraid that people could be hurt when hit with these hard objects. Did this attitude minister to the sense of legalism that, by his own confession, was so common among Lisu believers? Lisu believers today continue in the strict tradition inherited from their early teachers. They do not drink, smoke, eat blood, or dance. They strictly observe the Sabbath, even preparing food for Sunday on Saturday.[21]

Fraser believed that an essential requirement for the discipleship process was to create a script for the people and then to use it to prepare a catechism and Scripture portions. How would he find time to do this kind of concentrated work while living among the Lisu, who had no sense of privacy themselves or of granting it to others? He managed this by two trips to the Burma side of the border, where, with help from American missionaries, he first prepared a special script in 1913, and then in 1918 translated Mark's Gospel, prepared a dictionary and a primer, and wrote an enlarged catechism that included a number of hymns. As the churches matured, its leaders formed a large committee to give help to Fraser, and later to Cooke, in finding terms needed in Bible translation. The hymns were particularly useful in helping people to learn the new script, since they sang them over and over in their times of worship.

As the work among the Lisu continued to prosper and grow, Fraser and his growing number of colleagues[22] initiated the Rainy Season Bible Schools. These were held twice each year in February and August when the people were able to leave their fields of work and come away for a concentrated time of study. As many as one hundred came for this special time of training. The literature available in the Lisu language and script was the core curriculum taught in these sessions. In addition to starting Bible schools, the missionaries established a number of primary schools early in the work to give general training.

Missionaries never ceased in their efforts to make the Lisu think in these training sessions. One teacher noted that a question at the end of a Bible school examination asked, "Would you prefer to be pastor of the

21. Ming, "The Lisu Christians," 19.

22. Some of these were the Gowmans, the Cookes, John and Isobel Kuhn, Charles Petersen, and John Simpson.

church at Rome or at Corinth?" Students did not answer this question, for fear that at the end of school they might be sent off to Rome or Corinth.[23] From the inception of the Lisus' turning to Christ, many of their evangelists had been trained informally for the task of taking the gospel to their own people, as well as helping with other people groups who could understand and use their language. This was particularly true with the Nosu. When the Assembly of God missionaries commenced their work among the Black Lisu in the Weixi area in 1921, they requested that Fraser send two of his Flowery Lisu evangelists to help them in their work, a request that Fraser was only too glad to meet. Although different missions had slightly different doctrinal beliefs and although their methods of work were different, there was a basic unity that enabled the Lisu in diverse areas to understand that the church of Jesus Christ among them was one.

After John Kuhn, one of Fraser's colleagues in the Lisu work, led a Yunnan tribal survey in 1945 that identified at least one hundred groups who had never heard the Christian message, he laid the task of this new evangelistic outreach on the Lisu church.[24] Its leaders were only too happy to accept this challenge, but the advent of the new government in 1949, as at times of previous political rumbles in 1911 and 1927, created problems that hindered this new evangelistic effort.

On at least one occasion the gospel light penetrated to areas where neither the missionary nor Lisu evangelists had yet gone. Isobel Kuhn related the story of the small village of Goo-Moo-Ka on the Burma side of the border. Here in 1924 a woman who was demon possessed told her astounded neighbors that they should no longer worship demons, but must submit themselves to "God the Father, Jesus and God's Daughter." The people of the village did as she directed, setting aside one day of the week for worship. Agreeing with her exhortation, they also gave up the use of wine and opium. When this group of worshipers learned that the Lisu in Yunnan also worshiped Jesus, they tried to send some of their number to seek out these Yunnan groups. After two failures, they finally managed to get over the high mountains, "biting the snow," and came to the area where the Cookes and the Kuhns were working.

Meanwhile, the woman who had given the original revelation announced that Jesus was coming and urged her neighbors to build a home to welcome him. At about this time, "Jesus 'arrived' in the person of the Christian teachers and the Deputation of Three. Then, study of the True Way was started enthusiastically." In 1935, the first missionary arrived on

23. Dorothy Pape, "Interlude in Lisuland," *China's Millions,* July-August 1943, 28.

24. John Kuhn, "All Over Tribesland," in *Wide Open Doors: The Story of the Year 1946* (London: CIM, 1946), 145–53.

the scene, fully twelve years after the small group had been organized. With further instruction, these converts were baptized and a church was formally organized. A rational human explanation may exist for such a phenomenon, but, if so, the Lisu and the missionaries never discovered it. God had reached out, even beyond the bounds of the Lisu churches' aggressive evangelism, to prepare this village for his message.[25]

As this movement to Christ spread throughout Lisuland, what gave it continuity and stability? Fraser firmly believed that from the beginning the Lisu churches must be indigenous. This meant that the building of their grass-roofed chapels, financial support for their preachers, and money for their literature must come from the people themselves. The only foreign financial help was for the Bible schools and the literature. Such an approach was not a popular one in the 1920s and 1930s, for mission boards had assumed that people as poor as the Lisu could not support their own Christian activities. This method was successful among the Lisu, since there was no competing mission agency using a money-stimulated strategy that would violate Fraser's example and steal some of his sheep.

Lisu churches, particularly at the beginning, did not always agree with Fraser on this policy. He pressed his point vigorously in some long discussions on how his evangelistic helper was to be paid. Although he was willing to compromise a bit, he led them on to see that the money saved on opium and overly expensive wedding feasts was more than sufficient to care for all church needs. To pay converts was, to Fraser, a "vicious system":

> It is the line of least resistance, but is something like the broad road that leads to destruction. No! far better let our work go slowly, and tread the narrow way of self-support. We shall never regret it . . . what I want to see everywhere is the spirit of SACRIFICE for the Lord Who bought us with His blood—a desire to prove not what we can *get* but what we can *give*—and my heart burns as I write it.[26]

What was good for the people was also good for Fraser. He felt that if the Lisu churches were to be self-supporting, he also should do more to earn his living in China. So he arranged to teach in a government school for boys in the Chinese city of Dengyue, where he spent most of his time when not traveling about to Lisu churches. These extra monies—possibly eighty dollars a month—he contributed to mission funds.

Missionaries did more than preach among the Lisu. Fraser carried

25. Isobel Kuhn, "The Gospel in Lisu-land—How the Light Came to Goo-Moo-Ka," *China's Millions,* May 1936, 85.

26. Taylor, *Behind the Ranges,* 209.

medical supplies with him and treated the people's simple ailments. Carl Gowman, as a part of the curriculum of the Bible schools, taught converts to preach, drilling them vigorously until they knew how to proclaim God's message. Fraser delighted in teaching the young people how to sing. Universal church tunes such as "O Happy Day" were favorites at times of baptism, but Fraser helped converts to develop their own music. Two Christian lyrics with many stanzas, outlining Old Testament and New Testament history, were particular favorites and helped to fix Scripture truths in their minds.

Convinced that a better understanding of soil, climate, seeds, and methods would help the Lisu in farming and enable them to earn more money, Fraser also studied agriculture. He was helped in this project by a British botanical expert who advised him on the crops and flowers that would grow best in this section of Yunnan Province.

Despite the need to give a firm foundation to existing Lisu churches, Fraser never hesitated in responding to invitations to bring the gospel to unreached areas. Christians continued to multiply by hundreds of families. In the 1930s, when it seemed that Christians were waning in the vitality of their faith, he invited Anna Christiansen, a Danish missionary, to come into Lisuland and conduct revival meetings.

Another important feature of the work, never as successful among the Lisu as among the Miao in east Yunnan, was the use of Christian festivals. Fraser first introduced this idea at Turtle Village. Christians flocked there by the thousands for several days to sing, to praise God, and to encourage one another. Included in the first great mass meeting were numerous Jingpo families, because the work of God's Spirit had spilled over to them from nearby Lisu villages.

Any successful movement toward Christ among those with a traditional religious background will have at least one strong missionary or local leader. For the Sediq in Taiwan it was Ji Wang, a woman evangelist; for the Miao it was Adam of the CIM and Samuel Pollard of the Methodists; for the Lahu and the Wa it was William Young (chap. 10); and for the Lisu it was J. O. Fraser. Unlike Pollard, he did not often appeal to officials on behalf of the Lisu. But, in every other respect, he was a strong yet compassionate director of the work. He once confessed, "Imagine, what it is to have between five and six hundred families . . . looking to you as father, mother, teacher, shepherd, adviser, etc. etc. It is a big responsibility."[27]

Fraser's firm and tender leadership held his team together in a unified spirit, no small task in missions anywhere in the world. After his death in 1938, Isobel Kuhn, one of his colleagues, commented:

27. Ibid., 213.

> He was more than a Superintendent to us, he was our missionary ideal, a continual rebuke, challenge, and stimulus to maintain at any cost the apostolic methods of missionary work. His brilliant gifts, united with unfailing humility and a sympathy motherlike in its tenderness and thoughtfulness, made him our refuge at all times of perplexity and need. And to win a smile of approval from him was worth any extra effort.[28]

Principles of the Assembly of God Work

The Lisu people movement to Christ attracted the attention of many other Protestant mission groups. The Assemblies of God began work among the Black Lisu at Weixi, northwest of Dali and Lijiang, in 1921, and other missionaries associated with the Church of God, the Christian Church, and the Pentecostal Missionary Union also worked with the Lisu, as well as the Naxi, the Moso, and other minority peoples in this area.

Many features of the work in this area were the same as among the Flowery Lisu: the expectation of someone bringing to them the book they had lost, the extreme poverty of the people, their oppression by the landlords who taxed them heavily, and the basic structure of their religion and society. The missionaries put the same demands on the people to forsake opium and demonolatry. The people also responded in great numbers, and churches were formed quickly. Even the language differences did not preclude the use of the same script and the literature prepared for the Flowery Lisu. Evangelists traveled widely through all of the Lisu villages in Yunnan and were understood without too much difficulty.

Several distinctives marked the Lisu churches that developed in the Assembly of God work. Women were given a larger role in evangelism and leadership than was common among the Flowery Lisu, although Fraser mentions the use of young women for work among women. To know that Jesus loved them, that he had delivered them from demon control, and that he would use them to extend his work among all the people, not just among women, was a message of liberation.[29]

Missionaries urged their newly baptized converts to seek earnestly the baptism of the Holy Spirit to bestow on them his gifts, including the ability to speak in unknown tongues. Physical healing was emphasized by the missionaries, but, as they confessed, the people often carried this beyond their intentions. One elderly woman was totally dependent on her cow for ploughing her field. She testified that after it fell down sick and could

28. Ibid., 252.

29. The material about the work of the Assemblies of God is taken from Leonard Bolton, *China Call* (Springfield, Mo.: Gospel Publishing House, 1984).

not get up, she poured an entire bottle of oil on its head and prayed fervently. Immediately it got up, healed and ready to start ploughing again!

Why Such a Response by the Lisu to the Gospel?

To the missionaries, whether with the CIM or from these several other groups, the ultimate explanation for the Lisu people movement to Christ was the power of God. He had liberated these poverty-stricken mountain people from everything that had enslaved them and impoverished them. With the money saved and with the new motivation from their life in Christ, they cleaned up their villages and their lives. They became law-abiding and gained a new level of respect toward themselves and from the oft-amazed Chinese local officials. Not everyone, obviously, has been prepared to give God all the credit. T'ien Ju-'kang, a scholar from China, has traced these kinds of movements to several sociological and demographic features that cause people to seek release or an outlet in mass conversion. These are not necessarily antithetical to the ways in which God works in human society and shall be considered in the concluding chapter.

Other Chinese scholars, such as Zou Heping in an article in *Study of World Religions,* published by the Institute of World Religions of the Chinese Academy of Social Sciences, have not been as objective as T'ien in their analyses. Zou's investigation leads him to conclude that there are four reasons to explain the great response to Christianity among the Lisu in the Nujiang Autonomous Prefecture. His overall reason, popular with some Chinese scholars, is Western imperialism that manipulated and took advantage of the people as it preached a foreign religion. Religious imperialism, he contends, was carried out much more easily along the indefinite border between China and Burma, an area controlled very imperfectly by the Chinese government. His second reason was the lack of any systematic religious system or local tribal political base that could oppose the encroachment of the Christian faith. In the third place, he cites the financial liberation of the people from the money expended on demonolatry, marriage, and drinking. He is vague about whether this is good or bad. His fourth and final charge, much more serious than the rest, is that in the content and communication of the Christian faith, the missionaries "tribalized" their ministry to gain an advantage over the people. In expanding his obviously poor understanding of this subject, the author creates a catch-22 situation. The missionaries or local leaders are condemned if they do, and condemned if they do not.

Initially, Zou faults the missionaries for bringing a foreign product to China. In their use of maps, slide projectors, and medicine, they enslaved the local people. Better to really adapt to the local environment, he claims, and he gives some current examples illustrating how leaders have dressed Jesus in tribal clothes, as it were. Then he objects to the ways in which in Bible translation and script development they have used local culture terms. Moreover, he affirms, the way they talked about the Ten Commandments in different places was not consistent, sometimes emphasizing the religious dimension and at other times talking about the ethical. Unfortunately, he adds, the missionaries trained local leaders to carry out their policies. This, he tries to prove, has produced minority churches that do not love their country and who are opposed to the Communist Party.[30]

Scholars and local officials today, less driven with the need to prove their anti-imperialism stance, recognize the benefits of the gospel among the Lisu and other minorities of western Yunnan. Their churches, while under government supervision, have a large measure of religious freedom. Lay preachers, in the absence of trained pastors, shepherd hundreds of churches. Hymnals and Scripture are being reprinted, and new translation projects are in process. Many Lisu young people are studying at the Minority Seminary in Kunming. In times of persecution in China, some Lisu Christians have gone over the mountains into Myanmar to attend short-term training institutes, often sponsored by the CIM. Life is still on the perpendicular for the Lisu, but their relationship with God, also perpendicular, is sure. They face the future with confidence.

30. Zou Heping, "Dianxi Bufen Shaoshu Minzu Diqu Jidujiao Lisi Wenti Cutan" (An Initial Investigation into Questions About the History of the Christian Church in the Minority Areas of Western Yunnan), *Shijie Zongjiao Yenjiu* 3 (1987): 28–43.

7

The Crescent over Chinese Central Asia

Introduction

Chinese Central Asia is a vast territory inhabited by a confusing mixture of peoples whose appearance, languages, and lifestyle would seem to fit them for the Middle East. Although the focus of this chapter is on Xinjiang, China's New Province, the peoples whom the missionaries sought to reach lived in several areas: Qinghai, a province carved out from Tibet, Gansu, and Xinjiang in 1929, and Gansu, the province whose northwestern portion pierces like a sword toward Xinjiang between Inner Mongolia and Qinghai.

Bounded by Gansu and Mongolia in the east, by Tibet and Kashmir on the south, by the Pamir Mountains and the former USSR on the west, and on the north by Mongolia and the USSR, Xinjiang's six hundred thousand square miles of territory is almost totally walled about by high mountains. With only 2 to 3 percent of China's total population, it occupies one-sixth of its territory. While railway and bus lines and air travel have lessened the rigors for present-day travelers, missionaries were faced with mind-boggling distances. From Hankow along the Yangzi River in central China it took seventy-two days to get to Lanzhou, the major city at the southern end of the Gansu corridor. From there it was another seventy-two days to reach Urumqi in Xinjiang. A fifty-four-day journey took one west to Kashgar near the border of the Central Asia republics.

Although there are mountains, lakes, and scenic beauty in this territory, most of a day's journey was through hot, dusty deserts, from one small oasis to another, at altitudes varying from five thousand to fourteen thousand feet. Unbearably hot during the *da shu* or great heat of the summer, it was cold enough in the winter, one Catholic missionary complained, even to congeal the wine used in the Mass.

Xinjiang filled the heart of Chinese with fear, much as exile to Siberia terrified Russian peoples. The Great Wall of China extends to the west as far as Jiayuguan in Gansu, just five days east of Yumen, the Jade Gate, which is the formal entrance into Central Asia. The desert beyond Jiayuguan is known by the Chinese as *kou wai,* outside the mouth, a place of unwanted or enforced exile where vagrants, exiles, or criminals were sent. A Chinese writer has addressed it in a concise dirge: "When I leave thy gates, O Kiayukwan, my tears may never cease to run."[1] Today, Qinghai, the site of *lao gai* (reform through labor) for Chinese political prisoners, is the equivalent of the Russian gulag.

The Peoples of Central Asia: Racial, Linguistic, and Religious Background

Who are the peoples of Central Asia? Depending on how technical they wished to be, early Protestant missionaries in this area divided the populace into twelve or thirteen groups. What are these divisions and how do they relate to the names used by the PRC to define them today?[2]

Turkis (Chantou, "wrapped heads")	Uighurs
Kazaks	Kazaks
Kirghiz	Kirghiz
Tungans or Chinese Muslims	Hui
Taranchi (migrants from Russia)	Related to Uighurs
Salar	Related to Uighurs
Nogais	Tatars
Sarts (live largely in Russia)	
Badakshan (live on Afghan frontier)	
Kalmuk or Western Mongols	Mongols
Manchu	Xibo
Han Chinese	Han Chinese
Russian	Russian

1. Mildred Cable and Francesca French, *Through the Jade Gate and Central Asia: An Account of Journeys in Kansu, Turkistan and the Gobi Desert* (London: Constable and Co., 1927), 96.

2. These comparative materials have been taken from several sources. For the missionary perspective I have used George Hunter, "The Chinese Moslems of Turkestan," *Muslim World* 10 (April 1920): 168–71; Mildred Cable, Frank Houghton, R. Kilgour, A. McLeish, R. W. Stuart, and Olive Wyon, *The Challenge of Central Asia* (London: World Dominion Press, 1929), 46–47; and Cable and French, *Through the Jade Gate,* 219–21. For the modern classification and explanation, I have depended largely upon S. Robert Ramsey, *The Language of China* (Princeton: Princeton University Press, 1987), 178–216.

Uzbek
Tajik
Yugur

All of these except Russian (Slavic), Han Chinese (Sino-Tibetan), and Tajik (Indo-European) speak Altaic languages.

The population of the Han has increased during the Qing dynasty and into the Republican and Communist periods as the government has used them to colonize the area and to give more stability. The Russians have been White Russians or Bolsheviks, seeking to escape political turmoil in their homeland, or refugees from local disturbances. The Xibo, also found in other northern provinces, are the descendants of Manchu soldiers sent to Xinjiang in the eighteenth century to help pacify the border areas. Reports in late 1991 indicate that hard-line Communists from the Commonwealth of Independent Nations (CIN) are coming into Xinjiang, fleeing from the embryonic democratic process in their countries.

The Han Chinese settled in this area are non-Muslim Han and Hui, a religious minority who speak only the Chinese language. Despite the fact that the majority of the Hui have only Chinese ancestry and speak the Chinese language, they are still considered a minority, their only distinctiveness being their commitment to the Islamic faith. Ramsey comments: "The fact that they are the only religious group recognized as a national minority by Peking is certainly not unrelated to the trouble that all Chinese governments in the past have had in controlling them: Hui holy wars against the Han were still being reported in the 1950s."[3]

Do the Hui have any non-Chinese ancestry? They appear to be the descendants of Arab traders or soldiers who helped put down the An Lushan rebellion against the Tang dynasty in the eighth century. They entered China at that time, intermarried with the Chinese, and have become sinicized over the centuries. Muslims who came to China later, particularly during the Mongol dynasty, and intermarried with the Chinese are also included in their number. Scattered throughout every geographical area of China, they have had a love-hate relationship with the Chinese because of their commitment to the Islamic faith. The name *hui* is a shortened version of *huihui,* a name probably derived from the Huihe people or Ouigurs, ancestors to the present-day Uighurs, but distinct from them.[4]

3. Ramsey, *Languages of China,* 168.

4. Ma Yin, ed., *China's Minority Nationalities* (Beijing: Foreign Languages Press, 1989), 95. Marshall Broomhall, following Giles's dictionary, analyzes the term to mean "to return and submit," which would give it a meaning in Chinese similar to the Arabic *to submit. Islam in China: A Neglected Problem* (London: Morgan and Scott, 1910), 167.

As we examine the missionary enterprise in Central Asia, we will not consider its efforts to reach the Hui (for this, see chap. 8). Because the Hui are Chinese in everything except religion and lifestyle, both Catholic and Protestant missionaries did not really see them—that is, they were treated like potential Chinese converts. Minimal effort was made by the Christian population to relate to their unique Islamic context.

The dominant minority nationality group in Central Asia, particularly in Xinjiang, is the Uighur people, which explains why the area is named the Xinjiang Uighur Autonomous Region. It is very difficult to show a one-to-one correspondence between the old Uighur empire in Mongolia and later in the Zungarian district of Central Asia and the present-day Uighurs. Yet it is important to note that there is an indirect relationship between the two groups. When did Turkic peoples take the name *Uighur?* Previous to 1921, the majority of Turkic peoples of Xinjiang had called themselves by the name of whatever oasis they were living in. When Turkic peoples from Russia and China met in Tashkent in Soviet Turkestan in 1921, they chose the name *Uighur* as their mark of identity. The Yugur people, referred to by Ramsey as Yellow Uighur and numbering only fifteen thousand as compared to the six million Uighur, live in Gansu. They represent a more direct lineal descendent from the old Uighur empire, even retaining the old Buddhist faith that they followed in the eighth century in Mongolia.

Enough has been said to indicate that the use of names to identify various peoples in this area is very confusing. The only name that seems to work for all the people is *yerlik,* which means "local." A more significant division among the people of Xinjiang than the ethnic background is the matter of lifestyle. Several of the minority nationalities are sedentary farmers (Uighur, Uzbek, Tatar, and Taranchi), living in the sown land to the south, and several are nomadic (Kirghiz, Tajik, Mongols, and Kazakhs), living in the steppe country to the north. The Chinese, both non-Hui and Hui, tend to live in the cities.

Many religions have sought the allegiance of the peoples of Central Asia. Two thousand years ago, a bustling trade route ran from Xian in Shaanxi Province through the Tarim basin in Xinjiang. From there it went across the Pamirs and Central Asia to the eastern shores of the Mediterranean. Known for a portion of this long journey as the Silk Road, this route was the pathway for many religious emissaries and enabled India and Persia to influence the Middle Kingdom. Buddhism was introduced to China from India in the first century A.D., and the Bingling Temple Grottoes, Mogao Grottoes, and Mount Maiji Grottoes, all carved out in the stone cliffs along the Silk Road in Gansu, testify to the pervasiveness of this faith. Most of the peoples in Central Asia in this early period found it most convenient to follow the Buddhist faith.

During the Tang dynasty (618–906) missionaries representing Nestorian Christianity, Zoroastrianism, and Manicheanism came through this area, established bases in Xian, and tried to spread out across China. At this time, or even earlier according to some sources, the Jewish faith also entered China. The Islamic faith had its beginning in the early 600s A.D. By 751 the ruler of Tashkent in Central Asia, aided by the Arabs, defeated the Tang dynasty Chinese in the critical battle of Talas. As the Chinese then retreated for a period of nearly one thousand years from any direct control over Central Asia, the Muslim faith slowly penetrated the area and won over nearly all of the peoples living there. During the Mongol or Yuan dynasty there were many Nestorian churches scattered from Lanzhou in Gansu to Kashgar, but they were as small lights in an Islamic darkness.

Today, apart from the non-Hui Chinese, Russians, Xibo, Yugur, and Mongols, all the peoples of Central Asia are Muslims. Most of them are Sunni and belong to the Hanifi school of Islamic law. The nomads of the area—Kirghiz, Tajik, and Kazakhs—tend to be less orthodox in their religious observance than their sedentary brothers and sisters. They do not insist, for example, that they need to observe all rites regularly or have their women veiled. After the Cultural Revolution (1966–1976), when all religious groups were persecuted, the government relaxed its religious policy: as many as twenty thousand mosques are now opened, imams are being trained in several seminaries, and the use of the Arabic script is now permitted.

Relations of China's Central Government with Central Asia

In ancient times China did not have any direct knowledge of the area in Central Asia west of Gansu Province. During the Han dynasties (202 B.C.–220 A.D.), the Chinese made alliances with various groups in Central Asia to repulse and deflect the Xiong Nu (Hun) attacks. From that time until the present day, there has been an ebb and flow in the relationship: strong Chinese dynasties pushed into Central Asia when the barbarians were weak and then were pushed back when the barbarians threatened to overwhelm them.

These complex interrelationships between China and the barbarians became even more complicated during the Manchu dynasty because of what has become known as the Muslim question. Donald Leslie has divided the history of Islam in China into several periods:[5]

Tang period (600–800)	Foreigners in China
Sung period (900–1250)	Foreigners settled in China

5. Donald Daniel Leslie, *Islam in Traditional China* (Baleonan, A.C.T.: Canberra College of Advanced Education, 1986), 134.

Mongol period (1250–1350)	Muslims in China
Ming period (1368–1644)	Chinese Muslims—well acculturated
Early Manchu period (1650–1800)	Chinese Muslims in decline
Late Manchu period (nineteenth century)	Chinese Muslims in defeat

In general, the Manchu policy was to control the Muslims rigidly in Gansu, but to allow them a bit more free reign in Central Asia. This started the decline of which Leslie speaks, and the consequent failure of Muslim rebellions in Central Asia as well as in Yunnan where many Muslims had settled.

Several small Muslim rebellions broke out in 1818, 1826, and 1834. The most serious was one that started in Yunnan between Chinese and the Panthay Muslims, the descendants of those left behind by Kublai Khan after he had defeated the Dali alliance in 1257. These Muslims, always restive, established the *pingan guo* (Kingdom of the Pacified South) Muslim state in the Dali area from 1855 to 1873. The rebellion that led to this political state was sparked by a dispute between the Muslims and the Chinese over gold and silver mines. It spread to Gansu in 1862 and on to Central Asia by 1865.

The rebellion in Gansu started with local Chinese and Muslim disputes and was intensified by the presence of Taiping rebels seeking help for their losing cause. The leader was the fanatic New Sect headman, Ma Hualong, who was viewed by his followers as a virtual reincarnation of the Prophet Muhammad. Although his marauding bands wreaked havoc (see chap. 5) among Mongols in the Ordos region of Mongolia, missionary work, despite minor setbacks, was able to reap some advantage in a new openness by the people to the Christian message. This serious revolt was put down in 1873 by the Chinese general Zuo Zongtang, after much suffering by the local populace in all of the areas of fighting.

The rebellion in Xinjiang was not settled as easily. From the time the Emperor Qianlong asserted control over Xinjiang in 1759, the province had been governed as a military colony. The Chinese rulers oppressed the local Muslim populace so much that their religious leaders, who formerly ruled in the Kashgar area but who were now exiled across the border to Khokand, sparked a violent uprising. This enabled their leader, Yakub Beg, to gain control again over Kashgar and a portion of southern Xinjiang in 1870. The Chinese, weakened locally by corruption and occupied outside of Xinjiang by the Taiping and Muslim rebellions in other areas, offered little opposition. The situation was further complicated by politics among the great powers. Russia, wishing to promote her own commercial interests in the area and fearing that Yakub Beg might want to enlist British aid and thwart her efforts, occupied Ili in the Zungarian section of Xinjiang. The rebels were given tacit recognition by Russia and

Great Britain. However, before they were able to formalize any British financial or military support, General Zuo, the hero of victory over the Muslims in Gansu, defeated Yakub Beg and pacified Xinjiang for a while.

The Xinjiang unrest, initiated by the Hui but aided substantially by the Turkic groups, largely Uighur, resulted in the deaths of many Muslims and possibly as many as 130,000 Chinese. The wounds of this struggle were not easily forgotten. In Xinjiang and in Gansu missionaries talked repeatedly of local disputes, of how they destabilized their work, brought havoc and poverty, and resulted in the deaths of thousands. The struggles were not merely between the Muslims and the Chinese, but also between the Muslims and the Tibetans and the Muslims and the Mongols. Once the flame was lit, the fire burst out in all directions as people sought to settle old scores. They succeeded only in creating new ones.

Outwardly, many Muslims seemed to mind their own business, to keep somewhat to themselves culturally, and to do whatever was necessary to coexist within the majority non-Muslim society. But the Chinese were wary, recognizing only too well the ability of the Muslims and always a bit fearful of them. Two proverbs epitomized this attitude:

> A Tibetan can eat a Mongol, and a Chinese can eat a Tibetan, but a Huei-huei can eat the lot.
>
> A Chinese awake is not the equal of a Huei-huei sleeping.[6]

A new chapter in the ongoing tensions in Xinjiang came in October 1933, when some Muslim amirs from Khotan proclaimed the Turkish-Islamic Republic of Eastern Turkestan. This brought to an end the Swedish missionary work in Kashgar, Yarkand, and other western Xinjiang cities. A local warlord, Sheng Shihcai, with Russian help, managed to put down this independent state and retain control. Later, the Chinese government replaced Sheng with another governor who was faced with a new rebellion that again established an Eastern Turkestan Republic. The Chinese government was not able to repress the rebellion and so engaged in extended negotiations with the new provincial government that gave to the peoples of Xinjiang a greater degree of political autonomy. The advent of the People's Republic of China in 1949 began a new chapter in China-Xinjiang relationships, as the peoples of the area recognized the new government.

The conflicts continue, albeit on a smaller scale, but enough to show that the problem remains. For example, in October 1981, many Chinese

6. Mrs. Howard Taylor, *The Call of China's Great North-West,* or *Kansu and Beyond* (London: Religious Tract Society, n.d.), 157.

were killed in the Kaxi incident, when a Chinese quarreled with a Uighur and murdered him as they worked together on a water diversion canal. In the spring of 1990 nearly fifty people were killed when troops fired on Muslim peoples who were enraged because the government had halted the construction of a mosque. As recently as the fall of 1993 Muslim priests in Xining, Xian, and Lanzhou marched and rioted in protest against a book printed in Taiwan and distributed in Sichuan that they perceived as defaming Islam.[7] The government's policy of large-scale resettlement of Chinese in the area has enabled the Han population to increase to more than five million, nearly equal to that of the Uighurs. This, as well as the resurgence of ethnic nationalism and religious fervor sparked by new relationships with fellow Muslims in Central Asian republics across the border, has helped to rekindle the old animosities. Now these republics are independent within the CIN. As Xinjiang's peoples more than ever see their land as a colony of China, with most economic benefits coming out in China's favor, the potential for large-scale trouble continues. These Muslim peoples in Xinjiang, however, are still quite well off economically. This causes them not only to delay their own desires for independence, but also to attract their poor relatives across the border to join them.

The picture has not been totally negative. The government has helped the people to restore mosques destroyed in the Cultural Revolution, to build new ones, and to establish seminaries for the training of leaders. Muslims are encouraged to make pilgrimages to Mecca. The Arabic orthography has been restored for use, after earlier experiments with the *pinyin* and the Cyrillic script. Behind all of this is the "Law of Regional Autonomy for Minority Nationalities," which gives minority nationalities the freedom of religious belief and cultural expression. When these impinge upon or overlap with the political, with its overtones of independence, the government will increase its suppression.

The Christian Church in Xinjiang

During the Mongol dynasty (1260–1368), Franciscan and Dominican missionaries went through Central Asia and gave their witness to the regional Mongol rulers. They also had contact with some of the other peoples of Central Asia. We have no record of any ongoing Catholic work in the modern period until 1888, when the mission of Ili, sometimes called Kuldja, was separated from Gansu and assigned to the Scheut fathers. Over the years the church was able to establish a few small com-

7. *Beijing Review,* 1–7 November 1993, 5–6; see also *Challenges to Faith in Asia,* Traci New Review, September 1993, 33.

munities, largely among the Chinese Christian immigrants who settled in the Ili area. Catholic literature does not mention any work that was being carried on by either European fathers or local catechists among the minority nationalities of Xinjiang. The work in the province was made *Missione Sui Juris* 14 February 1930, and in 1946 it was related to the Vicariate of Lanzhou. Catholics in the area numbered fewer than 800 in 1941, with no seminaries listed for leadership training. The total Catholic population in the Lanzhou and Xining areas in Gansu Province was about 15,500.[8]

Among the Protestants, the two groups that exerted the most effort to bring the Christian message to Central Asia, particularly Xinjiang, were the China Inland Mission and the Swedish Missionary Union (Svenska Missionsforbundet). The Swedish missionaries worked in the far western section of the province and saw their work more as an extension of Russian Central Asia than of anything in China.[9] The China Inland Mission worked itself toward Xinjiang from initial bases in Gansu.

CIM Itinerant Evangelism in Xinjiang

The first two CIM missionaries, G. F. Easton and George Parker, arrived in Lanzhou in 1876. Previous to this Dr. James Cameron, who traveled more widely across China than did any of his contemporaries, was the first CIM'er to come into Gansu and Xinjiang, but he did not settle permanently. Easton used Lanzhou as his base and traveled into Xining and beyond in preliminary contacts with Muslim peoples. He engaged frequently in long conversations with "intelligent Mahometans" on weighty theological issues—Jesus' deity and the second coming—but also found time to distribute clothes and grain in a famine-stricken area.

The province of Xinjiang was created in 1892, and with its organization into a specific, coherent political unit, the area became increasingly attractive for missionary penetration. And Gansu itself, reduced somewhat in size, also seemed to be more manageable. The missionaries began to see conversions in Lanzhou, Xining, and Liangzhao, but none from among the Hui, who were the principal Muslim inhabitants of this area.[10] Whenever it seemed they were making some headway, the potential Muslim converts were bothered by teachers who came from Xinjiang and urged them to renewed dedication to the Koran and its teachings.

8. *Annuaire des Missions Catholiques de Chine 1941.*

9. Nothing may be found in the *Chinese Recorder* (1868–1942) about the work of this mission society. This includes places of work, names of individual missionaries, entry and departure news items, name of mission society, themes about work among Muslims or in Xinjiang. This agency did not consider itself part of the missionary enterprise in China.

10. The entire February 1892 issue of *China's Millions* was devoted to Gansu Province, with short articles written by the missionaries on several of the cities that they had occupied.

Among the CIM missionaries working in Central Asia, the names of George Hunter, Percy Mather, Mildred Cable, and Francesca and Eva French stand out. George Hunter, frequently labeled the apostle of Turkestan, first came to China in 1889. Disappointed at the death of a fiancée in Aberdeen before he went to China, Hunter pledged himself to a celibate ministry in the difficult Muslim areas of China—Hezhou, Xining, Ningxia, and Liangzhao. After the Boxer uprising, he went to Xinjiang, without question the most difficult place of all. Here he faced not merely the obdurate Muslim mind, but also the confusing variety of peoples and languages. The Chinese language worked as a stumbling trade language with some of these people, but literary work and local language acquisition were required if he were to be effective.

Hunter was a "nomad missionary among the nomads." He traveled incessantly and tirelessly to learn all he could about everything. He distributed in every language any literature and Scripture portions he could get from the tract or Bible societies, and engaged extensively in personal conversation. This was a tough life, and he, along with Mather who later joined him, felt it would be a crime to bring a wife into such a difficult and desolate area. Nor did he have any fellow missionaries to keep him company. This was probably just as well, because he was a loner and a maverick. Very austere and a man of violent likes and dislikes, he found it difficult to tolerate younger missionaries. If they wished to relax with some table tennis, he felt this was too light-hearted an attitude for missionaries faced daily with issues of life and death.

Hunter had a violent dislike for Roman Catholics. On one occasion he had accepted an invitation from the provincial governor of Gansu to attend a feast, but dismissed himself early when he found that a Dutch Catholic was present. Religious holidays, such as Christmas—he called it Christ Mass—or Easter, were anathema to him. A literalist in his biblical interpretation, he found it difficult to adjust culturally when it might give him the opportunity to relate better to his local environment. For a camel to go through the eye of a needle meant just this. He could not tolerate the idea that this might mean to go through a small gate, such as the many found in Urumqi or other Xinjiang cities.

He was very disciplined in his daily lifestyle. What Hunter ate never varied—morning porridge, boiled mutton and rice at noon, and leftovers from noon in the evening. He tried to keep food from being left over to the next day, because it seemed to deny God's day-by-day care and providence. His strict attention to daily finances and living was dictated in part by the slowness or uncertainty of his mission allowances getting to him or catching up with him.

Xinjiang was a difficult place to live. Hunter and other colleagues traveled widely except during the harsh winter months, when they gave themselves to study and to literature work. Chaos from Muslim-Chinese relationships or inter-Muslim squabbles was a constant menace. He once commented: "The government is despotic. No newspapers are allowed in any language. There is rigid censorship of letters. The people are rough and independent. The Chinese and Manchus are addicted to opium. The Turki people have all the immoralities of a debased Mohammedanism. The Mongols are drunkards, and men of the Qazaks and Tongans are thieves."[11]

In this sensitive border area, Muslims were fearful of being considered seditious. If a missionary sold a Gospel portion to a Muslim, he could be accused of causing the Muslim to be foreign. Because he had quoted a chapter of Scripture in one of his letters, a Christian believer had to get a guarantee that he was not plotting evil. At one time the government sent a notice to various post offices that they should confiscate any literature put out by the Swedish mission press in Kashgar, since it was not according to the Koran.[12]

In his travels Hunter helped as best he could in the Swedish mission work in Kashgar and with a community of two hundred families of strict Russian Baptists living in Kuldja (Ili), Chuguchak, and other nearby cities of the northwest portion of Xinjiang. In the years immediately preceding World War II, he was alarmed by the many "revivalists" who were coming into the northwest area. He feared that they would disrupt mission work in the same way he felt they had done in Shensi.

Hunter was an evangelist and a linguist. He did not really understand church planting. He believed his task was to win people to Christ, but, claiming to be like Paul, he did not wish to baptize those who had named the Name. He feared they would leave the faith and be a disgrace to the testimony of Christ. His approach to the missionary vocation in Xinjiang epitomized Kenneth Scott Latourette's observations about the work of the China Inland Mission and some of its missionaries, at least in its earlier years:

> The main purpose of the China Inland Mission was not to win converts or to build a Chinese church, but to spread a knowledge of the Christian Gospel throughout the empire as quickly as might be. To this end, when a province was entered, stations were opened in the prefectural cities and, later, in subordinate ones. Once the Christian message had been proclaimed, the fruits in conversions might be gathered by others. The aim was the presentation of the Christian message throughout the empire in the shortest possible time, not the immediate winning of the largest pos-

11. George Hunter, "Work among Turki and Tribes in Central Asia," *China Mission Year Book*, editor-in-chief Frank Rawlinson (Shanghai: Christian Literature Society, 1924), 237.
12. George Hunter in newsbrief in *Muslim World* (April 1923): 203.

> sible number of converts. In accord with this programme, the China Inland Mission did not seek primarily to build churches, although these were gathered. Nor, although Chinese assistants were employed, did it stress the recruiting and training of a Chinese ministry.[13]

Hunter was a capable linguist with the special interest in translating the Gospels for the Kazakh people. He studied each morning for three hours with a Turki *mullah* who lived among the Kazakhs, but whose mother tongue apparently was not Kazakh. After the two discussed the meaning of the text and the possible grammatical constructions, the *mullah* wrote it out on two or three sheets of wax paper. Using a small mimeograph machine, Hunter then printed off several hundred copies, took them out on the street, and preached to the people. After some rewriting and revision, more copies were prepared, cut and bound into a rough book form, and distributed to all who were interested. Often he combined simple medical work with his distribution of tracts and Scripture portions.

The British and Foreign Bible Society printed much of Hunter's translations into Kazakh (officially listed as the Altai dialect of Kirghiz Turkish), but it was always frustrated as to how to get the finished materials to him. Because the country was so lawless, the postal rate was increased to cover the risk of loss, making it to be one-third more than the cost of the book itself. So the Bible Society sent only one hundred copies by post and the others by caravan, with the possibility that the journey might take nine months or that the books would be ruined by rain or not get there at all. Was all this effort worth it? Missionaries gave a resounding yes, because they firmly believed that early Nestorian Christianity in Central Asia had failed because the Scriptures were never translated into local languages and distributed widely. Hunter even wished for Bibles for the many Russian refugees who often came to him begging for a "Beebel" in Russian.[14]

Did Hunter ever have as a goal the possibility of winning several converts, or even a village, and organizing them into a worshiping community of believers? Probably not, for in none of his many articles or in accounts written of his work do we have any missiological reflections on the work he was doing.[15] He was not averse to fitting his message to some extent into the local culture. After he distributed tracts to Kazakh people,

13. Kenneth Scott Latourette, *A History of the Expansion of Christianity,* vol. 6, *The Great Century in Northern Africa and Asia A.D. 1800–A.D. 1914* (New York: Harper and Brothers, 1944), 329.

14. *Reports of the British and Foreign Bible Society,* 1922, 214.

15. Material on Hunter may be found in several sources: Mildred Cable and Francesca French, *George Hunter: Apostle of Turkestan* (London: CIM, 1948); numerous articles in *China's Millions* and in *Muslim World,* such as the October 1918 issue, 427ff.

his opening statement was, "I belong to the people of the Holy Prophet, Jesus, who came down to earth and died for us all and, before ascension, told his people to go into all the world and preach the Gospel."[16]

The only person who could work with such a loner would have to be another confirmed bachelor, one willing to share with him the deprivations and dangers of this wild frontier area. Such a person was Percy Mather, who came to China in the early 1900s and worked for three years in China proper before sensing the need to get into a more pioneer work. A disciple of Roland Allen, Mather became disillusioned with getting bogged down, as his many colleagues did, in settled station work. Reading Hunter's letters from Xinjiang, Mather felt that this was real evangelism, and he joined Hunter in 1914, traveling throughout all the oases and distributing God's Word widely. Despite the pervasive illiteracy in Xinjiang, Mather was convinced that God's Word would not return void. Scattered as seed, even on hard soil, it would still lead to the evangelism of Xinjiang.

Like Hunter, Mather was also a linguist, although he was less aloof and mixed better with people. His particular focus was the Mongol people of the province. He played the fiddle, sang at their festive events, and entered with zest into their affairs, such as the erection of a tent, the control of horses, or the building of a campfire. Using his medical skills, he helped the sick, also praying with them and for them. He spent much time in the northwest city of Chuguchak, "the land of flies," and his name was known throughout the Russian, Tatar, Chinese, and Mongol sections of the city.

Mather's output in literature during the hard winter months of study and translation was prodigious. He completed a Manchu dictionary, grammar, and small book of proverbs. He also finished a small Tartar dictionary and one in Kalmuk or western Mongolian. As if this were not enough, he found time as well to help Hunter complete a dictionary in another Kalmuk dialect. All of this foundation work was necessary for the translation of numerous tracts, booklets, or Scripture portions in these several languages, all of which were then used in the wide itineration done by these two stalwarts. A question might be raised about the lasting value of this sacrificial translation interest: Mather, like Hunter, used a Russian teacher who did not speak as a mother tongue any of those languages into which Mather was translating. Not good translation theory for today, it may have been all that was possible in these frontier areas.

Mather's philosophy of missions was little different from Hunter's, although Cable and French credit him with "rethinking missions":

16. George Hunter, "Travelling among the Quasaqs," *China's Millions,* February 1918, 16–17.

> He never wrote about [rethinking missions], he never attended conferences, he did not even discourse on the subject—he merely did it. He never felt the need to rent a preaching hall or to have a Sunday service and no idea of 'opening a mission station.' He did not feel responsible for men who refused to accept God's gift. Thus he had no morbid sense of responsibility which seems to oppress many missionaries.[17]

No account of CIM work in Xinjiang would be complete without mentioning the work of the Trio: Mildred Cable, Francesca French, and Eva French. These three women operated as a team and were remarkable for their vivid descriptions of Central Asia, their fascinating writing, and their obvious commitment to spreading the Christian faith in this section of China. Like Hunter and Mather, these women did not jump right into the rigors of Central Asia. They commenced their ministries in Hezhou in Gansu and then worked for short periods in Liangzhao and Ganzhou. In 1923 they went to Suzhou, also in Gansu, which with Urumqi was their home. Wherever they went they showed special compassion for children, particularly for girls who had been abandoned. They did more than hold children's meetings; they cared for children during long winter months when they were cold and hungry. This opened the hearts of parents, who were often overwhelmed by the extent of their love, and led to invitations to visit local farmsteads where they were able to share their faith.

As they traveled, the Trio were always accompanied by a Chinese man, whom they referred to humorously as Thomas Cook. They needed more than humor on their treks. Once after Cable had been kicked in the head by a donkey, she noted that the owner "appeared to care nothing for the accident, merely seeming to view an 'infidel's' head as the legitimate kicking ground for a donkey privileged to belong to one of the 'faithful.'"[18]

The Trio were an oddity in this men's world. They were the first foreign women to travel through Xinjiang, but their foreignness aroused less curiosity than the fact that they were unmarried and were preachers. In the Islam of Xinjiang the men were in charge of all the religious rites, and the women were untaught and despised. This gave an opportunity for these "holy women," as they were viewed, to have a unique ministry within many harems. Nothing puzzled these Muslim women more than the message of forgiveness of sins through Christ, since their tradition taught them this was possible only by a life of religious works and sacrifice.

Whenever the Trio were not itinerating, they established a base in

17. Mildred Cable and Francesca French, *The Making of a Pioneer: Percy Mather of Central Asia* (London: Hodder and Stoughton, 1935), 253.

18. Mildred Cable, "From Tunhuang to Tihwa," *China's Millions,* October 1932.

Urumqi, where they lived in simple mud homes on the same compound with Hunter and Mather. They helped in the little church of six converts, largely Chinese, teaching women and helping in the work with children. Other responsibilities were taken by the Chinese Christian leaders. They also concentrated some of their evangelistic efforts at Suzhou in Gansu, where they were helped greatly by a pioneer band of Chinese believers from the Ganzhou church, several days to the southeast. A significant leader in this church was Dr. Gao, a Chinese medical doctor who had worked in the CIM hospital in Lanzhou, still farther to the southeast in Gansu. He felt called of God to the lonely outpost of Ganzhou where he might minister medically and spiritually to the Muslims in the city, as well as to those who passed through the city from farther west. Selling his comfortable home and abandoning a more affluent lifestyle, he moved to Ganzhou and sparked a movement to Christ which, by 1925, produced a thriving church of seventy-seven baptized members, largely Chinese. As local conflicts embroiled this area, Dr. Gao disappeared one day, never to be seen again.

The missionaries were not exempt from these difficulties. In 1932 the Trio were evicted from their home, which was taken over by Chinese soldiers. They were taken four days' journey across the Gobi Desert to the brigands' headquarters, a cold and inhospitable place. Released after several days, they were in poor shape but grateful to be alive. When the Trio retired in 1938, after fifteen years of service in Central Asia, the Queen of England received them at Buckingham Palace. They were also awarded the Lawrence of Arabia Medal of the Royal Central Asian Society and the Livingstone Medal of the Royal Scottish Geographical Society.[19]

A violent Muslim rebellion occurred in 1933, as more than ten thousand Muslims attacked Urumqi. Rumors were rife that Hunter and his colleagues, among whom were six new recruits who had come to augment the missionary forces in February of that year, were spies. Mather and Dr. Fischbacher were working in the dispensary there caring for sick and wounded soldiers. Both died of one of the deadly diseases going around.

George Hunter was arrested by the Russians, very active in seeking some position of power in the area during the 1930s and 1940s. He was detained and tortured by them for eighteen months in Tihwa (Urumqi). They sought in vain to extract from him a confession that he was a spy. After he was released, he returned to Lanzhou for four years and then went farther west to Ganzhou, still hoping in vain that he might be able to return to Urumqi. He died in Ganzhou when eighty-five years of age, with no missionaries closer than 250 miles, after a life of total commitment to the peoples of this vast area.

19. Leslie Lyall, *A Passion for the Impossible* (Chicago: Moody 1965), 172.

Protestant Christian churches continue in Xinjiang, with new converts being baptized regularly. Most of the members are Chinese, and they do not always have a deep concern for the local Muslim peoples. Xinjiang's Muslim peoples remain the most resistant among the unreached peoples of China. Would there have been more lasting results among the Uighurs, Kazakhs, or Kalmuk Mongolians had the missionaries concentrated on a more holistic, church-planting effort in a few specific centers? One key to answering this kind of question can be found by examining the work of the Swedish Missionary Union in the southwestern portion of Xinjiang around Kashgar.

A Thriving Christian Church in Xinjiang

All mission groups, both Protestant and Roman Catholic, working in Gansu, Qinghai, and Xinjiang came to their places of service from the China side. They had bases, lines of resource, and reinforcements from China, and it was most convenient for them to operate as China missions. This was not the case with the Swedish Missionary Union. Since its organization in 1878, it had been meeting the spiritual needs of Swedish workers who were employed in the Caucasus oil regions along the shores of the Caspian Sea. This ministry acquainted the missionaries with many Asians from Samarkand and Bokhara in Russian Turkestan, who also were employed as oil workers.

In the course of following up these leads, several missionaries went through Russian Turkestan in 1890 and as far as Kashgar, across the China border into Xinjiang. This was the most important city in the area, being the residence not only of the Chinese governor or *taotai,* but also of the British and Russian consuls for Xinjiang. When one of the missionaries, Mr. Hojer, visited with the Russian consul, Monsieur Petrowski, the diplomat showed him the clause in the 1858 agreement between Russia and China by which China was compelled to admit Christian missionaries into all of China.

As he returned to Russia, Hojer met the agent of the British and Foreign Bible Society (BFBS), Dr. Morrison, who long had been interested in having a base of operation in this region of China. Through Morrison's influence, Johannes Aveteranian was appointed in 1892 as the agent of the BFBS in what was then called Chinese Turkestan. Son of a Muslim *mullah* who served near the city of Erzerum in Turkey, Aveteranian, whose birth name was Mehmed Shukri, was converted to Christ through the help of Armenian Christians who had given him a copy of the New Testament. Saddened and confused by the death of his father who, on his deathbed, confessed his frustrations through life in trying to find the true God, Johannes was open to Christian truth claims. Even this possibility created a crisis for him, and he found it necessary to flee to Persia. Following baptism, he was given his new name, meaning "Son of the Gospel," and attended a school run by the Swedish Mission. Upon graduation he was seconded to the BFBS in Kashgar, where his gifts for ministry were put to wide use by the Swedish missionaries.[20]

Aveteranian was alone in Kashgar for two years, until he was reinforced by the arrival in 1894 of missionaries L. E. Hogberg and his wife, Sigrid, Anna Nystrom, and a Persian, Dr. Josef Massror. Within one year they were established in Kashgar, a city of about one hundred thousand, and had set up a station at Yarkand, about 140 miles southeast of Kashgar. They also made plans to occupy Hancheng (literally, "Chinese city," often called New Kashgar) just 7 miles away, as well as Yengi-Hissar, between Kashgar and Yarkand. Very soon Dr. Lacslund and missionaries Raquette and Backlund came to join the team and start a small medical ministry.

From their arrival in 1894 until the Boxer uprising in 1900 were "years of insecurity." Local Muslims were infuriated that there was a Christian presence in their sacred territory, and they refused to allow the missionaries to rent any residence. For an extended period they had to live in a garden area, and even then several riots occurred. Finally, the Muslims, together with the Chinese authorities, incited a riot at Easter in 1899. The mob threatened to tear down the newly rented dwellings of the missionaries and to topple the young mission. The women missionaries fled to the Russian consulate, but Hogberg, helped by the intervention of the British consul, George Macartney, refused to budge from the premises. The Chinese man who had rented his property to the missionaries for the dwelling was imprisoned because of his "crime." The situation calmed down when the Chinese mayor, who had instigated much of the opposition to the missionaries, was replaced by a new, much more friendly, mayor. The Boxer Rebellion stirred up new antagonism, but it did not result in any further loss of property or in danger to missionary personnel. The local populace became progressively more friendly as they realized that the missionaries were there to help them.

Of most help in allaying the suspicions of the people was the medical work carried on by the mission. Eventually a hospital was erected, and there were small dispensaries in other stations. In 1926 more than twenty-eight thousand people attended the mission medical centers, which were served largely by eight missionary nurses and only one doctor, G. Raquette. When a new ward was added to the hospital in Kashgar, this was made the occasion for a special visit by both the Russian and English

20. Samuel M. Zwemer, *Heirs of the Prophets* (Chicago: Moody Bible Institute, 1946), 128–29; Bishop B. La Trobe, "Our Neighbor Mission in the Heart of Asia," *Moravian Missions,* February 1916, 22–26.

consuls. Some time previous Raquette had been asked to give emergency treatment to a Russian colonel who had been taken seriously ill several days out in the desert. At the dedication of the new ward, the Russian consul presented the doctor with a beautiful cigarette case on which was the logo of the Russian eagle in a background of gold and diamonds.

In addition to the compassion they revealed through their medical ministries, the Swedish missionaries gave food in time of famine, provided clothes for the naked during the cold winters, and gave training in weaving as a means of providing work and compensation for the poor. The women missionaries also did Zenana work to help brighten the lives of the local women, who faced many tragic difficulties from divorce and polygamy in their Muslim households.

Schools were an important part of the effort of the Swedish Missionary Union to penetrate Muslim society. Altogether they ran at least ten schools, both on the lower and higher primary levels, for boys and girls, and with about half in the Turki language and half in Chinese. Bible training was given in connection with these schools. Some of the mission's most concentrated work among the Turki people (Uighurs) was done in Yarkand, where compared with Kashgar and its more lively population, the people appeared lethargic and listless. Here the work in the two orphanages, one for boys and one for girls, as well as in the three primary schools, was done in the Turki language.

The missionaries soon perceived that their work would experience less difficulty if it were divided between a Turki and a Chinese section. This lessened some of the intense opposition, although the first baptism in 1907 of two Muslims led to renewed animosity. The intense opposition did not come only from the Muslims. Communist influence from Russia was increasing because of the growing power of the Bolsheviks. Chinese officials walked a tightrope in trying to keep Russia and their own government happy.

A major contribution of the Swedish missionaries to Christian work among the Uighurs was their printing press in Kashgar. Here they issued for use throughout the province schoolbooks on history, arithmetic, and geography, as well as tracts, hymnals, and Scripture portions in the Uighur language. The press also prepared materials used for missionary language study; most of the missionaries became fluent both in Uighur and Chinese. The missionaries also used Muslim books, printed in Tashkent in Russian Turkestan, even though these were not written in the exact Uighur dialect used in Kashgar. One book, *Narratives of the Prophets,* the standard theological work of the Uighur people in Xinjiang, was used by new missionaries as they took their Uighur examinations in Yarkand and Kashgar. A large volume, weighing fifteen to twenty pounds, this was excellent material to familiarize budding missionaries with the Muslim mind and prepare them for their tasks of preaching and teaching.

What progress did the missionaries make in Bible translation? Johannes Aveteranian translated the entire New Testament, but since Uighur was not his mother tongue, it is not surprising that this version was soon afterward revised by Raquette and Hogberg. Uighur Scripture portions might work for the common people, but not for the *mullahs* of the area. They would only receive Gospel portions printed in Arabic, an extra literature project whose cost was borne by the National Bible Society of Scotland. A grammar of Uighur (called Kashgar-Turkish), commenced by Magnus Backlund, was finished by Raquette and printed in Germany with funds provided by German churches. Other missionaries worked on a variety of translation projects: a biblical history, textbooks in science, and the Old Testament.

Evangelism was at the heart of what the Swedish missionaries were about in Xinjiang. Medicine, education, and literature were the bow and arrow in their strategy, but the target was evangelism. Most of this was done in the several mission stations, but they took a few tours to the west and east to explore new possibilities. These they turned down, either because the population was too sparse or because the nomadic nature of the people made it impossible for them to have a settled mission. The staff of the mission in the early 1900s varied from twenty-four to thirty-two, and all of these had direct evangelistic contact with people.

The medical work was always begun with prayer and the preaching of the gospel message. The missionaries visited patients in the hospital and dispensaries to share their faith. Open-air preaching in the bazaars was conducted regularly. Worship services were held in the Uighur language at chapels and church buildings in the several centers where Uighur congregations were being developed. The best approach, particularly with the Muslims, was heart-to-heart conversations in which the Christian message was directed to specific needs of the listener.

Converts came with difficulty. The missionaries made haste slowly in accepting members into their churches. The first 2 baptisms came in 1907, and by 1914 the number had risen to 15. The largest number of baptisms at one time came in 1932, when 14 members, 10 Uighurs and 4 Chinese, were added to the church community in Kashgar. By 1933, the total number of baptized Christians was 163, mostly Uighurs and Kirghiz, but some Chinese. However, after a protracted period of persecution when Christians were imprisoned and tortured, the number dwindled, only to reach a new high of 200 after the missionaries were forced to leave.[21]

21. C. Persson, "Christianity in the Tarim Basin," *Friends of Moslems,* April 1940, 20–21.

Opposition and persecutions were the daily stuff of life for both missionaries and local Christians. One particularly bad time came with the change from the Manchu dynasty to the Republic in 1912. Murderers armed with swords came into the garden of the Yamen, the governor's palace, and killed him and the mayor of Kashgar. Their wives and attendants, along with the children, fled to the British consulate for asylum. One high official sought protection at the mission home, outside the city wall of Kashgar, near one of the gates on the northwest side. The missionaries feared, not without reason, that this might implicate them in local politics, but after the officials of the new republic arrived on the scene, they found they had nothing to fear. In fact, these new leaders were anxious to receive their medical help in caring for those wounded in the fighting.

The final blow to the missionary presence in this area of Xinjiang came in the mid-1930s when the Khotan amirs took control of Khotan 16 March 1933. By October 1933 the new leaders fought off rival factions, all seeking to control the south Xinjiang Muslim rebellion, and proclaimed the Turkish-Islamic Republic of Eastern Turkestan. They applied the Shariah Muslim law, issued new coins and currency, and hoped, as had Yakub Beg in the previous century, to be independent of China. However, without the support of the Ottoman Turks and the British, this proved to be a vain hope.

The new government swiftly imposed its will. Two hundred sixty-six Chinese were forcibly converted to Islam in Khotan, Hindi moneylenders were put to death, and the Swedish missionaries were ordered to leave the area. The most important leader of the Islamic government, Amir 'Abdullah Khan, came to Yarkand and immediately had the Swedish missionaries there arrested. They were bound and brought to 'Abdullah, who personally kicked and beat them. He threatened to kill them, because in their anti-Islamic teaching, he alleged, they were seeking to destroy this religion, and he had no choice but to kill them. They were saved by the intervention of a former local official who had previously worked for the British government. These Yarkand missionaries were imprisoned for a short period and then expelled from the country.

Missionaries were able to remain in Kashgar until 1937, when extreme antiforeign feelings, directed initially against Russia and Great Britain, turned into an anti-Swedish boycott. By February 1938 all missionary work came to a halt, and it was necessary for the missionaries to leave.[22] One of them, C. Persson, blamed directly the new Muslim government,

22. The material about the end of the work of the Swedish Missionary Union in Xinjiang comes from Andrew D.W. Forbes, *Warlords and Muslims in Chinese Central Asia* (London: Cambridge University Press, 1986), 84–87, 113–14, 147. See also India Office Records in London, L/P and S/12/2331 PZ 3558.1933.

stating that it was neither the zealous Muslim leaders, as opposed as they were, nor the people of the country who expelled them.

What hope did Persson have in 1940 that the Swedish work of forty-four years might survive? He pointed to the large number of Russian and German Baptist and Mennonite Christians near Ili, familiar to persecution in Russia, who would encourage the Uighur and Kirghiz Christians. He also put some hope in Uighur merchants. Although most were not Christians, they had often volunteered to distribute Scripture portions throughout the area for the missionaries at those times when their activities were being severely restricted. He quoted one of these friends who had said, "If the Swedish missionaries must leave here, Christianity shall not leave Turkestan with them."[23]

Missiological Reflections

What method was most effective—the widespread evangelistic itineration of Hunter, Mather, and the Trio? Or the long-time settled work of the Swedish missionaries in southwest Xinjiang? Both had their strengths and weaknesses. Itineration, at least to some extent, was needed to expose the many unevangelized peoples to the Christian faith. It might have been combined better with settled mission work and stations occupied more continuously by a larger number of missionaries. The Swedish approach worked well among a more sedentary population around Kashgar and Yarkand. The long-term, intensive commitment of the mission agency in personnel, energy, and finances was impressive, leading many to liberation through Jesus Christ.

Neither method could survive the ravages of local and national strife. The opposition of the Muslim *mullahs* and the people whom they found it so easy to mobilize to action was almost demonic. When these difficulties were combined with the formation of Islamic political states, anxious to court the favor of Russia and Great Britain, this could only result in adverse consequences for Christian missions and local churches. The opportune moment for the Christian faith did not come with Nestorian Christianity in an earlier period or during the nineteenth and twentieth centuries of the modern missionary enterprise. Political instability, ethnic animosities, and intense religious commitments do not augur well for any lasting Christian penetration into Xinjiang in the future.

23. Persson, "Christianity in the Tarim Basin," 22–23.

8

The Hidden Chinese Muslims

Introduction

Muslim peoples in Gansu and Xinjiang were very visible. Before large-scale colonization by the Chinese people, they were the dominant groups in the area. The Uighur, Kazakh, and Kirghiz peoples, as well as other smaller groups in Xinjiang and Qinghai, were committed Muslims (see chap. 7). In Gansu, missionaries talked about the Salar, originally from Samarkand, who spoke a Turki dialect mixed with Tibetan. They also mentioned the Dongxiang, who spoke a Mongolian dialect. To work among these peoples in either province required missionaries to learn another language, to get a working knowledge of Arabic, Islam's holy language, and to use methods appropriate for a non-Han ethnic population. The rigors of a harsh climate, a demanding geographical environment—impassable, high mountains and vast, desolate desert terrain—and a volatile political climate added to the difficulties of their mission task. Only a hardy few were prepared for the necessary long-term commitment and sacrifices.

Another Muslim people, the Dongan, were visible in both Gansu and Xinjiang. But, unlike the dominant peoples, these Muslims spoke only Chinese, and Arabic was used only by their *mullahs*. They tended to live together in close-knit communities, and missionaries in Gansu and Xinjiang included them rather naturally in their work of evangelism. Because they were far removed from the centers of power in political China, they were highly nationalistic and at the forefront of various dissident movements that rebelled against the local and national government.

Throughout the rest of China, however, these people, popularly referred to by the name of *huihui,* almost seemed to be invisible to the missionaries. Not that they looked exactly like the dominant non-Muslim

Chinese. Because of their historical intermarriage with Arab, Turkish, and Iranian merchants and soldiers who came to China during the Tang dynasty (618–906), they tended to be larger in build and have a longer face, deeper eyes, and a thicker beard than other Chinese.

Their Islamic faith, usually no less rigorous than that of the ethnic groups in Gansu and Xinjiang, and the cultural practices that went with this religious commitment also set them apart from other Chinese. Infrequently, their communities were dispersed among the non-Muslim Chinese. More usually, when separate, they were almost an inpenetrable enclave. Therefore, from the missionary view, they faded into the dominant Chinese Confucian and Buddhist background. They were the hidden Muslims of China and largely neglected in the missionary outreach.

Characteristics of the Hui People

These Chinese Muslims probably represent about 60 percent, or nearly eight million, of the total number of Muslim peoples in China. Apart from the number intermixed with the ethnic Muslims in Gansu and Xinjiang, they are concentrated in southwest China, with significant groups in Hebei and Manchuria. A large number live in Beijing and in Nanjing. Some provinces, like Jiangxi, have very few.

From one standpoint, the Chinese Muslims are an integral part of mainstream Chinese culture. Among them one can find Confucian scholars and government officials. They have adopted many Confucian virtues that characterize Chinese society as a whole. Few of them engage in farming, the principal Chinese vocation, but they have tea shops, restaurants, and jewelry shops. They sell cloth and mats and, like non-Muslim Chinese, engage in a wide variety of other business ventures. Because they are prohibited from eating pork, they are the exclusive sellers of beef. Eating restrictions can pose a problem for them. They often have to find employment with Muslim employers so as not to compromise themselves by eating, as is the usual Chinese custom, at their place of business.

How committed to the Islamic faith were the Chinese Muslims? It was difficult to probe into their innermost being, but missionaries noted certain outward observances that gave them clues to the depth of their convictions:

1. Their homes are not Chinese in appearance, since they do not put Chinese characters at the side or above their doors. Neither do they use the protecting wall often found opposite a Chinese door.
2. They do not usually intermarry with other Chinese; if they do, the non-Muslim partner converts to Islam.

3. On their restaurants or food shops they put up a sign indicating that this is operated by Muslims.
4. They refuse to give money for building temples, honoring idols, or supporting theatricals or puppet plays held in temples.
5. They usually practice the rite of circumcision.
6. They are monotheistic, recognizing only one God, and they do not use any symbols to worship him.
7. Every Chinese Muslim, in addition to a Chinese name, has an Arabic name that is given by the *mullah.*
8. Their burial customs are unique. The mound placed over the grave is square, not round as on an ordinary Chinese grave. If there is an enclosure inside the grave, it is also square. A special space is provided within the gravesite for the dead to kneel and pray toward Mecca.
9. Chinese Muslims frequently view themselves as aliens rather than truly Chinese. They are a people without a nationality, but with a religion. To be able to go to Arabia is to return to their native land. On several occasions efforts were made by Chinese Muslims to arrange with foreign governments to grant them the right of extraterritoriality in China, by which they would have some measure of protection in their religious and cultural observances. In this sense, they are more of a sectarian group within Chinese society than they are an institutional religion. Almost like a secret society, with an informal network throughout China, they are often seen as a dangerous political subgroup.
10. Wherever there are any number of Muslims there are mosques and a whole retinue of religious leaders—the *ahung,* teacher of religion or scholar, and an *imam,* who is responsible for leading the worship services. Most mosques have inscribed over them the three Chinese characters Qing Zhen Si, "the temple of the pure and true religion." The Muslim community is centered about the mosque and its worship, whereas the typical Chinese family's religion or ancestral rites is made up of the family kinship groups, the ancestral halls, and the trade guilds.
11. Despite the cohesiveness of the Muslim community, local groups of Muslims are completely independent of one another. There may be a Muslim association within one city.
12. Worship services are held in the mosques every Friday. With some exceptions, where women's mosques have been built, these are only for men. Women are not included.
13. Muslim schools are also held within the temple precincts, and children are given an education in Islamic doctrine and lessons in Arabic.

14. Chinese Muslims generally observe the five pillars of Islam, although most do not pray five times a day. Many attend mosque services only on important festival occasions, such as Lesser Bairan right after Ramadan, Corban, and Muhammad's birthday.

But if this seemed to be the usual Islamic orthodoxy, missionaries also noted many points where the Muslims' religious faith had been accommodated to the Chinese context:

1. Muslim women go into public without veils and observe the Chinese custom of footbinding.
2. With the exception of pork, they eat Chinese food. They often do not observe usual Islamic prohibitions against smoking or drinking alcoholic beverages. Even the restriction on pork might be conveniently overlooked either by calling the meat mutton or by ignoring the prohibition. A Chinese joke was that "one Moslem traveling will grow fat; two on a journey will grow thin."[1]
3. Chinese Muslims, possibly with the exception of those in Gansu and Xinjiang, often fast only the last three nights of Ramadan, rather than through the entire month.
4. Only a very few Muslims make the pilgrimmage to Mecca, even though this is considered essential to their faith.
5. They have so little missionary passion that fellow Muslims from abroad deny that they are true believers.[2]

Raphael Israeli argues that this contextualization enabled Islam to survive so well in China. He disputes the usual argument that Christianity was attacked in China because it was foreign. He affirms that Christianity was viewed as heterodox, and thus dangerous, because it was so zealous in propagating its truth. Islam, on the other hand, was despised by the Chinese because of its foreign origin and its strange customs, but not because of its heterodoxy. It had an alien ideology but did not impose it evangelistically on the Chinese. New converts were gained, not by proselytism, but by intermarriage. The spouse joined the new faith and the children were reared in the Islamic tradition.[3] Muslims did not use their mosques as a base for evangelization. Unlike the Christians, they did not

1. Marshall Broomhall, *Islam in China: A Neglected Problem* (London: Morgan and Scott, 1910), 245.

2. This material on the missionary view of Chinese Muslim characteristics comes from several sources: William Pettus, "Mohammedanism in Nanking," *The Chinese Recorder,* August 1908, 448–53, and "Chinese Mohammedanism," *The Chinese Recorder,* February 1913, 88–94; Raphael Israeli, *Muslims in China: A Study in Cultural Confrontation* (London: Malmo, 1980).

3. Israeli, *Muslims in China,* chap. 8, "Islam and Christianity in China," 91–106.

use street meetings, believing that their faith did not need this kind of public pleading. As a result, Muslims were less of a menace to the Chinese than were the Christians.

Protestant Missionary Interest in Islam

From the modern entrance of Christianity into China after the signing of the unequal treaties (1842–1844), Protestant missionaries were aware of the strength of Islam in the country. They soon saw that their task was not merely to win Chinese to the Christian faith, but also to evangelize Chinese Muslims. They were surprised to find that Islam was as strong as it was and had apparently not suffered the same degree of past failure in China as Christianity had. Israeli comments:

> The self-contained quality of Chinese Islam must have contributed to this dismay, for it showed how strong, independent and viable that religion was. After all the Muslims, far from appealing to the Chinese government with requests for privileges, on the contrary made efforts to be forgotten. Not only were the Muslims not backed by any foreign power, but they could muster enough power of their own to rebel against the regime.[4]

Missionaries had their initial, most direct confrontation with Islam in Gansu, south of Lanzhou in the cities of Hezhou, Minzhou, and Daozhou. Their aim was to penetrate into Tibetan territory, but the Muslims—Huihui (Dongan), Salar, and Dongxiang—were everywhere. It was inevitable that the missionaries would seek to bring the Christian message to them, but with almost no effect. One pioneer woman worker commented that in this area a missionary could put "one leg into Tibet, a hand into Mongolia, a foot into Turkestan, and an arm into Salar-country."[5] The work of Catholic and Protestant missionaries in Yunnan in the 1870s and 1880s was badly disrupted by the ravages of the Panthay Muslim rebellion in that province. Muslim conflicts with the Chinese in the late 1890s also brought the "Muslim problem" forcefully to the attention of the missionaries.

The most comprehensive early attempt by Christian forces to analyze Islam in China is to be found in Marshall Broomhall's *Islam in China: A Neglected Problem*. In this volume he traced the development of Islam in China, described Muslim unrest in northwest China, examined the origin of the term *huihui*, and brought readers up to date on Muslim literature. He had few specific recommendations to make on the evangeliza-

4. Ibid., 101.

5. Mrs. Mark Botham, *Two Pioneers: Life Sketches of Thomas and Mark Botham* (London: Religious Tract Society, 1924), 75.

tion of Muslims, because at this time little systematic analysis had been made as to how this might best be done. Articles on Islam are found in *The Chinese Recorder, China's Millions, The Chinese Mission Year Book,* and other publications. Some tracts were prepared specifically for Muslims, but all of these were in the Chinese language and did not relate directly to the Islamic context.

The spark that lit a flame of interest for the spiritual need of Muslims in China was the death in 1913 of William Borden, the heir of the Borden dairy organization. A graduate of Yale University and Princeton Theological Seminary, Borden had an unusual spiritual burden to evangelize China's Muslims, and he had been appointed to this ministry by the China Inland Mission in 1911. He sailed for Cairo in December 1912, where he had arranged to study Arabic and Islamics under the direction of Samuel Zwemer, the noted missionary to and scholar of Islam. After three months, Borden fell ill with spinal meningitis and died on 9 April 1913, within a few months of his twenty-sixth birthday.

Borden's family bequeathed large gifts to several organizations, with $250,000 specifically earmarked for the China Inland Mission and work among the Muslims in China. With this large donation, special literature was prepared and distributed freely for missionary use in China, and the Borden Memorial Hospital was erected in Lanzhou, one of the key cities for Muslim ministry in Gansu Province. Several committed CIM missionary and Chinese doctors worked at this hospital and contributed to the work of evangelism among Muslims. A branch of this hospital was later established in Hezhou, often thought of as the center of Islam in Gansu.

The beginning of the organized effort to evangelize Muslims in China came in 1917 with the visit of Samuel Zwemer. His daughter was about to come with her husband as a missionary to China, and he had also been a close friend and mentor of Borden's. His own lifelong concern for Muslims and his extended time of ministry among them in Arabia made the adherents of Islam in China a special concern for him. This was the right time for Zwemer's visit. Borden's death had created a high level of interest in the Muslims of China and raised up many prospective missionary candidates who desired to carry on his unfinished mission.

Zwemer's view of what God was doing in the world as a result of World War I also made this an opportune time to mount a new endeavor to win Muslims in China to the Christian faith: "The political unity of the Mohammedan world has disappeared by the abolition of the Caliphate and the fall of Mecca. The Moslem world, as Mr. Cash points out in his able little book, is in revolution, a revolution that is not only toward Christ, in a real sense, but also away from Christ."[6]

6. Samuel Zwemer, "The Call of Chinese Moslems," *China's Millions,* July 1925, 103.

The ascendancy of Great Britain, with many Muslims in its domains, and the demise of the Ottoman Empire were also hopeful signs to him that God's time for Islam had arrived. Zwemer observed that "from Gibraltar, Suez, and Bombay to Calcutta every great metropolis except Constantinople is under the power of Great Britain" and "all the strong and colonizing Moslem races are British subjects."[7] The editor of the well-known monthly, *The Chinese Recorder,* noted that "the capture of Bagdad by the British has given Mohammedanism a staggering blow and indicates that the 'drying up of the Euphrates' may be near."[8]

Zwemer's visit raised unparalleled enthusiasm among missionaries in China. He spoke at summer conferences for missionaries in Gigungshan, Guling, Beidaho, and Qifu, holding short workshops in which he helped the participants to understand Islam better and to formulate strategies appropriate for each area. He also visited several provinces with Charles Ogilvie, an American Presbyterian missionary, acquainting himself with the nature of Islam in China.

Zwemer's visit launched many new Muslim ministries. Missionaries at each of the summer conferences where Zwemer had spoken were unanimous in their recommendation that a special Muslim Committee become a permanent part of the China Continuation Committee. This body had been formed under the leadership of John Mott in 1913 as a firstfruit of the World Missionary Conference in Edinburgh (1910) and was intended to coordinate Protestant missionary forces in China. Such a Muslim Committee, with directors for different regions in China, would take the lead in several areas: producing literature, stimulating mission boards to appoint special workers for Islamic ministries, and mobilizing and educating missionaries in all provinces to minister to Muslims. Such an aggressive movement would enable Protestant Christian forces to test the conclusion that Zwemer and the missionaries had reached: "Chinese Moslems are more accessible to Christian work and workers than are their co-religionists in any other land."[9]

Sparked by Zwemer's visit, the Friends' Mission released one of its members, Isaac Mason, to work with the Christian Literature Society. He was interested not only in preparing literature for Muslims, but also in building up a library of Chinese Islamic literature. This collection had no equal, and at Mason's death it was bought by the New York Public

7. Samuel Zwemer, "A New Spirit Toward a New Moslem World," *The Chinese Recorder,* October 1917, 626.

8. *The Chinese Recorder,* August 1917, 485. The phrase "the drying up of the Euphrates" is found in Revelation 16:12. Many evangelical authors saw this to be an indication of the end time when false religions would be defeated.

9. This statement and the recommendations coming from each of these conference gatherings may be found in "Missionary News," *The Chinese Recorder,* October 1917, 676–82.

Library. Mason reminded his missionary colleagues in 1918 that the total amount of material prepared specifically for Chinese Muslims equaled about one-half of the New Testament, only four small booklets and twenty tracts. Other literature, he noted, was available, but this had been translated and was unsuitable for the Chinese context. In view of the fact that many converts from Islam were thoughtful, intelligent readers, he recommended that nonpolemical, conciliatory books and tracts be prepared that would focus upon the beauty of the life of Jesus.[10]

F. H. Rhodes of the China Inland Mission carried out another recommendation of the conferences—to make a thorough survey of Islam in China on behalf of the China Continuation Committee. Although no one could be positive about the number of Muslims in China (the figure varied from ten to fifteen million), Rhodes recommended that eleven centers—Beijing, Nanjing, Tianjin, Jinan, Kaifeng, Xian, Chengdu, Kunming, Guangzhou, Guilin, and Lanzhou—be pinpointed for special efforts to reach Muslims. Earlier in the conferences with Zwemer, missionaries also stressed that, although the majority of Muslims in China were Sunni, in certain areas, such as Henan, the dominant type of Islam was Sufism, the more charismatic variety of the faith. Thus, in each of the eleven centers the focus must always be on the local context.

The Muslim Committee met irregularly, hindered by its failure to persuade any mission board to second to it one of its members as a full-time director. Charles Ogilvie was one possibility, as well as Mark Botham of the China Inland Mission, but both of these men died early, partly as a result of their exhausting, unstinting efforts for the Muslims. After several years, the Muslim Committee was absorbed into the National Council of Churches in China, and all efforts to revive it under the name of the Moslem Evangelistic League were fruitless. Some Arabic literature, produced by the Nile Mission Press in Egypt, was translated into Chinese, and efforts were made to get help from the Moslem Work Committee of the British Mission Societies. In general, through the mid- and later 1920s, the impetus for work among Muslims lost much of its momentum. One very positive development was the formation of The Society of the Friends of Moslems of China in 1926. The other organization to which many missionaries belonged was The Fellowship of Faith for Moslems, which had been organized in 1915 and included workers among Muslims worldwide. The Friends of Moslems issued their first newsletter, *Friends of Moslems,* in January 1927. It was edited by Elizabeth Pickens, Zwemer's daughter. This helped to maintain some level of interest.

10. Isaac Mason, "Christian Literature for Chinese Moslems," *Muslim World,* April 1920, 164–67.

New momentum came in 1933 with still another visit from the peripatetic Zwemer. As on his previous visit, he met with missionary groups, visited mosques, and conducted workshops and special institutes to inform and inspire. This time, however, he lectured to Chinese Christians, spoke to large gatherings of Muslims, and conferred with *ahungs* in mosques. To Christians his message was straightforward: "fishers of Muslims" must know the sea, the context where Muslims live; the fish, the local people with their unique beliefs; and the net that would enable them to distinguish between the essentials and nonessentials of strategy.

By 1940 Leonard Street, acting superintendent of the China Inland Mission in the province of Gansu, characterized the work in that area of China, and it could well have applied to all of China, as marked by faithful effort ("Master, we have toiled all the night," Luke 5:5), failure ("and have taken nothing"), and faith ("nevertheless at Thy word I will let down the net"). Results were much more than "nothing" and were not to be reckoned merely in numbers of converts, but they were far less than what the missionaries had hoped, particularly since creative thought had been given to new strategies and methods from the post-World War I period until the demise of the missionary enterprise in 1949.

Theory and Strategy in Work among Chinese Muslims

The Fish

How did missionaries in China view the "fish," the Chinese Muslim? Some did not seem to see them, and, if they did, thought they were just like any other Chinese. More dangerous, some viewed them as Arab Muslims and tended to forget they were Chinese. Thus, they were lumped with Muslims everywhere. Rather than using unique literature prepared specifically for the Chinese, these missionaries wanted to translate tracts and books used for Muslims in other Islamic areas of the world.

Sensitive missionaries recognized that the Chinese *huimin* were a social organism in China committed to the Islamic faith and culture, but that they were Chinese. Montgomery H. Throop of the American Lutheran Mission felt that the right Christian message would "fulfil Moslem ideals" in the Chinese context. This, he claimed, would enable these converts to stand with the missionaries and Chinese Christians in the ongoing struggle against the atheism, pantheism, and idolatry so rife in Chinese society.

Throop stressed that the beginning point for such an approach was the person of God, seen by Muslims as a vengeful despot, but revealed as all-merciful, all-wise, "close to the human heart and a Lover of men," through Jesus Christ. He noted that the "rise and popularity of Sufism, a mystical school of thought and practice" in China came about because

Muslims view God as far off, rather than as one who is near and available. The stumbling block, of course, was the apparent conflict between the Islamic concept of the unity of God and the Christian doctrine of the Trinity. He and others had the usual illustrations that might defuse this difference, but they recognized this obstacle and also knew that argument, debate, and confrontation were counterproductive.

Throop then went on to explain how

> As Christianity fulfils and enriches the Moslem idea of God, so it does with the practical side of religion. Every Moslem has five religious duties, the five so-called "pillars of Islam" (1) Confession of Faith, (2) Prayer, (3) Fasting, (4) Almsgiving, (5) Pilgrimage. All of these duties are recognized, deepened, and spiritualized in Christianity. Of the first Christ said, "He that acknowledgeth me before men, him will I acknowledge before by Father who is in heaven." The second, third and fourth are inculcated and regulated and guarded against hypocrisy by Christ in the Sermon on the Mount (St. Matt. 6:1–18). The fifth finds its fulfilment in the public worship of God. "Where two or three are gathered together there am I in the midst of them"—that spot is holy ground.[11]

Throop was bold to claim that "the Moslem who accepts Jesus Christ as his Saviour is not disloyal to his former faith but is a true Moslem, which in the Arabic means, 'one who submits to God and in Him finds peace.'"

More so than in other countries, missionaries in China agreed that they should be conciliatory in their approach to Muslims. Without abandoning attempts at apologetics and a clear expression of Christian truth, the prevailing attitude was that

> Only harm is done by 'showing up,' at least in public, all that which the Moslem has been taught from earliest childhood to regard as most sacred. It is hard to reason with an angry man. Of course it was realised that such topics could not be altogether avoided, but it was thought that the best way was to deal with them tactfully in personal and private conversation, and if strong resentment seemed to be aroused, to change the subject at once and await a more favourable occasion, leaving him with some positive statement of Truth.[12]

11. Montgomery H. Throop, "The Fulfilment of Moslem Ideals in Christianity," *Friends of Moslems* 11, 1 (January 1937): 67–69. For a fine technical article on how to present the doctrine of the Trinity to a Chinese Muslim see Mark Botham, "Talks to Moslems—The Doctrine of the Trinity," *Friends of Moslems* 10, 3 (July 1936): 46–49.

12. "Review of Conferences," Sining, Tsinghai, 4 July 1933, *Friends of Moslems* 8, 4 (October 1933): 56.

Even as he emphasized the need for missionaries to understand Muslim thinking, Zwemer pleaded for returning to the missionary pioneers "who succeeded where we have failed." These men, he affirmed, had the qualities of "Vision; Knowledge (of the language and the people); Persistence; Passion for souls and Ability to Endure Loneliness." What was needed, he emphasized, was not "new methods" but a "new man."[13]

What mental attitudes did the Muslims have toward the Christian message as they heard it? George Harris, a veteran CIM missionary from Gansu Province, spoke for many missionaries in outlining the intellectual blocks that prevented the gospel message from making much of an impact:

1. Bigotry, an unwillingness to hear; rigid opposition to new converts; warnings about such things as a visit by Zwemer to Gansu.
2. Ignorance, by which illiterate Muslims hear the gospel, assent to it, add it to their superstitious beliefs, and claim that it is the same as Islam.
3. Indifference, often fed by the belief that God is willing to accept both Christians and Muslims, and that eventually there will be a union of these two faiths.
4. A dissatisfaction with orthodox Islam, shown in the growing power of sect groups, such as Sufism, the Djahariyah in eastern Gansu, the Qadiriya around Hezhou, and the Naqshbandiya near Xining.
5. Conviction or mental assent to the truth of Christianity, but still with an unwillingness to commit to Christ.
6. True belief, sometimes expressed openly, but more often secretly.[14]

Early missionaries always recognized that the extreme conservatism of Chinese Muslims—created by their separate communities, their distance from the centers of Middle Eastern Islam, and their isolation from intellectual currents both in China and in the rest of the world—was a major obstacle to their receiving the Christian message. Thus, they viewed with hope the New Forward Movement inaugurated in 1911 with the demise of the old Qing dynasty. This movement, sparked by the Republic's new broadening of popular education, meant the opening of new mosques, more Muslim schools for Chinese students, and more young people preparing for leadership roles—seemingly a more aggressive Islam. But, such a movement also augured opening up to outside influences. Teachers in Islamic schools used Chinese more than they did Arabic. Secular subjects

13. Ibid., 54.
14. George Harris, "The Moslem Mind and the Gospel in China," *Muslim World,* 403–6.

were put into the curriculum, and mosque schools, both on the primary and the secondary levels, were organized like those run by the government. As never before Muslim children, both boys and girls, were being affected by non-Muslim thinking, and many liberal ideas began crowding into their minds. While regretting that government regulations proscribed the offering of religious instruction, leaders saw that these schools were necessary if Islam were to compete with Christianity. One Muslim observer commented: "Civil education in Moslem communities, owing to scarceness of means and educators, is still in the first stages. A comparison between the Moslem schools and the Christian ones fills us with shame and regret: today the missionaries have all over China thousands of elementary schools, hundreds of secondary schools, and a dozen higher institutions."[15]

Women were more free than previously, and a few special mosques were established for their worship. Islamic leaders began to be interested in world religions and were more open to see how Christianity compared with Islam. New organizations were developed that would be comparable to the YMCA.[16] The sinister dimension of this renewal movement within Chinese Islam was a rash of new literature that pushed pan-Islamic ideals and an anti-Christian animus. In his address to the Annual Meetings of the China Inland Mission in Great Britain in 1925, Zwemer displayed dramatically to his audience *The Light of Islam,* a new Muslim magazine just published in Shanghai. The lead article proposed an International Moslem Association, one of whose goals was to invite foreign *ahungs* to come to China and propagate the faith. He saw Bolshevik efforts to unite Communism and Islam behind this new publication.[17]

The Net

How did understanding the Muslim mind in China and missionary theory result in a practical "net" of methods and strategy? Missionaries welcomed Muslims to the street chapels where they preached to non-Muslim Chinese, but they recognized that real progress would not be made until they were able to concentrate solely on a ministry to Muslims. The question was largely one of personnel. With the huge population of China and the relative scarcity of workers, was it sensible to take any among the few workers and assign them to a predictably unproductive ministry?

15. Lecture by Mohammed Ma Chien es-Sini Une, 1934, and printed in *Muslim World,* January 1936, 75.

16. The best analysis of this movement and its implications for work among Muslims is Mark Botham, "Modern Movements among Chinese Mohammedans," in Botham, *Two Pioneers,* 131–40.

17. Samuel Zwemer, "The Call of Chinese Moslems," *China's Millions,* July 1925, 103–5.

Any list of strategies or methods began with literature. Merely to use literature prepared for a general Chinese ministry was insufficient. These dealt with non-issues for Muslims: the evil of idolatry, Buddhist and Confucian ideas and idioms, and special terms and names. Tracts needed to "scratch where the Chinese Muslim itched." Many titles were suggested: Is Jesus only a *sheng-ren* (saint)? How can God have a Son? Is Mohammed a *Bao-ren* (mediator)? Did Jesus Die? Why Don't You Read Your Koran? *Fu, Zi, Maliya* (Father, Son, Mary)—Mohammed's Mistakes about the Trinity, and Confucius versus Muhammad. From these suggested titles, it is apparent that some would be appropriate for nominal believers, some for more ardent adherents, and some for the *mullahs*. Nearly all advocated a dialogue, possibly even a confrontational approach. These proposals for tract titles were made in 1913 (before Zwemer's first visit) and reflect an earlier, compulsive method of witnessing that would immediately lay all of the theological cards on the table.[18] A conference on Islam held by the Near East Christian Council in November 1938 suggested a lower rhetoric level for all publications:

> We must witness to Christ and even win them "without directly overcoming the special obstacles." Leave this to the Holy Spirit.
> Guard against the premature introduction of thoughts which divert the hearer from Christ himself.
> Get the hearer to read the New Testament and come to his own conclusions without our interpretation.

This conference also went so far as to suggest that workers among Chinese Muslims need to think of the spiritual equivalent of baptism. Would it not be better, the conferees suggested, to form small groups of believers, rather than seek large churches, so as to minimize the shock of a converted Muslim breaking his important social and cultural group connections?[19]

This more positive approach to literature centered on Jesus. Zwemer pointed out that John 5:46, "He wrote of me," is the basis for any publications to Muslims. So, increasingly, tracts focused on Jesus—the Light of the World, the Door, the Lamb of God. Missionaries recommended that Muslim inquirers read the Gospel of Matthew, whose geneological

18. "A Symposium. How to Adequately Meet the Recognized Need of the Chinese Mohammedans," *The Chinese Recorder,* February 1913, 98–103. This list of suggested titles comes from William R. Malcolm.

19. "Inquiry on the Evangelization of Moslems Findings," *Friends of Moslems,* July 1939, 53–55.

tables were so important to them, and search out for themselves the truth of the Christian faith.

This literature, it was agreed, should be available in both Arabic and Chinese. Many Chinese Muslims might have only a smattering of Arabic, but the tract or booklet would have greater credibility just by being written in the "language of heaven." Furthermore, the missionary must use it with great sensitivity and discretion because of the Muslims' great respect for the written page, particularly when written in Arabic. Raymond Joyce tells of the way George Harris visited an *ahung* who was not very receptive to his visit. He was careful, in entering the room, not to tramp upon the mat used for prayer. When he gave a copy of the Koran to the *ahung,* he took out his silk handkerchief, wiped the cover very carefully, and then began to read from it. This broke down whatever resistance the *ahung* had, and he was open to talk with Harris.[20]

What was the best delivery system to get this literature to Muslims? Missionary itineration was one favorite method. Should missionaries engage in public street preaching and then give out literature when their messages were completed? Or was it best to find a partially private courtyard where the message and the literature could be targeted more specifically to Muslims? Or was a home better yet? Missionaries had their own styles of evangelism that dictated their methods. They always needed to be aware that a generic message, with its usual polemics against idolatry, would not only not appeal to monotheistic Muslims, but would actually repel them. They saw themselves as totally different religiously from the Chinese, whose idolatry they despised even more than did the missionaries.

Some missionaries visited mosques directly and sought to converse with Muslim leaders, who often were very friendly and had long discussions with them. Usually theological in nature, these personal talks with the *ahungs* covered a wide range of topics: the person of Jesus, his relation to Muhammad, differences between the Koran and the Bible, and the importance of studying the Bible for oneself.[21] In contacting leaders, George Harris of the CIM stated that the missionary needed to distinguish three levels: the leader who has influence in farming areas; the teacher-class in Muslim villages; and then the Sufi leaders with their mystical bent. He warned that the missionary should avoid the "big frogs in little ponds," as well as those who were "leaders in villany" and who could quickly mobilize "gangs of ruffians" to oppose anything missionaries desired to do.[22]

20. News item in *Friends of Moslems,* January 1943, 13.

21. Paul A. Contento, "Personal Work Amongst Ahungs," *China's Millions,* December 1938, 187–88, is a good example of such a ministry.

22. George Harris, "Three Types of Moslem Leaders," *China's Millions,* July 1947, 29–32.

Where Chinese colporteurs distributed literature for Muslims, missionaries recommended that they not preach, for fear that they would get into involved theological discussions far over their heads. This might prove to be an embarrassment if they were unable to answer questions or to answer them incorrectly. Again, the preferred approach was to seek opportunities for personal conversation, where silence or mistakes would not harm the faith publicly.

One creative strategy was to send friendly letters written in Chinese to all of the mosques in the district where the missionary might be working or living. Sent by Chinese post and addressed ambiguously to "all the honorable scholars," this letter would invite the *ahungs* and other leaders to visit the missionary's home and see the literature he had in both Chinese and Arabic. Such a visit demanded special preparation. Missionary strategists recommended that a special inner room be readied where there would be no interruption and where the visitor would not need to have contact with "pork-eaters" or unbelievers. If refreshments were to be served, it would be best to have a clean kitchen where food and utensils would be uncontaminated by anything the Muslim viewed as unclean. Some Muslims might refuse tea because it is unclean, and a recommended substitute was fruit, such as oranges or peaches, with the skins intact.

The discussion itself should be calm, direct, and yet not a debate. F. H. Rhodes suggested that present salvation should be stressed and that all statements should be supported by Scripture. What if a missionary were asked, "Do you believe in the claims of Muhammad or the Koran"? Rhodes suggested an ambiguous reply, "Friend, please don't press me to answer your question, for my answer will be sure to give you sorrow!" Avoid anger at all costs, he insisted, even it means you must temporarily leave the room in order to gain your composure.[23]

No matter how hard the missionaries tried, they were constantly accused of being idol worshipers. Bible pictures that non-Muslim converts pasted up on the walls of their homes and posters caused Muslims to infer that Christians worshiped pictures. Roman Catholic usage of images in their worship heightened the problem, since Chinese people often found it difficult to differentiate between these two expressions of the Christian faith. Even to use the term *heavenly Father* seemed blasphemous to Muslims, who believe God to be so spiritual and transcendent that no human analogies can be used to describe him.

Harris related that taking his wife and two boys to join in visiting Muslim villages and families around Xining in Gansu opened up resistant areas to the gospel message. His wife had the opportunity to visit with

23. F. H. Rhodes, "Work for Moslems," *Friends of Moslems* 2, 4 (October 1928): 6–12.

Muslim women, and the children broke the ice much better than the most colorful poster. Many areas, particularly in northwest China, had been ravaged by famine, drought, or floods, and a ministry of distributing food and clothes demonstrated to the people, far better than preaching, the reality of a God who cared for them.

Missionary wives and single women missionaries tried to develop a strategy for reaching Muslim women. The ideal, of course, was that families might convert. For a woman to accept Christ without the permission of her husband and family would lead only to her being divorced and cast out. The nature and extent of opposition to a woman being converted varied with the area of China.

In the northwest the condition of women approximates most nearly that of their sisters in lands ruled by Muslims, and toward the south and east it conforms more to ordinary Chinese standards. This is due to the large and bigoted colonies of Muslims in the northwest, and to less intermixture of Chinese blood.[24]

Missionary women wanted to relate directly with Muslim women, fearing that general Chinese prejudice toward Islam skewed anything that a Chinese Bible woman might be able to do. Younger women were most open to hearing about the gospel, but only if older women, more bound by old traditions, and their husbands were not present. Muslim girls were best contacted with the gospel at mission schools, but their apparent interest soon ebbed after they reached home. One method that the women used in Henan and central China was to visit women's mosques, to talk with the women *ahungs,* and to make direct contact with women worshipers. Everyone seemed friendly at these visits, but it was only a superficial relationship.

Muslim tradition was far different from ordinary Chinese Buddhist traditions. This demanded a contextualized communication. Harris's goal in preaching was to latch on to ideas or aspirations common in Islam, such as how to obtain a pure heart. Muslim leaders in China, under the push of the New Forward Movement, produced a great amount of literature: tracts, booklets, catechisms, almanacs, and "The Three Character Classic for Moslems." The latter was an Islamic take-off of a well-known Chinese classic widely used in Chinese schools for instructing children. All of these publications were grist for the missionary mill in being able to understand what Chinese Muslims were saying. Not that these tracts were used by Muslims to evangelize; their only function was to nurture the faithful. But they were a reliable clue to the Muslim mind.

24. Olive Botham, "Moslem Women of China," *Muslim World,* October 1938, 360–61. See also Mrs. I.V. Soderstrom, "How Can We Best Reach the Mohammedan Women,"*The Chinese Recorder,* February 1913, 94–97.

Medical work was another means of distributing literature and of creating opportunities for sharing the message of Jesus. This was done in clinics and dispensaries, as well as by itinerating missionaries who carried simple medical supplies with them. The best-known hospital in northwest China, the Borden Memorial Hospital in Lanzhou, Gansu, had this specific goal:

> To convert sinners, to break down prejudice, and to show the fruits of Christianity. Of these the first is the greatest, though often the two latter are apparently more successful.[25]

In 1924 a branch of this hospital was established in Hezhou, where there was even a greater concentration of Muslims, both Hui and Turkic groups. But whether in Lanzhou or Hezhou, the number of Muslims who came for treatment constituted only 15 percent of the patients.

Was the medical work really attaining its goal with Muslim patients apparently unwilling to come, and with hardly any of these accepting the message of liberation in Jesus? This ministry of compassion did break down prejudice, and results may have appeared far from the hospital in isolated Muslim villages. Dr. George King, himself the son of a medical doctor who had died in China, gave himself to the training of Chinese medical evangelists who would dedicate themselves to Christian work in Gansu and Xinjiang. One of these, Dr. Gao, was inspired to serve Jesus effectively in Ganzhou, many days along the silk route toward Xinjiang.

Christian mission schools, particularly in Muslim areas, often enrolled students from Muslim families. How did missionaries follow up with these children once they left the school premises? No one had any good answers for this dilemma—only the hope that the seed of the gospel would not return void. Another potentially useful site for contacting Chinese Muslims was a hostel. The CIM ran one in Xining with mixed results. Muslims used the facility but held tightly to their own faith, not swayed by missionary efforts to win them. A hostel or like facility posed the old problem—will Muslims come for any period of time if there is not a Muslim cook? How can we be sure that the food is ritually clean for them? One of the difficulties that kept patients away from hospitals was the absence of a Muslim cook and the unwillingness of the relatives to bring special food to the patient.[26]

25. Frank Houghton, *George King, Medical Evangelist* (London: Religious Tract Society, 1930), 43.

26. For a discussion of some of these problems see an article by Olive Botham in *Friends of Moslems* 1, 3 (October 1927): 1–2.

Any Results?

What results can be reported from the extensive work that Protestant missionaries carried out among the Chinese *huimin?* They can be measured only by soft impressions. Harris sums these up well:

> In like manner we believe that the Water of Life has reached some of the barren souls among the Moslems in China. There are, first, some who have confessed Christ openly in baptism. From letters, mission reports, and personal experiences there is sufficient to know that ex-Moslem Christians are found in many of the provinces. One is Bishop over a large diocese, another is pastor of a church near the Moslem section of an important Central China city, and some are over other church responsibilities. They are found among teachers, soldiers, merchants, craftsmen and other classes of people.[27]

He goes on to point out that there were secret believers, as well as others upon whose hearts the Spirit of God was working. Will this latter group come to specific faith in Christ? This depends on the special grace of the Holy Spirit and the persistent, prevailing prayer of God's people. Missionary work was commenced in Ningxia Province in 1885, but the only significant response by the early 1990s was among the Han north of Yinchuan. Almost no impact has been reported among the dominant Muslims in the south of Ningxia.[28]

From the inception of their contact with Muslims, missionaries declared their belief that the resistance by Islam could be overcome only with prayer. Therefore, various groups, such as Fellowship of Faith for Muslims and Friends of Muslims, mobilized God's people to pray, as did all mission societies with work among Muslims. And countless other groups in mission-sending, western countries were formed to create awareness of need among Muslims everywhere and to develop prayer cells. The American Christian Literature Society for Moslems, Inc., founded in 1915, organized prayer groups of American Christians in many cities.

Not only have Chinese Muslims resisted efforts to reach them with the liberating message of the Good News of Jesus Christ. They and Muslims outside of China, in reflecting on this past Protestant missionary effort, have downplayed whatever results seem to have been attained. Were *ahungs* in some mosques open to the gospel? Not really, claims Israeli, a

27. George Harris, "Spiritual Results among Moslems in China," *Moslem World* 23 (April 1933): 156–63.

28. Tony Lambert, "A Visit to Ningxia Province," *China Insight,* August/September 1993, 1–4.

noted Muslim scholar: "Small congregations of marginal Islam seemed to be more receptive, perhaps due to the similarity that they could find between the Biblical stories that the missionaries told them and the Qur'anic versions that they had heard but were not able to read or verify for themselves."[29] "In places where Islam was strong, confident, viable," he argues, "the response was utterly negative, sometimes violently so."

The Hui Nationality Today in China

Most of the Hui people continue in their commitment to Islam. Within this basic system, however, they express their identity in several different ways. In the northwestern Sufi village of Na Homestead, located in the Ningxia Hui Autonomous Region, Islamic belief and ritual embody the most salient expressions of Hui identity. In the capital of Beijing city, the urban Hui of the Niujie Oxen Street community express their ethnicity in terms of occupational specializations and dietary restrictions. In the rural village of Changying, a Hui autonomous village on the Hebei North China plain outside of Beijing, Hui identity is often expressed in terms of ethnic marriage endogamy that has led to the establishment of national networks. Finally, in the Chendai Ding lineage on the southeast coast of Fujian Province, genealogical ideas of descent that reflect traditional Chinese constructions of ethnicity become the key marker of identity for these Hui who no longer practice Islam.[30]

Islam in China, whether among the Chinese *huimin* or among the Altaic-speaking minorities of Gansu, Qinghai, and Xinjiang, is undergoing renewal and revival like that among Protestant and Catholic churches. The reconciliation of Muslims to God and their liberation in and through Jesus Christ need to be high-priority items on the evangelistic agenda of the Christian churches in China. One hopes they will learn from the past missionary efforts how to use more effective missiological principles in this task.

29. Israeli, *Muslims in China,* 102.

30. Dru C. Gladney, *Muslim Chinese Ethnic Nationalism in the People's Republic* (Cambridge: Harvard University Press, 1991), xi. The author examines each of these four types in the remainder of his book.

9

A People Divided

The Tame Nosu of Yunnan and the Wild Nosu of Sichuan

Recent News

Beginning in mid-1944 and extending into 1946, news stories filtered out of China about American airmen who were lost as they flew supplies over the hump from India to the base of the Twentieth Air Force in Chengdu. Now and again, planes disappeared in the wild region near the top of the world known as Lololand. In this area located just north of the Yangzi River (River of Golden Sand) as it runs between Yunnan and Sichuan, not only were there high mountains, such as 24,900-foot Minya Gonka and 21,900-foot Mount Grosvenor, but also dense jungle and wild tribespeople. These Lolos both took slaves and killed people who came into their territory unprotected by guarantors.

In October 1944, an Air-Ground and Aid Section was organized by the Fourteenth Air Force in Kunming to seek and help any American personnel who might be lost in Independent Nosuland. This expedition, which originated in Lugu, thirty-five miles to the north of Xichang, and proceeded into the high mountains about Yuexi, Tianba, and Fulin, found the remains of a B–29 stripped of most of its guns. Further investigation to the southeast was made impossible by broken bridges and dense, impenetrable jungle.

Later in the fall of 1946, similar rumors of slave-held American airmen resulted in yet another expedition into this remote area. Several weeks of search yielded no results, and the investigative team left the area. Nothing in the few remaining years of the Kuomintang rule over China or in the subsequent period of the Marxist government lent any credence to stories of American personnel being held captive by the Nosu.

Interest over the Years

This was not the first time that the Nosu had been in the news. From early in the rule of ancient Chinese dynasties, the fiercely independent tribespeople living in this area had resisted control from various dynasties and at times had forged alliances with other groups more to the south to oppose the government. One notable example had been the involvement of the Lolo-type tribal groups in the Nan Zhao kingdom about Dali in what is now Yunnan Province. The Dali kingdom, a successor to the Nan Zhao, was defeated by Kublai Khan, the Mongol ruler of China in the thirteenth century.

The Lolo peoples have also attracted the interest of people from outside China, whether adventuresome explorers or missionaries. Everyone commented on their stature, the noble character and beauty of their women, and their Caucasoid features. Some wondered if these features of their physical appearance, so different from that of other minority peoples, might be traced to an earlier home in China's northwest, where they mingled with peoples of Altaic stock. One of the first travelers into the area was Marco Polo. During the time when he investigated the wonders of China and visited Chengdu and Yaan, he traveled down the Jianchang Valley, along the Anning River, to Xichang, then called Jianchangfu. To the present time, local people call this the interior silk route.

The first modern European to go through this area was E. Colborne Baber, British resident at Chongqing, who in 1878 traveled to the Jianchang Valley to discover its trading potential. In the same year, George Nicoll and Charles Leaman of the China Inland Mission also reached Ningyuanfu, a newer name for Xichang, and Huili. They crossed the River of Golden Sand and proceeded back to Chongqing, where Leaman had the opportunity to compare notes with Baber on the Nosu language and culture. In days of poor transportation and inaccurate maps, these two early journeys were amazing accomplishments.[1]

After these three trailblazers had pioneered the path into this wild country, others began to follow. Alexander Hosie, also stationed in Chongqing with the British consular service, made three expeditions through this area in 1882, 1883, and 1884. Vicomte D'Ollone, a major in the French army, engaged in a mission to interior China from 1906 to

1. A. J. Broomhall, *Assault on the Nine,* book 6 of *Hudson Taylor and China's Open Century* (London: Hodder and Stoughton and the Overseas Missionary Fellowship, 1988), 122–26.

1909, and a portion of his trip took him into Independent Nosuland. Like those who went before and after him, he agreed that the Lolos were a "black branch of the Caucasian race" with features that showed their kinship with the Indo-European race.[2] Samuel Pollard, a missionary among the Miao in southwest China, was the first European to travel into this country by crossing the River of Golden Sand from Yunnan Province in the south. His trip into Babuland, the name given to the territory by local Chinese (the word *babu* may be a corruption of two Chinese words meaning "hill climbers"), was done secretly and lasted for about six weeks. He noted that the Nosu, almost singly among the tribes in southwest China, had "withstood the advance of Buddhism."[3] In general, this was an uneventful venture, although he had to refuse politely the gift of a Nosu girl for a wife as well as foil the plot of several Nosu leaders to kidnap him and his companion.[4]

When visitors were not careful to arrange for guarantors or protectors (*baotou*), the usual procedure for outsiders going into the area, the results were tragic. In 1909 Donald Brooke, a Britisher accompanied by about a dozen men, was killed by the Nosu at the small village of Lianchanao. Those with him were taken captive and eventually sold as slaves. This incident led to difficulties between the British and the Chinese and sparked escalating hostilities over the next few years between the Chinese and the Lolos.[5]

Origins of the Lolo

The term *Nosu* means "black one" in the Nosu language and is most commonly used in Sichuan. The term *Yi,* including the Nosu of Sichuan, is a Chinese term that the Chinese from ancient times have applied to many non-Chinese nationalities, such as Lisu, Lahu, Naxi, and Bai. They are all minorities of the Tibeto-Burmese subgroup of the Sino-Tibetan minorities of China. Another term applied to these several peoples is the "Lolo group" of peoples. Thus, the terms *Yi* and *Lolo* may

2. Vicomte D'Ollone, *In Forbidden China: The D'Ollone Mission 1906–09 China-Tibet-Mongolia* (London: T. Fisher Unwin, 1912), 12.

3. R. Elliott Kendall, ed., *Eyes of the Earth: The Diary of Samuel Pollard* (London: Cargate, 1954), 68–69.

4. Samuel Pollard, *Tight Corners in China* (London: Andrew Crombie, n.d.), 59–70. For further information on the Lolos in the writings of early missionaries working in southwest China see Samuel Pollard, *In Unknown China* (Philadelphia: Lippincott, 1921); Samuel R. Clarke, *Among the Tribes in South-West China* (London: CIM, 1911); William Alexander Grist, *Samuel Pollard: Pioneer Missionary in China* (London: Gassell and Co., n.d.); and R. Elliott Kendall, *Beyond the Clouds* (London: Cargate, 1948).

5. Lin Yueh-hua, *The Lolo of Liang Shan (Liangshan Yi Chia)* (New Haven, Conn.: HRAF, 1980), 10.

apply to a specific nationality, or they may apply to the various peoples within this subgroup. As used in this chapter they refer both to the more domesticated (or sinicized) Yi of Yunnan and the wild, independent Yi living in the Great Cool Mountains of Sichuan, north of the River of Golden Sand in and on both sides of the Jianchang Valley. The precise origin of the Yi, Lolo, or Nosu peoples and the route by which they arrived in their present home in Yunnan and in the Daliangshan and Xiaoliangshan (the Great and Small Cool mountains) are unknown. They may have been known as early as the Zhou dynasty (1122–221 B.C.) under the name *Lu,* but the term *Lolo* appears first in records of the Yuan or Mongol dynasty (1260–1368).

By the time of the Ming dynasty (1368–1644), eleven Lolo tribes were listed in the records of the Nan Zhao as being subject to this Shan state located in Dali, the present Yunnan Province.[6] When the Mongols under Genghis Khan defeated the Dali kingdom, which succeeded the Nan Zhao, some of the Yi nationalities were dispersed throughout Yunnan, including the specific group known today as the Yi of that province. The area about the River of Golden Sand to the north remained unconquered, and tribal kings remained in power there as late as 1727. Even after the Manchus, with great savagery, suppressed the tribes and put their kings to death, thousands of Nosu refused to acknowledge defeat and withdrew across the River of Golden Sand to the Daliangshan area. Here they remained in haughty arrogance, resisting Chinese control, at least in the high mountains, until the advent of the People's Republic of China. The Yi of Yunnan accepted Chinese rule and gradually, with periodic resistance, adopted Chinese culture and many features of Chinese religion. Particularly in Sichuan, an intense hatred has existed between the Yi and Chinese who drove them into the mountains. These people, like Native Americans, feel that possession is ownership and resent the massacres of their ancestors and expulsion from their own land. When they raid Chinese villages to take slaves, livestock, and other provisions, they believe that they are only taking their rightful rent.

6. Several works discussing the origin and early history of the Lolo are Inez deBeauclair, *Tribal Cultures of Southwest China* (Taipei: The Chinese Association for Folklore, 1972), 3–39; Feng Han-yi and John Knight Shyrock, "The Historical Origins of the Lolo," 103–27; *Harvard Journal of Asiatic Studies*: Inez de Beauclair, *An Introduction to the South-Western Peoples of China,* West China Union University Museum Guidebook Series no. 7 (Chengdu, 1945); selections from the Weekly Bulletin of the China Information Committee, Chongqing, China, 22 September 1941; *Yi Zu Wenhua Yenjiu Wenji* (A Collection of Research on the Yi Culture) Chuxiong Yi Minority Cultural Research Center of the Yunnan Academy of Social Science (Kunming: Yunnan People's Publishing Company, 1985), and Liu Yaohan, *Zhongguo Wenming Yuantou Xintan Dao Jia Yu Yizu Hu Yuzhouguan* (A New Investigation into the Origins of Chinese Civilization: Daoism and the Tiger World View of the Yi Minority) (Kunming: Yunnan People's Publishing Company, 1985).

The Nosu of Sichuan

The Independent Nosu

The Nosu who live in this area of some three hundred thousand square kilometers number about 1.5 million, slightly more than the Chinese population. They are called Independent Nosu, in that by contrast with the "dependent" Nosu south of the Yangzi River, they have stubbornly and militantly refused to submit totally to Chinese authority or to be assimilated by Chinese culture. This does not mean that they do not speak Chinese or have many Chinese customs. The Chinese called them *sheng yi* or unripe ones, while the dependent Nosu they referred to by the term *shu yi* or ripe ones.[7]

Even many of the cities of the Jianchang Valley, where the less militant and more sinicized of the Independent Nosu live, were fortified with walls, and individual homes outside of the city walls looked like small fortresses. When missionaries in the late 1940s went even into the lower mountains, it was necessary to arrange for guarantors who would assure their safety from one place to the next. The day of kidnaping and selling people as slaves was not a thing of the past.

The simmering hostility, always present between the Chinese in the valley and the Nosu, frequently broke into open warfare. The issues were usually opium, rifles, and slaves. Chinese bands made quick raids into the mountains, often to wreak revenge for some Nosu offense. This included the taking of a few heads, and within a few days the Nosu made a retaliatory raid on a Chinese village, with the same bloody consequences. It was not uncommon in the 1940s to see Chinese soldiers walking through city streets carrying on their backs baskets filled with Nosu heads, still dripping blood.

Names

The term *Nosu*, "black person," is used by the people in their own language to refer to all the people. Originally, its primary designation was to members of the pure-blooded ruling class. This class distinction, where it still exists, is indicated more precisely by He Yi (Black Nosu) or Bai Yi (White Nosu). Frequently, the term *Lolo* has been used to designate these people. This name probably originated with the Chinese, who thought

7. All of this material, except where otherwise noted, is taken from Ralph R. Covell, *The Challenge of Independent Nosuland* (Chicago: Conservative Baptist Foreign Mission Society, 1947). The data in Covell's booklet came from research in the libraries of the Royal Geographic Society in Shanghai and the West China Union University in Chengdu. It was supplemented by material from Dr. James Broomhall of the CIM and Dr. Levi Lovegren and John Simpson of CBFMS from their travels in Xikang during 1947.

that the Nosu kept the souls of their parents in miniature baskets or hampers. The Chinese word for this basket is *lolo*. However, the connotations of the term were vile—roughly comparable to a derogatory expression like "nigger," "chink," or "wop." Even worse, when the term was written in Chinese, the dog radical was used. Because of these connotations and the smoldering hatred between the two groups of people, the Nosu reacted with resentment whenever the Chinese called them *lolo*.

However, there is a legitimate term *lolo* that is used by the people themselves. Their principal totem animal over the centuries has been the tiger and, in their language, the term *lolo* means tiger. They can even refer to themselves as the "tiger nationality." The men call themselves *lolo po* or *lopo*, and the women use *lolo ma* or *loma*.[8] The reason the people reject the term *lolo* is that the Chinese use it in a derogatory sense.

Daily Life

The Nosu live in villages, often perched in precarious positions on the mountainsides. Many do not dwell in villages at all, but in dispersed, independent homes. The house of a family is always a unit by itself, but sometimes several houses are built side by side to form a hamlet. The house is built of wood supported by poles, walled with stamped earth and roofed with planks. Stones are placed in rows above the plank roof to prevent the house from being shaken by the wind. Around the house is a square enclosure surrounded by earthen walls, built higher than the house itself. In one corner of the enclosure may stand a watchtower, two or three stories high, in which the people place guns and weapons to protect the house from raids. The Nosu have little in the way of utensils. They eat squatting around the hearth, using only their hands or a crude wooden spoon to take the food from a communal dish. In some areas there are brightly painted serving trays and individual bowls made of wood. Their ordinary food is very crude; the basic dish is a bread cake of buckwheat made of badly kneaded, unleavened dough and containing little or no salt. To this buckwheat cake is added rice, potatoes, boiled or roasted in the ashes, and sometimes meat, which they prefer when only half cooked. Wheat is sometimes used to make gruel. The people seldom eat vegetables, and no use is made of milk or butter, rather strange for a people owning great herds of cattle. For special occasions the meal is more elaborate, containing much more meat and accompanied by an abundant supply of beer or wine.

The chief occupations of the Nosu are pastoral and agricultural. They have sheep, cattle, ponies, pigs, and various types of poultry. Nosu territory can never be economically independent of its neighbors, since no salt

8. *Yizu Wenhua Yenjiu Wenji*, 37.

is found in the area. Other necessities, such as cloth, needles, firearms, and ammunition must be obtained by trading wool, sugar, coal, and opium.

Social Culture

The Independent Nosu were divided into two classes—the Black Nosu and the White Nosu. The Blacks were the princes, lairds, landowners, and wealthy farmers. They were the pure-blooded descendants of the early Nosu. The Whites were the serfs, the slaves, farm laborers, and freemen tenants, subject to control by the Blacks. They are an amalgamation of Chinese and many minority peoples, enslaved during the centuries and now freely intermarried. These White Nosu lived near Chinese villages, were subject to Chinese authority, often adopted the Chinese style of dress, and frequently chose surnames from the Chinese Book of Family Names. This class division was not confined to Independent Nosuland. It also existed among the Nosu farther south. And even within Independent Nosuland, notably in the Xichang area, there were both Black Nosu and White Nosu who had been subjugated by the Chinese.

The complexity of the divisions and ramifications of this caste system make it difficult to generalize. Within the White class there were three degrees of serfdom. The first degree was little removed from slavery, but those who passed into the third degree were practically freemen and could own property and have their own serfs.

This system was rightly called feudal. The lords or Blacks rented the land to the Whites. The Whites had to give a certain proportion of the produce of their land to their overlords. In times of warfare between clans, they had to give military aid. On special occasions of birth, marriage, or death it was obligatory to give tribute. The obligation, however, was not totally one-sided. The Blacks on their part pledged their power to protect their serfs or slaves in case of conflict with the serfs or slaves of another lord. The children of the Whites were born to be slaves and were the property of their fathers' overlords. The children of the Blacks did not need to learn any occupations, except hunting for recreation. Their daughters were trained to manage the household affairs and held a high position in the family.

The clan was the most important unit of the social organization. A clan was a group of blood-related families. Property was transmitted and descent reckoned through the male. A woman who married into the clan lived in the husband's locality. These clans occupied several consolidated villages or were interpenetrated by other clans, but clan solidarity was strictly maintained. Within the clan there was no fighting, and all disputes were settled amicably by the mediating efforts of the elders.

Between clans, however, there was much fighting. Frequently, they organized into parties against one another, usually the clans related by marriage. If there was fighting between these larger groups, the women connected with both by marriage sought to be reconcilers. If verbal means were insufficient, one went to the battlefield and prostrated herself naked on the ground between the warring groups. This resulted in peace, but the woman, ashamed of her conduct, committed suicide.[9]

Apart from such convenient temporary alliances, there was no overall organization of these clans into one tribe with one central government. To this extent it is a mistake to refer to the Nosu tribesmen. The clan was the basic unit, and there really was no tribe.

In common with other aboriginal peoples, the Nosu had elaborate ceremonies to cremate their dead. Located near their villages were sacred groves. Trees here were not used for any purpose other than cremation. An offering of wine was poured out, and then the light was put to the funeral pyre. If the body burned readily, it was taken as evidence that the deceased was a good person. If it was difficult to get the body to burn, this was taken as an evil omen. When the body was finally reduced to ashes, it was covered with dirt. The relatives and friends then returned to the home of the deceased, ate the flesh of the animal that was killed, and drank wine. At one time it was thought that the choice between cremation and burial depended on whether the family was poor or rich. Yi writers now stress the fact that to cremate fits best with the ancient Nosu tradition. The Nosu, it is believed, are descendents of the tiger, and only by cremation is the soul freed to return to its original tiger state.[10]

Religious Life of the Nosu

The Nosu follow a popular folk religion with some traces of monotheism. The people believe in and fear both good and bad spirits—those of their ancestors and demons with unlimited supernatural power. They are in the grip of the demons, and all of life is interpreted in terms of these spirits who control all events, for either weal or woe. Beneath this frenzy of belief and activity directed toward the spirit world, there is still a lingering belief in a "high god." The Nosu believe in a supreme creator spirit, known as the "sky god" or the "god of heaven." He is invisible and has no image. This high god has a son who busies himself in the affairs of human beings and is called Gee Nyo.

One expression of the continuing belief in a high god is the Nosu concept of the *tian pusa* (heavenly god). This is expressed by the tuft of hair

9. Another observer noted that a woman only "takes off her outer skirt, trails it between the fighters, then whirls this garment around her head several times and orders them to disperse, which they feel honor bound to do." Robert Wellwood, "Ningyuanfu," *Baptist Missionary Union,* 1908, 382.

10. See material in *Yizu Wen Hua Yenjiu Wen Ji.*

that remains on the shaven head of many men, both young and old. This hair lock is termed the *tian pusa* and is considered so sacred that even the man's wife is not allowed to touch it. When the man wears a turban, he rolls a portion of it around this forelock of hair, and it projects like the horn of an animal. Often the end of the lock escapes in a little pack. The people recognize that it is the heavenly god who made them and continues to care for them. They profess to know nothing about this god, nor do they worship him in any way.

Elements of Daoism, shamanism, and fetishism are found among the Independent Nosu. Nosu sorcerers adore Lao Zi as the founder of their religion and the organizer of their scripture. His image is often found in their homes, and the names of Daoist gods worshiped in their ceremonies. This indigenous Chinese influence is all the more significant when one recognizes that Buddhism has had no impact at all on the Independent Nosu.

Liu Yaohan, a well-known Nosu author, has written an entire book suggesting that the ancient Yi culture is the origin of many basic Daoist beliefs. He argues, for example, that the yin and yang concept, so basic to Chinese thinking, originated with the *ci-xiong* duality found thousands of years ago among the Yi. He analyzes at great length the ten-month solar calendar of the Yi and shows its influence upon Chinese life.[11]

The influence of shamanism is seen both by the significant position of the sorcerers and by the emphasis placed on divination. All the sacred ceremonies, ritualistic sacrifices, exorcisms, oracles, divination, and sacramental formulas are in the hands of a sorcerer-priest known as the *bimo*. The name literally means "old man who understands moral and religious doctrines, teachings, and sacred books."[12] He is in charge of the religious life in each clan, and no religious ceremony would be complete without his presence and authority. All he does conforms to the formulas of the sacred books. He is the only master of the literature, and he fills the role of public writer or scribe for the nobles and princes and tutor for the small children. He encourages the nobles to know the national literature, of which the serfs and slaves are totally ignorant.

In common with beliefs of these traditional religionists worldwide, Nosu life was filled with taboos, incantations, and black magic. They elevated to the status of gods the forces of nature, such as thunder, lightning, the wind, mountains, sun, and moon. When an important leader got sick or died, hundreds or even thousands of sheep and cattle were slaughtered to fulfill all the demands of the spirit world. This, along with

11. See Liu, *Zhongguo Wenming Yuantou Xintan*, preface 1–25.

12. David Crockett Graham, *Folk Religion in Southwest China* (Washington, D.C.: Smithsonian Institution, 1961), 78.

the ravishing oppression of opium, kept the Nosu people in a never-ending cycle of poverty.

Nosu Writing

The Nosu language is a part of the Tibeto-Burman branch, which in turn is a part of the larger Sino-Tibetan family. Like Chinese, it is monosyllabic and tonal. Scholars of the Yi language recognize at least six major dialect areas in Sichuan, Guizhou, and Yunnan provinces.

The Nosu writing system was probably both phonetic and ideographic in ancient times—that is, it expressed both a meaning, often in picture form, and a sound value. Similar to the Chinese characters, the Nosu symbols represent an entire syllable and not just a single consonant or vowel. The writing was the property of the *bimo*. A priest's reputation rested on the number of written symbols he could read and write. This led each priest to invent new symbols, the better to confuse a neighboring *bimo*. In the early postwar years, each *bimo* probably had an inventory of five to six thousand symbols.

The manuscripts of the Independent Nosu represent Nosu thought. They are filled largely with religious sentiment and many magical incantations. From these manuscripts it is possible to get a picture of the myths and legends of the people. In common with other minority nationalities of southwest China, the Nosu have elaborate legends on the origin of the universe and of mankind. Some Nosu believe that they came from the calabash, and they give reverence to it as a symbol of fertility. Others of the independent Nosu and some dependent Nosu near the city of Chuxiong in Yunnan believe that the heavenly god created the people out of the snow that he sent down to the earth. This type of belief, among people who live in areas where it may snow heavily, lends some support to Chinese scholars who assert that the people's religion originated from their tendency to personify the forces of nature.

Nearly all of the minority peoples have a legend of a flood. The usual account is that only one couple, male and female, survived, married, and produced children. The Nosu twist to this tradition is that only one person survived and went to the heavenly kingdom, where he took a female genie (*xiannu*) as his wife.

The manuscripts contain material that reinforces the belief that the major totem animal for the Nosu is the tiger. We have already noted that the name *lolo* means tiger. Pictures may be found in the ancient Nosu manuscripts showing a tiger moving the universe, setting it in motion and sustaining it. The Nosu call Mount Omei, where some of them once lived, *lomo shan* or mother tiger mountain. At an earlier time in the history of the Nosu people, their priests wore a tiger skin. In some areas the Nosu put a drawing on the door of their homes that is pronounced *nie loma*. This is a type of ancestral tablet and means the "spirit of mother tiger." Scholars have also taken this to indicate that early Nosu society was matriarchal.

In some mythical way the mother tiger was involved in the creation of mankind. One interesting Chinese expression tells how "tiger blood became water and gave birth to mankind." One of the reasons the people give for cremating the dead is that this will enable the person to return to his or her original tiger state. Some manuscript material relates how the Nosu believed in a kind of "tiger divination" that enabled them to obtain success in planting good crops, in hunting, in building homes, in marriage, and in warfare.

More recently, some Nosu writers, possibly hoping to cause the Chinese to have a more progressive view of their people, suggest that this primitive tiger world view was later conceptualized in a more abstract way by Lao Zi and Zhuang Zi to become the *dao* of Chinese philosophy.[13]

The Yi of Yunnan Respond to the Christian Message

The Yi of Yunnan have been very similar, at least in general culture although not in language, to their cousins to the north. The fact that they assimilated to Chinese culture, lived closer to Chinese villages, and had long abandoned the savage customs of their ancestors meant that they were more receptive to both Catholic and Protestant missionaries and the message they brought.

Roman Catholic Efforts

During the seventeenth century it is probable that missionaries of the Society of Jesus came to Yunnan for survey trips and evangelization, although there is no reliable records of these forays. In 1702 Yunnan was committed to the care of the Foreign Mission Society of Paris (MEP) and Monsieur Leblanc was named the vicar apostolic of that province. Monsieur Gleyo began a work among the Lolos in the Zhaotong area in 1780 and felt that the best way to encourage faith among them would be to transplant a few "pious families," presumably Chinese, from Sichuan to live among them. No record exists as to the result of this effort.

In 1802 Monseigneur de Philomelie went into the area of Caojiang, about two-thirds of the way to Zhaotong from Kunming, to begin a pioneer work among the Lolos. The people were delighted to have their own priest. Wherever he and his helpers went, the Lolos wished to become Christians in groups. In five or six days he counted as many as five

13. This material on the tiger world view and its relationship to Daoism and ancient Chinese thought is found in Liu, *Zhongguo Wenmin Yuantou Xintan*.

hundred adorers. There were not sufficient catechists or school principals to give any grounding in the faith, and much of this momentum was lost. Eventually the missionaries mobilized more resources and sent two or three catechists from village to village to instruct catechumens, to baptize both adults and infants in danger of death, and to teach against the remaining superstitions of the people.

Local authorities resisted Catholic evangelism among the Lolos, preferring that the missionaries go instead to the nearby Miao areas. Eventually the MEP priests had to go to Kunming in order to obtain an edict that would enforce the treaties granting freedom of religion. These provisions not only granted liberty to preach the Christian faith, but also made it possible for the converts to be exempted from participating in the pagan superstitions.

In this early outreach, Catholic missionaries or their Chinese colleagues went as far north as Huili in what is now the southern part of Sichuan. In 1809 Monsieur Hamel sent Thomas Tsin into this area, and he founded five stations, baptized seventy-four adults, and registered the names of thirty-six catechumens.[14]

People Movements to Christ among the Protestants

The Lolo turning to Christ among the Protestants was part of the great Christian people movements among the neighboring Lisu and Miao peoples. Work among the southwest minorities began among the Miao in the Anshun area of Guizhou in 1896 (see chap. 4). The movement spread from there to Zhaotong and the nearby villages of Gebo, Hezhang, Zhenxiang, and Bijie in the Wu Mao mountain area near the Guizhou-Yunnan border. From there it jumped to Sapushan and Salowu in the Wuding area of Yunnan. The Miao believed in the thousands, and the Yi, initially at least, responded only by the tens and hundreds.

In the beginning, the Nosu in the Zhaotong and Wu Mao mountain areas were like an appendix to the Miao church, but their only hope for growth was to loosen this attachment. For the Miao to believe in Christ

14. The material in these several paragraphs comes from two principal sources: Adrien Launay, *Histoire des Missions de Chine Mission du Se-tchoan,* vols. 1 and 2 (Paris: P. Tequi, 1920), and M. Pourias, *La Chine Huits Ans au Yunnan* (Paris: Lille, Desclee, de Brouwer et Cie, 1892). Another work, George F. Wiseman, trans., *Kwangsi Land of the Black Banners* (London: Herder, 1942), mentions work among the Yi in the province of Guangxi. Paul Vial has written a large volume entitled *Les Lolos: Histoire, Religion, Moeure, Langue, Ecriture* (Changhai: La Mission Catholique, 1898), but he says nothing about Catholic missionary work among the Lolo. It is difficult to know about Catholic work into the twentieth century among the Lolos of Yunnan, because Catholic works seem to treat the minority peoples as an integral work of everything they do among the Han Chinese. Thus, it is difficult to determine from descriptions of churches, statistics, and other materials what is Han Chinese and what refers to any of the minority nationalities.

was itself an incentive for the Nosu not to accept the Christian doctrine. The Nosu needed their own buildings, organization, pastors to lead them, and a school. Although they had believed in much smaller numbers than did the Miao, even these numbers fell off when they understood that the Christian faith did not guarantee the economic and legal privileges they believed the foreign missionaries had brought.[15]

The springboard for reaching the Nosu in the Wuding area came from a group whom the Chinese called the Gopu, but who referred to themselves as the Gan Yi. Probably one of the branches of the Nosu, these people began to "study" Christ at Xinshao, after which some of them went on a preaching tour among the Nosu.[16] Their trumpet, unfortunately, did not give a true sound: "It is sad to say that their object was only worldly profit, promising converts freedom from taxation, sickness, calamity and death. They gave a false version of the Second Coming, telling the people they must repent by a set date—or it would be too late. Incidentally, they sold Christian books at double profit!"[17]

News that the Nosu were ready to receive Christ came to G. Porteous in 1910, and he responded to the invitation to be their missionary. Soon several churches were organized, and groups formed to reach out in evangelism. Lisu evangelists were prominent in this effort and gave much help in dealing with the many inquirers.

The revolution that deposed the Manchu dynasty in 1911 disrupted the work for a short time, but by 1912 the male missionaries returned to the area and continued their work. By 1914 each minority in the area had a few churches, and G. Nicholls, an Australian missionary with the CIM, helped to form the Six Nationalities Christian Association of North Yunnan. Each group had a specific center: the Lisu at Taogu, the Black Yi at Aguomi, the Dai at Laoban, the Miao at Sapushan, the Gan (Dry) Yi at Salowu, and, in 1917, the Gopu at Xunxun Xingshao.[18]

How many Nosu Christians were there in Yunnan in this initial period? Nicholls ordered seven thousand hymnals in 1916 and thousands of copies of Mark, but these may have only been inquirers, for by 1932 the number of church members was put at only six hundred.[19] Baptisms did not come easily. Inquirers were usually instructed for two to three years, both by Lisu evangelists helping in the work and by the missionaries. An equal number of men and women were numbered among those bap-

15. For an account of the experiences of some Christians in the Zhaotong area consult James Broomhall, *Strong Tower* (London: CIM, 1947).

16. With many in the traditional religions the term *study* means to inquire about Christ, to learn about him, or even to believe in him.

17. T. Mulholland, "Amongst the Tribes," *China's Millions,* July 1932, 131.

18. "Minority Churches in Yunnan," *Bridge,* May-June 1987, 11.

19. See *China's Millions,* January 1916, 12, and Mulholland, "Amongst the Tribes," 131.

tized. While missionaries were important in the work, they were also the prime targets of the bandit groups that roamed unimpeded through this territory. Wisdom dictated that responsibility in the ministry be turned over to local leaders as quickly as possible.

Very soon, then, the missionaries established training programs to produce leaders. A primary school was started in Salowu, two one-month Bible schools were held annually in Salowu for deacons, elders, and preachers, and eventually a permanent Bible school was established there. All three served not only the Nosu, but other nearby nationalities as well. The United Tribal School was often shifted to other areas in Yunnan, so as to be more accessible to all the minority peoples. Instruction was in Chinese and had a practical emphasis, teaching students to preach, to evangelize, and to be able to form singing groups in churches. Finances were always a problem, but usually parents and local churches were willing to help. Beginning in 1937, revival meetings, sparked by Dan Smith of the CIM and local minority evangelists, resulted in several hundred families embracing the Christian faith over the following three years. Beginning at this time, some of the Yunnan Nosu committed themselves to the task of evangelism among their highly resistant cousins to the north.

The Nosu New Testament was completed for the Black Yi[20] in 1941, but the war of resistance against Japan meant that the churches could not get it before 1949. Following the advent of the People's Republic of China in 1949, the Nosu church in Yunnan went through the same ups and downs, zigs and zags as the Han Chinese church. By the mid-1980s the number of Nosu Christians in the Salowu area had increased to at least five thousand, and their church building, seating two thousand, is now the largest Protestant church building in Yunnan Province. Their New Testament, using the Pollard script, was reprinted by the Amity Press in Nanjing in 1988, and the hymn book was reprinted as well. At present, local pastors from both the Black Yi and Gan Yi are participating in a translation project sponsored by the United Bible Societies that will revise old translations and create new ones, both in a romanized script more functional than the old Pollard orthography.

While the obstacles from brigandage, persecution, hard travel, and the usual resistance to the gospel message have been present, Christianity has taken deep root among the Yi peoples of Yunnan. In Guizhou the Yi are often a small percentage of villages that are largely populated by Miao. In Yunnan, north and west of Kunming, the Yi exist more as separate, dis-

20. In Sichuan there was a rigid distinction between the aristocratic Blacks and the servile Whites, who had been enslaved by them over the years. In Yunnan these distinctions were being erased, and all of one group of Yi were referred to as Black Yi. The Gan Yi belong to another group.

crete communities. The total church population may be as high as thirty to forty thousand. Why has this not happened among the Yi of Sichuan? The key for resolving this question can come only by analyzing both Roman Catholic and Protestant efforts among the Independent Nosu, high in the Great Cool Mountains, only two hundred miles north of Salowu.

Resistance to the Christian Faith among the Independent Nosu in Sichuan

Roman Catholic Penetration among the Savage Lolo

The first Catholic mission was a small school for Lolo[21] priests in far north Yunnan in the 1790s. Missionaries did not begin a formal work north of the Yangzi until 1802, when they came to Huili at the southernmost edge of the territory. For Catholics this isolated area in eastern Tibet was "too high and too far," but they gave it their best effort. Gradually other priests and catechists worked their way north, until by the late 1800s chapels, schools, and even dispensaries could be found in the larger centers of Mianning, Lugu, Lizhou, Xichang (then Jianchangfu or Ningyuanfu), and Dechang, as well as in the larger villages surrounding these cities.

Very soon the work divided itself naturally into three areas: the Lolo area in the high mountains; the plains areas that were not under the immediate control of Chinese officials; and the plains areas controlled by the Chinese.[22] The desire of the missionaries was to plant a strong church among the savages in the mountains, but the opposition from both the Nosu and the Han Chinese was too great. They had to settle for spreading the faith among the Chinese.

Not that the missionaries did not itinerate in the high mountain areas or have significant contacts with Nosu leaders and their followers. Monseigneur de Guebriant, the first apostolic vicar when the area was elevated to this status in 1910 and later to become the Superior General of the Foreign Mission Society of Paris, lived in several cities in the Jianchang Valley from 1893 to 1898 and again from 1903 to 1910. He traveled constantly among Chinese centers, but also to isolated villages in the mountains. Here he found Xifan minorities or the Lolo, and occasionally some Tibetans or other minority peoples.

21. I use the term *Lolo* in the text to follow the usage of the missionaries working among them at that time.

22. The sources for this account of the Roman Catholic work are *Les Missions Catholiques,* particularly 1924–1945; *Annales de la Societe des Missions-Etrangeres,* 1924–38; *Bulletin de la Societe des Missions-Etrangeres de Paris,* 1924, 1927; *Echos de la rue du bac,* January 1990; and a large volume on the life of Monseigneur de Guebriant.

Roman Catholic Missiological Principles

Wherever he went, de Guebriant looked for significant chiefs whose conversion might spark a mass movement to Christ. He spoke of one Lolo chief in the mountains near Ningyuanfu who wanted to embrace Christianity and bring with him into the church thousands of his serfs. All were prepared to call themselves Christians and claim Christianity as their only religion. De Guebriant was ready to follow through on this. He was not certain about the local priest. This man was pleased that a mass conversion would reduce the dangers the mission faced from the Lolos. He was also frightened, not knowing if he was ready to lead such a large movement. Apparently the chief changed his mind or the Catholic priest continued in his fears.

At a later time de Guebriant related the story of another chief, Lan Haoyan, who possessed much land and many slaves and Chinese tenants who wished to become Christians. De Guebriant held Mass for him in his home, the first time for this kind of religious ceremony among the Lolos. What blocked this effort? Apparently local Chinese officials who were nervous about this type of foreign incursion into a sensitive minority area. In his many travels, this ambitious, creative Catholic missionary seemed always to be on the verge of seeing important clan chieftains ready to declare their faith. How sincere were these apparent inquiries about the Christian faith? Clan leaders were always anxious to obtain missionary help for medical clinics or schools. They may have believed that the missionaries possessed power to give them an advantage over their enemies. However, if any one of these efforts had succeeded, it might have created a foothold for an ongoing work with more possibility of success than that produced by individual, isolated conversions.

Unfortunately, the favor of one clan chief and his followers often produced enmity with another one. Father Baptistin Biron, originally stationed at Suifu, had well-developed plans for living in Lolo country. He first settled in Mabian, and then, with permission from his Catholic authorities and from the local clan chieftain, Zhouke, he moved to Cheu Peu Nia Kia in 1931. All seemed to be in place and orderly, with every necessary precaution taken. But then a few Lolos, controlled by another chief, possibly irked that Biron had not come to live in his territory, argued with the priest and killed him. The annals of the MEP described him as "a victim of the savage Lolos."

Once, when de Guebriant was visiting with Lolos above the village of Ya Long, hoping to have a breakthrough for faith, another clan attacked the village, burning the chief's home, killing his sister, and seriously injuring his wife. The independence and isolation of each clan, with its ongoing cycle of being attacked and taking revenge, defeated hopes of any interclanal turning to the Christian faith.

Missionaries often had their first contact with the Nosu when they attempted to rescue Chinese Christians and their villages from the ravages of fierce Lolo raids. The village of Yang Cao Ba, the center of a large revenue-producing area purchased by the mission, had been badly pillaged. Eventually, as a result of missionary favor to the clan chief, he promised not to harm the Christians and to allow other Christian families to be moved to this territory. This village was in the plains, but still in territory controlled by the Lolos. Nothing was more fearful for Chinese in the Jianchang area than to face nightly attacks by the Lolos.

On one visit to Eul Se Yn, slightly to the northwest of Lugu over the mountains, de Guebriant found a group of Christians who had been released from captivity by the Lolos. Should he organize them into a church and arrange for the beginning of services? He concluded that this was too precarious, for the vindictive Lolos wanted to kidnap them again.

Another type of relationship that the missionaries had with the Lolos was to seek to rescue Chinese, Christian or non-Christian, who had been kidnaped by them. The Christians found it easy to rebuke the missionaries for their impotence, to pout and forsake the Christian faith, or to move to another area where there was less danger. But to rescue a captive was complex, often involving ransoms and complicated negotiations over a long period of time. Kidnaping was a long-standing Lolo custom—this is how they had developed their feudal society with its blacks, whites, serfs, and slaves. Why give it up under the vain threats and/or inducements of the Catholic church?

At times, the church did not need to intervene. Jeune Pen, the young daughter of a catechumen at Yang Cao Ba, was kidnaped about 1920 and held for ten years before she managed to escape and make her way back to Chinese society. She had tried to get away several times previously, only to be recaptured by a different clan that then sold her back to the clan that had kidnaped her. Now that she had returned safely to Chinese society, church leaders used her knowledge of the Lolo culture and language by making her the mistress of a Lolo school.

The missionaries were always disturbed by the incessant fighting between the Lolos and the Chinese, who periodically mounted campaigns to exterminate them, often engaging in barbarous acts that went beyond even the horrors of war. De Guebriant specifically mentioned the time in 1908 when soldiers from Chengdu went to the village of Gailaho and massacred women and children. Three hundred of the men were led away captive and then decapitated. De Guebriant mentioned a special "sacrifice to the flag," at which time the blood of a cow was sprinkled on the flag as a type of good omen to prepare the Chinese soldiers for battle.

On this occasion a Lolo hostage was sacrificed five hundred meters outside the Ningyuanfu wall, his blood sprinkled on the flag, his throat cut, and his heart and liver taken home to be eaten by the soldiers. As late as the early 1930s the Chinese were executing Lolos by the hundreds, crucifying their chiefs and burying them alive. None of these activities subdued the Lolos; if anything they always retaliated viciously against Chinese villages. Fighting was a way of life for them, and the loss of even a large number of people did not deter them.

One missionary task, then, was to promote reconciliation between the Nosu and the Chinese. A particularly wrenching case involved a fifteen-year-old Black Nosu boy, the son of a Nosu chieftain, who was studying at the Catholic school in Ho Si. When a dispute broke out between his father's clan and the Chinese, he was pressed into duty as an intermediary and was killed in the process. A Catholic priest was nearby as he was dying and received from him a clear confession of his faith in Christ. De Guebriant called him the first Black Nosu to die as a Christian and then referred to his death as a type of "expiation for the crimes of his race."

Obstacles to Roman Catholic Work

What kinds of obstacles did the Catholics face in their work, apart from the difficulties of establishing satisfactory relationships with the Nosu? Chinese officials, often with what the missionaries called an anti-French bias, opposed them at nearly every step, refusing to allow new priests to take their posts, resisting the free preaching of the gospel, persecuting local converts, and taking no steps to protect them from Nosu raids. The priests also deeply resented the opposition they faced from converts in the churches that had been established by the American Baptist Foreign Missionary Society. Accusing the Baptists of aligning with secret societies, they frequently asked local magistrates to solve their inter-religious disputes. The situation was particularly tense in the early 1900s, immediately after the Baptists had commenced their work.

Internally, the greatest problem that the Catholics faced was the lack of local catechists who could break the ice with pagans and new Christians in front-line evangelism and prepare the way for follow-up work by the priests. Schools were established in every center, and eventually there was a seminary in Ningyuanfu, but these were predominately for Chinese leaders. Despite their hopes, the Catholics never had any real breakthrough with the Nosu. Some individual Nosu believed, but these were absorbed into Chinese churches that, by their very nature, were not bridges for outreach into the minority communities. The Franciscan Sisters of Mary arrived in the 1920s, but they had no more success in penetrating Nosu society than did the priests of the Paris Missionary Society.

De Guebriant commented that this area was more "a Chinese colony than a territory of the Chinese empire." Any change on the national scene produced tidal waves in this part of China, so infested was it with bandits, potential rebels, and many unlawful elements, all doped by the ever-present opium. Father Castanet was killed south of Huili by bandits in the revolution of 1911. A serious Nosu revolt in 1917 totally disrupted the work. Missionaries and many of their students fled south from Ningyuanfu in 1935, when the encroaching Communist forces destabilized society. Father P. Boiteux was killed in the disturbances of 1945.

Catholic Christians continue to live out their faith today in Xichang, Mianning, and Dechang. Their churches in these cities are for Han Chinese, and there is no Nosu church. Their well-intentioned effort, led often by capable and energetic missionaries and planted by the seed of several martyrs, has produced no lasting result among the minority peoples of Independent Nosuland.

American Baptists Prepare a Steppingstone to Burma

The American Baptists had established a strong mission base in Sichuan, with centers in Chengdu, Suifu, Leshan, and Yaan. To try to do something in the distant Jianchang Valley, twelve difficult days of walking over high mountains from Yaan to the north, represented a formidable challenge. The new station was to be a steppingstone mission station toward Burma, which, since the days of Adoniram Judson, had been one of the Baptists' great mission fields.

Robert Wellwood and his wife, the family most identified with the Baptist work among the Nosu, first reached Ningyuanfu in the summer of 1905. He was born in Ireland and she in Germany. They met when both were serving with the China Inland Mission in west China. After their marriage, they were appointed with the ABFMS, and in 1905 assigned to work in Ningyuanfu. No sooner had the Wellwoods arrived in this distant station than they were caught up in a struggle with the Roman Catholics. The precise nature of this unfortunate dispute is unclear. Wellwood saw it as "Catholic oppression and persecution," fomented by priests and local leaders who were in an ongoing battle with Chinese officials who opposed them. The struggle was a "work for humanity." He reported that local people regarded the French as "without conscience."[23]

23. This quotation is from Wellwood letter file, 18 September 1905. These files are to be found at the American Baptist Archives, Valley Forge, Penn. Other materials used in this section on the American Baptists are ABFMS West China, Field Minutes; *The West China Missionary News;* and *The Baptist Missionary Magazine.*

The Catholics accused the Baptists of siding with the Chinese officials against the French, of uniting with the secret societies against them, of stirring up their Christians to attack the Catholics, and of being totally "without conscience." The religious warfare brewed for two or three years, and then it seemed to disappear—or at least it no longer was in the headlines. If it was no longer active, it was not soon forgotten, and when new missionary forces arrived in this area in 1947, local people gave a blow-by-blow account of what had happened.

Within two years Wellwood had purchased, leased, or rented suitable premises for mission work in nine cities or villages. He had already engaged in long itineration trips from one end of the field to the other. The response to the Christian message was encouraging. The First Baptist Church of Ningyuanfu was organized on 29 September 1907 with ten recently baptized men of "good social standing, highly intelligent and well-regarded." By the end of 1908 forty more were baptized, thirty-seven men and three women from fifteen districts. Two years later about the same number were baptized. Although the new converts were from the entire area, this response was an encouragement to other missionaries—evangelists, doctors, nurses, and teachers—who were coming to augment the work. One notable problem was evident—none of those baptized were Nosu, the group for whom the Baptists had expressed a special concern and who were one of the main reasons for their coming into the area.

The revolution of 1911 slowed down the flow of baptisms for at least two years. Although this area of China was hardly in the mainstream of Chinese life, the anti-Christian movement was very active. Missionaries also feared that England's position in advocating independence for Tibet might increase the antiforeign attitude. The results might be even more disastrous if the tribes, wishing to be as independent as Tibet, rebelled against the new government. It appeared that a new anti-Republican government might be established in Chongqing that in turn might stir up rebel activities about Ningyuanfu.

Some of the fears were justified. When the revolution of 1911 brought an end to the Manchu dynasty, a group of local rebels called the Railway League, with compatriots in Chengdu, attacked government offices in Ningyuanfu, beheaded the magistrate, commenced a battle with the prefect and his soldiers, and released all the prisoners in the jail. The rebels soon retreated to Lushan, a sacred mountain across Qionghai Lake from the city, only to return a day later to continue the battle. Eventually, forces loyal to the new Republican government won the day, beheading 350 people in the rebel force. Foreigners were not exempted from the danger, and the missionary women left the Baptist compound to stay overnight with some of the church members. Wellwood and his colleagues in this danger zone reflected long on the fact that they in Ningyuanfu and one missionary in Yaan, of all the missionaries in west China, had failed to heed the consular warning to evacuate to a safe place until the troubles subsided.

The population of Huili, one hundred miles to the south, was also ready to erupt in a strong antiforeign animus. Public signs had been put up saying that "foreigners are to be protected according to the treaties." These were erased with the substitute phrase that foreigners were to be exterminated. Unlawful rebels dismantled the chapel, stole books and furniture, and destroyed everything else. The Baptists claimed a small indemnity for the losses they suffered at this time.

Two years later, the zigs and zags of Yuan Shikai, as he went from president to emperor to president, sparked a new wave of troubles. The troops in the Jianchang area were sent south to suppress the Yunnan Rebellion whose leader was opposed to Yuan, either as emperor or president. With the troops protecting Ningyuanfu off on this foray to the south, groups of Lolo descended on several villages around the city, kidnaping and selling for slaves several hundred people. These were raids to avenge a serious Lolo loss near Huili a few weeks earlier. Chinese soldiers surprised a group of Lolo near Huili, killing several hundred of them. Jubilant in victory, the Chinese loaded four ponies with Lolo heads to bring them to Ningyuanfu. Since this load was too heavy, the Chinese cut off the ears and brought them into the city to be presented to their commander.

With the political changes in China in 1911 and the subsequent confusion, the new government issued paper money unacceptable to the local people. When soldiers could not exchange one dollar of this new money for one dollar's worth of the old silver dollars, they rioted, plundering homes and shops. This in turn disorganized trade and commerce, caused the merchants to fear investing their capital, and brought the economy to a standstill. The widespread planting and use of opium throughout the area, worse now than before the Manchu dynasty fell, only added to everyone's economic miseries.

Baptist work in Ningyuanfu and the entire area had many facets. Evangelism was primary, and Wellwood took some long evangelistic trips that lasted for two or three months. A small hospital and several dispensaries were established, and medical personnel busied themselves treating goiters, leprosy, and other diseases. They also held clinics giving treatment for opium addiction and binding up the wounds of the attackers and attacked in the many local conflicts. In one year they handled as many as eight thousand patients, but they were always short of personnel, facilities, medicine, time, and money. Of even more concern was their inability to follow up spiritually the many to whom they were bringing some measure of physical healing.

Unsettled political and social conditions and adverse health problems made it difficult for medical personnel to continue in the work. And, as they left, it meant that other missionaries, often with small children, were not willing to live and work in this isolated area where they were not able to deal adequately with family medical emergencies.

In Wellwood's view, the key to the work in the Jianchang area was to have good schools. Preaching halls and schools went together in all of the centers of work. In most villages the schools were small, but in Ningyuanfu there were nearly one hundred students in each of the boys' and girls' schools. In this central city missionaries held Bible training institutes for two months in the summer. In view of their expressed need for twenty evangelists and fifty teachers, the missionaries also held a Bible training class in Ningyuanfu for seven months, with heavy emphasis on biblical studies, preaching, and church history. Anyone who wished specific, long-term training for church ministry was sent to the seminary in Chengdu.

Missionaries came and left in rapid succession, finding the isolation and local difficulties more than they could manage. The Wellwoods delayed their furlough for one year in 1915, but the needs of their children demanded that they return to America in 1916. He felt it good to leave the teachers and pastors on their own for one year. Beyond this, he feared that the schools would need to close down and the parents, students, and government would lose faith in the mission. While his wife remained in Dayton, Ohio, Wellwood, as did many other missionaries during the war years, went to France to serve alongside many Chinese in the work of the YMCA. There he was killed in a bombing attack by the Germans in May 1918.

Wellwood's death accelerated the process of disengagement of the mission from Ningyuanfu. Few missionaries, the isolation of the field, the inability to have a productive work among the Nosu, unusually volatile local conditions—all of these led to this conclusion. Even more definitive was the recommendation of Henry Robins, the Foreign Secretary for Asia of the ABFMS. In his report of 1921 he concluded that the work in Ningyuanfu should never have been started—it could not be integrated with the other stations, it was a detached work, and, most important, it did not fit in with the "intensive policy" in west China. He commented, "We may there spread ourselves more or less ineffectively over wide stretches of country to find the same number of people that we have right at our door in such cities as Suifu, Chengdu, Kiating and Yachow." This was good general policy for the mission around the world, but once again it meant that the unreached Nosu were still unreached.

When the American Baptists left, they turned their work over to the local Chinese, but then, in 1921, they invited the Australian Church of Christ to take over the field. The Australians were never able to occupy more than Huili at the very southern end of the area. By 1926 they reported that the scenario had not changed: soldiers not sufficient to protect the city from "barbarians," work in chapels and schools curtailed, antiforeign placards and demonstrations, missionaries coming and going, not enough personnel to do what they wished to do. They continued to send a few missionaries in the late 1920s and 1930s, but by the time of World War II they turned the mission over to the China Home Mission Society, who maintained work among the Chinese until 1950.

Whether the Australians or the China Home Mission Society, the focus of the work gradually shifted to the Chinese, always more ready to respond, albeit in small numbers, than were the Nosu.

A Chinese-Controlled Church Mission Agency Enters Nosuland

Every effort until 1940 to bring the Christian message to the Nosu and to other borderlands of China had been spearheaded by foreign mission agencies and expatriates. But several Chinese had a different vision. Made refugees in west China during the war of resistance with Japan from 1937 to 1945, they learned by experience for the first time of the large number of nationalities in the "back water of the human stream." How could these people be served in Jesus' name? With the encouragement of Cheng Chingyi, moderator of the Church of Christ in China, and H. H. Kong of the Kuomintang, Christian leaders organized the Border Service Department of the Church of Christ in China. A department of the Church of Christ in China, but with an autonomous board of directors, this was a church-centric service organization to work cooperatively with appropriate government agencies in serving the needs of peoples in border areas of China.

The Border Service Department (Bianjiang Fu Wu Bu) had three areas of ministry: the Qiang people of Sichuan; the Xifan people, numbering about one million, who lived west of the Qiang toward Tibet; and the minority peoples of the Xikang Province, particularly the Nosu. Its personnel saw the Nosu as unique: "the black sheep among the minorities of China" and "the spoiled child of the China family throughout history."

Headed by W. B. Djang, who had served as professor of New Testament at the Cheeloo School of Theology in Jinan, Shandong, this service agency made a balanced use of trained Chinese men and women professionals and foreign missionaries willing to work with it in a cooperative relationship. It was funded by Chinese churches and foreign mission societies. Unfortunately, finances were always the weak point of the effort:

> The problem of support is the most baffling of all. The Border Mission has been leading a life of stringency from the beginning. After the first year it was in debt all the time. On more than three occasions the very meagre support of the workers had to be suspended in part; and even boiling water for office staff had to be rationed to a very limited extent.[24]

The lack of finances created a crisis for the organizational structure of the Border Service Mission. To receive more money from western sources, as one of the leaders commented, meant that "we need to have western friends in control of things, whether openly so or in a submerged form." This tendency was resisted, because those expatriates in the best position to influence the direction of the mission, such as Archie Crouch, had a clear vision of the unique role that the agency must fill at this point in China's Christian history.

For Crouch, the advantages of such a mission were several. First, it was a united approach bringing together Chinese and expatriates, as well as various expatriate groups, for a focus on the minority peoples of China. In his view, "if Western agencies carry out their program as independent and competitive Western ventures, they are predetermined to comparative failure with a heavy loss of previous human energy and hard-earned funds." Second, it had the possibility of receiving government subsidy to meet the types of needs that churches alone would not be able to meet. Third, the gospel will meet less resistance in these sensitive areas if the first contact for Christ is not made by westerners. Fourth, in meeting a wide range of human needs, personnel will be able to present the "Gospel of Attraction" that "without great public excitement, disturbances and bizarre street scenes" will be able to live out the Christian faith in community and attract by the power of the Christian life. Crouch feared that in sensitive minority areas, everything could be ruined by evangelistic methods that would only repel, rather than attract.

In keeping with this policy, the work of the Border Service Mission was broadly holistic, aiming to integrate medicine, education, economic improvement, social service, and evangelism. The policy of the mission on evangelism received different emphases in different documents. Whole statements were devoted to amplifying what was meant by evangelism, how it was to be done, in what language, in what manner, and with what hopes. In other documents, it was never mentioned. Cooperating with government agencies that were nonreligious undoubtedly dictated the type of policy statements to be made for particular situations.

24. This quotation, as well as the other material in this section, is taken from the Border Service Department files deposited in the John Mott Archives at the library of the Yale Divinity School.

In actual ministry, the prominence of evangelism depended to a large extent on the particular workers who were involved.

What specific types of ministries did the Border Service personnel have in the Cool Mountain area? In Xichang (the new name for Ningyuanfu) they had a church for the Chinese, a hospital with one hundred beds, a kindergarten for Chinese and Nosu children, and a Nosu hostel. In five outstations they ran schools, clinics, hostels, experimental farms, and rural industrial work. Three of the schools they ran in the outstations were entirely for the Nosu, and one was for both Chinese and Nosu. The mission personnel had hopes that within a few years they would be able to open a total of fifteen stations, with a staff of at least twenty expatriate missionaries and one hundred Chinese colleagues in various posts.

The primary focus of the mission was on the Nosu, but it was inevitable that many of its services would also benefit the Chinese. Certainly the church in Xichang did not attract many Nosu to Christ—it was largely Chinese. The same could be said about some other types of institutional work that was done in the cities and larger towns. What the mission called its Type B work—primary schools, vocational training institutes, citizenship and leadership training classes, peasant gospel schools, and social and economic improvement work—was directed toward mountain areas and needed the approval and cooperation of clan chieftains.

One of the more useful features of the work in Xichang was the hostel for the Nosu. This provided shelter and protection, the opportunity in the city for fellowship and entertainment, first aid, and advice on how to carry on business in the large city, so different from their mountain homes. Missionaries used hostels extensively in north China for contact with Tibetans, Muslims, and Mongolians.

The folk schools in the mountains gave the best ongoing services to the Nosu community. Built of adobe, these simple buildings serviced up to thirty children who were taught a variety of useful subjects, including the Christian faith. The aim was to produce strong local Christian leaders. The students lived on the school premises throughout the school year. A teaching post in the mountains was not exempt from its problems—one teacher was murdered and another one was imprisoned for a short period.

As I noted at the beginning of this chapter, Nosuland came into worldwide prominence with the loss of American airplanes in its wild jungles as they were flying over the hump from Burma to Chengdu. The Chinese government or its air force was not viewed favorably by the Nosu, because of the longtime hatred between the Nosu and the Chinese. So the government turned to the Border Service Mission as an intermediary to negotiate with the Nosu for the safety and return of any

U.S. air personnel lost in the area. The mission negotiated with both sides in seeking to deal with this matter. The best that was turned up was the location of downed aircraft. Presumably the crews were killed in the crash.

Any lasting work among the Nosu requires far more time than that allotted to the Border Service Mission from the early 1940s to 1950. Its work was impressive and was gaining momentum. The Nosu seemed open and receptive, both to its social services and its presentation of the Christian faith. Years of resistance, suspicion, hostility, and indifference, however, are not whisked away in a span of eight or nine years. This short time, however, might have been even more productive had the China Inland Mission and the Conservative Baptist Foreign Mission Society (CBFMS), both of whom came in the post-World War II years, felt themselves free to cooperate with the Border Service work.

Two New Agencies Enter Nosuland in the Post-World War II Period

The China Inland Mission had long been interested in the Independent Nosu. Various ones of their missionaries, beginning with George Nicoll and Charles Leaman in 1878, had traveled through or near the area and were concerned to bring the gospel to them. Dr. James Broomhall, a CIM medical missionary, had formerly lived in Jiegou, Guizhou Province, and from this base had had considerable contact with the wild Nosu who lived across the Yangzi River in what was then the province of Xikang, or eastern Tibet. This renewed for him his vision of seeing these people come to Christ in the same way as the sinicized Nosu had responded in Guizhou and Yunnan provinces.

By the mid-1940s Broomhall had organized a team of five expatriate adults. They used Xichang as a supply base, but pushed on to Zhaojue, at that time five days by horse or mule east of Xichang, in the very heart of Nosu country. In contrast with groups who had worked earlier in this area and seen their focus on the Nosu diluted by access to and the response of the Chinese, Broomhall and his party wanted to immerse themselves in Nosu life.

Soon Broomhall had a home built for himself and his family, commenced language study with his colleagues, established a small medical facility, and ministered to the Nosu in and about Zhaojue. The people were grateful for this demonstration of compassion and care. They listened, usually respectfully, to the gospel message. Apart from the early conversion in 1947 of Broomhall's interpreter, however, there was little response right up until the new government was about to come and the missionaries were prepared to leave. About thirty-five trusted Christ at this time, both Nosu and Chinese, but no time remained to organize them into a worshiping community that has had any continuing Christian witness in Zhaojue.

More than any other group up to this time Broomhall sought to draw upon the resources of the Nosu church in Yunnan. Several Nosu Christians came from Yunnan and Guizhou to help. They found it very difficult to adjust to the differences in language, culture, and general lifestyle and soon returned to their homes in the south. Despite the difficulties of using Christians from these southern churches, this still seems to be the most fruitful pattern to bring the gospel to Independent Nosu today. Government bans on travel and on preaching, as well as the strictures of the "three designates," imposed by the Sichuan Provincial Three-Self Committee, militate against this.[25]

The CIM team was made up of old China hands who knew Chinese well, who understand China's culture, and who jumped in immediately to this new minority language and culture. By contrast, the Baptist team that entered Nosuland in 1947 to 1948 consisted of eighteen members, only four of whom had had any China experience at all.[26] The remaining fourteen were well educated in a variety of disciplines, largely theology, committed to Christ and his church. Culturally, however, they were ill-prepared for the rigors of the task before them.

These missionaries quickly spread out from Xichang as the center of their work to Lugu in the north and to Huili in the south. They hoped, ultimately, to have personnel in Yuexi, Mianning, and Lizhou to the north and possibly in Dechang in the south. Apart from Dr. and Mrs. Lovegren, Esther Nelson, and John Simpson, all were deeply involved in the study of Chinese. This meant that the chapels opened, the Bible studies conducted, and the rural evangelism focused on the Chinese. No time and energy were left to learn the Nosu language or to focus on this minority people who were the *raison d'etre* of the mission.

The missionaries took survey trips into Nosu country, always accompanied by the necessary guarantors. They made some beginning efforts at language study, spent a few days in Nosu villages, and witnessed to

25. I asked Bishop K. H. Ting what might be the problems for Nosu evangelists from Yunnan to proclaim the gospel among their cousins to the north. He mentioned that the basic difficulty might be the use of the "three designates" by the Sichuan Provincial Three-Self Committee. He noted that this was not a national policy, but that some provincial committees had developed it. It means that only a designated *person* can preach in a designated *place* at a designated *time*. The material on the work of the CIM in Nosuland comes from several issues of *China's Millions,* the book written by James Broomhall, *Strong Man's Prey* (London: CIM, 1953), and from personal conversations with Dr. Broomhall.

26. The detailed story of the Baptist work may be found in Ralph R. Covell, *Mission Impossible: The Unreached Nosu on China's Frontier* (Pasadena: Hope, 1990).

them as they strayed into Chinese-speaking chapel services. They also ministered to their physical needs at a medical clinic in Lugu and through weekly mobile medical trips to a few villages around Lugu. Good personal contacts were developed with a few Nosu clan chiefs, but these tended to be those who were more friendly to the Chinese and had become partly sinicized.

As was the case with the Border Service Mission and the CIM, the work might have stabilized and accomplished some of its goals had there been the possibility of thirty years of ministry. These people do not respond readily to new people, to new world views, to new messages, to a new life. Could the message proclaimed have been more relevant? Probably.

> Such tribes . . . seem so unapproachable that sometimes one wonders whether work among them should not be given up. But are they really barren soil? Are they actually irreligious or merely unresponsive because they cannot accept our presentation of the Gospel? May it not be that they are more difficult because they take religion more seriously, or because they are not wordminded so that word-preaching does not appeal to them, or because they need more adequate ways of approach than have yet been found?[27]

External obstacles made the task of those missions who came during and after World War II to be a "mission impossible." Very poor or nonexistent transportation, a hopeless Nosu script under the control of the priests, the rampant use of opium, interclan warfare among the Nosu and mutual head-taking raids between them and the Chinese, constant strife between a number of local Chinese armies, the isolation of the area, and the ongoing civil war with an uncertain outcome made most of the work ineffective.

Would any of these problems have been easier to solve had there been a unified approach by these three mission groups? That is difficult to say, but the Border Service leaders did make overtures to the CIM and to the Baptists. "Going it alone" is a luxury of the western world and its churches. But in such a sensitive area as Nosuland it would have been most useful, albeit a bit clumsy, to present a united Christian front to people who have resisted the gospel over nearly two hundred years. They had little idea of what the Christian faith was all about, let alone to distinguish among the differences in its expression.

An armed uprising by the Nosu was put down by force by the Chinese army in 1958,[28] but they hardly view themselves as subdued by the Chi-

27. Ts'ai Yung Ch'un, "The Call of the Border Tribes," *The Chinese Recorder,* April 1941, 186.

28. *London Daily Express,* 18 February 1958.

nese. Although more sinicized than in 1950, they still maintain their old clan independence. Most still believe in the heavenly Pusa and participate in their ancient religious traditions. But many of the earlier external obstacles—poor transportation, no useful script for the language, an economy based on opium, constant warfare and head-taking—are no longer present. God may yet use Chinese or other minority churches to bring them the liberating message of Jesus.

10

Cutting the Ancient Cords

The Lahu and Wa Are Liberated from Demons

Introduction

The people who approached William Young on that day in 1904 at Kengtung, Burma, close to the southwestern border of China, had a strange request. "Come and cut the cords from our wrists and neck," they implored. Taken back by their evident sincerity, he could only ask them to explain what they wanted. The leader, a member of one branch of the Lahu people, gave the puzzled missionary a full explanation of why they had come:

> From ancient times we have had the custom of wearing cotton cords around our wrists and neck. They are a constant reminder to us not to forsake our tradition of belief in one God and our pledge not to drink liquor or follow after any evil. They also remind us that one day a foreign teacher will come and teach us more about the God we worship. Only then are we free to cut the cords, for it shows that our longing has been fulfilled.[1]

Young was no neophyte missionary. He knew well the traditions among the Karen, Kachin, Lisu, and many other groups in southwest China about the book—on paper, palm leaves, or parchment—that God,

1. This is adapted from an account in document B-502 in the William Young files in the American Baptist Archives, Valley Forge, Penn.

after a short sojourn on earth, had left to reveal himself and that was then lost or destroyed. The great priests and storytellers remembered parts of it, particularly the stories of creation and the flood, and practiced it as best they could. But the full truth would need to wait until God sent a foreigner with a Book that would tell his full truth.

With these simple Lahu, however, the story had added dimensions. Over the past several years, spurred on by unusual dreams, some villages had built chapels, prescribed strict moral regulations not unlike the Ten Commandments, and worshiped this one great spirit as best they could. The cords were a constant reminder that the day was coming when once again they would be liberated, not only spiritually, but also economically and politically.

Fear of Demons among the Lahu and Wa

William Young and his American Baptists colleagues worked in Burma, largely among the Buddhist Shans, cousins to the Dai minority in China. The hill people in this area of northeastern Burma were the Lahu and Wa, and each group had several divisions, with dialectical differences and unique cultures. While Young rejoiced that some of the Lahu, and the Wa influenced by them, retained their cords and remembered their ancient traditions, he soon learned that among both groups there was a great fear of evil spirits.

Lahu

The Lahu are another of the Loloish nationalities in China, closely related to the Yi of Yunnan and Sichuan. They number about six hundred thousand, of whom half live in Burma and the other half in China, west of the famed Xishuangbanna in the prefectures of Lingcang and Simao. The people probably came originally from the northern section of Yunnan and were forced to the south over the centuries by the pressure of the Chinese and other minority nationalities.

The Lahu had a belief in one superspirit, either G'ui Sha, "a male heavenly spirit," or G'ui Ma, a "female heavenly spirit," whom they worshiped by offering sacrifices on festive days and at times of birth, marriage, or death. But their day-to-day lives were obsessed with placating evil spirits. Particularly was it necessary to cooperate with these evil spirits to assure good crops. Because of the influence of Chinese Hinayana Buddhism in the area, Lahu food sacrifices were a combination of their ancient traditional religion and Buddhism.

In August and September, for example, at the time of the rice harvest, each family took some rice home to cook. The entire village feasted on their fattest pigs, after which the first bowl of new rice was offered to their ancestors. The next step was to take the rice to the Buddhist temple, where it was offered as a sacrifice to the evil spirits. The new rice was first eaten by the parents the next morning, and at noon by all members of the community.

When a waste area was opened for the planting of crops, when the seed was sown, and when the time of harvest came—each of these events called for elaborate ceremonies with the sacrifice of pigs and food to the evil spirits, by whose good or evil will the village either was impoverished or enjoyed plenty. The elaborate procedures necessary to manipulate the spirit world were controlled by several levels of witches, white, red, or black, all of whom were designated to this role by heaven.[2]

Wa (Va)

The Wa are a Mon-Khmer or Austroasiatic minority and not Sino-Tibetan like the Lahu. Consequently, the two languages, as well as cultures, are very different. The ways in which their villages are interspersed, the one with another, means that they have learned much from each other. Therefore, the people movement that brought thousands of Lahu into the kingdom of God greatly influenced the turning of the Wa to Christ.

The Wa, numbering about three hundred thousand, live on the southern border areas of Yunnan in and near the villages of Cangyuan, Ximeng, Lancang, and Gengma. Their name means "mountaineer," indicating that from ancient times they have dwelled in the mountain areas along the border of China and Burma.

Whereas the Lahu used food sacrifices to placate the evil spirit world, the Wa sacrificed humans. Each year during March, April, or May the Wa took heads, from distant enemy or nearby neighbor villages, to sacrifice to the evil spirits. They gave priority to a head with a thick beard, believing that their crops would then grow thick like the man's beard. Such a custom kept each village in a state of preparedness, never knowing when it would be attacked or its members ambushed along the roadway.

What was the nature of the ceremony of sacrifice? The bloody heads were nailed to a stake under a house where special drums were kept. The chief of the village prayed before the heads, asking that the spirits protect his villagers from illness, famine, or other calamities. He then pressed ashes onto the still-dripping heads and divided the ashes among all the families to take home. At springtime the villagers took the ashes to the fields and buried them together with the seeds they were planting. This would guarantee a plentiful crop.

2. The material on the backgrounds of the Lahu and Wa are taken from Tseng Hsiu (Carol) Li, *The Sacred Mission: An American Missionary Family in the Lahu and Wa Districts of Yunnan, China,* an unpublished M.A. thesis at Baylor University, Waco, Texas, 1987.

Over the years this sacrificial ceremony was modified. First, the heads of slaves of the Wa replaced the use of Wa heads. The next change was to use the heads of dead people. Finally, by the 1950s, the heads of oxen, pigs, or chickens replaced human heads. Not every area practiced this ceremony in the same way. Farther to the north, for example, families under a particular headman had to take turns in providing a head. If the family could not take a head, it was responsible to give up one of its own children. Under this kind of pressure, many families fled from this "wild Wa" area and sought refuge farther south.[3]

An integral part of the sacrifice ceremony was the beating of a special wood drum, which only the chief or the witch of the village was allowed to use. This drum was regarded as holy and was built in accordance with strict religious regulations. Many of the Wa villagers worshiped this wood drum, effective, they believed, in calling back the spirits of the dead. They kept it in a special place.

The Lahu-Wa People Movement to Christ

The American Baptist work among the Lahu and Wa has been called "a miracle of modern missions." William Young, the apostle of this movement, has, in the words of Carol Li, a researcher at the Yunnan Institute of Minority Studies, "written an important page of the Yunnan ethnic people's religious history."[4] Young came to Burma in 1896 and spent his first five years working with the Shan and learning their language in Mong Nai and Hsipaw. He moved to the Shan state of Kengtung in 1901, still with the prime responsibility to evangelize the Shan.

Almost immediately, however, Young began to trek among the hill people, thoroughly despised by the Shan, who called them Muhso. His first convert came in April 1903, and shortly after, two Lahu teachers who claimed they had been believers for one year came on a three-day journey from Mongmong, Yunnan, to visit him. A short conversation convinced them that Young's message fit with their tradition. Excitedly, they went to the marketplace and rounded up about a hundred Lahu to whom they announced the good news. These in turn returned to their homes to "tell it on the mountains." For the next few weeks the mission compound in Kengtung was crowded with people wanting to learn more. Shan opposition checked the stream of visitors for a while, but the interest continued. Young's first baptisms came 30 October 1904, delayed for at least two years by the opposition of the Shan, who did not

3. C. G. Gowman, "On the Burmese Border," *China's Millions,* October 1928, 155.
4. Li, *Sacred Mission,* 3.

wish foreigners living and working among the backward hill peoples. This was followed by another delegation of Lahu from China, one member of whom exclaimed, "I have been seeking for the true God for fourteen years, and have just found him."[5] This led to Young's touring among several villages, to a few more baptisms, and then, about Christmas 1904, to a mass meeting attended by representatives from one hundred villages. Larger and larger groups kept coming, until, by May 1905, Young had baptized 1,623 converts, mostly from the Lahuna (black) and Lahushi groups.

Since this movement had been sparked by a few visitors from China, and some of those baptized were from China, the newly Christian Lahu were convinced that the biggest harvest awaited them in China. With this prospect, Young made his first trip to China in 1905, accompanied by a noted Wa chief who had been influenced by the Lahu Christians. Young could not respond to the many invitations to go everywhere along the China border, but he arranged to send Shan Bibles and Gospel portions and tracts into hundreds of Wa villages.

This only increased the desire of both Lahu and Wa villages to learn more. Since Young was somewhat bound to his assigned work in Kengtung and could not travel to China, the people came to him. Nearly 6,000 were baptized in 1905 and 1906. Accompanied by another missionary and a Karen Christian leader, Young made another extended tour of China in 1907 and baptized 1,567. Furlough and unsettled conditions in China hindered the work for several years, but in 1916 William, accompanied by his son Vincent, went to China again for two months and baptized 1,600 Wa and Lahu.

By this time, it was apparent that the best prospects for the work were in China, and in 1920 Young and his family established a mission station in the Chinese city of Menglem (alternative spellings are Mein Ning or Menglien). This was not a matter of merely crossing the border, a fairly short trip. Rather, they entered China via Haiphong and the French railway to what is now Kunming. From there the governor of the province, Tang Zhiyao, gave them special permission to go into border territory and sent a military guard to protect them through this robber-infested territory. Located now in China, the Youngs were able to respond more effectively to the unusual demands of a people movement.

With her husband traveling so tirelessly to the many villages demanding his time, the burden of overseeing the station, of superintending the school, and of guiding the local workers fell on Mrs. Young. Already weakened by the long, arduous trip to Menglem, her health failed, and

5. W. M. Young, "The Awakening of Keng Tung," *The Missionary Review of the World,* March 1906, 215.

within a few months she died in Rangoon, where she was taken for treatment.

In the next few years after his move to China, Young's outreach was responsible for the baptism of another ten thousand converts, increasing the total number of those baptized to sixteen thousand by 1926. With the help of William's two sons, Harold and Vincent, and the Buker twins, Raymond and Richard, the work continued to grow with the development of a school system, local church associations, and a modest medical ministry. William retired in 1933, but his sons and the Bukers carried on among the responsive Lahu and Wa. By 1936 Vincent reported that among the Wa alone fifteen thousand had been baptized and that there were ninety Christian Wa villages. The number of Christians among the Lahu was slightly less.

Harold Young and his family were forced out of China by the Japanese in 1942, but continued to live and work in Burma and Thailand. In 1948 he aided the Burmese government put down a Wa rebellion against it. An article in the *New Times of Burma* described him as a "Burma citizen born in the Shan state, but he is of British extraction."[6] Vincent and his family managed to return to China at the end of World War II, but then had to leave again in 1950 with the coming of the People's Republic of China. Although he was in Rangoon at the time, he arranged for getting many minority friends across the border into Burma, where they could continue their religious life without any interference.

Despite the loss of missionary personnel and the consequent difficulties faced by the churches from 1950 until China's opening to the west in 1979, the Lahu and Wa churches continued to grow. During times of particular difficulty, Christians fled across the border to Burma, there to take up a more stable and settled life. Remaining in China today are about thirteen thousand Wa Christians living in forty villages in the Lancang area, and thirty to thirty-five thousand Lahu Christians in twenty-four villages in Banli, Mujia, Gengma, and Menglien.[7]

Overcoming the Spirits in Lahu and Wa Societies

So much for the details of how thousands of Lahu and Wa became Christians. But what is the story behind the story? Were there dynamics

6. Harold Young file in American Baptist Archives, Valley Forge, Penn.

7. These most recent statistics come from articles by the staff of *Bridge: Church Life in China Today*, September-October 1990, 12–15. Statistics from the Yunnan Institute of Ethnic Religion Research indicate that from 1887 to 1950 missionaries belonging to thirty-one organizations built at least 965 churches, chapels, and stations in Yunnan. A total of 150,000 in 118 cities or districts were converted to Christ from among the Han, Miao, Yi, Lisu, Dulong, Jingpo, Bolong, Wa, Lahu, Dai, and Bai. This report is in Li, *Sacred Mission*, 8.

at work that help us understand how this happened? Did the missionaries operate according to any strategy? What was the opposition faced, and how did the missionaries deal with it? How truly Christian is a people movement of this extent?[8]

One important dynamic, already mentioned, was the ancient tradition of the Lahu that led them to expect a foreigner who would come and bring the true religion that they had lost. Not so well known is the political dynamic in the early 1900s along the China-Burma border. Two peasant revolts occurred in Yunnan, one led by Du Wenxiu, a Hui Muslim, and another by Li Wenxue of the Yi. After the government put down both of these uprisings, the survivors fled to Shuangjiang county in Yunnan and continued their anti-Qing resistance under the cloak of the Buddhist church.

One leader who arose was a Buddhist monk, Tung Jing, who, with great compassion, alleviated the sufferings of the people and was affectionately called a Living Buddha. When he was killed by government troops in 1903 in Lancang, his followers fled to Kengtung, where they heard William Young preach the gospel. Some of these may have been among the early inquirers whom Young received into his home in Kengtung in 1903 and 1904. They liked what they heard: Young's message of salvation had implications for the needs of their suffering people as they opposed the corrupt Qing dynasty. To them Young seemed to be Living Buddha II.

When these dissidents returned to Yunnan, they proclaimed that Tung Jing was not really dead, but that he had returned in a representative called Living Buddha II. They related that to find this representative they must follow the white horse that Tung Jing had left. Suffering as they were from heavy taxes and poverty, often so extreme that they had to sell their children, the people were ready to grasp any straw of hope. The white horse crossed the border, came to Young's chapel, and kicked the door down. Out came Young in surprise, and the people accepted him as the new Tung Jing, their leader in the fight against poverty and oppression. Did Young know about this story, still remembered by old people in Shuangjiang? Possibly not initially, but at a later time, he used his alleged friendship with the monk and his possession of a smoking pipe with the monk's signature on it to gain footholds in Buddhist villages that would otherwise not have welcomed him.[9]

8. Some observers of the Lahu and Wa societies believe that the Young family overemphasized the place and power of evil spirits. They observe that William Young never learned the Lahu language and culture and did not give sufficient weight to their belief in a single God *(G'ui Sha)*.

9. This unusual story comes from a letter written to Li on 10 December 1986 by Wang Jingliu, then director of the Yunnan Ethnic Research Institute in Kunming. Li, *Sacred Mission,* 41–45. Paul and Elaine Lewis, missionaries with the American Baptist Foreign Mission Soci-

William Young himself was a strong, charismatic figure, not afraid of confrontation, whether with human or demonic opposition. His obvious interest in meeting any human need created such an aura about him that the people thought he must be a heavenly being. Certainly his appearance was different from anyone whom they had seen before, and he was not afraid of anything.

An initial confrontation was in the border village of Lofu, inhabited at that time by the Lahu and a few Dai families. The chief, an ardent believer in the evil spirits, ordered his followers to drive Young out. Young left, but not before, with the help of a relative of the chief, he had the chief's house fenced off with some large wires. The next day Young again asked the chief for permission to build a chapel in the village. Again he ordered him to leave. At this moment, Young's friends pulled on the wires and simulated an earthquake, which so frightened the chief that he yielded a bit. "You can build a church here, but only on the ground under the ox skin that I am giving you."

Young was not to be outsmarted. He cut the ox's skin into long strips, which his helpers used to fence off a large piece of land, and then he started to construct the church building. The chief was enraged, but saw that Young had outwitted him. Not only did he not oppose the building of the church; he later converted to Christianity and became one of Young's most ardent supporters.[10]

Banay village in Cangyuan was almost totally Buddhist. Even after the people believed Young's claim that he was a friend of Tung Jing, they were not willing to receive his message; it seemed too different from what they believed. Finally, he convinced them that his aim, like that of Buddhism, was to relieve the sufferings of people. He settled down in the village for a period of time, helping the disabled, treating people medically, providing food and clothes, and showing them his love and concern. Eventually, the villagers were convinced by these works of compassion that this new message was true, and they became a Christian village.

The opposition in Gongnong village came not from Buddhism, but from the chief, who followed the evil spirits meticulously. He refused to

---

ety, later lived in Young's home in Kengtung, Burma. They report that many legends have circulated about the horse. The story they knew best was not about a white horse. Their version had it that several travelers came with a horse to Young's home. The horse stopped by a well that Young was digging. They called down and Young emerged, confirming for the travelers that he was the one to whom their messianic legend referred. In general, the Lewises doubt some of the myths that grew up among the people about Young's exploits (personal conversation, May 1992).

10. A letter from Li Chayo, an aged resident of Lofu, who wrote to Li 18 November 1986. Li, *Sacred Mission,* 47–50.

let Young even enter the village to talk with him. Three days later, according to a report that people later related to Young, the rope holding up the cooking pot in the chief's house broke suddenly. The pot was considered holy, and such an event was the omen of a coming disaster. The chief had what we might call a nervous breakdown, not eating or drinking and able only to lie on his bed, convulsed with chills and mumbling incoherently. No amount of praying to or sacrificing to the spirits brought any relief. Finally, the villagers sent for Young, who gave the chief some medicine. Upon his recovery, he and the entire village converted to the Christian faith.

The village of Bangkah, Lancang, presented unusual problems. After being repulsed from entering the village by men with long knives and bows, Young and his helpers camped outside the village for several days. One day, as he took some morning exercises, Young stumbled on a man left for dead, reckoned incurable by the witch doctor. Young carried the man back to his tent, washed him, gave him medicine, and treated his sores with ointment. A few weeks later, completely restored to health. the man reentered his village and was viewed first as a ghost, and then as a miracle. Obviously, the people concluded, the foreigner's God was stronger than the evil spirits. With the chief and the witch doctor leading the way, they came to Young and asked him to cut the cords from their necks, arms, and wrists.

Young's exploits spread widely through the area, and whether it was he himself or his helpers who were doing the preaching, the people responded by families and villages. "Jesus Christ is Lord" was the cry among countless numbers of Lahu and Wa villages, as people tore down their evil-spirit altars and turned to God. The new faith had many side effects: villages cleaned up, no more drunkenness, no more fighting, no more fear of the evil spirits, no more economic losses from the widespread slaughter of animals for sacrificial purposes.

Young's work was not without its opposition, sometimes from the Shan, who held responsible positions in border areas, or directly from the Chinese officials. This took the form of mob attacks on Young and his helpers or on the Wa and Lahu Christians. Young did not take this passively, and gave himself vigorously to protect the rights of those who had accepted this new faith. After one particularly difficult time, he protested both to the Chinese government and to the American consul, with the result that in 1926 the highest official in Lancang issued an edict for all the border areas:

> It is written in the constitution that the people of China have the liberty to join any religion they like . . . the American missionary family's religion is the Yesu religion which teaches people how to be kind and help

> people too. They have gotten the permission from our governor that allows them to carry out their missionary service in the district. So long as they do not violate our law, we should help them and protect them. It is a good thing that since the people joined their religion, they abide by the law, and we can not see them drink or smoke any more. They know how to be clean and polite to people, and it is wonderful that the foreigner's religion does not need any sacrifice, big ceremonies, idols, or altars, which teach people to do away completely with the old superstitious customs. Those who do not want to be Christians are not allowed to do anything to hurt them. . . .For these Christians should not discriminate against the believers who worship their gods with altars or idols. No matter if you are Christians, Buddhists or Moslems, you might be neighbors or relatives, you should live in peace, should love each other and respect each other and work hard![11]

How effective were the methods Young used in his work with the Lahu and Wa? What was the nature of the gospel he preached? What missiological principles guided him? When Young began his ministry in Burma, he learned the Shan language and culture. As he began to preach to the Wa and the Lahu, he either did it in Shan, hoping that the people might be able to follow the gist of his language, or had one of his helpers translate for him. If it were a Karen from Burma, as was often the case, the possibility of miscommunication was always present. One American Baptist observer commented, "He told the people that if they believed in Jesus, they would live forever. When some died, the survivors were mad!"

Much of the work, of course, was conducted totally by local evangelists who prepared the inquirers in a village for baptism when Young arrived. He himself did very little of the follow-up, since the demands on his time were so great. Although the critics of his work admired his evangelistic zeal and knew well that he was a staunch fundamentalist in his doctrinal views, they questioned whether his converts were ready for baptism. The questions preparatory for baptism were simple: Do you wish to be a Christian? Have you forsaken the evil spirits? Do you have just one wife? Do you refuse to go to the bazaar on Sunday? If the answers were all affirmative, the person was baptized.

When others, dismayed by what they viewed as a superficial process, sought to question further about Jesus and God and the people's faith, the roadblock was usually the same: "We do not read. We do not know the answers to these questions." By this standard, a Christian village was one where the people wanted to be Christians, where they worshiped God

11. From Pen Guierh, *A Glance at Shuangjiang* (Shuangjiang: Yunnan Shuangjiang Normal College, 1926), 26, and quoted in Li, *Sacred Mission,* 66–67.

on Sunday rather than go to the bazaar, where some break had been made with placating evil spirits, and where a man had only one wife. Critics said that it was more cultural than biblical. Donald McGavran, well-known exponent of people movements, viewed this stage as discipling, during which time people turned from the past and were ready to think about a true commitment to Christ. With Young and his helpers, however, this *was* their commitment to Christ, and whether or not they were followed up and "perfected," to use McGavran's term, depended on the lay leaders in the village and/or the teacher sent to lead the local school. The former knew little more than fellow believers, and the latter had little extra time to devote seriously to pastoral concerns.

This pattern was difficult to change, for the local evangelists were extremely loyal to Young, who had hired them and paid them from mission funds. Ray Buker, one of Young's colleagues, proposed a new strategy. Less likely to produce converts in a hurry, this approach took the missionary into a village for two weeks at a time. Here he rented a local-type home, preached and taught intensively, and, at the end of this time, if people truly understood what it meant to be a Christian, he baptized them.

Buker tried this method for about a year and was gratified that it produced ten churches. The people provided all that was needed for their pastor's livelihood, and they recognized that the church belonged to them and not to the missionary. In fact, the itinerant missionary often retired early in the evening, and the local leaders would continue their conversations with the village elders until well after midnight.

Young's strategy was to reach out constantly in an ongoing program of evangelism. He was not sure of his board's policy on this—was it truly committed to *extensive* evangelism or was it *intensive*, focusing largely on the nurture of Christians? He had no compunctions about leaving a village with no outside local leaders, even for as long as seven or eight years, as long as the whole village had committed itself and there were several nearby villages with the same commitment. He had good financial connections in America and believed that when home churches knew of the need, they would send him the money needed to employ native workers. By 1926 he spoke of two Lahu associations of churches and two Wa associations. All the churches involved were within one day's walking distance of one another.

Buker questioned this approach. He found many areas where he could have baptized several villages, but he was not willing to do so unless he was able immediately to put a native teacher there. Unlike Young, he had few channels for funds in America, and his local missions budget was not sufficient to hire personnel for this task. He took whatever time he could on his preaching tours to meet with the deacons and to discuss problems that plagued them: drinking, the planting of opium, extramarital affairs, and the matter of self-support. On the latter subject he was at a disadvantage: Young was the father figure whom the people obeyed on every matter, and Buker ranked only as a stepfather. So the leaders were happy for the financial arrangements to remain as they had been at the beginning: let the mission pay.

Nothing stands out as being distinctive in missionary preaching among the Lahu and Wa. The villagers were urged to forsake the evil spirits, but no special emphasis was placed on the person or power of the Holy Spirit to help them in this. Buker relates that his messages stressed the awfulness of sin, salvation through faith, and the power of prayer. On one tour his preaching topics included the Lord's Prayer, the resurrection of Jesus, salvation, John the Baptist, and Mary. Strangely, none of the missionaries reported that they preached on the Old Testament, essential subject matter for adherents of traditional religions. Buker's homiletical style was not one-way; he used topical sentences, drilled the people on their meaning, and had them repeat the sentences after him. The use of colored picture posters on salvation or New Testament stories always attracted the people.

Some of the missionaries in the Baptist work among the Lahu and Wa stressed the need for schools. Conversion to Christ and education seemed to follow logically in the people's thinking. Sometimes Young had money from America for special scholarships to give to those who were trained as pastors in places like Menglem, or even in Burma, and they were expected to return to their own village churches to work after graduation. To qualify to study in a compound school at a central station, a student had to first finish three years of studying Bible and general subjects in a village school. No efforts were made to start schools in non-Christian villages.

The schools were a blessing to the people but a frequent bone of contention among the missionaries. How necessary were schools? Young often argued that if Jesus were returning soon, was it not better to get a smattering of education and then go out to win souls? Compared with later well-educated missionaries—the Bukers, Andrew Telford, and Paul and Elaine Lewis—the Youngs, although brilliant, had only a limited education. They did not wish to overeducate local converts and possibly make them unfit for their local context. Other questions were raised. How could qualified Christian teachers be found to teach? How would they be paid: by local funds, from the mission budget, or by special funds from America? What should be the qualification for students? How can the educational work be kept from outranking the emphasis on evangelism? These ongoing questions were never fully and finally resolved.

In such a frontier area, the pattern followed by the missionaries in relating to the local culture became a model for the Christians to follow. Vincent Young found the Lahu very hospitable and responded warmly to invitations to join in their New Year and Grain Spirit Finding festivals. He reports, "My wife and I always dressed like a Lahu couple. I played a bamboo flute, and my wife danced like a young Lahu woman." Little wonder, then, that as the people turned to Christ, the Vincent Youngs were asked to preside over the celebration of these festivals in the churches.[12]

Not every situation was this easy. Ray Buker relates how a Shan friend invited him to give help in running down a cow thief who had stolen animals from both him and Buker. He had a footprint of the thief and wished to use this along with an effigy to invoke the evil spirits to curse him. Buker refused to participate.[13]

In their observance of certain events today, such as the birth of a child, marriage, death, and baptism, the Lahu and Wa churches hold strongly to the traditions taught them by the missionaries. Some special occasions reveal patterns of accommodation to their context: "They will cook some good food as a sacrifice to Jesus Christ, and when the food is ready, they will say, 'Come, Yesu, Lord, come and help yourself; this is made specially for you to thank you for protecting us.'"[14]

When the message is overaccommodated, it may become garbled. Yang Liuxiang has observed in *The Christians in Cangyuan*:

> Jesus Christ was a man whose mother was a widow. Before he was born some fortune-tellers told his mother that she was going to have a son who would be strong enough to conquer the whole world. When the chief heard that, he was so angry that he decided to kill Jesus' mother. With the help of the villagers, Jesus' mother escaped to a horse stable, where Jesus was born in a horse manger. His mother took him home, and he jumped down from his mother's arms. No sooner had he stepped on the floor than there appeared a golden chair for him to sit in. When he grew up, the chief sent three hundred people to kill him. They caught him, killed him, and buried him with a big stone pressed on his body. But three months later the stone broke up, and all these bad people were killed by the fragments of stone. After Jesus Christ was resurrected, he told all the people of the world that he was going to Heaven, but he would not stay there long, just three days (in fact three thousand years). During the three days of his absence, there was to be a great disorder in which more sinners would appear in this world. Jesus told the people not

12. Li, *Sacred Mission*, 31.

13. Buker files, letter to ABFMS, 7 December 1927.

14. Lei Hongan, *Traditional Religious Beliefs of the Minority Nationalities* (Kunming: Yunnan Ethnic Research Institute, 1984), 82, quoted in Li, *Sacred Mission*, 98.

> to worry, but to do good things to help poor people and trust God to protect them. Then he said they would have a happy and peaceful life. Three days later, when Jesus was to return to earth, there was going to be a fierce earthquake in which the bad men would be killed, but God would protect the good people so long as they stayed in the church. Even if they died, death for them only meant that they would be transferred to a better place called Heaven, where there was no worry, no hatred, no poverty, no starvation, but peace and perfection. In order to go to Heaven, people were to do good things and go to church. If they did not do as Jesus said, they would be sent to hell where they would suffer for many generations.[15]

In a portion of the vows used in a Lahu or Wa marriage ceremony, the pastor asks the bride and bridegroom some very specific questions: "Do you still love him when you see some other man who is stronger and more handsome than your husband?" and "How about you, do you love her when you see some woman prettier and healthier than she?" When the two have responded with the expected answers, "Yes, I do," the pastor gives them a cup of honey or sugar water to drink and expresses his desire that their lives together will be as sweet as honey.[16]

A people movement for Christ cannot be grounded until there is a written language; Christian literature, including the Scriptures, has been translated; and the people have been taught how to read. The alphabet for Lahu was first worked out by a missionary grandson of Adoniram Judson. It was perfected by a Lahu teacher, Ai Pun, and then used for various Scripture portions. Vincent Young, born in Kengtung, Burma, spoke the Shan, Lahu, and Wa languages. He prepared the Wa alphabet, and by 1938 had translated the Bible into Wa. Published in Rangoon, it was enthusiastically welcomed by Wa readers both in China and in Burma. Even after his family returned to America in 1953 and he in 1954, Vincent continued to have a literature ministry to the Lahu. After he completed his translation of the Lahu Bible in 1959 in southern California, he had it published privately in Taiwan with the money furnished by one of his sons and Dr. Richard Buker, one of the twins, who finished his medical missionary career in Thailand. These Bibles were shipped to Kengtung for distribution in Burma and China. A stiff, formal, word-for-word translation, it was never used widely and needed extensive revision. After he had completed this translation, Vincent put most of his efforts into preparing Bible stories and hymnals in the Wa language.

15. (Kunming: Yunnan Ethnic Research Institute, 1958), 72, quoted in Li, *Sacred Mission,* 99–100.

16. Li, *Sacred Mission,* 102.

Good mission theory emphasizes that the Bible ought to be translated early in a people movement, in order that new believers might be grounded properly in Christian truth. Scripture portions were available after about ten years of the Lisu work, but with the Sediq in Taiwan and the Lahu and Wa in China, a full Bible was not available to the people until twenty-five or thirty years after the first converts had been received. During the transition period, oral preaching in the tongue of the people and written Bible portions in the trade language—Shan in China and Japanese in Taiwan—were used. These kept the movements going and allowed them to expand.

Disputes on Missiological Principles

Even though the Baptist work among the Lahu and Wa prospered, the missionaries faced a number of tensions. First was a dispute with the Presbyterians who worked in Laos but wanted to follow up some of their believers who had gone into the area about Kengtung, Burma. The Baptists denied that any Laotian believers spoke the languages of Burma and accused the Presbyterians of sheep-stealing. This led to charges and countercharges. One Presbyterian medical doctor, harboring secret Baptist convictions, resigned because he did not like the way a colleague was "baptizing illegitimate children." His colleague countered that he would "prefer to be dead than be a Baptist."[17]

This dispute festered for many years, even though a basic division of the field was made late in 1905. The Presbyterians agreed to restrict their activities to Kengtung city, where they would work only with those who used the Laos language and its written characters. The Baptists would continue to concentrate on the Shan and the illiterate tribes in the hills. They both agreed that they must let God providentially rule in their work, and that the total need was beyond what either mission could meet.

Not that there were only two mission agencies that wished to evangelize this border area. In the 1920s Swedish Pentecostals baptized several hundred Lahu converts in Gengma. Their work was stimulated by a Chinese evangelist who felt that speaking in tongues made it unnecessary for outsiders to use the Lahu language, and that, since Jesus had incarnated himself as a Chinese, this was the proper language to use. Young strongly opposed speaking in tongues, since Lahu converts felt that to do so was a reversion to their ancient belief in demons. He also criticized this Chinese brother for not giving any instruction previous to baptizing new be-

17. This material is from the Young family letter file in the American Baptist Archives, Valley Forge, Penn.

lievers. He failed to add that in practice he also followed this pattern. Young conversed extensively with Pentecostal leaders and arranged that their work, numbering more than one thousand baptized adherents, be turned over to the Baptists late in 1926.

Young also conferred with missionaries Allyn Cooke and Carl Gowman of the CIM, since they wished to work among the Lahu in some areas intersected by Lisu villages. Their attitude toward Young was critical, convinced that his methods of using financial aid, baptizing quickly without much instruction, and leaving villages unattended by trained Christian workers for a long period to be much less effective than Fraser's meticulous approach to the Lisu. Young resisted the CIM desire to enter the Baptist area, since he felt that to oppose the Pentecostal work and to allow the CIM to come in was unfair. Furthermore, he argued, to have several mission agencies and their respective churches among the Lahu and Wa would confuse simple believers. He also apparently had his doubts whether the CIM had enough well-trained missionaries to occupy the area adequately. Cooke accepted most of Young's arguments, but he claimed that the CIM and the Pentecostal mission believed that the Lord was coming soon, that the time was short, and that everyone needed to be involved.

Personal disputes on the field among missionaries and between them and the home board threatened to bring down the work. Not everyone wanted to see a rigid division between the Baptist and Presbyterian work, feeling that they ought to try to work cooperatively. The Baptist Board in America was not convinced that the hill work was important. Why not decrease continued outreach and use more educational work to deepen the spiritual experience of already committed Christians? Young and others bitterly criticized the board policy. They claimed that it poured money into the Bengal-Orissa field that had seen only 145 converts in an eight-year period and did not increase their own budget for the hill work that in 1918 to 1919 had had more converts than the work in Japan, the Philippines, and other areas of China combined.[18]

Part of the board's questions about the hill work stemmed from its perception of the way in which Young was doing it. Some of this was fed by criticism on the field, as well as from the observations of those who visited the border areas. Young, as is the case with most strong leaders, was perceived as unable to work with fellow missionaries, unwilling to follow field policy and regulations, desiring to control all the work, viewing all differences of opinion as personal opposition, and having an attitude of superiority to his colleagues. More serious were the questions

18. Letter of William Young to J. C. Robbins, 21 April 1919, found in Young letter file in American Baptist Archives, Valley Forge, Penn.

about the way he did his work: uninstructed converts gained through salaried workers with little attempt to develop self-support and local responsibility; total funding of schools in local villages with little attempt to get community support; and the unwise use of money to lure native workers from other mission agencies.

If Young and his family had been working by themselves, the same problems vis-a-vis the board would ultimately have arisen. They came to a head earlier, because other missionaries, notably the Buker twins, had come to the field. They admired Young for his pioneering efforts, but their methods in the work were diametrically different from his. As the board brought Young's methods under scrutiny, he opposed the approaches advocated by Ray Buker. He perceived Ray as too kindhearted, too ready to spend time with those having problems, and less willing than he to "beat sinners." Buker was more reluctant than Young to intervene for local Christians with the Shan or Chinese officials. Most seriously, he felt, Buker was not as free with money. On this matter Buker observed, "My methods of introducing self-support pinch the foot of luxury which the Lahu preachers were getting used to as preachers of the Gospel, and receivers of the white man's money."[19]

Buker believed that Christian nurture was very important. He urged local Christians to support their own evangelists, whom he trained to preach and to deal with the various problems they would meet in each village. He often accompanied them, modeling for them how to preach and how to use a catechetical, question-and-answer approach, even in public meetings, that would help people grasp the truth firmly. He confessed that he was often discouraged as he visited many villages and was confronted with great backsliding, for which the only solution seemed to be to pay out more money and strengthen the people's spiritual commitment.

The board in America and the missionaries on the field were never able to find a final answer to these problems. Both Young and Buker were asked to meet with the board's Reference Committee when it came to Rangoon. The usual solution seemed the best one—divide the work and the missionaries. Menglem was closed down as a station, and Harold Young was given a specific sphere at Bana. The Bukers were furloughed because of Mrs. Buker's health, and returned later to work among the Shan in Burma. William Young was allowed to continue

19. Letter of Ray Buker of 14 January 1930 to Auntie and Cousin Ida. In Buker family archives held by the family. With respect to his "laxness on sinners," Buker commented that he felt it necessary to go and pray with sinners, not just denounce them. He often preached on 1 Corinthians 13 and tried to carry on a pastoral ministry. This led to the claim that he was responsible for "developing all kinds of sins in the church." This comes from a letter of 29 March 1929.

until his retirement two years later. Such a dispute, although not fatal to the work, created a sense of division among the supporters of both factions, and this fact undoubtedly destroyed some of its effectiveness.

William Young, aggressive in traveling into politically sensitive border areas restricted by the authorities, often found himself in trouble with the Chinese government. It felt constrained to report his activities to the United States' State Department, which requested the American Baptist Board to relieve him of his responsibilities and return him to America. The board, uncertain of the muddled charges and countercharges between Young and the officials, negotiated with the State Department for him to remain in China.

Obstacles in the Work

The external pressures facing missionaries among the Lisu, Yi, and Miao were also common with the Lahu and Wa. Drunkenness, opium, sexual immorality, a back door of reversion that was as open as the front door to faith—all of these were part of the Baptist work. Political disturbances, such as those in 1911 and 1927, frightened the people and created difficulty in the work. Ruth Young, Harold's wife, reported in 1927 that Chinese magistrates had ordered them to turn all mission schools over to the Chinese, to dismiss all native workers, to cease using Lahu in preference to Chinese in their teaching, and to quit preaching outside a radius of thirty miles from the mission station.[20]

Despite the physical hardships of living and traveling, the chaotic conditions of countrysides infested with robber gangs, the external pressures from political changes in China, the villages obsessed with evil spirits, the educational backwardness of the people, and the unfortunate disputes among the missionaries, God was in control of the work and it prospered, bringing thousands to accept Jesus as the great Liberator. What were the motivations for faith?

Reasons for Growth

If one were able to go into a Lahu or Wa village and ask each of twenty believers, "What led you to believe in Jesus?" he would receive twenty answers.[21] Very few would be theologically sophisticated. A common

20. Letter by Ruth Young of 11 May 1927. This is found in Young family files in American Baptist Archives, Valley Forge, Penn.

21. The writer once accompanied Donald McGavran as he went to a Sediq village near Dong Men, Taiwan, in 1956 to ask this very question. Predictably, the answers all differed as to the precise motivation for belief. The temptation was to answer the question from the convert's current, more mature perspective, rather than from the actual situation at the time of conversion.

theme among those who believed was that they were afraid of evil spirits, and Jesus was stronger than the spirits. Some were impressed that Jesus would make life better for them: they would not be as poor, the crops would do better, they would be free from sickness, they would live forever, they would be delivered from wild animals and many other dangers lurking in the dark forests. Very few, at the time when they first believed, would articulate that they had been saved from sin. This theological refinement came much later. That was Ray Buker's fear. Would it ever come, if the only thing done to encourage the new believers was an endless round of meetings with little biblical content to give foundation to their faith? The first impetus to faith might not be too important, but what happened after faith and baptism by ongoing instruction was essential.

As Li has analyzed the current situation in the Lahu and Wa districts of Yunnan, she lists several reasons for a "widespread conversion to Christianity." Topping her list is the economic factor. The people save money by not following the old paths of sacrificing to the evil spirits. Eventually, the old religion will disappear. This has led Li and others to conclude that it is "possible that Christianity will eradicate the evil-spirit belief in most of the districts in the future." She further observes that "in the areas where the Youngs did not reach, where evil-spirit belief was popular a few years ago, now about two-thirds of the population has been converted to Christianity."[22] Some researchers have estimated, possibly too optimistic, that 40 percent of the Lahu and Wa people are Christians: some villages are totally Christian, some two-thirds Christian, and others one-third Christian.[23]

The second reason that Li gives for belief is "cultural entertainment." Life in a mountain Lahu or Wa village is boring. Government organs and educational institutions do nothing much to allay this situation. The church, in addition to being a religious institution, is a social and educational center for the village. It puts on entertaining programs of singing, dancing, storytelling, and the playing of musical instruments. Visitors come from Myanmar (Burma) to tell them interesting things from another country. The economic, cultural, and social factors are very significant. So also is the sense that the Christian faith has delivered the people from oppression by majority groups and given them a new identity as followers of the Christian faith. As with the Sediq in Taiwan, the Lisu, the Miao, the Yunnan Yi, and the Karen in neighboring Myanmar, the Lahu and Wa have been revitalized, with the new religion as the center of their lives.

22. Li, *Sacred Mission,* 95.
23. Ibid., 97. Here she is quoting Lei, *The Problems of the Christians,* 81.

Buttressed by all these supports for faith is the central affirmation: "Jesus is Lord over the spirit world, and he has freed us from this which has dominated our lives for so long." With this bedrock conviction, the Lahu and Wa churches face the future with certainty, undeterred by the outward pressures that have been so much a part of their lives in the troubled border areas of China.

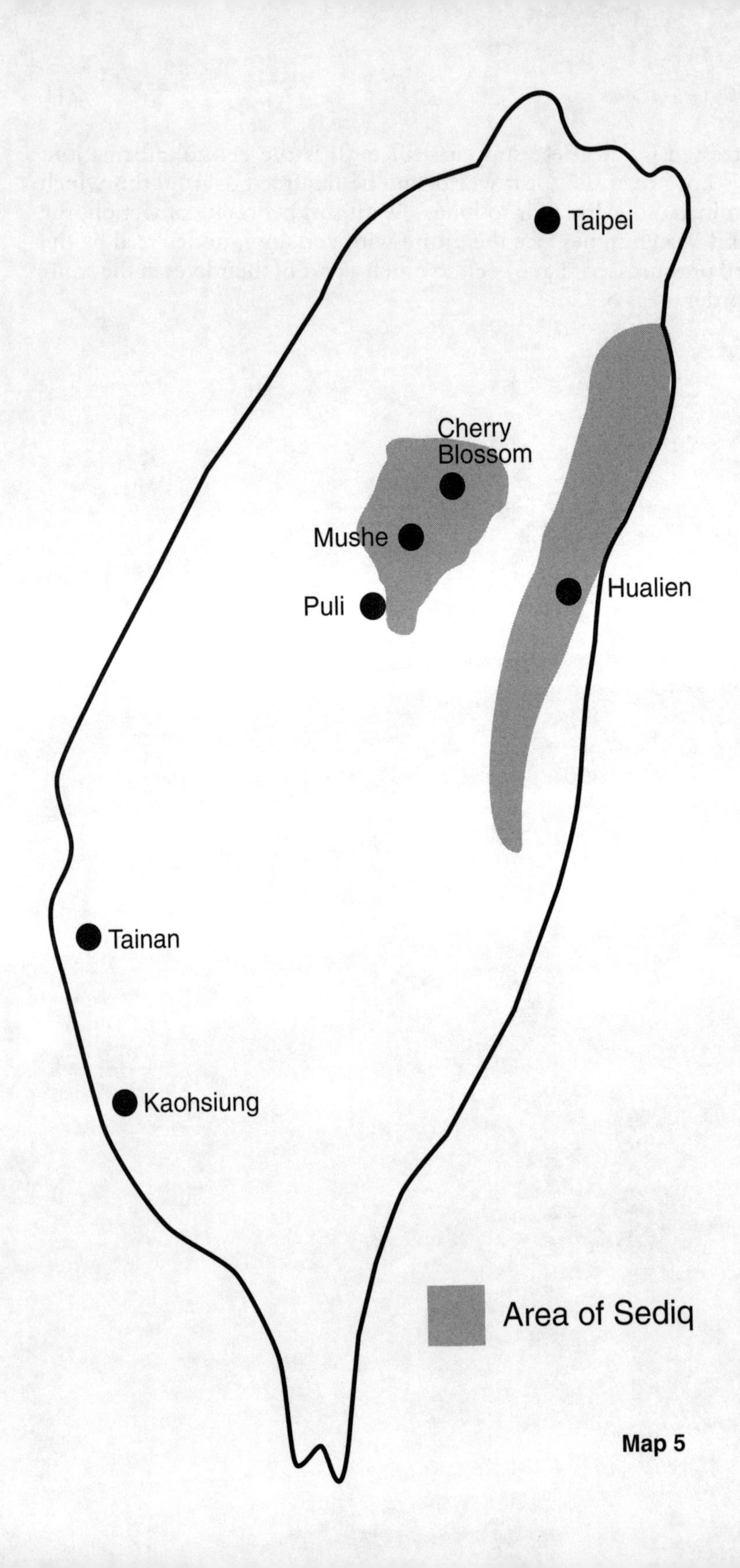
Taipei
Cherry Blossom
Mushe
Puli
Hualien
Tainan
Kaohsiung
Area of Sediq

Map 5

11

Headhunters Turn to Christ

The High Mountain People of Taiwan

On a Cliff Overlooking Cherry Blossom Village

The village of Cherry Blossom high in the central mountains was deathly silent. Unlike a usual day for farming, when men, their wives, and their children might be expected to be working on their mountainside land plots, today was different. The men were working their way toward the village of Mushe, no more than a half-hour's walk from their homes. They were prepared for fighting, not farming. The women and children were on a steep cliff overlooking Cherry Blossom. As if responding to some prearranged signal, the wives began jumping off the cliff with their children in their arms. No hesitation was apparent, no screaming, only the heavy thud of bodies falling on the sharp rocks below.

Not present to view this final episode of their wives' commitment, the men, with heavy hearts, pressed on to do battle with the Japanese forces proceeding toward the village from Mushe. Now they could and would fight to the death, unburdened with the fear of what might happen to their families should they die in the upcoming skirmish.

The mass suicide by the women and children of this small village was only the latest phase of the ongoing struggle between the Japanese colonial forces and this village of the Sediq minority, one of ten Malayo-Polynesian groups of aborigines living in Taiwan. Then known as Formosa, "the beautiful isle" as the Portuguese called it, Taiwan had had many rulers. For centuries these several peoples had the island to themselves. They originally had been inhabitants of the Asian mainland, but then migrated to Taiwan from the islands of the South Pacific, a home they later shared with their Polynesian, Melanesian, and Micronesian cousins. The Dutch ruled the island for thirty-seven years, from 1624 to 1661, following which time the Chinese on the mainland of China took control. Gradually the Chinese pushed these various minority groups from the more fertile plains into less desirable land in the mountains. The tribes retaliated by cutting off Chinese heads.

Following China's defeat by Japan in 1894, Taiwan was ceded to Japan. The Taiwanese people did not accept this treaty arrangement and sought to be independent. This led Japan to land its naval forces on Taiwan and to put down the opposition. The minorities in the mountains continued the struggle. They resisted the way the Japanese tried to change their social organization by substituting a village council with an elected chief, rather than allowing them to have a hereditary chief. Neither did they bow to the Japanese attempt to impose their state religion, Shintoism, on them.

The southern minorities, largely the Paiwan, Bunnun, and Amis, and the Atayal to the north realized that continued resistance to such overwhelming force and superior weaponry was futile and finally accepted Japanese rule. The Sediq, a small minority with only twenty thousand people, continued to fight on.

The Crucial Issue

For the Sediq the crucial issue was headhunting. More than a means to settle a blood feud, headhunting was at the heart of their world view and the center of their religious life. The Sediq people have given two basic rationales for headhunting. First, it affirmed and upheld the moral order of the universe. A person accused of any crime, great or small, resorted to taking a head to prove his innocence. If he failed in his bloody endeavor, all the people of the village knew that he was guilty. If he succeeded in his venture, he brought the head back with him and hung it over the doorpost of his accuser. This proved that he was innocent, and his accuser was put to shame before the entire village.

The second reason was that taking a head proved that a man was a "real man." Only real men could enter the abode of the spirits, the final resting place for the Sediq. When a person died and his spirit came to the bridge entering the abode of the spirits, he had to give proof that he had taken a head. He held out his hand so that the judge standing by the bridge could see if it had a bloodstain. If the judge succeeded in washing away the stain, the man was recognized as a fraud and was turned away. If the stain remained, he was granted entrance. In the land of the spirits lived all of the Sediq ancestors. To be joined once again with them was the highest religious aspiration that a person had. The myth of the bridge and the judge who granted or refused entrance was deeply held and was a part of the folklore drilled into the minds of the young as they heard it repeated endlessly around mountain campfires.

Fortunately, it was easier to become a "real woman." Girls were taught at an early age how to weave beautiful garments. This became their pass across the eternal bridge and into the abode of the spirits.

The Sediq practiced headhunting on members of their own tribe and on enemies from other tribes. But after the Treaty of Shimoneski in 1895, when Taiwan was ceded to Japan, it was the Japanese who lost their heads. To be shamed by these "uncivilized" mountain people was more than they could stand, and they exerted every possible pressure on the Sediq to change their ways. A favorite method was to station a contingent of troops in the mountain area where they could closely monitor and control tribal life.

One of these detachments of troops, along with accompanying family members, was placed in Mushe, a small village about twenty miles north of the city of Puli, up a tortuous, winding, washboard road. Very disciplined in all of their activities, the Japanese troops, numbering over one hundred, made life miserable for the Sediq in the surrounding mountain villages. But one festive day, the Japanese community rested and amused itself with recreational games in a large public square. Little suspecting that the Sediq had much fight left in them, the soldiers had placed their weapons at the side of the field and were enjoying the day with their families.

The Sediq, no mean warriors, had waited for such an opportunity. Stealthily, several hundred of them surrounded the village and suddenly swooped down on the soldiers, taking them completely by surprise. The Sediq, ruthless in their revenge, killed off all but one person gathered at the athletic field, inflicting on the Japanese the worst defeat they had ever had in their colonial empire.

The one survivor fled in panic to the city of Puli and reported the massacre. Quickly the Japanese sent a large number of troops toward Mushe. The Sediq were prepared. At one point along this narrow road—a very precipitous section rightly named "no-man's pass"—they were waiting with huge boulders. As the troops tried to move through this narrow pass, the tribespeople dropped the boulders down on them, effectively blocking travel to Mushe.

The technology of warfare was not well developed in the late 1920s, but the Japanese had a number of biplanes and flew these into the area, bombing Cherry Blossom and other nearby villages. This resulted in the death of many Sediq and led ultimately to the opening of the road. Since Cherry Blossom village was believed to be the center of this revolt, the Japanese troops concentrated their efforts there.

Despite their resolve not to surrender at the Mushe battle, some of the Sediq men were taken prisoner. Rebellious to the end, they leaped into a river gorge, taking their guards with them. A restless quiet followed this tragic incident, but the area was ready to explode at any time. Both the Japanese and the Sediq recognized that continued conflict was a no-win situation. Any continued fighting, even with victory, would be shameful for the Japanese, and the Sediq, although tragic losers, felt they had shown they could stand up to the Japanese. Three decades later when I lived off and on in the village of Cherry Blossom, I was frequently entertained by evening dances that gave a visual presentation of how their ancestors had defeated the Japanese!

Ji Wang the Reconciler

The tragedy at Mushe should never have happened, because long before this the Sediq and the Japanese had negotiated a settlement meant to avoid just this kind of incident. Three decades earlier, from 1896 to 1906, the Japanese had used a Sediq woman, Ji Wang (Chi Wang), to bring peace between them and the headhunting tribespeople. Twenty-four years old and married to a Taiwanese merchant living in the city of Hualien on the east coast of Taiwan, she was fluent in Taiwanese and her own language and understood enough Japanese to be a good interpreter.

The Japanese soldiers gave a large red flag to Ji Wang. They put her in a sedan chair and took her to areas where the fighting was most fierce. She waved the flag back and forth, crying loudly, "Do not fight each other! Do not kill each other!" Her reputation was such, even as a young woman, that the antagonists listened and laid down their weapons of warfare.

Since both sides were prepared to come to a peaceful settlement, they entered into a period of cooperation. The mountain villagers around Mushe were not affected by this earlier peace settlement, but those living near Hualien above the Taroko Gorge, sometimes called the eighth wonder of the world by admiring tourists, were moved out to the foothills at the western edge of the plain that runs along the eastern sea coast. Some villages were relocated in the lower mountains along the long valley running between Hualien and Yuli.

The Japanese claimed that they wished to protect the Sediq in their new environment. They feared that Taiwanese merchants would exploit their naiveté and take advantage of them. So the government had a wire fence, most of it electrified, put about the areas occupied by the Sediq and other tribes. Ever-present police stations at two or three places about the villages made it almost impossible for outsiders to get in. And, of course, this enclosure prevented the Sediq from having contact with the outside world.

With permission, the Sediq could return to their old habitats for hunting deer, wild boar, monkeys, flying squirrel, and bear. They followed an elaborate ceremony of inquiring of the *sisil* bird to find out if there were favorable omens. Their religious life, as long as it followed the old traditions of taboos and the worship of ancestors, was not disturbed by the Japanese. The conquerors knew that this would fit comfortably with their efforts to impose shrine attendance, more a patriotic duty than a religious ceremony, on the people. Christianity, the Sediq would later learn, was not viewed favorably by the government.

In general, the Japanese respected minority languages and cultures. The police who lived in the Sediq villages learned the tribal language and did not interfere with tribal customs. Erin Asai, a Japanese scholar at the Institute of Linguistics of Taihoku University, prepared two massive volumes on *The Myths and Traditions of the Formosan Native Tribes* and also wrote simple grammars on the Sediq and Yami languages. This attitude toward minority cultures and languages, although not without its ethnic chauvinism, was far more enlightened than later Chinese nationalism that had no room for minority peoples.

Reconciliation between the Sediq and God

The Sediq have often exclaimed, "The Japanese prepared us to accept the gospel." Without seeming to be too Calvinistic, I tried to help them see that this was God's purpose, and the Japanese were merely his unwilling servants. How did these past experiences of the Sediq prepare them to receive Jesus Christ?

Factors Leading to Faith

After making peace with the Japanese, first through Ji Wang and then after the Mushe incident, the Sediq lost their sense of tribal identity. The name *sediq* means "person," and it is applied, not only to themselves, but to all humanity. As is the case with other groups in Taiwan and in the rest of the world, it is the old story, "We are the people!" With headhunting, the basic building block of their world view, gone, the Sediq were questioning whether they really were "the people." Their confidence was shaken and life had lost much of its meaning. How could they relate to the moral order of the universe? What hope was there for the future? What meaning did any of their taboos have, related as they were to the spirit world? How was a person justified from the claims of accusers or from his failure to live by the old taboos? Was there a way to get rid of the sense of shame? And with the moral framework of life in disarray, the fear of evil spirits became more intense.

An American anthropologist, Anthony Wallace, has analyzed the way in which a society is thrown into disequilibrium when its basic premises have been destroyed. An original steady state has been challenged, and society has gone into a long, downward slide, leaving the people grasping for a new center, a force that might revitalize them. This enables them to recapture momentum, to move upward toward new goals, and to maintain a fresh steady state that will enable them to meet future challenges.[1] From this standpoint, the gospel message became this new center, something that gave life new meaning and direction. Christianity was a type of functional substitute for the old practice of headhunting. Its form was far different—peace between God and his creation and among one another, replacing the taking of heads—but it performed the same function. The Christian faith gave to the people a way of coping with their new environment and restored to them a sense of the identity, lost with their defeat by the Japanese. As they faced the growing, inevitable need to assimilate to the larger, majority Chinese civilization, how would they do so? The Christian faith gave them courage and hope.

When the Christian faith was at its height among the Sediq, World War II was drawing to a close. The Japanese police often warned the people, "Do not to believe in the 'American God.'" They urged them to commit themselves with new fervor to the Japanese *kami*. This reinforced in the people's thinking a seed that had been planted much earlier—maybe victory by the Americans in the war would deliver them from their Japanese oppressors. And the way the war seemed to be going in its later years, the Japanese gods were not doing too well. The closer the day of victory came, the more evident it was to the people that the American god was stronger and the people should believe in him. This yearning to be on the victorious side was undoubtedly a further stimulus for the people to turn to Christ in great numbers.

New identity, new hope in a new environment, a new attachment to the god winning the war—these were all important. God works in the human scene in ways we may not understand. These are not sociological reasons for faith; they are the God of history controlling all human events for his purposes. But also crucial for his purposes are the human instruments who helped to stimulate a vital faith. What greater evidence of his grace and providence that the instrument who brought about recon-

1. See *The American Anthropologist,* April 1958, 264–81, for Wallace's presentation of this theory. Eugene Nida, *Message and Mission* (New York: Harper, 1960), 144–47, gives a summary of Wallace's view.

ciliation on the human level, Ji Wang, was now the mediator for reconciliation between the Sediq and God.

Key Harvesters

Ji Wang had been raised in a traditional fashion in a Sediq village in the mountains, but she had more ambition than the usual young tribal woman. Eager to know more about the outside world, a very pressing motive for minority young people even in the late 1800s, Ji Wang married a Taiwanese husband in 1890, when she was eighteen, and went into a lucrative business with him. This was six years previous to her decade of peace-making efforts with the Japanese. Within three months her husband was murdered by two Sediq who tried to rob him. She again married and was widowed; in 1906, she married another Taiwanese. The marriage was not a good one, as this husband often gave himself to drinking, gambling, and womanizing. The final straw came seventeen years later when, returning with him to his old home on the western plains of Taiwan, she discovered that he had another wife and three children. He finally left Ji Wang in 1925, burdening her with his many debts. His creditors took all that she had, including her house, and she was left destitute.

Because of these many difficulties in her life, Ji Wang began to think about God and her relationship to him. Through the help of a Presbyterian Taiwanese pastor in Hualien, she made a decision to follow Christ and was baptized on 1 June 1924. For at least five years following her conversion she lived the life of a secret Christian among her people. In 1929 James Dickson, a Canadian Presbyterian missionary with a heart for getting the gospel into the mountain areas, learned about Ji Wang and visited the east coast to see her. He urged her to go to the Presbyterian Bible school in Dan Shui to receive Bible training. Now fifty-seven years old, Ji Wang was not an average candidate for a Christian training school. Also, she resented the fact that the Taiwanese still viewed the mountain people as savages. She gradually learned to live with this, saying to her neighbors, "You call me Savage. But since I have accepted Christ, and you refuse Him, it is *you* who are acting like savages."[2] Although she was literate in both Taiwanese and Japanese and able to speak her own language, Ji Wang's limited educational background had not prepared her for hard study. She was a woman in a society dominated by men, older than most students, and not in good health. What future could a Bible school training give her?

Dickson was very persuasive, however, and she accompanied him back to Dan Shui. She enrolled in a two-year program, but lasted for only

2. Margaret Copland, *Chi-Oang, Mother of the Taiwan Tribes Church* (Taipei: General Assembly of the Presbyterian Church of Formosa, 1962), 4.

six months. She complained that it was much easier to work in her fields all day long than to sit on hard chairs and listen to people speak and watch them write on a blackboard.

But if she was not a dedicated student, Ji Wang was an ardent witness for Christ. She was living in Kaliawan, just north of Hualien, near the present airport. This was a Taiwanese village and outside the strict control imposed by the police on Sediq villages. However, as some of her tribal friends learned about her Christian faith, they found ways to visit her. Their favorite time was late at night. No more than four or five would come at any time and usually only from nearby villages to which they could return before the break of day.

Weiran Takoh, the best-known disciple, explained the precautions that they took. The men went inside to listen to Ji Wang, and Weiran's wife was posted at the door where she could give warning of a police raid. He did not need to say that should there be a raid, his wife would be the one most quickly apprehended. Ji Wang's message was a simple one: one creator God ruled over everything and must be worshiped above all other gods; he sent his Son, Jesus Christ, to save all who believed in him; faith was shown by repentance from all those things that displeased God; prayer was essential to the Christian faith; persecution was the inevitable result of following Jesus.

Very few of those who came were able to read the Japanese Bible. The Bible in Japanese used very literary language and was difficult even for the Japanese. How much more so was it impossible for these uneducated mountain people to understand it. Japanese was the trade language that they used in all of their relations with police, government officials, and Taiwanese merchants. And yet it was spoken Japanese that was used for the oral transmission of the gospel. With minds well honed by memorizing their myths and ancient traditions, these simple mountain believers memorized many Scripture stories that helped to establish God's truth in their lives.

When those whom Ji Wang instructed returned to their own villages, they sought out family members and friends to whom they could give the great news of the creator God who not only ruled over the entire universe, but also loved them. The numbers who believed were not many at first, but gradually they increased to the point where they wanted to meet for worship. To gather in a group was not easy because of constant police surveillance. Ji Wang's teaching had not gone entirely unnoticed, and although the police were reluctant to put pressure on her, they were not kindly disposed toward her followers.

These early Sediq Christians knew that Sunday was a day of worship. Early in the morning they took all their implements of work and headed out of the village in four or five small groups of related family members.

Far up on the mountainside they assembled at a prearranged location where they worshiped God as best they could.

These believers had hidden a few Japanese Bibles under rocks, and they brought these out for use in their simple service. Usually no Scripture portion was read and no message delivered. No leaders were yet ready for this. Testimonies were very important, because the believers were learning the power of God to answer prayer and deliver them from many difficulties. They prayed for deliverance from persecution, for good harvests, for success in hunting, for healing from illness, and for their non-Christian friends to repent and follow Jesus.

On occasion Ji Wang went on teaching tours to evangelize and to encourage those who had believed. The people did their best to hide these activities from the police, but with little success. It was a cat-and-mouse game played out over several villages. The people knew how to hide Ji Wang, a tiny woman, often carrying her in a large bag like a sack of potatoes. When they smuggled her onto the small railway cars running on the narrow-gauge tracks up the valley, they put her under a large blanket or locked her in the lavatory. Believers carried her from home to home, always just a step ahead of the authorities who were more and more alarmed at the Christian following that was snowballing despite everything they tried to do.

It was hardly a mass movement, because there were no large meetings and no evidence of many believing at one time. But it was a people movement by this definition given by Donald McGavran: "The joint decision of a number of individuals—whether five or five hundred—all from the same people, which enables them to become Christians without social dislocation, while remaining in full contact with their non-Christian relatives, thus enabling other groups of that people, across the years, after suitable instruction, to come to similar decisions and form Christian churches made up exclusively of members of that people."[3] Not until World War II was over and the Japanese had been defeated was it possible to baptize believers and form churches. In almost every village, however, small groups of believers were worshiping and witnessing.

Another Sediq evangelist was Dawai. Trained for two years in the Bible school at Dan Shui, Dawai specialized in traveling throughout the mountains, preaching wherever he found listeners, and smuggling Japanese Bibles to believers. Some could read a bit, although very poorly, and found security in having a copy of God's Word. For his efforts, Dawai was badly beaten, accused of crimes against the state, and imprisoned for seven years. Upon his release, he was not as effective as previously in pro-

3. Donald McGavran, *Understanding Church Growth* (Grand Rapids: Eerdmans, 1970), 297–98.

claiming the message. He is remembered by the people as one of God's early messengers, but not as one who persevered to the end.

The most respected of Ji Wang's early disciples was Weiran Takoh. Until the Japanese departed, he carried on a witness that was to individuals or to small groups. Threatened repeatedly by the Japanese police, he refused to cease talking about Jesus. This earned him many beatings, some so severe that he was mentally impaired. The climax came when they imprisoned him in a small cage that measured about 8 feet by 4 feet by 4 feet. This was placed in the yard of his mountain home along the east coast, also in a village named Cherry Blossom, and he remained there for one year. The police released him for a few minutes two or three times a day, and his wife was allowed to give him food and drink. The police finally relented and restored his freedom, since it was obvious he feared neither them nor death and was committed to following and serving Jesus.

From the beginning there were devoted Bible women who followed in the footsteps of Ji Wang. They encouraged the women particularly, but they also had a ministry to the men. One of these, Labai, was the adopted daughter of Ji Wang, and the people's respect for the leader of their faith rubbed off on her as well.

The Christian movement among the Paiwan, Bunnun, Amis, Atayal, and Yami was helped by devoted Sediq evangelists like Weiran, by Taiwanese pastors, by missionaries, and eventually by their own local leaders. At the present time about one-half of Taiwan's high mountain peoples have become Protestant or Roman Catholic Christians. This turning to Christ has often been referred to as the Pentecost of the Hills.[4]

Grounded in Christ

The people movement to Christ, coming as it did without missionary presence during World War II, excited churches in the plains among the Taiwanese and also the returning missionaries. But they all had one question: Will it last?

Warnings from the Past

This question made sense, because earlier movements of a similar nature had long since passed out of existence. During the period when the

4. The technical Chinese name used for the minority nationalities in Taiwan is Gao Shan People. In English this means "high mountain people." Mainland Chinese in their publications on Taiwan refer to the Gao Shan language, culture, and history as if Gao Shan referred to one specific group. This is comparable to talking about the "Indian" language or culture in America, rather than using specific names: Kiowa, Apache, Comanche. The term *gao shan* is generic, and any references to language, culture, society, or religions must be specific as to which of the ten minorities is being referred to.

Dutch ruled Taiwan (1624–1661), the missionaries who accompanied the merchants and diplomats concentrated their efforts on the tribes in the mountains. They incarnated themselves among the people, a few even taking tribal girls as wives. The Gospel of Matthew was translated into one of the tribal languages, and other literature was prepared.

After a relatively short period of time, six thousand believers had been baptized, and in 1657, a theological college was founded to train leaders for the many churches. This early turning to Christ had an unfortunate political twist—Dutch authorities reserved government jobs for those who had become Christians.

Such a special privilege for Christians was both a blessing and a curse. When the Chinese general Koxinga, fleeing from the new Ming dynasty rulers in China, invaded Taiwan in 1661, he killed both the Dutch and the Christians. He had no particular anti-Christian animus, but Christianity was so closely identified with the foreign rulers that it died with them.

So thoroughly was the Christian faith of this period exterminated that no traces of the gospel remained in the traditions of the people. The movement was apparently stronger in southern Taiwan than in the north, and this may explain why the southern tribes did not practice headhunting after the Dutch period.

Another people movement that suffered extinction was among the Pepohoan, a group formed from the intermarriage of Malayo-Polynesian peoples and early Chinese settlers to whom they assimilated. The term *Pepohoan* means "savages of the plains," but they were at least one step removed from the savagery found in the deep mountains.

At its heyday in about 1900, this movement numbered nearly sixty churches in both north and south Taiwan and appeared to have the potential for much more expansion. Missionaries were thrilled, because these people were so much more responsive to the gospel than were the Chinese. These hopes were dashed as the Pepohoan churches lost their vitality, and their members assimilated to the dominant Chinese civilization.

What would keep the Sediq community of believers from suffering the same fate as these two movements? Was it possible to lay a better spiritual foundation? Were the cultural factors of a "foreign religion" and the escalating assimilation to Chinese civilization, the fatal factors during the period of Dutch role and with the Pepohoan, still operating?

The First Baptisms

As World War II was coming to a close, Ji Wang helped the mountain believers organize into informal communities in which they found mutual help and encouragement. She also selected small committees with head men to lead them. Those who lived close to the city of Hualien often made secret visits to the pastor of the church to receive spiritual nourishment. Close surveillance by the Japanese police made this a risky venture.

As soon as the war was over and it was clear that Japan had been defeated, this quasi-underground movement came to the surface. The first evidence of this were believers nearby Hualien coming to the large Presbyterian church in that city and seeking baptism. In the first year alone more than five hundred were baptized in that large church. By 1949, nearly five thousand Sediq had confessed their faith through baptism.

Baptism to these tribal Christians was no mere formality, a kind of anticlimactic event to be appended to an earlier confession of faith. Baptism, like marriage vows, was the final ratification of a slowly culminating decision process. Weiran stated, "By our own endeavor we can't leave the old bad habits and do the will of God, but God helps us through baptism. We received baptism and were cleansed from our old sins; thus we became the children of God."[5] To some American Christians, such a statement smacks of baptismal regeneration, but it also is remarkably similar to Paul's testimony on what baptism meant to him (Acts 22:16).

Organization of Churches

Before the believers were organized into churches and had their own buildings, they crowded out the services at the Hualien church. At first they mixed in with the Chinese congregation, but then it became necessary to have a separate Sediq service. Sermons were translated into Japanese, for only a very few of these mountain Christians knew Taiwanese, the local Chinese language.

Dickson, who spoke at one of these gatherings in 1946, noted the poor appearance of the Japanese Bibles that some of the people carried—moldy, weather-beaten, and tattered. Upon inquiry, he learned that the people had hidden their Bibles under rocks or clumps of leaves or even buried them to keep the police from confiscating them. The same was true of their Japanese hymnbooks. As he heard the people sing enthusiastically and noted their avid interest in the message, which they expected to go on for at least an hour, Dickson had to repeatedly pinch himself to realize that these were former headhunters.[6] What could have changed them so dramatically except the living power of Jesus Christ?

At this point in the movement, no evangelizing church gave impetus and direction to outreach and nurture. The key tribal leaders were continuing to evangelize, but they had no idea of how to organize a church

5. George Vicedom, *Faith That Moves Mountains* (Taipei: China Post, 1967), 59.

6. Edward Band, ed., *He Brought Them Out: The Story of the Christian Movement among the Mountain Tribes of Formosa* (London: The British and Foreign Bible Society, 1950), 25–26.

congregation or how to erect a church building. They had enthusiasm, and without them all would have come to a standstill, but more leaders were needed.

Pastor Wu, the young Taiwanese pastor of the church in Hualien, gave critical help at this juncture. Before he baptized the first believers, he insisted that they must have believed for at least two years. He made time in his busy schedule to visit in many villages, instructing in the faith and teaching many hymns. With Ji Wang's help and advice, he selected for special training young men and women with leadership potential. Bringing their own food, they came and lived with Pastor Wu for several months. During this time he gave himself unstintedly to them, not only instructing in the Bible but also helping them to understand the constitution of a church, bookkeeping procedures, and better farming methods.

Pastor Wu organized a total of seventeen Sediq churches in this early period. Because he was Presbyterian he organized them along the lines of this denomination, and eventually the churches were associated with the Presbyterian Church in Formosa. No trained pastors were available, but he appointed elders and the church community elected its deacons. A sense of order was far preferable to the potential anarchy in church affairs. Some observers have wondered, however, if it would not have been better to allow the churches to develop patterns of church life more congenial to their own traditions.[7]

If the new Christians did not know how to organize a church, they seemed to know even less about erecting church buildings. Some groups living in the mountain areas above the Taroko Gorge came to Pastor Wu and asked him, "How do you build a church?" Taking out a piece of paper, he sketched a rough drawing of a bamboo building with thatched roof and gave it to them, promising that when he visited in a few weeks he would fill out the detail. A few weeks was too long to wait, however, and when he arrived the crude building had already been erected.[8]

The fact that the people lived in or close to the mountains and that simple building materials were available to them freely meant that they did not need to depend upon assistance either from Taiwanese churches or from foreign missionaries. The church buildings were very simple, utilized crude logs on a bare dirt floor for seating, and, apart from a rough-hewn pulpit, were devoid of any other trimmings. For festive occasions, such as Christmas, Easter, and the harvest festival, the people strung colorful paper decorations from wall to wall.

Over the years these structures, appropriate in the early days of faith, have been replaced by wood, stone, and reinforced concrete buildings.

7. Vicedom, *Faith That Moves Mountains,* 69–71.
8. James Dickson, *Stranger Than Fiction* (Toronto: Evangelical Publishers, n.d.), 37–38.

The east coast of Taiwan has strong earthquakes and violent typhoons, and these church buildings have proved to be far more secure. Sediq Christians take pride in the fact now that their buildings are no less attractive than those of the Taiwanese and Chinese churches in the plains. The homes of the people in the Sediq villages are also more sturdy and beautiful than they once were, but to the Christians nothing is more important than to have an adequate church building in which they may worship God.

A Special Training School

With the exception of Ji Wang and Dawai, none of those leading the Sediq church at that time had received any special leadership training. Dawai no longer had any influence, and Ji Wang died in the spring of 1946 at the age of seventy-four. Who would lead this church that was bursting at the seams? Informal training given by some of the more concerned Taiwanese pastors was important. It was hardly sufficient, however, for the demands of this new day when the gospel could be taken, almost without restriction, into all mountain areas.

Pastor Wu helped to organize a training school, but two major needs must be met. First, there must be a school building, with classroom space and dormitories. The Christians themselves had a solution for the facilities. They brought the wood from the mountains, and they assigned to each of several village churches a quota of thirty or forty workers to come in succession each week until the buildings, sufficient to accommodate thirty-five students, had been completed.

Who would have the time to head up this new school and to give full time to teaching the students? The Canadian Presbyterian Mission enlisted one of its missionary couples from Japan, Mr. and Mrs. McIlwaine, to take over this task. The first class, which commenced in 1946, consisted of twenty-one Sediq, two Amis, and one Saiset. All of the instruction was conducted in Japanese, the only language the McIlwaines knew and the only trade language available to any of the tribal groups.

Many years later I asked Pastor Tailong Litok (Li Shouxin), my longtime colleague in Bible translation and a member of the first class of students, about some problem in the interpretation of a passage in Romans. He replied that he first encountered this problem in Bible school, but that the solution always eluded him. Then he added, "Our instruction was in Japanese, and the Japanese Bible is very difficult to understand."

Ultimately the Bible school, now Yu Shan Theological Seminary located on a mountainside above a beautiful lake south of Hualien, would have believers from ten or more tribal groups. Japanese has long been replaced by Mandarin Chinese as the language of instruction. Ideally, each group would have instruction in its own language, but this would have demanded several schools, each with separate languages, or one school where separate languages would be used with each group. Neither of these solutions was possible for the Presbyterian Church in Formosa, from the standpoint of either finances or personnel. Unfortunately, this has meant that tribal leaders have not learned adequately how to express the gospel message with precision in their own language. For difficult concepts, they often revert to either Japanese or Chinese.

Bibles for the Sediq

Conventional mission thinking has said that a group of people need God's Word in their own language before there can be a significant movement to Christ. This would be ideal, but it did not happen with the Sediq, the several other groups in Taiwan, and the Miao, Lisu, Lahu, and Wa in China who were swept into the kingdom of God through dynamic people movements. Faith came first through the oral proclamation of the gospel, led by a few leaders who had learned stories from the Japanese Bible. Only later was there a Bible in the people's own language.

Dickson contacted the leaders of the Wycliffe Bible Translators in 1952 to see if they would assign missionaries to learn the several mountain languages of Taiwan and to translate the Bible. They replied that several missionaries from other mission agencies were either in or soon coming to Taiwan and would be able to do the work.

By 1953 many of these missionaries or Taiwanese pastors were in place and ready to start their work: Hu Wenchih, a Taiwanese pastor, for the Bunnun; Clare McGill, Canadian Presbyterian, for the Atayal; John Whitehorn, English Presbyterian, for the Paiwan; Ed Torjeson, The Evangelical Alliance Mission, for the Amis; Grace Wakelin, independent, for the Yami on Orchid Island; and myself with the Conservative Baptists for the Sediq. Although the translators helped in evangelism and nurture among the Presbyterian churches, these tasks were carried out largely by local leaders.

Translators met regularly as a consultative group for Bible translation and found that, with little differences here and there, the problems were similar. For example, what kind of alphabet should be used? Translators wanted to use the English romanized alphabet. But the Kuomintang government in Taiwan, nervous that the new government on the mainland was using *pin yin*, its own form of romanization, let it be known that this would not be acceptable. So, with the help of Zhu Zhaoxiang, a fine Presbyterian Christian, who was in the Department of Education, each translator adapted a Chinese phonetic system, usually employed only to help Chinese people learn to read Chinese. Most minority translations in the 1950s, 1960s, and 1970s used this unwieldy orthography. Beginning in the early 1980s it was possible, albeit without official permission, to use a romanized alphabet.

What term should be used for God? How did the rather passive structure of Malayo-Polynesian languages fit with the more active sentence structures of the biblical languages? What should be done with key biblical concepts, such as "save," that seemed to have no equivalents in the tribal languages? Often there were more questions than answers. But in frequent discussions with fellow translators and with the ever-available help of translation consultants from the United Bible Societies, the translators prepared hymnals, catechisms, study booklets, individual books of the Bible, the entire New Testament, and eventually the entire Old Testament.

Whatever the expenditure in time, money, and energy, the reward was that the people now saw that "God speaks our language." Sediq Christians often prayed, "Lord, you know that we are as the beasts here in the forest about us—with nothing written in our language." For them now to see that God's Word could be inscribed in their own language was an answered prayer far beyond their wildest expectations.

How true this was for the leaders who preached so constantly, but who had nothing to depend on except their often faulty memories to give the biblical message. A Bible woman, Tomon Awi, had a regular routine. She was a *Bible* woman, and therefore she felt she must teach the Bible. When she stood before a congregation in the early days, she would take out her Japanese Bible. Then she lifted it before her as if to read, only to stop, take out her eyeglasses from her blouse, and wipe them off carefully. After putting on her glasses, she once again raised her Bible as if to read it. Finally, with a little gesture of hopelessness, she gave the Bible to a young man on the front row and asked him to read it.

As soon as individual books of Scripture were published, Weiran, Labai, Tomon, and many other local leaders now for the first time read God's Word in Sediq and proclaimed it with a new vigor and authority. Weiran often told friends that his Bible was to him more precious than either silver or gold, and that once he picked it up, he knew neither how to lay it down nor when to stop underlining.

Faith and Repentance

Sediq believers in their witness for Christ referred to themselves as "we who have repented." Life in Christ was a new direction, no longer walking in the ways of the past but following in the way of Christ. The emphasis was on the positive—believing in the one Creator God, worshiping him with other believers, believing in his Son who had died on the cross, trusting him to overcome evil spirits and sickness, praying for him to help in all aspects of their lives, and talking about him to their friends.

Not much cognitive information was involved—possibly less than what an average American teenager might learn in Sunday school—but what these Christians did know they obeyed with a total commitment.

Sediq preachers were always careful when witnessing to start with "brothers and sisters." Even though they knew that not all those listening were their brothers and sisters in Christ, they did not want to convey any feeling that they were outsiders and not included among those who had repented and truly trusted Christ. This attitude of corporate identity with all of the people is needed to sustain a people movement, and not turn it into a church activity.

The negative dimension was not omitted. Traditional folk religion lives by taboos, not precise moral precepts. Dark demons filled the life of the Sediq, and they prescribed and controlled the system of taboos. Taboos embraced every part of life—all those things that could and could not be done, spelled out in great detail and taught faithfully to each succeeding generation. They had a high sense of shame, brought when they violated societal taboos, but no concept of guilt.

When the gospel came into their lives, the risen Christ set them free from this fearful bondage. Believers now trusted in a loving God whose good hand ruled over them in grace and who, through the death of his Son, had defeated the demons. Not that many of the customs associated with these taboos did not continue. Cultural features such as those related to marriage, the birth of a child, planting of their crops, the building of a home, and hunting in the high mountains continued as they always had, but with no sense of fear.

The major celebration of the Sediq year was the harvest festival when the people rejoiced over the good harvests that they had received. This had been a time to sacrifice to the spirits and give them thanks for the abundant food supply. Now, apart from Christmas, this feast in August is the major Christian festival and is celebrated in church, with the people bringing to God not only their thanks but also a portion of their harvest to be used in his service. In many instances, the way they observed an old custom was changed, but the intended purpose continued. Instead of inquiring of the *sisil* bird to determine omens for hunting, the hunters came to the church with their weapons. The pastor prayed for them publicly, asking for safety and success, before they went on their way.

In time, it became apparent to the Sediq that some old customs must be abandoned. Sediq fathers had taught control and discipline to their sons, since this was demanded if they were to succeed in headhunting. When a son was growing up, for example, he was required to sleep naked with a young woman for several nights and refrain from sexual relations. He was warned that should he fail in this, the *otox*, the spirits, would bring calamity upon him and upon his family. Some Sediq households continued with this practice after they had become Christians. It led only to sexual orgies by the young people, who now felt they were under no constraints and could give free rein to their passions. The legalistic system of taboos had a dynamic restraining force through fear. The gospel of God's grace brought freedom, but the people were slow to realize that they must avoid temptation.

In the first few years after conversion, the Sediq continued with their dance festivals, many of which had to do with headhunting and other activities related to the spirit world. Gradually they realized that to rethink and re-act these old customs did not help them in living for Christ.

A prominent part of old Sediq life had been the endless reciting to younger generations of their ancient myths. These tales were the Sediq way of explaining and rationalizing the world in which they lived. Some of these were morally neutral and talked about their ancient origin, about a great flood, and about the pleasant way of life in the past. Other stories were very risqué and dealt with many sexual matters. Once the people became Christian, it was very difficult to get them to recite these tales, even when they were told that the grammar, syntax, and specific vocabulary found in them were needed for Bible translation purposes.

Drunkenness was and is the besetting sin of the Sediq. Drinking was an indispensable part of all festivals and ceremonies. The people honored their ancestors with special libations of wine; no serious discussions took place without heavy drinking, and agreements were sealed by the two parties to the contract imbibing wine together out of one cup. It seemed impossible for the people to drink socially and then stop. All drinking led to drunkenness. When the people believed in Christ and joined Presbyterian churches, the elders made nondrinking a requirement for baptism. Some were able to honor this commitment, but many found it very difficult and violated their pledge. Failing in this often led to lying, adultery, bad hunting accidents, brawls, and killing. This problem continues to plague the Sediq church, even its leaders, and obstructs it from having the dynamic witness that it desires.

Even though the early emphasis of the gospel was on Jesus as liberator from evil spirits, Christians, through reading and hearing the Word of God, have come to know him as savior from sin. They have learned what it is to be guilty before a holy God, and their faith has become more well-rounded. Christian truth is like a many-faceted diamond. The entering point of faith is different for people of different cultures, even for individuals within one culture. As people grow in Christ, the other dimensions of the gospel gain in prominence.

Shortly after he had written his well-known book *Bridges of God* in the early 1950s, Donald McGavran, the leading exponent of church growth philosophy, visited a small Sediq church. After the service was ended, he asked the people to stay. One by one he questioned them as to what motivated them to believe. The answers varied widely: fear of spirits, hope to be healed of a sickness, the desire for a wife to become pregnant, belief that Jesus would bring back a drunk husband. Later McGavran commented wisely, "It does not matter so much where the person started, but where they are now."

Before Sediq Christians had the Bible in their own language, they depended heavily on dreams as a way of knowing God's will. One brother who claimed that he had gone to heaven in his dream regaled wide-eyed listeners in many churches with his description of all that he had seen there. Dreams were obviously a subjective and shifting foundation for faith, and they became less prominent after people had God's written revelation.

God's Continued Work among the Sediq

The Sediq churches remain vital in their walk with Christ. The years have brought many changes. Churches can be found in all villages. The Sediq have their own Presbytery within the General Assembly of the Taiwan Presbyterian Church. Their young aspiring leaders attend Yu Shan Theological School or one of the other Presbyterian seminaries. Some have been sent abroad for study.

In August 1989 the Sediq church celebrated the completion of a revised New Testament and a shorter Old Testament. In contrast with the beginning of Bible translation in the mid-1950s, all of the most recent work on revision and the Old Testament was done by Sediq translators. God has raised up a new group of leaders who can go forward without outside help.

Since those early days when there were only Presbyterian churches, Roman Catholic missionaries have established their churches, and the True Jesus Church, an indigenous hybrid of Pentecostalism and legalism, has also entered some villages. Rivalry and interchurch squabbles have caused the police in some villages to force a truce on believers, requiring them to abstain from evangelizing and to maintain the status quo in church membership boundaries.

Many problems plague all mountain church groups. Chief among these is the encroaching power of Chinese culture and modern urban life. Many of the young women, reluctant to face a lifetime of hard farm labor if they marry a Sediq husband, have gone to the large cities to seek work and, they hope, a Chinese husband. Failing in these goals, they have ended up in prostitution.

Sediq Christian leaders are well aware of these problems, and, even as their forebearers faced and overcame critical difficulties during the Japanese period and in the early years after the end of World War II, they are prepared to move forward into this new, challenging era in Taiwan's history.[9]

Conclusion

The gospel revitalized the culture of the Sediq, becoming the main building block in a new society that arose out of the ruins of their old life. So has it been with many other minority groups in Taiwan and nationalities in China that have responded to the gospel.[10] The Miao, Lisu, Yi, Lahu, Wa—found largely in Yunnan and Guizhou in southwest China—were all oppressed people whose lives were being overwhelmed, either by the Chinese or by other minority landlords. The human oppression was made even more bitter by bondage to demons.

The gospel, as proclaimed by sensitive missionaries of the cross who treated them as human beings, did not despise them. It took their side against the oppressors as a message of glorious liberation. People were free and renewed in Christ, and they responded even as the Sediq did. Their churches today are filled with tens of thousands of believers, most usually led by local lay leaders with no formal theological training.

The Christian message is a catalyst for revitalizing a culture that has been challenged. Not an isolated event, it is the principal key that has opened the door of faith to many of China's minorities with a traditional religious background.

9. Where other sources have not been listed in this chapter I have depended on my own notes and oral histories given to me by many Sediq friends.

10. This chapter is only illustrative of the great turning to Christ among the Atayal, Amis, Bunnun, Paiwan, and Yami. The Republic of China, beginning in the fall of 1992, instituted a new educational thrust in public primary schools to encourage minority students to learn to read material in their own languages.

12

Why Did Some Receive and Others Refuse the Liberating Gospel?

The Story Has Not Been Fully Told

One hundred million people divided into fifty-five minority nationalities living in an area of 3,692,244 square miles, a territory greater than that of Europe or the continental United States! Into this mix add hundreds of outside Protestant and Catholic mission agencies, many with an agenda to have a part in evangelizing minority peoples. How can the story be told fully? We have analyzed the major groups that have consistently refused to accept the Christian faith—the Mongolians, the Tibetans, and the Uighurs in Central Asia. In their resistance they represent other Altaic (Turkic, Mongol, and Tungus-Manchu) peoples in north, northwest, and northeast China. We have said nothing about the Zhuang, the Naxi, the Tujia, the Yao, the Dong, the Li of Hainan Island, and the Bouyei. These all have followed traditional folk religion. Were they totally neglected by missionaries? Not at all. But the results have been so minimal, usually no more than a 1 percent response at best, that they must be classified as resistant.

In some instances, groups named by missionaries in the past, such as the Diois of Kui-chow, among whom Catholic missionaries reported three thousand converts in the 1920s, are no longer listed among minority nationalities.[1] Who are the Chung-chia, a large group in Guizhou and Guangxi, sometimes identified with and other times differentiated from

1. Joseph Esquirol, P.F.M., "Among the Diois of Kui-chow (China) Superstition and Sorcery," *Annals of the Propagation of the Faith* (New York: The Society for the Propagation of the Faith), July-August 1921, 131–37.

the Zhuang?[2] The four hundred thousand She people of Zhejiang were not even considered a minority until well after the coming of the People's Republic of China.

We have not been able to include every "successful" effort among the minorities of China. The Sediq (Gao Shan), Miao, Yunnan Yi, Lahu, Wa, and Lisu stories have been told. Were there other responsive groups? Yes! In this category are the Amis, Bunnun, Paiwan, Atayal, and Yami in Taiwan and the Bai, Hani, and Jingpo in China. Their stories were intermingled often with those of other minorities, or the details of how the gospel came to them were not precisely told in accessible records.

Even though the Protestant minority Christian population of Guizhou and Guangxi is not great, it outdistances the number of Han Chinese Christians. In Guizhou the number of Christians from the Miao, Yi, Bai, Bouyei, and Dong nationalities has reached 90 percent of the total. In Guangxi there are thirty thousand Protestant Christians from the Han and eleven different minority groups, such as the Zhuang, Miao, and Dong.[3] Zhuang converts are probably half of this number, and the Catholic Zhuang community may be equally as numerous. Extensive people movements occurred among the Amis, Bunnun, Paiwan, and Atayal in Taiwan in the 1940s and 1950s.

Small Protestant Christian populations are found among the Hani, Dai, Bai, and Jingpo minorities in China and the Yami in Taiwan. The Hani, living in the Hani Autonomous County, have several thousand Christians, many of whom were first exposed to the gospel message through the Assembly of God mission in the years just previous to the downfall of the Kuomintang. The name *Dai* is synonymous with Buddhism, and yet in the very midst of the Dai area is the Christian village of Mengyun near Xishuangbana, the remnant of evangelism ninety years ago by the American Presbyterian Mission in Burma. A small congregation meets in a home in Jinhong, and several small churches have been established in the surrounding areas. No reliable estimate can be given of the size of the Dai Christian church.

Known as Kachin or Jingpaw in Burma, but as Jingpo in China, this minority nationality has seven or eight thousand Christians in the Chinese counties of Ruili, Huibeng, and Bangda, all straddling or near the border between Myanmar (Burma) and China. Related to the work of the Baptist mission in Burma, most of the evangelism and literature work

2. Cyril Edwards, "Glimpses of Tribal Survey," *China's Millions* (British edition), March-April 1948, 18–19. He refers to the Chung-Chia as Tai, which then relates them to the Zhuang.

3. "Minority Christians Become a Majority in Two Southern Provinces," *Chinese Around the World*, July 1991, 13.

was done by Ola Hanson, assisted ably by several local Kachin evangelists. A recent visitor observed that the Jingpo Christians have baptized their folk traditions and dances to the use of the gospel, thereby maintaining an ongoing contact with their nonbelieving friends.

The number of Bai Christians, found largely in the area around Dali in western Yunnan, may be as high as thirty thousand, although many have turned back to their pre-Christian traditional religion. The number attending the large, colorful church in Dali has been greatly reduced over the last few years.[4]

Missiological Issues of Resistance and Receptivity

To understand past Christian effort among the minority nationalities of China is far more than an interesting historical footnote. History is not merely past; it is present. It forces us to ask hard questions about the nature of the gospel itself, the way it was proclaimed and lived, and the important issues that determined whether it was received or rejected. We have taken a quick look at these matters in the foregoing chapters. As we now examine the issues in more depth, it is necessary to consider the *receptors* and the *source* of the Christian message.

The Receptors of the Message

General Observations

That Buddhist and Muslim minority nationalities in China should respond slowly or not at all to the Christian message is hardly surprising. The same pattern has been seen in Africa and in other parts of Asia. An ancient, complex, classical religious tradition, accompanied by strong social cohesiveness and a high sense of corporate identity, has always resisted Christianity. Particularly is this so when Jesus has been presented in a pietistic, individualistic, other-worldly pattern. Not that there may not be large numbers of conversions when the classical faith is merely a thin veneer over a basic foundation of traditional religion, such as with the Wa and some of the Lahu.

Western Protestant mission societies, as well as some Catholic groups, have lamented the lack of response from China's resistant minority na-

4. Most of the material on the Hani, Dai, Bai, and Jingpo has been taken from the September-October 1990 issue of *Bridge: Church Life in China Today* that had as its subtitle "Ethnic Groups in Yunnan." See also a chart from Huafu Lianlo Zhongxin Zixun Fuwubu and included as an appendix to an article in *China Churches Today,* May 1992, "Who Will Respond to the Call of China's Minority Peoples?" 39–43. The estimates given of Christians among China's minorities are very tentative.

tionalities. They responded to what they believed was God's call in going to China. Using numerous Scripture passages to motivate them, they mobilized young people, raised millions of dollars, and educated their constituencies with slogans and promotional material that raised the expectation that these "pagans" would soon respond to the gospel. And yet, one hundred years later, the task may be less completed than it was originally. How have they explained what anyone in business would call a failure?

Most of the blame has been placed on the receptors of the message. Theological rationales have always been ready at hand. Has God really elected these people to salvation? Maybe God never intended many Tibetans or Mongolians to enter his heavenly kingdom. Were they possibly too reprobate? Appealing to Romans 1, missionaries wondered if God had "given them up." Does God reveal himself only once in time to a given people, and its response becomes then a one-time critical corporate decision that determines its spiritual destiny? Even as the human race has "sinned in Adam," its federal head, has the course of future generations been determined by earlier decisions? Because a people has refused God's love in some specific way, has God abandoned them to a corporate hardness of heart? Or does God continue to seek this people in each generation, irrespective of previous response? Or has a group become more resistant because of progressive hardening of the heart in successive generations? From another perspective, is it possible that resistant peoples in Central Asia, Tibet, and Mongolia were evangelized much earlier in the Christian era by the Nestorians?

Some evangelicals, particularly those with a dispensational hermeneutic, were committed to a called-out small church, and a great response to the gospel among any people group would have been surprising, unexpected, and even suspicious. The way into the kingdom of God is straight and narrow, and only a very few will enter. Possibly, in the last days, there will be an eschatological outpouring of the Holy Spirit that will open the floodgates of converts. Nothing much, however, can be expected in the present dispensation. Extreme dispensationalists have affirmed that the final phase of world evangelization will be done by a converted Jewish remnant of 144,000 after the church has been taken to be with Christ in the first stage of his second advent. This does not diminish their zeal for evangelism, but they can be more relaxed since they know the ultimate outcome. The results are totally in God's hands.

Claiming support from Daniel 10:12–14, in which the "prince of the Persian kingdom" resisted an angelic messenger sent to help Daniel, some missiologists affirm that the most resistant areas of the world are controlled by demonic beings whose principal work is to thwart the spread of the truth. To proclaim the name of Jesus in these areas demands that Christian emissaries not only overcome ignorance, but also do battle with Satan and his hosts. All of God's resources of signs and wonders are required if territorial demons are to be overcome, and the lands they control are to be released from spiritual oppression.

Serious exegetes of Scripture, often unacquainted with personal demonic oppression found in many parts of the world, tend to interpret Paul's statements on powers, authorities, and principalities as references only to oppressive economic, political, and cultural structures of society. A case may exist for this, but it does not rule out the reality of personal demonic forces. Protestant missionaries may not have given enough attention to this reality in their past work. John Nevius, an American Presbyterian missionary to China and Korea in the late 1800s, commented: "No Protestant missionary, so far as I know, has ever given native converts instructions as to casting out spirits; and few, if any, have dreamed that their converts would have the disposition, the ability, or the opportunity to do so."[5]

Most missionaries, at least theoretically, have not denied the pervasive power of demons in creating a corporate resistance to the gospel. What is new in the current emphasis is to recognize territorial demons, to discover their precise names, and to develop elaborate procedures of prayer and national exorcism to defeat them. Missionaries are almost required to be spiritual SWAT teams. The validity of this approach has not been buttressed by responsible exegesis that considers cultural factors. Moreover, the detailed procedures are ad hoc and subjective.

Religious, Social, and Cultural Factors in Receptivity and Resistance

The specific situations of receptor groups are a part of the bigger picture of crosscultural religious diffusion. The study of diffusion has concentrated on technological innovations and social and cultural practices; how a religion passes from one culture to another has not been given equal attention. Robert Montgomery suggests that a fruitful area for investigation is what he calls a "sociology of missions—the sociological study of the spread of religions." To do this he proposes that scholars pay attention to "corporate self-identity—that part of an individual's self-concept which derives from his knowledge of his membership of a social group (or groups) together with the value and emotional significance attached to that membership."[6]

5. John Nevius, *Demon Possession,* 8th ed. (Grand Rapids: Kregel, 1968), 14.

6. These quotes and the following material on a sociology of missions come from Robert Montgomery, "Some Research Directions for the Sociology of Missions," an unpublished paper presented at the Annual Meeting of the Religious Research Association, Pittsburgh, Penn., 8–10 November 1991.

Religion is a valued aspect of social identity, and, unlike race or sex, is changeable. Whether or not it will change depends on several complex intergroup relations that involve domination and subordination. A dominant group will probably see no need to change its religion; a subordinate group may feel that an outside religion cannot help it. It then would resist a new religious faith, certainly one associated with the dominant group. It responds either by strengthening its traditional religion or by mixing it with some outside elements.

A group that is dominant politically, economically, or culturally may feel that its social identity can be enhanced by taking the religion from a culture it perceives as superior in this respect to its own. Does this, along with other factors, explain the success of Buddhism, a foreign religion in China? Likewise, a subordinate group threatened by a dominant group may find great help and new strength in the religion of some nonthreatening group. To determine the dynamics of change a careful analysis must be made of all of the internal groups within a given receptor society.

T'ien Ju-k'ang, a scholar from mainland China, has made an extensive analysis of Miao, Lisu, and Lahu societies to find reasons for their large-scale conversions to Christianity. He finds a key in the relationships between dominant and subordinate groups. Each of these three minority nationalities was oppressed, either by the Chinese or by other minorities, such as the Yi, Bai, and Naxi. They responded by rebellions, migrations to other areas, and seeking out the top of the mountains for their villages and farmlands. Some were easily assimilated and became those called "tame" *(shu)*. Those who resisted were considered "wild" *(sheng)*. Between these two extremes were variations on a long continuum. He adds a further dimension to Montgomery's sociological analysis—those groups that responded best to the Christian faith were decentralized in their political and religious structures. Thus, they were unable to resist cohesively, either in their overall internal tribal structure or on the village and temple level, the invasion of a new religion. To use Montgomery's phrase, this introduced a new "social identity," with all of the values associated with the Christian faith.[7] Anthony Wallace paints a broader picture of the crisis into which any society may fall. The crisis need not come from a dominant group oppressing a subordinate one; it may derive from strife among equal groups or it may be stimulated by internal social and economic problems. These provoke disequilibrium within society, leading to a decline and collapse. Then, new leaders, new ideas, new

7. T'ien Ju-k'ang, "Cementation of Segregatory Tribes—the Protestant Church Among Minority Nationalities in Yunnan," an unpublished paper, 1990. See also his *Peaks of Faith* (Leiden: Brill, 1993).

goals, new values may lead to revitalization, putting the society back again on a steady state.[8]

Historians have noted some of these same features in their analysis of resistance and receptivity. Paul Cohen has observed:

> When resistant peoples were oppressed by the Chinese, they had close-knit communities and systematic religious beliefs and they focused on these and resisted even more vigorously. The past was a path for the future. Only a few on the margins dared to think of change, and these were the ones who encouraged the missionaries, but their power was limited for the most part to small enclaves.
>
> With the responsive groups there was not such a close-knit community cohesiveness, and nothing in their overall framework that could resist, except maybe a clan leader. As the people went through persecution or oppression, they found the Christian faith and its emissaries to be their protectors, and, in one way or another, the faith became the focal point of a new identity for a large number of people.[9]

Kenneth Scott Latourette extrapolates a broader principle from these and many similar situations around the world where the Christian faith has spread rapidly: "Never has Christianity been adopted where the pre-Christian culture remained intact. In some regions of high civilization (Persia, India, China, and Japan) it has won the allegiance of minorities . . . Christianity has seldom since its early expansion in the Mediterranean world succeeded in becoming the predominant faith of any people which at the time of their conversion possessed an advanced civilization."[10]

Lamin Sanneh, professor at Yale Divinity School, raises a mild objection to this when he notes that even Latourette admits that the Christian faith won out peacefully over a vigorous neo-Platonism, which was hardly a primitive tradition.[11] To this comment Latourette would probably reply that this was a part of its early expansion in the Mediterranean world and is not to be taken as normative of Christianity's worldwide expansion.

Many find this quotation from Latourette to be profoundly disturbing. What sort of power is resident within the Christian faith that it needs po-

8. Anthony F. C. Wallace, *Religion: An Anthropological View* (New York: Random House, 1966), 30–37.

9. Paul Cohen, "Reflections on the Missionary Movement," in *The Cambridge History of China,* vol. 10, *Late Ch'ing, 1800–1911, part 1,* ed. John Fairbank (Cambridge: Cambridge University Press, 1978), 543–90.

10. Kenneth Scott Latourette, *A History of the Expansion of Christianity,* vol. 1, *The First Five Centuries* (New York: Harper and Brothers, 1937), 7.

11. Lamin Sanneh, "Gospel and Culture," in *Bible Translation and the Spread of the Church,* ed. Phillip Stine (Leiden: Brill, 1990), 9.

litical, social, and cultural forces to destroy the original culture before it can take root? How can the Christian faith incarnate itself in a culture that is destroyed by all of those forces accompanying its propagation? Is it true that only a primitive people with no so-called high civilization can become Christian in any large-scale movement and have Christianity as its predominant faith? Perhaps the charge made against the missionary movement that it has engaged in "cultural imperialism" and been an agent of a domineering western civilization is true!

But before we give up too quickly on Latourette's statement, let us probe its implications. How may a pre-Christian culture fail to remain intact? Several paths are possible:

1. A particular nation, continent, or people group may be colonized by outside forces whose culture is then imposed on it. Was this not true of the Spanish conquistadors who conquered Central and Latin America? After the conquest, many tried to humanize the conquest, or to establish "reductions," or, as did Bartolome de Las Casas, to protest against such oppression of the Indian peoples. But these several options of nurturing the people came only after much of the original culture had been destroyed.

2. A people may willingly give up its culture in whole or in part as it receives the gospel. This was true of the Lahu, who asked William Young to cut the cords from their necks and wrists to symbolize their readiness to give up the evil features of their old culture.

3. A minority people within a dominant culture may be almost totally assimilated into that culture. This has happened in China with the sinicization of the Manchu people, who ruled China from 1648 to 1911. They no longer speak their own language. Nothing about their lifestyle indicates that they preserve anything of their ancient culture. In this instance, the Manchu have not received the gospel, because they became as resistant to the Christian faith as the Chinese to whose culture they assimilated.

4. Force or some combination of external influences may result in a people in whole or in part giving up its culture and accepting another one, such as the Sediq, one of the Gao Shan peoples in Taiwan.

Protestant and Catholic missionaries working among China's minorities, whether or not aware that any large-scale movements to Christ required the replacement of the pre-Christian culture, sought coercively or noncoercively to gain partial control of the receptor culture. We have noted how the Belgian Scheut fathers tried to gain the favor of the several kings who ruled over large fiefdoms in Mongolia. Their best success came when fanatic Muslims overran Mongolian villages, destroying not only their faith, but their culture as well. Missionaries in Tibet with the Paris Foreign Mission Society were not reluctant to appeal to the French Protectorate to gain an advantage with Chinese and Tibetan officials.

Nor were the Protestants slow to use such power tactics, even though they often condemned the Catholics for doing so. Victor Plymire nearly entered into a blood covenant with a Tibetan clan chieftain that would have given him opportunity to do what he wished over an extensive area of Tibet. And what shall we say about George Patterson, who, with a platform of human rights, sided with one political faction in Tibet and hoped, with its victory, to have a Christian foundation for a new Tibetan society based on biblical principles?

To raise questions about these power plays is not to condemn appeals to appropriate decision-making centers in any society. These efforts, however, must not be confused with power politics, manipulation, or unwise use of missionary clout and money. Neither should missionaries be compulsive in seeking an advantage when one society (as Muslims) has ravaged another one (as Mongolians). In all of these situations, the very character of God and the nature of the gospel are at stake.

We may or may not agree with the theories generated by sociologists, anthropologists, and historians or with the tactics followed by some missionaries. Be this as it may, the relationships among dominant and subordinate groups have played a major part in the resistance or receptivity to the Christian faith by China's minority nationalities. A simple, tentative paradigm is this:

Receptive

Oppressed by dominant group, submits, and is partially sinicized. Finds a new social identity through Christian faith (Yunnan Yi, Sediq, Lahu, Wa, Miao, Lisu, and Koreans).

Resistant

a. Oppressed by dominant group, but does not submit; essentially independent. Retains its own social identity and resists any new religion (Sichuan Yi).
b. Oppressed by dominant group, submits partially, and/or sinicized totally or in part. Adopts a new social identity that has elements of Chinese social identity or reinforces features of traditional religious beliefs and values (Mongols, Tibetans, Islamic peoples in Xinjiang; traditional religious groups like Zhuang).

Although only three positions are represented, the situation is more complex, with many gradations along a continuum from receptivity to resistance.

Issues of dominance-subordination and of crises within societies may create the conditions favoring response or resistance to new ideas and values. Could we then rephrase Latourette and say "that Christianity has never been adopted where the pre-Christian culture has not been dominated in some way (socially, culturally, psychologically) by another culture"? Psychological, social, and cultural factors may also aid or hinder transcultural communication. Charles Kraft has identified the basic relationships between two societies that influence the diffusion of ideas (see table 2).

TABLE 2

Factors Influencing Acceptance/Rejection of New Ideas

Factors	*Hinder Acceptance*	*Help Acceptance*
Basic premises of source and receptor cultures	Very different	Very similar
Attitude of receptors toward own culture	Very positive	Very negative
Attitude of receptors toward source culture	Despised	Respected
Openness to new ideas	Closed	Open
Pace of change	Slow	Rapid
Borrowing tradition	None	Strong
Morale	Proud	Demoralized
Self-sufficiency	Strong	Weak
Security	Threatened	Stabilized
Flexibility	Resistant	Adaptive
Advocate	Nonprestigious	Prestigious
How ideas relate to felt need	Unrelated	Related
Fit of new idea with present ideology	Incompatible	Compatible

From Charles Kraft, "Ideological Factors in Intercultural Communication," *Missiology* 2, 3 (July 1974): 300.

In one sense, this table draws out the characteristics of an oppressed people. For example, with the Sediq in Taiwan and the Lahu, Wa, Miao, Yi (Yunnan), and Lisu, they were demoralized and weak. They were threatened, but not by the people from whom they were receiving the Christian faith. They were negative toward their own cultures, and, because of what they had suffered, they were relatively open to new ideas, adaptive, and even willing to undergo rapid change. These peoples respected the source culture and perceived it as prestigious. When the gospel was presented with some degree of cultural sensitivity, the people saw it as related to their felt needs and compatible with their spirit-filled lives. The peoples of Yunnan and Guizhou, with many of their villages intersecting with one another, often borrowed social, cultural, and religious ideas, as well as implements and methods related to their work and living.

On the other hand, those oppressed groups who are unwilling to submit to a dominant authority, or who submit partially and are still independent in spirit, manifest nearly all thirteen factors that hinder the acceptance of new ideas or a new ideology. They all have a high sense of social identity, usually despised those groups bringing them the gospel, and did not recognize anything in the Christian message that related to their felt needs.

Do these many factors in the receptor cultures relegate God to a spectator and not an active participant in the culture? A popular proverb notes that "man's extremity is God's opportunity." Whenever an individual or a society has particular needs, a readiness is created to receive new information and values and to adopt new goals that will remedy the problems. The Spirit of God is able in these situations to bring God's message to bear. But God is not the sole actor; other religious ideas, ideologies, and deities are prepared to move in and take control. The critical factor at this point is the source, the messengers who come with the Christian faith, and the nature of their message.

The Source of the Message

The environment in which Catholic and Protestant missionaries worked in China in the last century was not favorable for proclaiming the kingdom of God. China was often in turmoil. A weak central government, local rebellions, a full-scale civil war, struggles by outside nations to gain economic and political rights, a change from dynasty to republic to warlords to a Marxist society, anti-colonial, anti-imperialistic, anti-Christian movements, massive rural and urban unrest, a never-ending, unsuccessful search for national identity, hatred between the Chinese and the minorities—all these and many other factors were constant thorns to the missionary enterprise. That missionaries and their national colleagues accomplished as much as they did in this chaotic context is remarkable. Is it too much to expect that more might have been done?

As missionaries pondered their lack of success among resistant peoples, they were very self-flagellating. For example, they bemoaned the fact that they prayed or fasted so little, appealing to Jesus' prescription for casting out demons: "this kind can come out only by prayer [and fasting]" (Mark 9:29). Or was it a lack of faith, with Mark's observation (6:5) as a prooftext: "Jesus could do no great works there because of the people's unbelief"? Many regretted they had so little vital spiritual power that could help them face up to the demonic world with courage and boldness. They sensed that they were ready to preach the gospel, but not to engage in spiritual warfare. One brother left his mission agency to enter a more charismatic one. However, mission history among the minorities in China, resistant or responsive, indicates no better success by Pentecostal mission agencies than by non-Pentecostal ones. Did any of us as missionaries pray enough or have enough faith, love, wisdom, or power? Certainly not! But did these spiritual weaknesses have a one-to-one, cause-effect relationship in explaining the paucity of results? Probably not. The picture is far more complex.

Any who worked among the resistant peoples of China can list, and not merely on the fingers of two hands, the foolish mistakes that plagued the work. Most of these related to cultural insensitivity, poor language acquisition, naive theological assumptions, an inability to understand the social dynamics set in motion when outsiders came into these kinds of encapsulated areas. To these can be added a failure to learn, understand, and apply the lessons from the past. God can and does overrule human frailty and fallibility, but these qualities did not help to promote his kingdom in China.

On a more positive note, what lessons may be learned from what missionaries did poorly or failed to do? Of prime importance is the nature of evangelism. Among the responsive minorities of Yunnan there was clearly a *preparatio evangelica*, a providential preparation within the receptor culture for the Christian faith. Was the same true in Tibet, Mongolia, and among the many Islamic groups in Xinjiang? The question seems never to have been raised seriously. Whenever anyone inquired as to how God was related to these pagan cultures, "he was quickly consigned to the dump heap of 'compromiser' or 'syncretist.'" The general approach, with some fine exceptions, was to rule out any good in the ancient religions of these countries.[12]

Missionaries operated on the assumption that they were bringing God to the receptor culture; somehow he belonged to them exclusively. They reflected little on the fact that the very religions that confronted them were the results of God's prior activity. The people were at once seeking God and rejecting him, desiring the truth and suppressing it. God had revealed himself, but the satanic kingdom had perverted his truth. Where could the missionary find remnants of his truth, partial insights on which to build, points of contact to the hungry hearts? This is far different, and much more hopeful, than assuming from the beginning that the religions of China are the creations of Satan and his evil forces.[13]

12. J. H. Edgar, *High Altitudes: Missionary Problems in Kham or Eastern Tibet* (Chengdu: Canadian Mission Press, n.d.) notes, even as he acknowledges the errors of Lamaism, that "a wholesale condemnation of Lamaism would proclaim us to be victims of a fatuous prejudice. Its long life alone should set us thinking" (p. 4).

13. This approach is presented clearly by John Herman Bavinck, *The Church Between Temple and Mosque* (Grand Rapids: Eerdmans, 1966). Clinton Bennett points out that in the nineteenth century there were two types of British missionaries seeking to reach Islamic peoples.

When a point of contact was discovered, the western missionaries were prone to be word-oriented and compulsive about presenting linear propositions that must be accepted, often memorized to meet catechetical requirements. Where all resistance has been broken down, this will work as well as any other approach. Where there is great resistance, missionaries will need to think more creatively. How may they lead the hearer from an experience-related, existential situation to an understanding of the gospel? It will be an economic, political, or allegiance encounter much more than a question of ontological truth. The biblical understanding of salvation, particularly in the Old Testament, has a wide range of meaning: peace or welfare, preservation in society, deliverance from an unhappy situation, rescue in danger, deliverance and victory, and eschatological deliverance from guilt and sin. Almost any sincere motivation can be a starting point for faith in Jesus Christ; postbaptismal instruction will lead to a fuller approximation to the biblical norm. Missionary preaching to people bound in oppressive demonic systems usually jumped in with forgiveness of sins as its central message. More productive, probably, would have been to explain how Jesus liberates from fear, spirit control, and taboos and restored people to a relationship with God the Creator. Ultimately, the entire gospel would be proclaimed when the people had a foundation on which to build. This type of decision-making process requires time. It is not accomplished with one fell blow. To give out the story of Jesus orally or with literature does not mean that the gospel has been communicated. The missionary must take people where they are in their understanding and their life situations and help them move along to a point where the gospel message and its lifestyle make sense.

To use this type of approach—attention to the beliefs and points of contact of specific individuals and careful follow-up to nurture immature motivations to faith—requires time and continuity of contact. It will best be done where a full-service community, the church of worshiping and fellowshiping believers, uses the full range of God's concern in ministries of education, medicine, and compassion. The best long-term results among resistant peoples, whether among Uighurs in Xinjiang, Tibetans in China or India, Mongols in north China, came where a stable church community had been established. Here missionaries and local leaders gave

---

One group was "predisposed to think positively about Islam. Its representatives looked for God's hand and found it. Consequently, their picture was, on balance, a positive one, which stressed a genuine spirituality and vindicated Muhammed of many traditional Christian charges." Another group "began convinced that Islam was morally and spiritually bankrupt and at best of human origin." Clinton Bennett, "Victorian Images of Islam," *International Bulletin of Missionary Research* 15, 3 (July 1991): 115–19.

themselves over a long period of time to evangelism, education, medicine, industrial vocation, and relief. The missions prepared to pay the price in money and personnel over an extended period in two or three central locations reaped the best harvest and had the most solid impact.

Also noteworthy is that some of the most successful ministries among China's minorities had bases (India, Central Asia, and Burma) outside but near the immediate area inhabited by the minorities. This enabled the mission to bring in outside nonwestern workers easily. These were more familiar with the local situation and language. They often were converts from the religion of the host society. Their testimony had much more impact than that of the western missionary.

An alternative understanding of evangelism may not be as productive. Many missionaries, trying to follow in the steps of the apostle Paul, as interpreted by Roland Allen, constantly engaged in missionary trips, itinerating compulsively over hundreds of miles, distributing all variety of literature to illiterate, semiliterate, or functionally illiterate people, and making converts on the run. Not that people did not meet Jesus Christ in this fashion. They did, and some were organized into small churches, usually widely separate from one another. Christians had little sense of belonging to a community or participating in its benefits.

The fuel for such wide scattering of the gospel seed came from a sense of urgency. People were lost spiritually, and their only hope was to acknowledge Jesus as their Savior. In the spirit of an American revival meeting, this might be their last chance. The message must reach them, even if the messenger must hurry on his way. Conversions came from point decisions. If the person were truly converted, spiritual growth would follow, even in the absence of anyone to follow up. This was the work of God the Holy Spirit. If God had brought people to this decision, they would not fall away. No allowance was made for a gradual process that would take a long period of time and required repeated contact with the messengers.

At the heart of this urgency was a belief in the imminent second coming of Jesus Christ. Evangelism must be done quickly, before the day of grace was passed with Christ's advent. Only when the evangelistic proclamation was completed would it be possible for Jesus to return (Matt. 24:14). To itinerate as widely as possible, to distribute tracts, to witness to individuals here and there—this was evangelism. Such an approach makes more sense in a world where there is already some understanding of God's biblical revelation, as in Paul's world in the Roman Empire or in some western "Christian" countries. Lacking this, much more time was needed to lay the foundation for the Christian church among the resistant minorities of China. And, well beyond the missionaries' control, these resistant peoples probably needed several more centuries of exposure to Christianity before any great progress could be seen. Buddhism entered China roughly in the last decade of the first century of the Christian era. It did not take root and escape the epithet of a "foreign faith" until at least five centuries later. Missionaries sought to import an instant Christianity among Mongolians, Tibetans, and Islamic peoples in China in one century. If the message did not get through, it was because "the god of this world had blinded the minds of unbelievers, so that they cannot see the light of the gospel of the glory of Christ . . ." (2 Cor. 4:4). This attitude allowed no room for all of the complexities of communication in an environment strange to the communicator. Nor were missionaries patient enough to await God's *kairos*, which may yet be at some distant time.

The urgency often expressed itself in hurried Bible translations. Missionaries used nonnative translators, worked hastily, had few or no procedures for checking what they did, and rushed materials into print as fast as possible. Was there no other way? Maybe not, given this mindset, but a moderated pace and more care would have communicated the message more clearly. This also is important! Most people movements get along well for a long time with a trade language that will be understood better than a garbled message in the local patois.

This urgency meant that foreigners were in high profile. Insufficient time, money, and energy were devoted to training local leaders who could work out front and reduce the sense that Christianity was foreign. In responsive areas the presence of highly visible missionary leaders was of little consequence. With resistant peoples, it was a critical obstacle.

Missionaries must be urgent—the Great Commission is serious business! God's glory among the peoples of the earth is very important. Clark Pinnock, John Sanders, and others have argued persuasively that there is a "wideness in God's mercy." This may allow more to enter his kingdom without overtly naming the name of Christ. However, the proponents of this possibility agree that the wider hope gives no excuse for not exerting every effort to fulfill the Great Commission.[14] But this urgency must not tempt us to develop fancy slogans, to project unrealistic goals that later, with no apology, are redefined and downgraded, and to spread promotional material among agency constituencies that generate enthusiasm but little light. What precisely does it mean to "reach Tibet for Christ"? Limited or restricted access areas require precise strategies, measurable goals, and disciplined procedures. These, far more than "flying by the seat of their pants" by insensitive and untrained neophytes, can be honored and directed by God's Spirit to effective ends.

14. See John Sanders, *No Other Name* (Grand Rapids: Eerdmans, 1992); Clark H. Pinnock, *A Wideness in God's Mercy: The Finality of Jesus Christ in a World of Religions* (Grand Rapids: Zondervan, 1992).

An overdone urgency in the missionary enterprise also meant that evangelism was more of a priority than the establishing of local churches. Only following World War II and its damage to earlier mission work did evangelical mission agencies sense the importance of church planting and the development of strong local leaders.

An overcompulsive urgency might be tempered in some areas by asking hard questions as to whether or not the specific people group has been evangelized at some point in the past. If Matthew 24:14 is interpreted to mean that the proclamation of God's kingdom is necessary before Christ can return, does this imply that all of this proclamation is to be completed within one specific generation—notably this one? Or is it possible that this proclamation has been completed in stages: some at various times in past generations, as with the Nestorians in Mongolia and Chinese Central Asia, and some in the present generation? This would not void the church's responsibility to continue its witness to some of these groups, but it might lead to prioritizing the remaining work, so that those groups obviously neglected in the past will be included in present outreach.

Not too much attention was paid to matters of receptivity and responsiveness in past work among the minorities. Yunnan and Guizhou were obvious harvest fields, and yet much of the harvest was not gathered because of the lack of missionaries and national leaders. The name *Laka people* is repeatedly mentioned in missionary literature about Yunnan. Always it appears with the sorry refrain that although people wanted to believe, no one could be sent to them, either to evangelize or to disciple. Many mission agencies continued to pour inequitable amounts of money and personnel into obviously unproductive areas of China, both among the Han and resistant minorities, and to neglect areas that were ripe for harvest in Yunnan and Guizhou.

The missionaries working in China in the 1840s and 1850s, long before the later thrust to China's minorities, were no less urgent than their later, more revivalistic colleagues. In theory, at least, they doubted the wisdom of the indiscriminate distribution of literature. They argued that biblical Christianity always implied the presence of a teacher, at least an informal kind of magisterium, that would help to guarantee continuity with a historical understanding of the faith. Thomas Meadows once commented: "While un-annotated copies of the Bible may answer well enough among illiterate Polynesians or Africans, who *must* read it under the guidance of a teacher; such copies, spreading among millions of reading Chinese, who may never see a foreigner, cannot fail to give rise to much greater diversities of opinion than exist in Western Christendom."[15]

15. Thomas Meadows, *The Chinese and Their Rebellions* (London: Academic Reprints, 1856), 412.

People movements to Christ in southwest China among the Miao, Lisu, Lahu, and Wa were served by missionaries who wished to liberate them from every bondage. These missionaries courageously confronted systemic religious oppression and helped new converts break cleanly from the demonic world that enslaved them. The missionaries worked on their behalf to free them from the feudalistic social system that bound them politically and economically. In their thinking, this was the task of the gospel, not a compassionate footnote added to their religious work. They refrained from the use of military and political power, but they were committed to liberation theology long before it was popularized by Latin American theologians and their followers.

Did the missionaries working with resistant peoples think creatively enough about the possibility of group movements to Christ? Those in contact with clan leaders and chieftains in both Mongolia and Tibet had this possibility in mind. Catholic missionaries in Tibet were ready to encourage and accept entire villages to faith in Christ. Protestants preached regularly in bazaars and marketplaces. They concentrated on winning individuals, rather than trying to lead families to faith and then expanding the work into a village conversion. An obvious response to this observation is that "if we cannot win individuals, how can we win families?" On difficult soil, this is a natural question. But it might be turned around. "Until there is the possibility of a family or part of a village believing, preserving some degree of social cohesion, what hope is there that one person will step out against the crowd?" To spark a group movement to Christ may be a difficult goal, but it deserves to be high on the agenda of all those working in a context where community is so important.

God's ultimate goal is that the church include many diverse peoples. Where the geographic situation makes it possible, this heterogeneity reaches to local congregations. Whether because of this good theory, or more likely from the nearness of more responsive Han Chinese people, missionaries assigned to reach minority peoples bogged down with the responsibilities of Chinese work as well. This diluted their concentration on the unique situations of the minority peoples. They lumped people and gave them a generic gospel not tied to specific needs in context.

An imperative need is that the missionary enterprise pay greater attention to developing a common witness for Christ among unreached minorities. Most mission agencies developed and implemented their own strategies. They wanted unique identities. They often knew little and cared less what others were doing. Although they were usually not divisively competitive, neither were they overly cooperative. They had their own agendas and hoped to gain a promotional, and thus financial, edge over some other agency. Many groups reaching out to one area is a luxury that only American Christianity can afford. This mistake is fatal in reaching out to peoples who have no understanding of the gospel and to whom access is limited. Can American mission agencies ever come to the point of combining their efforts for Christ, even with considerable promotional loss, among minority groups such as those in China? Reports from beginning efforts in the People's Republic of Mongolia are not encouraging regarding this.

Where Do We Go from Here?

Churches among responsive minority nationalities in Taiwan, Guizhou, and Yunnan continue to grow and prosper. They face great needs for leadership development, for literature to face a new, modernizing context, and for creativity in proclaiming the gospel of the kingdom to their unreached neighbors and villages.

What can we say about Mongolia, Tibet, and the many Muslim peoples of Xinjiang? Will they ever again have as good an opportunity as in the past? Will God create among them the types of situations that will open the door of opportunity for the gospel message? Will the gospel be proclaimed and seen as relevant to their needs—to exchange or modify their social identity so that the Christian faith may be a viable alternative to their ancient beliefs and traditions? What role can the Chinese church play in proclaiming the gospel to them? Particularly does this question need to be addressed by the increasing number of Han Chinese whom the government is sending into these sensitive areas and who are despised by the local people. Is there any role for well-trained, culturally sensitive, disciplined outsiders? How would they relate to the government and to the Chinese churches already there?

The past has not been a long past, but we neglect it to our own peril. It contains signposts, trails, and paths toward whatever future and whatever messengers will be involved in the spiritual destiny of one hundred million minority peoples in China.

Bibliography

Journals and Magazines

American Anthropologist
Annales de La Propagation de la Foi
Annales de La Societe Missions Etrangeres de Paris
Annuaire des Missions Catholiques de Chine 1941
Annual Reports of the British and Foreign Bible Society
Annual Reports of the Directors to the General Meetings of the LMS
Annual Reports of the Korean Mission of the Presbyterian Church in the U.S.A.
Annual Reports of the Presbyterian Church, U.S.A.
Baptist Missionary Magazine
Beijing Review
Bible Society Record
Bridge
Bulletin de la Societe Missions Etrangeres de Paris
Catholic Missions Annals of the Propagation of the Faith
China's Millions
China Year Book
Chinese Around the World
Chinese Recorder
Christian Alliance Foreign Missions Weekly
Collectanea Commissionis Synodalis
Ethnology
Evangelical Magazine and Missionary Chronicle
Friends of Moslems
Hong Kong Jewish Chronicle
International Bulletin of Missionary Research
International Review of Missions
Journal of the Institute of Muslim Minority Affairs
Journal of the West China Research Society
Les Missions Catholiques
Missionary Broadcaster of the Scandinavian Alliance Mission
Missionary Review of the World
Mongolian Society Bulletin
Moravian Missions
Moravian Quarterly of the London Association in Aid of Moravian Missions
Muslim World
Newsletter of the American Christian Literature Society for Muslims, Inc.

New Yorker
Sign
Scottish Geographical Magazine
Standard
West China Missionary News

Archives

American Baptist Archives, Valley Forge, Pennsylvania
Buker Archives, Boca Raton, Florida
China Inland Mission Archives (partial), Billy Graham Center, Wheaton College, Wheaton, Illinois
Christian and Missionary Alliance Archives (partial), Billy Graham Center, Wheaton College, Wheaton, Illinois
Covell Archives, Denver, Colorado
John Mott Archives, Yale Divinity School, New Haven, Connecticut
Passionist Archives, Union City, New Jersey
Smithsonian Institute Historical Archives, Washington, D.C.

Books

Amundsen, Edward. *In the Land of the Lamas: The Story of Trashilhamo A Tibetan Lassie*. London: Marshall Brothers, 1910.
Anderson, Flavia. *The Rebel Emperor*. New York: Doubleday, 1959.
Andrew, F. Findlay. *The Crescent in North-West China*. London: Religious Tract Society, 1921.
Band, Edward, ed. *He Brought Them Out: The Story of the Christian Movement among the Mountain Tribes of Formosa*. London: The British and Foreign Bible Society, 1950.
Bavinck, John Herman. *The Church Between Temple and Mosque*. Grand Rapids: Eerdmans, 1966.
Bawden, Charles R. *Shamans, Lamas and Evangelicals*. London: Routledge and Kegan Paul, 1985.
deBeauclair, Inez. *An Introduction to the South-Western Peoples of China*. Chengdu: West China Union University, 1945.
Blunden, Caroline, and Mark Blunden. *Cultural Atlas of China*. New York: Facts on File, 1983.
Bolton, Leonard. *China Call*. Springfield, Mo.: Gospel Publishing House, 1984.
Botham, Mrs. Mark. *Two Pioneers: Life Sketches of Thomas and Mark Botham*. London: Religious Tract Society, 1924.
Broomhall, James. *Strong Tower*. London: CIM, 1947.
———. *Strong Man's Prey*. London: CIM, 1953.
Broomhall, Marshall. *Islam in China: A Neglected Problem*. London: Morgan and Scott, 1910.
———. *The Bible in China*. London: CIM, 1934.

———. *Some a Hundredfold: The Life and Work of James R. Adam among the Tribes of South-west China*. London: Morgan and Scott, n.d.

———. *The Chinese Empire: A General and Missionary Survey*. London: Morgan and Scott, 1907.

Brown, Arthur Judson. *The Mastery of the Far East*. New York: Charles Scribner's Sons, 1919.

Browne, Laurence E. *The Eclipse of Christianity in Asia from the Time of Muhammed till the Fourteenth Century*. Cambridge: Cambridge University Press, 1933.

Bull, Geoffrey T. *When Iron Gates Yield*. London: Hodder and Stoughton, 1955.

Cable, Mildred. *The Fulfillment of a Dream of Pastor Hsi's*. London: Morgan and Scott, 1917.

Cable, Mildred, and Francesca French. *The Gobi Desert*. London: Hodder and Stoughton, 1946.

———. *Dispatches from North-west Gansu*. London: The Religious Tract Society, 1925.

———. *Through the Jade Gate and Central Asia: An Account of Journeys in Kansu, Turkestan and the Gobi Desert*. London: Constable and Co., 1927.

———. *Something Happened*. London: Hodder and Stoughton, 1934.

———. *The Making of a Pioneer: Percy Mather of Central Asia*. London: Hodder and Stoughton, 1935.

———. *George Hunter: Apostle of Turkestan*. London: CIM, 1948.

Cable, Mildred, Evangeline French, and Francesca French. *A Desert Journal: Letters from Central Asia*. London: Constable and Co., 1934.

Cable, Mildred, Frank Houghton, R. Kilgour, A. McLeish, R. W. Sturt, and Olive Wyon. *The Challenge of Central Asia*. London: World Dominion Press, 1929.

Callery, Joseph-Marie, and Melchior Yvan. *History of the Insurrection in China with Notices of the Christianity, Creed, and Proclamations of the Insurgents*. New York: Harper and Brothers, 1853.

Carey, William. *Adventures in Tibet*. Chicago: Student Missionary Campaign Library, 1901.

Carlsen, William. *Tibet: In Search of a Miracle*. New York: Nyack College, 1985.

Charbonnier, Jean. *Guide to the Catholic Church in China 1989*. Singapore: China Catholic Communication, 1990.

China's Minority Nationalities. Beijing: China Reconstructs, 1984.

Christie, Mrs. Dugald, ed. *Thirty Years in the Manchu Capital in and around Moukden in Peace and War: Being the Recollections of Dugald Christie*. New York: McBride, Nast and Company, 1914.

Clarke, G. W. *Kwiechow and Yun-Nan Provinces*. Shanghai: Shanghai Mercury Office, 1894.

Clarke, Samuel R. *Among the Tribes in Southwest China*. London: CIM, 1911.

Copland, Margaret. *Chi-Oang, Mother of the Taiwan Tribes Church*. Taipei: General Assembly of the Presbyterian Church of Formosa, 1962.

Covell, Ralph. *The Challenge of Independent Nosuland.* Chicago: Conservative Baptist Foreign Mission Society, 1947.

———. *Mission Impossible: The Unreached Nosu on China's Frontier.* Pasadena: Hope, 1990.

Chung, Henry. *The Case of Korea: A Collection of Evidence on the Japanese Domination of Korea and on the Development of the Korean Independence Movement.* New York: Revell, 1921.

D'Avezac, M. *Relation Des Mongols ou Tartares Par le Frere Jean du Plan de Carpin.* Paris: Des Societes Geographiques de Paris, n.d.

Dawson, Christopher. *The Mongol Mission.* New York: Sheed and Ward, 1955.

Desgodins, C. H. *Le Thibet d'Apres la Correspondence des Missionnaires.* Paris: Libraire Catholique de Saint-Paul, 1885.

Dessaint, Alain Y. *Minorities of Southwest China.* New Haven: HRAF, 1980.

Dickson, James. *Stranger Than Fiction.* Toronto: Evangelical Publishers, n.d.

Dieu, P. Leon. *La Mission Belge en Chine.* Bruxelles: Office de Publicite, 1944.

Drochon, Jean Emmanuel. *Un Chevalier Apotre Celeatin-Godefroy Chicard Missionnaire du Yunnan.* Paris: Typographie Augustinienne, 1891.

Duncan, Marion H. *The Mountain of Silver Snow.* Cincinnati: Powell and White, 1929.

Ekvall, Robert L. *Gateway to Tibet.* Harrisburg, Penn.: Christian Publications, 1938.

———. *Cultural Relations on the Kansu-Tibetan Border.* Chicago: 1939.

Edgar, J. H. *High Altitudes: Missionary Problems in Kham or Eastern Tibet.* Chengdu: Canadian Mission Press, n.d.

Fairbank, John, ed. *The Cambridge History of China,* volume 10, *Late Ch'ing, 1800–1911, part 1.* Cambridge: Cambridge University Press, 1978.

de Fillipi, Fillipo. *An Account of Tibet: The Travels of Ippolito Desideri of Pistola, S.J. 1712–1727.* London: George Routledge and Sons, 1932.

Flachere, R. P. A. *Monseigneur de Guebriant Le Missionnaire.* Paris: Libraire Plon, 1946.

Forbes, D. W. *Warlords and Muslims in Chinese Central Asia.* London: Cambridge University Press, 1986.

Gilmour, James. *Among the Mongols.* London: The Religious Tract Society, 1882.

Graham, David Crockett. *The Customs and Religion of the Ch'iang.* Washington, D.C.: Smithsonian Institution, 1958.

———. *Folk Religion in Southwest China.* Washington, D.C.: Smithsonian Institution, 1961.

Gratuze, Gaston. *Un Pionnier de la Mission Tibetaine le Pere Auguste Desgodins (1826–1913).* Paris: Apostolat des Editions, 1968.

Grist, William Alexander. *Samuel Pollard: Pioneer Missionary in China.* London: Gassell and Co., n.d.

Hawley, Joshua David. *The Kingdom of God Is Near: Christian Conversion and Political Change in the Highland Zone of Mainland Southeast Asia.* Unpublished M.A. thesis at the University of Wisconsin, Madison, 1991.

Hayes, Ernest H. *Sam Pollard of Yunnan.* London: Livingstone, 1928.

Hickey, Edward John. *The Society for the Propagation of the Faith: Its Foundation, Organization and Success (1822–1922).* Unpublished Ph.D. dissertation, Catholic University of America, 1922.

Horne, Charles H. *The Story of the London Missionary Society.* London: London Missionary Society, 1908.

Houghton, Frank. *George King, Medical Evangelist.* London: Religious Tract Society, 1930.

Hu, Chang-tu. *China: Its People, Its Society, Its Culture.* New Haven, Conn.: HRAF, 1960.

Huc, M. l'Abbe. *Christianity in China Tartary, and Thibet 1844–46.* Vol. 2. London: Longman, Brown, Green, Longmans, and Roberts, 1857.

Huc and Gabet Travels in Tartary, Thibet and China 1844–46. Vol. 1. London: George Routledge and Sons, 1928.

Hudspeth, William H. *Stone Gateway and the Flowery Miao.* London: Cargate, 1937.

Hutton, Samuel King. *By Patience and the Word: The Story of the Moravian Missions.* London: Hodder and Stoughton, 1935.

Isering, Marku. *Sharing Christ in the Tibetan Buddhist World.* Upper Darby, Penn.: Tibet Press, 1988.

Israeli, Raphael. *Muslims in China: A Study of Cultural Confrontation.* London: Malmo, 1980.

Jack, R. Logan. *The Back Blocks of China.* London: Edward Arnold, 1904.

Jagchid, Sechin, and Paul Hyer, *Mongolia's Culture and Society.* Boulder, Colo.: Westview, 1979.

Jiang, Wenhan. *Zhongguo Gudai Jidujiao ji Kaifong Yotairen.* (Ancient Chinese Christianity and the Jews of Kaifeng). Shanghai: Zhi Shi Press, 1982.

Kendall, R. Elliott, ed. *Eyes of the Earth: The Diary of Samuel Pollard.* London: Cargate, 1954.

Larson, F. A. *Larson Duke of Mongolia.* Boston: Little, Brown, and Company, 1930.

Latourette, Kenneth Scott. *A History of Christian Missions in China.* London: SPCK, 1929.

———. *A History of the Expansion of Christianity.* Vols. 1 and 6. New York: Harper and Brothers, 1937, 1944.

Launay, Adrien. *Histoire de la Mission du Thibet.* Paris: Desclee, de Brouwer et cie, 1930.

———. *Memorial de la Societe des Missions-Etrangeres.* 2 vols. Paris: Seminaire des Missions-Etrangers, 1912–16.

Learner, Frank Doggett. *Rusty Hinges: A Story of Closed Doors Beginning to Open in North-East Tibet.* London: CIM, 1933.

Lee, Chae-Jin. *China's Korean Minority: The Politics of Ethnic Education.* London: Westview, n.d.

Lei, Hongan. *Traditional Religious Beliefs of the Minority Nationalities.* Kunming: Yunnan Ethnic Research Institute, 1984.

Leslie, Donald Daniel. *Islam in Traditional China.* Beleonan, A.C.T.: Canberra College of Advanced Education, 1986.

Leyssen, J. *The Cross over China's Wall*. Peking: The Lazarist Press, 1941.

Li, Tseng Hsiu (Carol). *The Sacred Mission: An American Missionary Family in the Lahu and Wa Districts of Yunnan*. Unpublished M.A. thesis at Baylor University, Waco, Texas, 1987.

Li, Dun J. *The Ageless Chinese: A History*. 3d ed. New York: Charles Scribner's Sons, 1978.

Life and Lifestyles. Beijing: Foreign Languages Press, 1985.

Lin, Yueh-hua. *The Lolo of Liang Shan*. New Haven, Conn.: HRAF, 1980.

Ling, Shunsheng, and Yihfu Ruey. *A Report on an Investigation of the Miao of Western Hunan*. Shanghai: Academia Sinica, 1947.

Liu, Yaohan. *Zhongguo Wenming Yuantou Xintan Dao Jia Yu Yizu Hu Yuzhouguan*. (A New Investigation into the Origins of Chinese Civilization: Daoism and the Tiger World View of the Yi Minority.) Kunming: Yunnan People's Publishing Company, 1985.

Loftis, Z. S. *A Message from Batang*. New York: Revell, 1911.

Loup, Robert. *Martyr in Tibet: The Heroic Life and Death of Father Maurice Tourney, St. Bernard Missionary to Tibet*. New York: David McKay Co., 1956.

Louvet, M. Louis-Eugene. *Les Missions Catholiques au XIX Siecle*. "L'Eglise de Chine, 1800–1890." Paris: de Brouwer et Cie, 1898.

Lovett, Richard. *James Gilmour of Mongolia*. London: Religious Tract Society, 1893.

Lyall, Leslie. *A Passion for the Impossible*. Chicago: Moody, 1965.

Lyall, Leslie, ed. *The Phoenix Rises*. Singapore: OMF, 1992.

Maguire, Theophane. *Hunan Harvest*. Milwaukee: Bruce, 1946.

Manna, Paulo. *The Conversion of the Pagan World*. Translated by Joseph McGlinchey. Boston: Society for the Propagation of the Faith, 1921.

Marston, Annie W. *With the King: Pages from the Life of Mrs. Cecil Polhill*. London: Marshall Brothers, 1905.

———. *The Great Closed Land: A Plea for Tibet*. London: S. W. Partridge and Co., n.d.

Martin, W. A. P. *A Cycle of Cathay*. New York: Revell, 1900.

Ma Yin, ed. *China's Minority Nationalities*. Beijing: Foreign Languages Press, 1989.

Ma Yin, chief comp. *Questions and Answers about China's Minority Nationalities*. Beijing: New World Press, 1985.

McGee, Gary. *This Gospel Shall Be Preached*. Springfield, Mo.: Gospel Publishing House, 1986.

McLean, Archibald. *The History of the Foreign Christian Missionary Society*. New York: Revell, 1919.

Meskill, J., ed. *An Introduction to Chinese Civilization*. New York: Columbia University Press, 1973.

Mingana, Alphonse. *The Early Spread of Christianity in Central Asia and the Far East: A New Document*. Manchester: The University Press, 1925.

De Moreau, Edward, and Joseph Masson. *Les Missionnaires Belges de 1804 Jusqu'a Nos Jours*. Bruxelles: Editions Universitaires Les Presses de Belgique, 1944.

Myland, David W. *The Latter Rain Covenant and Pentecostal Power.* Chicago: Evangel, 1910.
Nairne, W. P. *Gilmour of the Mongols.* London: Hodder and Stoughton, n.d.
Nevius, John. *Demon Possession.* 8th ed. Grand Rapids: Kregel, 1968.
Nida, Eugene. *Message and Mission.* New York: Harper, 1960.
D'Ollone, Vicomte. *In Forbidden China: The D'Ollone Mission 1905–09 China-Tibet-Mongolia.* London: T. Fisher Unwin, 1912.
Palmer, Spencer J. *Korea and Christianity: The Problem of Identification with Tradition.* Seoul: Hollym Corporation, 1967.
Panskaya, Ludmilla, with D. D. Leslie. *Introduction to Palladii's Chinese Literature of the Muslims.* Canberra: Faculty of Asian Studies, Australian National University, 1977.
Paik, George. *The History of Protestant Missions in Korea.* Seoul: Yonsei University Press, 1927.
Patterson, George. *God's Fool.* New York: Doubleday, 1955.
———. *Requiem for Tibet.* London: Aurem, 1990.
Payne, Joseph, and Wilhelmine Payne. *I Beheld the Mountains.* New York: Vantage, 1969.
Peissel, Michael. *Cavaliers of Kham: The Secret War in Tibet.* London: Heinemann, 1972.
Pen, Guierh. *A Glance at Shuangjiang.* Shuangjiang: Yunnan Shuangjiang Normal College, 1926.
Piolet, J. B. *Nos Missions et Nos Missionnaires.* Paris: Libraire Bloud et Cie, n.d.
Pollak, Michael. *Mandarins, Jews and Missionaries: The Jewish Experience in the Chinese Empire.* Philadelphia: Jewish Publication Society of America, 1980.
Pollard, Samuel. *The Story of the Miao.* London: Henry Hooks, 1919.
———. *Tight Corners in China.* London: Andrew Crombie, n.d.
———. *In Unknown China.* Philadelphia: Lippincott, 1921.
Pollard, Walter. *The Life of Sam Pollard of China.* London: Seeley, Service and Co., 1928.
Plymire, David. *High Adventure in Tibet.* Springfield, Mo.: Gospel Publishing House, 1959.
Plymire, Wardella, comp. *Assemblies of God in China.* Unpublished manuscript held at Central Bible College Library, Springfield, Mo.
Rachewiltz, Igor. *Papal Envoys to the Great Khans.* Palo Alto: Stanford University Press, 1971.
Ramsey, S. Robert. *The Languages of China.* Princeton: Princeton University Press, 1987.
Rhodes, Harry A., ed. *History of the Korean Mission Presbyterian Church USA 1884–1934.* Seoul: Chosen Mission Presbyterian Church, n.d.
Richardson, H. E. *Tibet and Its History.* London: Oxford University Press, 1962.
Rijnhart, Susie Carson. *With the Tibetans in Tent and Temple: A Narrative of Four Years' Residence on the Tibetan Border, and of a Journey into the Far Interior.* New York: Revell, 1904.

Roberts, James Hudson. *A Flight for Life and an Inside View of Mongolia*. Boston: Pilgrim, 1903.

Robson, Isabel Suart. *Two Lady Missionaries in Tibet*. London: S. W. Partridge and Co., n.d.

Rutten, R. P. J. *Les Missionnaires de Scheut et leur Fondateur*. Louvain: Editions de L'Aucam, 1930.

Sandberg, Graham. *The Exploration of Tibet: Its History and Particulars from 1623–1904*. London: W. Thacker and Co., 1904.

Sawyer, Eva M. *Mildred Cable*. London: Pickering and Inglis, 1962.

Schmidlin, Joseph, edited by Matthias Braun. *Catholic Mission History*. Techny, Ill.: Mission Press, S.V.D., 1933.

Shelton, Flora Beal. *Shelton of Tibet*. New York: George H. Doran Co., 1923.

———. *Sunshine and Shadow on the Tibetan Border*. Cincinnati: Foreign Christian Missionary Society, 1912.

Snead, Alfred C., ed. *Missionary Atlas: A Manual of the Foreign Work of the Christian and Missionary Alliance*. Harrisburg, Penn.: Christian Publications, 1950.

Spuler, Bertold. *History of the Mongols Based on Eastern and Western Accounts of the Thirteenth and Fourteenth Centuries*. Berkeley: University of California Press, 1972.

Stewart, John. *Nestorian Missionary Enterprise: A Story of a Church on Fire*. Edinburgh: T. and T. Clark, 1928.

Streit, P. Karl. *Katholischer Missions Atlas*. Verlag der Missionsdruckerei in Steyl, 1906.

Sturt, Reginald W. *The Call and Challenge of Mongolia*. London: Alfred Holness, 1910.

Swan, William. *Letters on Missions*. Boston: Perkins and Marvin, 1831.

Taylor, Annie R. *Pioneering in Tibet*. London: Morgan and Scott, n.d.

Taylor, Mrs. Howard. *The Call of China's Great Northwest, or Kansu and Beyond*. London: Religious Tract Society, n.d.

———. *Behind the Ranges: Fraser of Lisuland in S.W. China*. London: Lutterworth, 1944.

Thompson, Phyllis. *Desert Pilgrim: Mildred Cable's Venture for God in Central Asia*. London: CIM, 1957.

T'ien, Ju-k'ang. *Peaks of Faith*. Leiden: Brill, 1993.

Torrance, T. *China's First Missionaries*. London: Thynne and Co., 1936.

Van Dyck, Howard. *William Christie, Apostle to Tibet*. Harrisburg, Penn.: Christian Publications, 1956.

Van Hecken, Joseph. *Les Reductions Catholiques de Pays des Ordos Une Methode d'Apostolat des Missionnaires de Scheut*. Schoneck/Beckenried, Suisse: Administration der Neuen Zeitschrift fur Missionswissenschaft, 1957.

van Melckebeke, Carlo. *Service Social de L'Eglise en Mongolie*. Bruxelles: Editions de Scheut, 1968.

Van Oost, Joseph. *En Butinant Scenes et Croquis de Mongolie*. Chang-hai: Imprimerie de la Mission Catholique, 1917.

———. *Monseigneur Bermyn Apotre des Ortos*. Louvain: Museum Lessianum, 1932.

———. *Au Pays des Ortos (Mongolie)*. Paris: Editions Dillen et Cie, 1932.

Vial, Paul. *Les Lolos: Histoire, Religion, Moeure, Langue, Ecriture*. Changhai: La Mission Catholique, 1898.

Vicedom, George. *Faith That Moves Mountains*. Taipei: China Post, 1967.

Wallace, Anthony F. C. *Religion: An Anthropological View*. New York: Random House, 1966.

Waters, Curtis, and T. W. G. Waters. *A Modern Pentecost*. London: Morgan and Scott, n.d.

Wessels, C. *Early Jesuit Travellers in Central Asia 1603–1721*. The Hague: Martinus Nijhoff, 1924.

Willeka, Bernard H. *Imperial Government and Catholic Missions in China During the Years 1784–1785*. St. Bonaventure, N.Y.: The Franciscan Institute, 1948.

Winnington, Alan. *The Slaves of the Cool Mountains*. London: Lawrence and Wishart, 1959.

Wolferstan, Bertram. *The Catholic Church in China from 1860–1907*. London: Sands and Company, 1909.

Woodward, David. *Sky-High in Tibet*. Unpublished manuscript.

Zhang Tan. *"Zhai Men" Qian Di Shihmen Kan Jidu Jiao Wen Hua Yu Chuan, Dian, Qian Bian Miao Zu She Hui* (The Stone Threshold in Front of the "Narrow Door": Christian Culture and Miao People's Society on the Border Regions of Sichuan, Yunnan and Guizhou Provinces.) Kunming: Yunnan Educational Publishing House, 1992.

Zwemer, Samuel. *A Primer on Islam and the Spiritual Needs of the Mohammedans of China*. Shanghai: Special Committee on Work for Muslims, 1919.

Index